PUBLIC **SEX** / GAY **SPACE**

Between Men ~ Between Women
Lesbian and Gay Studies

Lillian Faderman and Larry Gross, Editors

PUBLIC **SEX** / GAY **SPACE**

Edited by William L. Leap

Columbia University Press / New York

COLUMBIA UNIVERSITY PRESS

Publishers Since 1893

New York   Chichester, West Sussex

Copyright © 1999 Columbia University Press

All rights reserved

Library of Congress Cataloging-in-Publication Data

Public sex/gay space / edited by William L. Leap

     p.   cm — (Between men—between women)

    Includes index.

    ISBN 0–231–10690–4 (cloth). — ISBN 0–231–10691–2 (pbk.)

    1. Homosexuality.   2. Sex customs—Cross-cultural studies.

  3. Public spaces—Health aspects.   I. Leap, William.   II. Series.

  HQ76.P8   1999

  306.76'62—dc21   98–26490

                                              CIP

Casebound editions of Columbia University Press books are printed on permanent and durable acid-free paper.

Printed in the United States of America

c 10 9 8 7 6 5 4 3 2 1

p 10 9 8 7 6 5 4 3 2 1

"Tearoom Trade: Impersonal Sex in Public Places" by Laud Humphreys first appeared in Society v. 7, n. 3 (1970). Copyright © 1970 by Laud Humphreys. Reprinted by permission of Transaction Publishers.

Contents

Preface   vii

Contributors   ix

Introduction   1
    WILLIAM L. LEAP

1 Reclaiming the Importance of Laud Humphreys's "Tearoom
    Trade: Impersonal Sex in Public Places"   23
    PETER M. NARDI

2 Tearoom Trade: Impersonal Sex in Public Places   29
    LAUD HUMPHREYS

3 A Highway Rest Area as a Socially Reproducible Site   55
    JOHN HOLLISTER

4 Speaking to the Gay Bathhouse: Communicating in Sexually
    Charged Spaces   71
    IRA TATTELMAN

5 Beauty and the Beach: Representing Fire Island   95
    DAVID BERGMAN

6 Sex in "Private" Places: Gender, Erotics, and Detachment in
    Two Urban Locales   115
    WILLIAM L. LEAP

7 Ethnographic Observations of Men Who Have Sex with Men
    in Public   141
    MICHAEL C. CLATTS

8   Self Size and Observable Sex   157
        STEPHEN O. MURRAY

9   Baths, Bushes, and Belonging: Public Sex and Gay Community
    in Pre-Stonewall Montreal   187
        ROSS HIGGINS

10 Homosex in Hanoi? Sex, the Public Sphere, and Public Sex   203
        JACOB ARONSON

11 Private Acts, Public Space: Defining the Boundaries in
    Nineteenth-Century Holland   223
        THEO VAN DER MEER

12 "Living Well Is the Best Revenge": Outing, Privacy,
    and Psychoanalysis   247
        CHRISTOPHER LANE

    Index   285

Preface

Public Sex/Gay Space is the product of several years of discussion about the relationships between public location, sexual practices, and male-centered, same-sex identities and desires. Many of the participants in this discussion have submitted papers for this collection. Other participants chose not to be represented here, but their influence resonates throughout the collection in powerful ways. Ralph Bolton and Gilbert Herdt have been particularly important in that regard. Both of them have done much to champion the need for detailed, descriptive studies of sexual practices and sexual cultures, goals that this collection also seeks to address.

My thanks to Columbia University Press for supporting this project at a time when other presses were much less eager to be associated with its content. Particular thanks go to Ann Miller, senior executive editor at CUP, for the support she has given to this project throughout its development, and to Alexander Thorp (Ann's assistant), Joan McQuary, and Brady McNamara for valuable services during production.

Contributors

Jacob Aronson is the pseudonym of a North American researcher who has made numerous visits to Vietnam over the last decade.

David Bergman is the author or editor of over a dozen books and three volumes of poetry, the latest of which is *Heroic Measures* (1998). His *Gaiety Transformed: Self-Representation in Gay American Literature* (University of Wisconsin, 1991) was designated an Outstanding Book of the Year by *Choice* and the Gustavus Myers Center for Human Rights. He edits the *Men on Men* series and is working on a study of the Violet Quill gay writers group. He teaches at Towson University, Maryland.

Michael Clatts is a medical anthropologist whose principle area of interest is the development of community-based public health programs. He was one of the first social scientists to become involved in AIDS research. Since 1982 he has conducted a number of studies of AIDS preventions issues among out-of-treatment drug injectors, homeless youth, and other groups in New York City.

Ross Higgins is an anthropologist and cofounder of the Archives gaies du Quebec, of which he has been president since 1975. He has written a number of scholarly and journalistic articles on gay life, history, and community in Montreal. He teaches courses in ESL, applied linguistics, and sexuality studies at the Université du Quebec á Montreal and at Concordia University.

John Hollister lives in the desolate setting of Binghamton, New York, where he has been constructing an infrastructure to enable the local gay population to transform itself into a more creatively imagined community. He dwells in cyberspace, runs the g/l/q social science e-mail list (GLQSOC-L), plays "go," jumps into the moshpit at OI shows, and spins websites.

Laud Humphreys, an Episcopal priest and sociologist, pioneered the study of men-having-sex-with-men in public places. His *Tearoom Trade: Impersonal Sex in Public Places* (Aldine, 1970), in which his chapter in this collection first appeared, received the C. Wright Mills Award of the Society for the Study of Social Problems.

Christopher Lane is associate professor of English at Emory University. He is the author of *The Ruling Passion: British Colonial Allegory and the Paradox of Homosexual Desire* (Duke, 1995) and *The Burdens of Intimacy: Psychoanalysis and Victorian Masculinity* (Chicago, 1999), as well as editor of *The Psychoanalysis of Race* (Columbia, 1998).

William L. Leap is professor of anthropology at American University in Washington, D.C. His research examines connections between language, culture, and power in lesbian and gay life in the United States, Cuba, and South Africa. He is author of *Word's Out: Gay Men's English*, editor of *Beyond the Lavender Lexicon* and (with Ellen Lewin) *Out in the Field*.

Stephen O. Murray is a San Francisco sociologist, author of *American Gay*, *Latin American Male Homosexualities* and author or coauthor of ten other books.

Peter Nardi is professor of sociology at Pitzer College (California). He is coeditor of *Social Perspectives on Lesbian and Gay Studies* (Routledge, 1997), *In Changing Times: Gay Men and Lesbians Encounter HIV/AIDS* (Chicago, 1997), and *Growing Up Before Stonewall: Life Stories of Some Gay Men* (Routledge, 1994). He serves as book review editor for *GLQ* and is the special features coeditor for *Sexualities*.

Ira Tattelman is an architect. artist, and independent scholar. He has exhibited his photo-constructions and design work in New York City, Baltimore, Washington, D.C., and Boston. His articles about queer space have appeared in the *Harvard Gay & Lesbian Review*, the *Journal of Architectural Education*, and the *Journal of Homosexuality*, as well as the collections *Queer Frontiers*, and *Queers in Space*.

Theo van der Meer is a fellow of the Foundation for Historical Research of the Netherlands Organization of Scientific Research. He is author of *De Wesentlijke Sonde van Sodomie en Andere Vuyligheeden* and other studies of same-sex sexuality in the Netherlands.

PUBLIC **SEX** / GAY **SPACE**

Introduction

WILLIAM L. LEAP

How important to gay men's lives is the pursuit of male-centered sexual pleasure?[1] Is men-having-sex-with-men really the centerpiece of contemporary "gay culture," as some authors have recently claimed? Or does the subject matter of gay desire stretch sexual imagination and erotic practice, and position gay culture within broader fields of reference—and, if so, what do those fields of reference actually contain?

Questions like these have prompted much discussion within Gay Studies/Queer Theory classrooms, conferences, and scholarly journals. Additionally, much of this discussion has focused on the constructed, negotiated, and situated nature of categories like "gay" and "straight" and on the close ties (and the conflicts) linking gayness, straightness, and other gendered identities with claims to ethnicity, race, nationalism, class position, and privilege. Now, as the instability of these categories has become more firmly documented, discussion turns to the locations within which gayness and its related claims become constructed and negotiated, and, more specifically, to the particular intersections of location, gay identity, and male-centered sexual practices.

In *Public Sex, Gay Space*, anthropologists, sociologists, architects, geographers, literary critics, and historians join forces to explore these intersections as they unfold in parks, truck stops, secluded beaches, alleyways, health club saunas, bath houses, bookstore backrooms, and other sites of male-centered sexual opportunity in the urban and rural United States, Canada, Mexico, Great Britain, the Netherlands, and Viet Nam. All of the locations explored in this collection are, in some sense, *public* places, and for some of the participants, the public nature of the location and its on-site possibilities intensify the power and pleasure of the erotic moment. For other participants, public condition erases interests in on-site erotics, and lead them to locate sites sexual privacy elsewhere. And for others, sexual activities become assertions of privacy, the public location of the site notwithstanding.

One of the themes in this collection is the multiple meanings of public vs. private as this distinction applies to sites of male-centered erotic opportunities. A related theme centers on the effects which claims to a public or private location impose have on site-specific erotic practices. Here, discussions in this collection overlap uncomfortably with the analysis of location, gay identity and erotic practices offered in two recent critiques of the weaknesses bespoiling contemporary gay culture, e.g. Gabriello Rotello's *Sexual Ecology* and Michelangelo Signorile's *Life Outside*.[2]

According to Rotello and Signorile, "gay identity" has become synonymous with an unending pursuit of promiscuity, sexual risk-taking, and ultimately (given the realities of the AIDS pandemic) willful self-destruction. They argue, further that sexual risk-taking is particularly likely to occur when men have sex with other men in *public* locations, that is, in the same types of sites which are of interest to the essays in this collection. To counteract this trend, Rotello and Signorile demand that gay men renounce all participation in casual sex with multiple, anonymous partners, support a strict policing of the locations where men-have-sex-with-men, and agree to the aggressive prosecution of anyone found to be participating in on-site erotic exchange.[3]

Rotello and Signorile use these intersections of public site, gay identity, and sexual risk-taking to speak deliberately and forcefully in favor of the close-the-baths/police-the-parks approach to AIDS prevention, which has enjoyed considerable appeal within the Public Health community (and among some AIDS activists) over the years.[4] And by doing so, they speak in support of those who want to curtail all forms of gay-related sexual experience, and who want to see the state, and not the citizenry, become the architect and manager of sexual culture(s).

Public Sex/Gay Space did not begin as a response to these expressions of sexual fascism. But responding to these claims has become an unavoidable outgrowth of the studies in sexual geography which the authors of this collection now provide. Unlike Rotello, Signorile and colleagues, we are unwilling to assume that public sex and sexual risk-taking are fundamental and inseparable components of gay culture. Instead, we propose to examine the connections between risk-taking and male same-sex desire as these connections are attested within particular locations, and to draw conclusions about gay-related sexual practices (and AIDS prevention strategies) in equally situated terms.

Accordingly, this collection offers ethnographic snapshots of male-centered sex in public places.[5] Rather than talking in abstract or generalized terms about gay (and other male) promiscuity or about the public courtship of sexual risk, this collection uses *participants' own narratives* and, in some instances, *the authors' own voices of experience*, to document localized

conditions public sexual practices, safety and risk. Rather than assuming
that the participants in public sex are (in some essentialized sense) "gay"
men, this collection explores the *identities and other self-descriptions* of the
men who participate in sex-with-other-men at these sites, the overlap
between sexual experiences and gender-identity, and the connections
between sexual practices, ethnic/racial identity, class position and claims to
privilege. Finally, rather that assuming that the "public" basis of a "public
location" is unproblematic, this collection looks carefully at *the locations
where men-have-sex-with-men*, examines the social and historical processes through which certain locations come to be favored as site for sexual
encounters, as well as the social and historical consequences of certain
sites being designated as sexualized locations.

Our focus on erotic experiences, participant identities and the construction of sexual spaces aligns this collection with several other studies of public sex and its discontents which have appeared in recent months, e.g.,
Mapping Desire (Bell and Valentine, eds. 1995), *Policing Public Sex* (Dangerous Bedfellows, eds. 1996), *Queer Space: Architecture and Same-Sex
Desire* (Betsky 1997), *Queers in Space* (Ingram, Bouthillette, and Retter,
eds. 1997), and *Stud: Architectures of Masculinity* (Sanders, ed. 1996).

Mapping Desire, for example, focuses on particular instances of "eroti-
cized topography," including physical as well as imagined locales, all to
show how "the spaces of sex and the sexes of space are being mapped out
across the contemporary social and cultural terrain" (Bell and Valentine
1995: 1). *Stud* narrows the focus of this theme, by exploring how "the precise organization and distribution of materials, objects and bodies in space
[enables] physical structures [to] assist in the fabrication of masculine
identities at specific sites and moments in history" (Sanders 1996: 12).
Queer Space reverses the direction of the argument: "because of the particular place that [gay men] occupied [during the 20th century]," gay men
"produced spaces which we might call queer [which] infected and inflect-
ed our built environment, pointing the way toward an opening, a liberating
possibility" (Bretsky 1997: 5). *Policing Public Sex* and *Queers in Space*
remind us, however, that efforts toward "built environment" and sexually
"liberating possibility" occur in the midst of the hetero-mainstream's fasci-
nation with sexual irregularity and provocative display. As Dangerous Bedfellows, eds., explain,

> Late capitalism has . . . more than a passing interest in shirtless men with
> nipple rings and braless women in tight t-shirts. For queers especially, the
> late 90's are not so much about identity coming out as about sex going
> public.

> . . . stepping into messy debates where Snoop Doggy Dogg's music,
> Madonna's music videos, Mapplethorpe's art, and Holly Hughes's perfor-
> mance art are all on the line.   (Dangerous Bedfellows, eds., 1996: 15).

As Dangerous Bedfellows also note, discussions of public sex in that collection (as is also the case in ours) raises questions about the meaning of
public, and the sources which give the term its regulatory power. Dangerous Bedfellows and colleagues respond to these questions by presenting a
working definition of public sex which highlights the commonalities
between homo-sex and paid-sex, privileges activities over identities as they
both pertain to public locations, and generally "plays with the dividing line
between public and private" (1966: 14).

Public Sex/Gay Space responds to these questions somewhat differently.
As noted, we examine the complex linkages between gender-based identities and sexual practices as they unfold in particular (that is, queer and not-
so-queer) locations. But we argue (and I highlight this argument in some
detail below) that the regulatory power of the state has *already* established all
of these locations as *public* locations, and that claims to sexual (and other)
privacy are constructed in spite of public regulation. In other words, the concern of this collection is not just the contested nature of sexual visibility, the
architectural/spatial representation of masculine identities, or the subversive
nature of queer locale, but the complex intersections of these themes as
they unfold in the lives of men-who-have-sex-with-men and as they shape
the participants' claims to sexual experience and gendered identities.

Moreover, the authors contributing to this collection are gay men, and gay
subjectivity has had significant effects on the preparation of these essays.
Even before we began the research described in these chapters, we knew
about the pleasures and dangers associated with sex-in-public-places, either
through our own experiences or through the experiences of others. We are
writing here about issues which have been, and for most of us still are, closely
tied to our personal as well as scholarly lives. These ties have made it difficult
to frame these essays in terms of detached description, objective commentary or other forms of scientific neutrality. Instead, we deliberately try to highlight the personal, the emotional, the sensual, and other components of lived
experiences that male-centered sex-in-public-places so richly contains.[6]

Overview

The organization of this collection builds directly on a commitment to study
"public sex" from an "insider," gay-positive perspective.

The collection begins with Peter Nardi's review of Laud Humphreys'
classic exploration of men-having-sex-with-men in public restrooms.
Besides being the first American monograph to give serious discussion to
male-centered public sex, *Tearoom Trade* has also received attacks
because of Humphreys' seemingly unorthodox research methods, particularly his violation of informant anonymity and his direct involvement (as
"watch queen" and in other ways) in the erotic activities he was trying to
explore.

The following item in this collection is a reprint of Humphreys' own summary of his research findings (Humphreys 1970); it allows readers to draw
their own conclusions regarding the effectiveness of his research methods
and findings.

The continuing validity of Humphreys' claims are attested in Hollister's
report on his study of male-centered public sex in a highway rest stop.
"Public sex" is still highly cooperative and highly anonymous, says Hollister, but those factors provide only part of the site's appeal as an male-centered erotic space. Tattelman's description of gay bathhouse architecture
and Bergman's reflections on public sex at Fire Island raise additional
questions about "site-specific appeal"; and like Hollister, their essays
underscore the need to distinguish how particular locations provide place
(e.g., neutral, accessible terrain) for some of its inhabitants, while at the
same time functions as space (a constructed, situated, "claimed' terrain)
for other inhabitants.

Leap's comparison of sexual activities in two different locations, the
locker room of a "straight" health club and the backroom of an adult/gay
adult bookstore, reminds us that "public" and "private" are also locally constructed and may be applied differently to conditions at different sites.
Clatts' description of erotic experiences in and around a gay bar in Greenwich Village discloses other ways in which the public/private distinction is
artificial and misleading, and so do the explanations which the men give for
their pursuit of public sex in Murray's essay.

The next set of papers explores the complex connections linking particular instances of male-centered sexual activities and the surrounding politics of society and community. Sex-between-men in a public park in mod-
ern-day Hanoi (Aronson) invokes a set of meanings which are very different
from those growing out similar activities in pre-Stonewall Montreal (Higgins)
or early nineteenth-century Holland (van der Meer). Public, male-centered
sexual practices in Hanoi resurrect colonial and post-colonial messages
about exploitative homosexuality. In Montreal, those practices created ties
between men who were otherwise separated by social and economic differences, and created the basis for claims subsequent claims to a Montreal

"gay community." In Holland, these practices were assigned a series of meanings, each reflecting the Dutch government's increasing attempt to impose moral authority on its citizens, and to use gender-related pariah categories as scapegoats when moral failures could not otherwise be repaired. The tensions between gay-baiting and outing, the two public stances examined in Lane's essay, remind us that gay-related transgression and pariah-status are still a part of today's discourse of moral authority.

And here the collection returns full force to the critique of gay cultural practices offered by Rotello and company, to offer our own reflections on the shortsightedness of their claims. The essays demonstrate quite convincingly that male-centered public sex is *not*, as Rotello and Signorile maintain, a spontaneous, unstructured product of unrestrainable bio-erotic urges, something manageable only in terms of the regulatory authority of the (patriarchal) state. Instead, as we show in these essays, male-centered public sex is *culturally* constructed—with physical, historical, as well as imaginary terrains, negotiated risks and negotiated safety, verbal declarations and silence, as well as gay pride, closeted desire, and heterosexual identity all contributing to such constructions.

And so, while none of the authors will deny the presence (or even the prominence or the attractiveness) of unsafe sex in contemporary gay America, all of us argue powerfully that the reasons why men—straight and gay—engage in unsafe sexual practices when having-sex-with-other-men cannot be reduced to self-contained sound-bites of journalistic commentary, but are part of a larger aggregate of social and cultural practices whose details still need to be more fully disclosed.

Understanding Public Sex: Place, Space, and Landscape

The starting point in the disclosure of those social and cultural practices is the distinction between *place* and *space*. The meanings expressed through that distinction frame many of the current debates in the study of cultural, and specifically sexual, geography.

Michel de Certeau (1984: 115ff) explains the distinction develops this contrast with the following example. Urban planners define the geometry of the city when they lay out its gridwork of streets and avenues, designate locations for public parks, and identify other features of the city's formal design. But the inhabitants of the city reconfigure that gridwork, and transform its abstract, objective geometry into a more meaningful and personalized configuration of space(s), each time they walk through these streets and avenues as they go from home to work, to the market, to visit friends, and on other urban journeys. Walking the city is a form of cultural practice, de Certeau observes, and through such cultural practices "place" becomes transformed into "space."[7]

Under this formulation, *place* designates a location that has been natu-rally formed or constructed, but whose meaning-potential has yet to be fully developed. *Space* emerges when practices are imposed on place, when forms of human activity impose meanings on a given location, and trans-form "neutral" terrain into landscape, that is, into a particular "way of see-ing" (Cosgrove 1984: 13ff) relevant to that particular locale.

Echoing arguments from Raymond Williams' (1973) discussion of *The Country and the City* , Cosgrove reminds us:

> A cultural concept like the landscape idea does not emerge unprompted from the minds of individuals or groups . . . Landscape is a way of seeing that has its own history, but a history that can be understood only as part of a wider history of economy and society. (Cosgrove 1984: 2, 1)

It is possible, then, that what some people consider to be a naturally formed or "neutral" terrain, others will claim as space by means of particular cul-tural practices—or may already have done so. In fact, Hirsch refers to place and space as

> moments or transitions possible within a single relationship, analogous to the experience of a person momentarily losing his/her way on a familiar journey before relocating him/herself by reference to an external perspec-tive; or to the . . . the 'empty place' which periodically fills the foreground experience before receding into its customary background location.
> (1995: 4–5)

In other words, the "ways of seeing" relevant to a particular sense of landscape, as well as the distinction between *place* and *space* itself, are not static arrangements, but topics continually being constructed, negotiated, and contested. This makes it important for studies of cultural geography (of the sort presented in this collection) to focus on the readings which individ-uals give, e.g., to the urban terrain as they walk through the streets and avenues of the city—or to whatever the location under study. But it is equal-ly important to ask questions about context, situation, and personnel: which city (continuing the focus of de Certeau's example) is under discussion here? Are all features of the city's terrain amenable to such readings? Or do some areas resist attempts to impose such meanings on their terrain? And how does walking through the streets overlap with other components of urban opportunity structure? Whose constructions of landscape actually recast the urban terrain and create new and enduring claims to landscape? Whose constructions, while personally valuable, are disregarded, devalued, or erased by the larger urban aggregate? What relevance does urban land-

scape have when a person's health problems, employment schedule, or
concerns with safety limit the possibilities of movement through the city
streets? What happens when the person is simply not interested in walking
through the streets at all?

How This Collection Develops These Themes

These and related questions provide the foundation for the discussion of
male-centered sexual practices—the subject matter of this collection. For
example, David Bergman explores the complex meanings that gay writers
and other gay men have associated with the same "gay resort" (Fire
Island), and shows how the creation of these meanings diversify the category
"gay tourist" relevant to this site.

Tattelman suggests, in contrast, that the physical arrangements of one
gay bath house encouraged patrons from various social and economic
backgrounds to make similar assumptions about the availability of erotic
opportunities that are available there.

Clatts shows how hustling, cruising, and scoring construct a complex
sexual geography in "the heart of Greenwich Village," and how money-for-
sex, money-for-drugs, homelessness, and loneliness further diversity and
intensify erotic opportunities available within this terrain. Leap shows how
self-descriptions of patrons' sexual identities help explain their conflicting
assessments of the appropriateness of erotic activities at a health club
sauna and a bookstore backroom, as well as their conflicting interests in
pursuing erotic activities at each location.

Higgins shows how the social bonds formed by men having sex with
other men in public parks in pre-Stonewall Montreal promoted the emergence of "gay community" in that city during the years after Stonewall, and
created the basis for additional forms of gay experience. Aronson shows, in
contrast, how men having sex with men in Hanoi's public parks has created
a sense of continuity for Hanoi's "gay" men that stretches from the time of
colonial occupation to the more recent years of political liberation—even if
it has not prompted the emergence of a distinctive gay community.

Understanding Public Sex: The Public/Private Distinction

The claims to (gay) space described in this collection are associated in
complex and unpredictable ways with notions of place and landscape,
with particular sexual practices and with sexual identities. But these
claims are also dependent on a distinction between *public* and *private* terrain, and the details of that distinction also requires some introductory
comment.

In general usage, *public* vs. *private* does not refer to properties inherent in any locale, so much as it specifies two different interpretations (or "ways of seeing," in the sense of the preceding section) of the visibility or accessibility of a particular locale; that is, *public* identifies a location which appears to be "open," "accessible," and "unrestricted," while *private* suggests a location which seems more "sheltered," "secluded," or (using Sisela Bok's wording), "being protected from unwanted access by others" (Bok 1982: 10).

Defined in terms of such contrasts, *public* and *private* become relative, almost subjective interpretations of local terrain. And as is always the case with questions of landscape, those interpretations always have to be read against broader forms of regulation and control.

The U.S. Supreme Court's ruling in *Bowers v. Hardwick* (478 U.S. 186 [1986]) speaks directly to this point.[8] Hardwick and his male sex-partner may have believed that Hardwick's bedroom was a private location and that the presumption of privacy offered them some protection from the state of Georgia's prohibitions against practicing sodomy. The Court ruled, however, that while such a right to privacy certainly holds in instances of (heterosexual) marriage, family, and procreation, " 'none of [those] rights bears any resemblance' to a sexual privacy right—at least for homosexuals" (Hunter 1995: 81, quoting directly from the court's decision). Even though the charges against Hardwick were dropped and the case never actually went to trial, the Supreme Court upheld the reasonableness of the police officer's intrusion into Hardwick's bedroom, and reaffirmed the regulatory authority of the state as expressed through Georgia's anti-sodomy statue. Understandably, then, Mohr (1989: 94) writes: "that an act occurs behind four walls does not give it even a prima facie presumption of substantive immunity from the state."

Move outside of the bedroom and conflicts between "sexual privacy" and "public authority" become even more acute. David Bell, writing about "public homosex," has observed:

> In terms of the location of the sex act, then, nominally [public homosex] is taking place in public space: the park, the public toilet, the alley, the beach, the parking lot, the woods, the docks, the street. But in terms of the identities of the participants, their knowledge of each other, and the wider 'public' knowledge of the activities that go on in a particular setting, [it] can be very private, *only attracting attention* when the lives and loves of the rich materialize there, or when the police or queerbashers target a particular site for their own kinds of nocturnal activities. (1995: 306, emphasis mine).

Similarly, Lee Edelman, writing about the "ambiguity of the [men's room's] positioning" as public vs. private space, observes that:

> efforts to provide a space of privacy interior to the men's room itself, a space that would still be subject to some degree of public regulation and control, had encouraged by 1964 the increasing popularity of the coin-operated toilet stall within the public washroom.

Ironically, he continues:

> (i)t was in the anticipated privacy of just such a stall that Walter Jenkins [the White House chief-of-staff under President Lyndon Johnson] would be spied upon by representatives of the DC police department as he engaged in illegal sexual acts with a Hungarian born veteran of the US Army.   (1994: 159).

Similarly, Dr. Mervyn Silverman, San Francisco's director of Public Health, defended his October 9, 1984, decision to close nine of the city's bathhouses (as well as three bookstores and two movie theaters) by explaining that he found it necessary to: "bring to an end commercial enterprises that involve exploitation for profit of an individual's willingness to engage in potentially lethal forms of recreation" (Murray (1996: 110–117). Silverman recognized that "altering sexual activity is a matter of individual privacy" but, he continued: "when sexual activity takes place in a commercial setting, the government has the prerogative and duty to intercede" (cited in Murray 1996: 116, n.60).

The designation "commercial" in Silverman's statement responds to the fact that local licensing regulations had previously designated San Francisco's bathhouses as "private membership clubs" and not "public" facilities. By identifying the bathhouses as "commercial" facilities, Silverman envoked the city's authority to regulate behavior in commercial settings, whatever the intrusions on privacy which might also obtain.

Ultimately, the Superior Court ruling rejected the county's case for closure and allowed the bathhouses to reopen. At the same time, the court's ruling: "ordered (the clubs) to remove private rooms, to hire monitors to survey the premises every ten minutes to ensure that no unsafe sex acts were occurring, and to expel patrons observed to be engaging in 'unsafe sex practices' " (Murray 1996: 117).

The bathhouses remained open, but public sovereignty triumphed over "private" space, all the same.

Rethinking the Meaning(s) of Privacy

The possibility of intrusion by police, the threat of attack by queerbashers, the "false security" of the bedroom, toilet stall, or bathhouse membership, the pervasive presence of regulatory authority—all of these realities reframe the meanings of "private" and "privacy" as they apply to sites of sexual practice. In such settings, and through various means, people may claim "protect(ion) from unwanted access by others" (Bok 1982: 10) or attempt to establish "control over the access that others have to one" (Mohr 1992: 12), but those efforts are always subject to the intrusion, supervision, and/or disruption of others. In this sense, *all* sites of sexual practice are public locations, and any claims to privacy which unfold there are *fictional* claims.

I use the term "fictional" in this statement for several reasons. First, claims to privacy are fictional in the sense of everyday English usage: they stand in opposition to "fact"—in this case, the fact of public regulation, intrusion, and disruption. At the same time, following arguments from post-modernist literary theory, claims to privacy are fictional because they reference features which are not "inherent" in a local terrain, but are constructed, assembled, and imposed. Understandably, as McHale has observed (1986: 27–33, as cited in Harvey 1989: 56), "the essential trope of fiction [is] a technique which requires a willful 'suspension of belief as well as disbelief.'" Claims to privacy within sites of sexual practice require similar acceptance of suspended dis/belief. In fact, it is only through the suspension of dis/belief that secluded location, "watch queen" surveillance, nonverbal communication, and other space-constructing practices are able to surround sites of sexual practices with the *appearance* of safety, security, and "controlled access by others" (citing Bok's phrasing yet again).[9]

But appearances do not necessarily impose obligations on the local terrain. Claims to privacy certainly benefit the participants who pursue sexual activities in these settings, but these claims may not have any relevance for others who share access to these sites, e.g., men using a public toilet for personal (rather than sexual) relief, couples enjoying an picnic in a secluded area of a park or beach, motorists interrupting their driving at a highway rest stop; in some cases, in fact, others may consider such claims highly objectionable. So here is another sense in which privacy is "fictional." Privacy may be only one of several readings which different groups of people impose onto a given landscape, and it may not be the reading that the majority of those persons impose. In this sense, the fictional nature of privacy ensures a convergence of opportunity, vulnerability, and danger. Unavoidably, then, assertions of privacy, as they apply to sites of sexual practice, depend heavily on questions of status and privilege. This helps explain why the dominant figures in the category "participant" at these sites are more likely to be "men," rather than "women." This also helps explain why "sex in public places" is so closely associated with male, rather than female, identities.[10]

Sexual-site-as-public-site, sexual-privacy-as-fiction—these are the corner-stone claims for the essays in this collection. While the sites under discussion here range rather widely—highway rest stops, beaches, health club saunas, bookstore backrooms, bathhouses, street corners, bus terminals, parks, and gay resorts, these case studies describe efforts to create opportunities for sexual privacy in the face of public access, objection, and regulation. All of these studies show how claims to privacy created within the erotic moment extend beyond the boundaries of the sexual site, to become, e.g., a starting-point for "gay community" in post-Stonewall Montreal (as described in Higgins's essay), a rationale for tighter enforcement of "public morality" in nineteenth-century Holland (van der Meer), an enduring feature of resort geography on Fire Island (Bergman), a basis for (re)defining identity in Viet Nam (Aronson), or an incentive for outing "closeted" officials in Margaret Thatcher's England (Lane).

Public versus *private* becomes a source of tension in these examples, and resolutions of that tension play out in various ways, e.g., the architectural design of the St. Marks' baths (Tattelman's essay), the isolated location of the highway rest stop (Hollister), the invented opportunities of the health club sauna (Leap), the sexualized geography of Greenwich Village (Clatts), Hanoi (Aronson), or early nineteenth- century Amsterdam (van der Meer).

Finally, the forms of sexual privacy explored throughout this collection are closely linked to transformations of place into space (in other words, to the construction of landscape) in the sense of the definition from the preceding section. In fact, by considering *privacy as a form of space*, these essays underscore the fictional qualities which both "ways of seeing" impose on local terrain.

Understanding Public Sex: Ethnography, Representation, and Ethics

Previously, researchers who studied "sex in public places" remained "at a distance" from the erotic activities they were describing, and they described their research findings in equally distanced terms. "Public sex" was a form of "deviance," they claimed, whose occurrence depended on conditions of silence, identity concealment, and a reliance on "fronts" behind which a "social management of embarrassment" (borrowing Goffman's phrase) could then safely unfold.[11]

The research described here has moved far beyond these earlier concerns with silence, concealment, and embarrassment. Our goal is to unpack the "logic" which underlies the appeal that men find in having sex with other men in public places and the personal investment some men bring to, and gain from, these "impersonal" and "anonymous" encounters. We address this goal by focusing data-gathering "at the site" and "in the moment" of the sexual encounter, and by using the participants' own voices, not the detached impressions of outsiders, to provide the framework for analysis and interpretation of those data.

Similar goals and research strategies guided the preparation of Laud Humphreys' now-classic *Tearoom Trade* (1970a). Humphreys' interests in understanding "the social organization of impersonal sex" and "the mechanisms that make [impersonal sex] possible" (1970a:14) led him to make regular visits to public toilets where men had sex with other men, and to prepare detailed observations of the range of erotic activities that took place there. On several occasions, Humphreys served as "lookout queen" so that other men could enjoy their erotic interludes without fear of sudden interruption. He also conducted follow-up interviews with many of the men he had observed in these settings, eliciting information on their personal backgrounds and other components of their lives. Some of these men (he referred to them as his "the group of twelve" in his book) became key informants for the duration of the research period.

While some of these interviews grew out of conversations which began at the "tearooms," Humphreys located most of his informants by recording license-plate numbers of cars parked nearby, retrieving home addresses of the drivers from the Motor Vehicle Commission, and contacting them under the guise of conducting a "social health" survey. These actions (which Humphreys himself later admitted were inappropriate [1975: 230]), combined with his seeming disregard for these men's rights to privacy, his descriptions of activities which participants assumed were taking place "in private," as well as his participation in those activities on more than one occasion, prompted colleagues and others to accuse him of unethical research practices.[12]

Today's studies of sex-in-public-places take place within a climate which differs somewhat from that which greeted the publication of *Tearoom Trade*. Broader discussions of ethics in social science research, the creation of Codes of Professional Ethics in many academic disciplines, and the constraints of institutional review boards and federal regulations governing the protection of human subjects limit the extent to which participant/observation can be employed in such studies, without giving full disclosure to the research goals and obtaining the informed consent from the intended research subjects.

At the same time, the emergence of lesbian/gay studies (and of culture/sexuality studies, more inclusively) as subfields within many academic disciplines, the greater visibility claimed by gay presence in U.S. society, and the unyielding urgency of the AIDS pandemic has prompted an awareness of the limitations of such constraints and, in some instances, led to alternative proposals for ethical compliance. [13] Understandably, while some of the research projects described here may not meet the traditional imperatives of "full disclosure" and "informed consent," all of these projects have maintained high standards of ethical representation, and those standards have had visible and productive effects on the development of this collection.

To begin with, the AIDS pandemic, and AIDS-related research, are relevant to concerns of these essays, even in those instances where the researcher does not mention the pandemic directly. By identifying issues which shape male-centered sexual practices in public places, the authors in this collection are mobilizing information that can be useful for effective AIDS education and can also reveal the shortcomings of the pejorative, gloom-and-doom prophecies of sexual fascism. The challenge we face in this work is to make sure that our data-gathering, data analysis, and research findings actually *do* address both goals. Our efforts to meet that challenge establishes the foundation for the ethical stance affirmed in this collection.

Second, we agree with Ralph Bolton (1996: 161; see note 13), that discussions of ethics, while certainly important, should not become impediments to effective inquiry. So while we would agree to make a full disclosure of research goals and plans for informant protection prior to beginning a formal interview with a willing informant, we would be much less willing to defer any observation of men participating in public sex activities until we obtained informed consent agreements from all participants. Attempting to do so would irreparably disrupt the situated intimacy which we are attempting to describe. Moreover, it would limit our regulation of on-site identities during subsequent visits to that site.

At the same time, we are ethically committed to safeguarding the anonymity and confidentiality of our research subjects, and to that our actions result in "no deliberate harm."

Anonymity is particularly an issue for participants in these "public sex" encounters who actively conceal their erotic interests in men once they move outside of these settings. If a participant's perspective on the erotic moment is as valuable to our research as we claim, then it is our job, as responsible ethnographers, to maintain that concealment in our research and writing. In some cases (my fieldwork in Washington D.C. health club locker rooms, for example), that concealment means reproducing the conditions of "the closet" or other forms of gendered privilege—conditions which, in other areas of our personal lives, many of us are eagerly trying to dispel.

Avoidance of deliberate personal harm raises an additional, and equally difficult, set of ethical concerns. For example, the papers in this collection describe "sex in *public* places," but the locations themselves are not always common knowledge—or commonly acknowledged—within the surrounding community, and neither are the erotic activities taking place there. By identifying these locations and describig these activities, our research draws outside attention to these sites, and may increases the likelihood of outside disruptions by thrill-seeking spectators, law enforcement officials, and/or by queerbashers.

Other, equally serious, forms of disclosure, with serious consequences, could also emerge from the publication of our research. Public health authorities in Washington D.C. could use the information of the sort presented in my chapter to close the health club (or the bookstore) I described, since sexual activities at these sites violate licensing agreements and health codes. Law enforcement officials could use information in Hollister's chapter or Murray's chapter to help them rid the highway rest stops in upstate New York or the beaches in San Francisco of sexual "undesirables." Members of Congress could use the sexually explicit narratives contained in Clatts's essay to raise new complaints about federal endorsements of "the homosexual lifestyle," since much of his research has been supported by federal funds. The description of "homosexual presence" and disclosure of male same-sex experiences presented in Aronson's essay could prompt the Vietnamese government to deny his future requests for visas and/or research permits. Indeed, Aronson's concerns about this issue, and other forms of retaliation led him to adopt a pseudonym and to disguise his identity in other ways.

None of us can prevent regulatory authorities from pursuing any of these actions, if they choose to do so. However, we can make certain that the effectiveness of our presentation offsets any risks we may incur and which we may inadvertently impose on others, as our research findings gain broader circulation. A commitment to effective presentation need not compromise our commitments to anonymity and avoidance of deliberate harm; and that commitment is the final component of the collection's ethical standards I want to discus here.

By effective presentation, I mean nothing more than describing the details of ethnographic observation concisely, clearly, and unambiguously. As far as details of the erotic moment are concerned, effective descriptions raise several issues regarding language choice. Do we use the scientific vocabulary, or some form of the vernacular, to describe the detail of male-centered sexual activity? Do men "perform fellatio" at these sites, or "give each other blow-jobs"? Do they "engage in anal intercourse" or "fuck each

other in the butt"? The scientific language is more elegant and less abra-
sive, but does little to convey the realities of the participant voice. The vernacular phrasing coincides with the lived experience of the erotic moment,
but the bluntness of such usage is likely to alienate readers who can benefit
from the insights these essays proclaim.

Some of the insights here address issues in AIDS education and with
sexual fascism, as I have already explained. Other insights focus more
directly on the subject matter of this volume: men having sex with men in
public (and private) locales is part of the sexual culture of contemporary
America, whether participants consider themselves to be gay, homosexual,
bisexual, straight, curious, or horny, how they self-identify is not a barrier to
participation in male-centered sexual practices.

By acknowledging that men have sex with men in public places,
researchers draw attention to components of male sexuality, erotics, and
desire that are not consistent with the expectations of the hetero-mainstream. Traditionally, male-centered public sex has been assumed to
belong to the margins and the shadow-worlds of American sexuality, and
have been assigned marginal/shadowed status in formal discussions of
sexual themes. Understandably, as Lee Edelman (1994: 132) has noted:

> The crucial question informing the discourse of homosexual sodomy in
> America, then, is not so much what individuals, or individual bodies, can
> be permitted to do in private, but what these bodies can *publicly be repre-*
> *sented* [emphasis in original] as being permitted to do in private; it is a
> question in other words of whether or not sodomy is *susceptible* [my
> emphasis] to representation.

The essays in this collection to speak directly to Edelman's question. Instead
of positioning their subject matter "at distance" from heteronormative practice, the essays locate the center of the analysis "on the margin" — focusing
directly on men-having-sex-with-men in public places, and on the effects of
male-centered sexual practices on constructions of space, claims to privacy,
and broader expressions of gender, desire, and sexual identity. By doing so,
this collection makes "sodomy" and other issues connected to male-centered sexuality susceptible to (public) representation, and, following the tradition of *Tearoom Trade*, our representation of these issues more public.

ENDNOTES

My thanks to Brett Williams and Liz Sheehan, to the students in my Spring 1997 Linguistics and Lesbian/Gay Studies seminars, and to the outside reader who reviewed
this collection for Columbia University Press; their comments were very helpful as I
prepared the final wording for this Introduction.

1. Other recent volumes addressing weaknesses in gay culture include Daniel Harris's *Rise and Fall of Gay Culture*, Andrew Sullivan's *Virtually Normal*, Frank Browning's *Culture of Desire*, and Bruce Bawer's *A Place at the Table*. While the particulars of these studies vary considerably, their arguments (with one exception—see below) support the position outlined forcefully by Rotello and Signorile: gay men's efforts to move beyond the constraints of "the closet" have created lifestyles that are excessive, imbalanced, and dangerous. Their solution to this problem also parallel's Rotello's and Signorile's solution: refocus gay culture around the conventions that provide moral stability to middle-class heterosexuality, e.g., monogamy, fidelity, "marriage," child-rearing, and elimination of all forms of public indecency.

Harris is the one author in this grouping who does not argue in favor of cultural repair. For him, the sexual (and other) excesses described by other critics are proof that gay culture has outlived its usefulness, so we should simply allow it to disappear.

2. As alternatives to sexual promiscuity, Rotello and Signorile encourage gay men to enter into long-term monogamous relationships, to explore gay adoption and child-rearing, and to pursue other activities which bring gay culture into closer alignment with heterosexual norms. These arguments resemble Andrew Sullivan's defense of "same sex marriage," and echo Bruce Bawer's proposals to help gay men and lesbians secure their rightful "place at the table."

3. Steve Murray (1996: 99–124) reviews the debates surrounding the closing of the gay bathhouses in San Francisco; Eigo (1995) reviews similar events in what he terms "NYC's war on sex." Alexander (1996) and Gilfoyle (1996) remind us that the same arguments have been directed at public sex involving female prostitutes and their clients.

4. Ethnography is the anthropologist's term for a site-specific descriptive study of human behavior. Sociologists, economists, and political scientists address similar interests when they call for a microlevel, rather than macrolevel, analysis of social, economic or political systems.

5. Critics of the subjective stance we have adopted here will argue that we need to protect ourselves (and our readers) from the distortions stemming from our close involvement with these issues, and not celebrate these connections. This disagreement speaks to a larger debate over appropriate research ethics I explore in the final section of this essay.

6. "Walking the city" calls to mind references to the nineteenth-century Parisian flaneur, the man (gender deliberately chosen) who imposed his own meanings on the urban terrain as he leisurely sauntered through the city. Baudelaire once depicted the flaneur as a man walking a pet turtle on a silken leash. The image speaks to notions of male privilege—only a select group of men would be in a position to spend time in that fashion. Moreover, as Wilson (1992) and Mundt (1995) explain, women as a category could be objects of a (male) flaneur's attention, but women were the sources of that gaze only under particular (and often socially devalued) conditions. So to understand the cultural practices at issue in forming "space" as "practiced place" (de Certeau 1984: 117), the practices in question have to be *fully* situated within their social and cultural contexts.

7. *Hardwick* references conditions in the United States, but the principle here has a much wider relevance. Even in South Africa, where the new constitution guarantees nondiscrimination on the basis of sexual orientation, "sodomy laws" have not been repealed, and sexual activity conducted in "private" between persons of the same sex still carries the possibility of arrest and prosecution by "public" authorities. Lane's discussion shows the presence of similar threats in the United Kingdom; Aronson's description of homophobia in Hanoi shows similar threats persist in Vietnam. The point is, as I will argue in the remainder of this section, a "private" location affords no guarantees of protection from "public" authority, and in that sense, it is not really "private" at all.

8. Equally fictional, according to this argument, is the idea that the domestic sphere (e.g., the home, the family) is a site of privacy, especially as contrasted to the "public" domains that lie outside of the domestic context. This classification of gendered spaces into "domestic" versus "public," "natural" versus the "cultural," "female" versus "male" spaces was an important early argument in feminist anthropology (Ortner 1974) and has been a cornerstone of American gender ideology for some time (Martin 1992: 15–19). But as Sacks (1989: 538) explains, this classification obscures the fact that the domestic sphere is a site of production, as well as consumption and emotion, and domestic relations are political and economic relations, and not merely "natural" social ties. In this sense, "home" and "family" are deeply embedded within public economic process, even if they claim the appearance of "privacy."

9. Esther Newton (personal communication) explains the absence of outdoor cruising areas for women in Cherry Grove (Fire Island) and in similar locations where women's presence was otherwise powerfully displayed. Even in lesbian/gay-positive spaces, threats of discovery and danger are still associated with such outdoor spaces, and those threats are enough to discourage women' enjoyment of same-sex erotics in public locations.

10. Studies using "at distance" research perspectives include Delph (1978), McKinstry (1974), Ponte (1974), and Weinburg and Williams (1975). Styles (1979) reports that he began his studies of gay baths in these terms, but once he found that his "asexual observation became more and more tiresome, more tedious, and more frustrating," he decided to "[give] up observing without sexual intent and plunged fully into the sex life of the baths" (1979: 142). The remainder of his article (1979: 142–152) shows how greatly this shift in research strategy benefited his inquiry.

11. For example, journalist Nicholas von Hoffman questioned the moral legitimacy of the project, paralleling Humphreys's deceitful conduct to that of then U.S. Attorney General John Mitchell. The chancellor of Washington University terminated Humphreys's teaching contract and his participation in a major research grant, and attempted (ultimately without success) to have his doctoral degree revoked. Humphreys responded to von Hoffman and other critics in several essays, later appended to the second edition (1975) of *Tearoom Trade*. Peter Nardi (in Nardi 1995 and this volume) reviews the controversy and Humphreys's responses in more detail.

13. Ralph Bolton, whose own highly participatory studies of gay men's sexual behaviors have also been branded as "immoral" (see his comments, 1996: 161), offers the following suggestion:

> Like all of you, I must confront ethical issues every day in this epidemic, in my personal life as well as in my professional decision-making. It is my view that while these issues are important, we cannot spend much time agonizing over them; we need to consider them seriously, resolve them quickly, and then get on with the job as best we can.   (1995: 302).

REFERENCES

Alexander, P. 1996. Bathhouses and brothels: Symbolic sites in discourse and practice. In Dangerous Bedfellows, eds., *Policing Public Sex*. City: Pub, 221–250.

Bawer, B. 1993. *A Place at the Table: The Gay Individual in American Society*. New York: Touchstone Books.

Bell, D. 1995. Perverse dynamics, sexual citizenship, and the transformation of intimacy. In D. Bell and G. Valentine, eds., *Mapping Desire: Geographies of Sexualities*, 304–317.

Bell, D. and G. Valentine, eds. 1995. *Mapping Desire: Geographies of Sexualities*. London: Routledge.

Betsky, A. 1997. *Queer Space: Architecture and Same-Sex Desire*. New York: Morrow.

Bok, S. 1982. *Secrets: On the Ethics of Concealment and Revelation*. New York: Pantheon Books.

Bolton, R. 1995 Rethinking anthropology: The study of AIDS. In H. ten Brummelhuis, H. Herdt, and G. Herdt, eds. *Culture and Sexual Risk: Anthropological Perspectives on AIDS*, 285–314.

——. 1996. Coming home: The journal of a gay ethnographer in the years of the plague. in E. Lewin and W. Leap, eds. *Out in the Field: Reflections of Lesbian and Gay Anthropologists*, 147–169.

Browning, F. 1993. *The Culture of Desire*. New York: Crown.

Cosgrove, D. 1984. *Social Formation and Symbolic Landscape*. London: Croom Helm.

Coxon, A. P. M. 1996. *Between the Sheets: Sexual Diaries and Gay Men's Sex in the Era of AIDS*. London: Cassell.

Dangerous Bedfellows, eds. 1996. *Policing Public Sex*. Boston: South End Press.

de Certeau, M. 1984. *The Practice of Everyday Life*. Berkeley: University of California Press.

Delph, E. W. 1978. *The Silent Community: Public Homosexual Encounters*. Beverly Hills: Sage.

Duggan, L. and N. Hunter, eds. 1995. *Sexual Dissent and Political Culture*. New York: Routledge.

Edelman, L. 1994a. Capitol offenses: Sodomy in the seat of American government. In *Homographesis: Essays in Gay Literary and Cultural Theory*, 129–138. New York: Routledge.

—— 1994b. Tearoom and sympathy; or, The epistemology of the water closet. In *Homographesis: Essays in Gay Literary and Cultural Theory*, 148–170. New York City: Routledge.

Eigo, J. 1995. NYC's war on sex: Some notes from the fore (& the aft). *Steam* 3 (4): 414–423.

Gilfoyle, T. J. 1996. From soubrette row to show world: The contested sexualities of Times Square, 1880–1995. In Dangerous Bedfellows, eds. *Policing Public Sex*, 263–294.

Goffman, E. 1967. *Interaction Ritual*. New York: Anchor Books.

Harris, D. 1997. *The Rise and Fall of Gay Culture*. New York: Hyperion.

Harvey, D. 1989. Postmodernism. In *The Condition of Postmodernity*, 39–66. London: Blackwell's.

Hirsch, E. 1995. Landscape: Between place and space. In E. Hirsch and M. O'Hanlon, eds., *The Anthropology of Landscape*, 1–30.

Hirsch, E. and M. O'Hanlon, eds. 1995. *The Anthropology of Landscape*. Oxford: Oxford University Press.

Humphreys, L. 1970a. *Tea Room Trade: Impersonal Sex in Public Places*. Chicago: Aldine. 2d ed., 1975.

——. 1970b. Tearoom trade: Impersonal sex in public places. *Transaction* [Society] 7 (3): 11–26.

Hunter, N. 1995. Banned in the USA: What the Hardwick ruling will mean. In L. Duggan and N. Hunter, eds., *Sexual Dissent and Political Culture*, 80–84.

Ingold, T. 1993. The temporality of landscape. *World Archaeology* 25: 152–157.

Ingram, G. B., A. M. Bouthillette, and Y. Retter, eds. 1997. *Queers in Space: Communities, Public Places, Sites of Resistance*. Seattle: Bay Press.

Jacobs, J. ed. 1974. *Deviance: Field Studies and Self-Disclosures*. Palo Alto: National Press Book.

Lewin, E. and W. Leap, eds. *Out in the Field: Reflections of Lesbian and Gay Anthropologists*. Urbana: University of Illinois Press.

Martin, E. 1992. *The Woman in the Body*. Boston: Beacon Press.

McHale, B. 1987. *Postmodernist Fiction*. New York: Methuen.

McKinstry, W. C. 1974. The pulp voyeur: A peek at pornography in public places. In J. Jacobs, ed., *Deviance: Field Studies and Self-Disclosures*, 30–40.

Mohr, R. 1989. Why sex is private. In *Gays/Justice: A Study of Ethics, Society, and Law*, 94–133. New York: Columbia University Press.

——. 1992 The outing controversy; Privacy and dignity in Gay ethics. In *Gay Ideas: Outing and Other Controversies*, 11–48. Boston: Beacon Press.

Mundt, E. 1995. The lesbian flaneur. In D. Bell and G. Valentine, eds., *Mapping Desire: Geographies of Sexualities*, 114–125.

Murray, S. O. 1996. The promiscuity paradigm, AIDS, and gay complicity with the remedicalization of homosexuality. In *American Gay*, 99–125. Chicago: University of Chicago Press.

Nardi, P. M. 1995. "The breastplate of righteousness": Twenty-five years after Laud Humphreys' *Tearoom Trade. Journal of Homosexuality* 30: 1–10.

Ortner, S. 1974. Is female to male as nature is to culture? In M. Z. Rosaldo and L. Lamphere, eds., *Woman, Culture and Nature*, 67–88.

Ponte, M. R. 1974. Life in a parking lot: An ethnography of a homosexual drive-in. In J. Jacobs, ed., *Deviance: Field Studies and Self-disclosures*, 7–29.

Rosaldo, M. Z. and L. Lamphere, eds. *Woman, Culture, and Nature*. Stanford: Stanford University Press.

Rotello, G. 1997. *Sexual Ecology: AIDS and the Destiny of Gay Men*. New York: Dutton.

Sacks, K. 1989. Toward a unified theory of class, race, and gender. *American Ethnologist*, 534–550.

Sanders, J., ed. 1996. *Stud: Architectures of Masculinity*. Princeton: Princeton University Press.

Signorile, M. 1997. *Life Outside: The Signorile Report on Gay Men: Sex, Drugs, Muscles, and the Passages of Life*. New York: Harper-Collins.

Styles, J. 1979. Outsider/insider: Researching gay baths. *Urban Life* 8: 135–152.

Sullivan, A. 1995. *Virtually Normal*. New York: Vintage Books.

ten Brummelhuis, H. and G. Herdt, eds. *Culture and Sexual Risk: Anthropological Perspectives on AIDS*, 285–314. Newark: Gordon and Breach.

Weinberg, M. S. and C. J. Williams. 1975. Gay baths and the social organization of impersonal sex. *Social Problems* 23 (2): 124–136.

Wilson, E. 1992. The invisible flaneur. *New Left Review* 195: 90-110.

Reclaiming the Importance of Laud Humphreys' *Tearoom Trade: Impersonal Sex in Public Places*

PETER M. NARDI

Whenever I teach introductory sociology, publishers are quick to send me copies of their latest textbooks. Not too long ago, I received an examination copy of *Sociology* by David Ward and Lorene Stone (West Publishing, 1996). One way I evaluate the quality is to read how topics on gay men and lesbians are presented. It is not uncommon for texts to leave out such issues or, at most, include a token mention or paragraph. Typical of many, the Ward and Stone book devotes a "Social Diversity" half-page sidebar in "The Family" chapter on gay and lesbian families. That's really about it for this 500-page text, except for a half-page titled "Invasion of Privacy" under the "Ethical Issues in Sociological Research" section of the chapter on doing social research.

Once again, Laud Humphreys' infamous study on "impersonal sex in public places" has made the cut. Alas, like many textbooks that discuss his research, the focus is on the ethical questions raised by his methodology. Only two sentences are devoted to mentioning what the study actually discovered sociologically about the men who participated in sexual activity in a public park toilet. (A "tearoom" in American slang or a "cottage" in British slang is a public toilet where same-gender sexual acts occur).

How is it that this book, more than twenty-five years later, could still be used as an exemplar of ethically problematic research? What is it that made this study so scandalous? Debates arise about Humphreys' "voyeur-lookout" or participant observer role in the tearooms, his recording of the license plate numbers of the participants, his search for their home addresses and names through public records, and his interviews a year later with fifty of them while posing as a survey researcher for a study on mental health. What some have described as an ingenious way to uncover difficult-to-study forms of hidden behavior, others have attacked as unethical and an invasion of privacy.

When the study appeared as the lead article in *Trans-Action*, a monthly sociology magazine (now called *Society*) edited by Irving Louis Horowitz, it

was denounced in a January 1970 *Washington Post* column by Nicholas
von Hoffman as immoral and a violation of the participants' basic human
rights to informed consent: "No information is valuable enough to obtain by
nipping away at personal liberty" (reprinted in Humphreys 1975: 181).
Sociologists Irving Louis Horowitz and Lee Rainwater jumped to the defense
of Humphreys' work and methods in a May 1970 editorial in *Trans-Action*
(reprinted in Humphreys 1975). They strongly stated their belief in the
research and "in its principled humaneness, in its courage to learn the
truth and in the constructive contribution that it makes toward our understanding of all the issues, including the moral, raised by deviant behavior in
our society" (Humphreys 1975: 185).

Horowitz and Rainwater responded that the behavior of tearoom participants is not private but public behavior; that full disclosure of the purpose
of the follow-up interviews would have compromised the findings and
research; and that the researcher's intentions in this case do matter ("the
pursuit of truth, the creation of countervailing knowledge, the demystifica-
tion of shadowy areas of human experience," Humphreys 1975: 188).

Yet Humphreys himself later had doubts about one portion of his
methodology. Although he felt that observing tearoom behavior was not a
violation of privacy or unethical since it occurred in a public place, he did
come to believe that tracing license numbers and interviewing participants
in their homes may have placed his respondents "in greater danger than
seemed plausible at the time" (1975: 230). If he were to do the study over,
Humphreys wrote, he would spend more time cultivating additional willing
participants for the interviews.

However, rather than endlessly argue about these ethical and method-
ological issues, let the following excerpt of his study reclaim what has been
lost over the years, namely the important sociological findings about the
participants and what the research has taught us about the social organization of same-sex sexual encounters in public places (see also Nardi 1995).
Humphreys often stated that he wished "other sociologists would give more
attention to some of my substantive findings that I believe provide an incre-
ment of understanding of social behavior in our society" (1975: 231).

Sociologically, Humphreys' research contributed several key findings, as
will be seen in the selection that follows. One finding was the structure of
the collective action in the tearooms. Humphreys found that maintenance
of privacy in public settings depends heavily on the silence of the interaction and on a special ritual that must be both noncoercive and noncommit-
tal. Making analogies to Goffman's work on games, he analyzed the
encounters in terms of the flexible roles and standard rules that characterize a game. Humphreys illustrated the collective actions of positioning, sig-

naling, maneuvering, contracting, foreplay, and the payoff. Since there is
such an elaborate social structure, he concluded that being propositioned
against one's will or recruited into homosexuality in public restrooms—as
some antigay rhetoric proclaims—is an unlikely occurrence.

A second important finding from Humphreys' work was that many of the
participants in tearoom sexual encounters were married (54%), were
Roman Catholic (42%), and were politically and socially conservative
(32%, as measured on a social/economic liberalism scale). In addition,
based on their appearances and demeanor during the interviews,
Humphreys (1975: 135) concluded that most of the participants put on a
"breastplate of righteousness"—"a protective shield of superpropriety . . .
[with] a particularly shining quality, a refulgence, which tends to blind the
audience to certain of [the wearer's] practices." The participants—especially those who were married or were closeted single men—engaged in
various forms of minimizing revelations about themselves through a strategy of information control designed to misdirect from their behaviors. Many
of these men took a defensive shield by advocating moral crusades,
endorsing vice squad activities, and creating a presentation of self-
respectability.

Another important sociological conclusion was Humphreys' discussion
about why people engage in public sex and what the costs are. Just as
games of chance attract and thrill participants, so also does the kick from
risk-taking behavior, as we see all too well today among those knowingly
taking a chance with unsafe sexual acts. But Humphreys went beyond simple psychological explanations and noted the importance of certain structural reasons: the availability, invisibility, variety, and impersonality of tearoom encounters. Finally, he raised important theoretical and sociological
questions about the social control of sexual behavior and public policy. The
real harm of public sex, Humphreys felt, was putting these men at risk for
blackmail, payoffs, and destroyed reputations at the hands of the police.
This was a strong statement to make in its day—perhaps even to this day—
when entrapments were a routine method of police work.

It is especially important to remember when this book was written in
order to understand fully the reasons for its notoriety. *Tearoom Trade* was
first published in 1970 as a revised version of Humphreys' 1968 Ph.D. dissertation at Washington University in St. Louis. Relying on the classical
sociological theories of Erving Goffman, Harold Garfinkel, and Howard
Becker, Humphreys developed a proposal to study the social structures of
sexual interaction in a public place and the social characteristics of those
participating in the behaviors. When he began collecting his data in the
mid-1960s, there were no "gay studies programs," only a few publications

in sociology and anthropology focusing on homosexuality, and certainly very little by openly gay men and lesbians. Psychoanalytic publications were also widely available but, typically, these pathologized homosexual behavior. Furthermore, media information and the public's attitudes about gay men and lesbians were almost all negative and erroneous. And the militant resistance to routine raids by the police on gay bars had only just begun: the "Stonewall" rebellion occurred a scant six months before publication of the book, and about a year after completion of the dissertation research.

In such a climate, Humphreys' thesis became a minor scandal. It was opposed by Alvin Gouldner, a noted professor in Washington University's now-defunct sociology department, which resulted in some physical shoving between him and Humphreys (see Goodwin, Horowitz, and Nardi 1991). There was an attempt by the chancellor of the university to revoke his Ph.D. degree on the grounds that Humphreys committed a felony by observing and facilitating fellatio; after that failed, an agreement was reached to keep the dissertation from being published for at least a two-year period. However, the book version, published by Aldine in 1970, was awarded the C. Wright Mills Award by the Society for the Study of Social Problems. Two years later, Humphreys left his position at the State University of New York, Albany, and joined the sociology department at Pitzer College, one of the Claremont Colleges located near Los Angeles, where he remained until his death in 1988 from smoking-related lung cancer .

More than twenty-five years after its publication, *Tearoom Trade* continues to provide a strong foundation and framework for any research done today on public spaces and sexuality. Humphreys' work raises the kinds of questions that queer studies pose today about what it actually means to call someone "straight" or "gay." For example, other studies in recent years on sex in public places have confirmed some of Humphreys' findings. Desroches (1990) analyzed Canadian police case materials and interviewed officers about arrests in shopping mall restrooms and also found that the interactions were silent and impersonal, were not coercive, and involved married men in 58 percent of the cases.

An unpublished report from the Los Angeles Gay & Lesbian Police Advisory Task Force in 1992 estimated that about half of those arrested for "lewd conduct" in a public park were heterosexually married men, although only 24 percent of those completing the survey were married (around 75% of those arrested did not complete the survey). And in Australia, where public places for sex between men are termed "beats," Moore (1995: 324) wrote that "Brisbane-based surveys from the 1990s show that the majority of men who cruise urban and highway beats are ostensibly heterosexual married men with families, the same pattern uncovered by Laud Humphreys in his 1960s study from America, *Tearoom Trade*."

Such is the legacy and the enduring power of quality academic research and why the following selection is included in this collection. Humphreys' work, for all the controversy about its methods and findings, remains a salient part of the international gay studies canon and a pioneering model for all those who continue to do research about the diversity of human sexual behavior.

REFERENCES

Desroches, Frederick J. 1990. "Tearoom Trade: A Research Update." *Qualitative Sociology* 13(1): 39–61.

Gay and Lesbian Police Advisory Task Force, Los Angeles. 1992. *Questionnaire Results for 1992 Griffith Park Activity*. Unpublished report.

Goodwin, Glenn A., Irving Louis Horowitz, and Peter M. Nardi. 1991. "Laud Humphreys: A Pioneer in the Practice of Social Science." *Sociological Inquiry* 61(2): 139–147.

Humphreys, Laud. 1975. *Tearoom Trade: Impersonal Sex in Public Places*. Enlarged ed. (1st ed., 1970). Hawthorne, N.Y.: Aldine de Gruyter.

Moore, Clive. 1995. "Poofs in the Park: Documenting Gay 'Beats' in Queensland, Australia." *GLQ: A Journal of Lesbian and Gay Studies*, 2:3, 319–339.

Nardi, Peter M. 1995. " 'The Breastplate of Righteousness': Twenty-Five Years After Laud Humphreys' *Tearoom Trade: Impersonal Sex in Public Places*." *Journal of Homosexuality*, 30(2): 1–10.

LAUD HUMPHREYS

At shortly after five o'clock on a weekday evening, four men enter a public restroom in the city park. One wears a well-tailored business suit; another wears tennis shoes, shorts, and teeshirt; the third man is still clad in the khaki uniform of his filling station; the last, a salesman, has loosened his tie and left his sports coat in the car. What has caused these men to leave the company of other homeward-bound commuters on the freeway? What common interest brings these men, with their divergent backgrounds, to this public facility?

They have come here not for the obvious reason, but in a search for "instant sex." Many men—married and unmarried, those with heterosexual identities and those whose self-image is a homosexual one—seek such impersonal sex, shunning involvement, desiring kicks without commitment. Whatever reasons—social, physiological, or psychological—might be postulated for this search, the phenomenon of impersonal sex persists as a widespread but rarely studied form of human interaction.

There are several settings for this type of deviant activity—the balconies of movie theaters, automobiles, behind bushes—but few offer the advantages for these men that public restrooms provide. "Tearooms," as these facilities are called in the language of the homosexual subculture, have several characteristics that make them attractive as locales for sexual encounters without involvement.

Like most other words in the homosexual vocabulary, the origin of *tearoom* is unknown. British slang has used "tea" to denote "urine." Another British usage is as a verb, meaning "to engage with, encounter, go in against." According to its most precise meaning in the argot, the only "true" tearoom is one that gains a reputation as a place where homosexual encounters occur. Presumably, any restroom could qualify for this distinction, but comparatively few are singled out at any one time. For instance, I have researched a metropolitan area with more than 90 public toilets in its parks, only 20 of which are in regular use as locales for sexual games. Restrooms thus designated join the company of automobiles and bath-houses as places for deviant sexual activity second only to private bedrooms in popularity. During certain seasons of the year—roughly, that period from April through October that midwestern homosexuals call "the hunting season"—tearooms may surpass any other locale of homoerotic enterprise in volume of activity.

Public restrooms are chosen by those who want homoerotic activity without commitment for a number of reasons. They are accessible, easily recognized by the initiate, and provide little public visibility. Tearooms thus offer the advantages of both public and private settings. They are available and recognizable enough to attract a large volume of potential sexual partners, providing an opportunity for rapid action with a variety of men. When added to the relative privacy of these settings, such features enhance the impersonality of the sheltered interaction.

In the first place, tearooms are readily accessible to the male population. They may be located in any sort of public gathering place: department stores, bus stations, libraries, hotels, YMCAs, or courthouses. In keeping with the drive-in craze of American society, however, the more popular facilities are those readily accessible to the roadways. The restrooms of public parks and beaches—and more recently the rest stops set at programmed intervals along superhighways—are now attracting the clientele that, in a more pedestrian age, frequented great buildings of the inner cities. My research is focused on the activity that takes place in the restrooms of public parks, not only because (with some seasonal variation) they provide the most action but also because of other factors that make them suitable for sociological study.

There is a great deal of difference in the volumes of homosexual activity that these accommodations shelter. In some, one might wait for months before observing a deviant act (unless solitary masturbation is considered deviant). In others, the volume approaches orgiastic dimensions. One summer afternoon, for instance, I witnessed 20 acts of fellatio in the course of an hour while waiting out a thunderstorm in a tearoom. For one who wishes to participate in (or study) such activity, the primary consideration is finding where the action is.

Occasionally, tips about the more active places may be gained from unexpected sources. Early in my research, I was approached by a man (whom I later surmised to be a park patrolman in plain clothes) while waiting at the window of a tearoom for some patrons to arrive. After finishing his business at the urinal and exchanging some remarks about the weather (it had been raining), the man came abruptly to the point: "Look, fellow, if you're looking for sex, this isn't the place. We're clamping down on this park because of trouble with the niggers. Try the john at the northeast corner of [Reagan] Park. You'll find plenty of action there." He was right. Some of my best observations were made at the spot he recommended. In most cases, however, I could only enter, wait, and watch—a method that was costly in both time and gasoline. After surveying a couple of dozen such rooms in this way, however, I became able to identify the more popular tearooms by observing certain physical evidence, the most obvious of which is the location of the facility. During the warm seasons, those restrooms that are isolated from other park facilities, such as administration buildings, shops, tennis courts, playgrounds, and picnic areas, are the more popular for deviant activity. The most active tearooms studied were all isolated from recreational areas, cut off by drives or lakes from baseball diamonds and picnic tables.

I have chosen the term "purlieu" (with its ancient meaning of land severed from a royal forest by perambulation) to describe the immediate environs best suited to the tearoom trade. Drives and walks that separate a public toilet from the rest of the park are almost certain guides to deviant sex. The ideal setting for homosexual activity is a tearoom situated on an island of grass, with roads close by on every side. The getaway car is just a few steps away; children are not apt to wander over from the playground; no one can surprise the participants by walking in from the woods or from over a hill; it is not likely that straight people will stop there. According to my observations, the women's side of these buildings is seldom used at all.

What They Want, When They Want It

The availability of facilities they can recognize attracts a great number of men who wish, for whatever reason, to engage in impersonal homoerotic activity. Simple observation is enough to guide these participants, the researcher and, perhaps, the police to active tearooms. It is much more difficult to make an accurate appraisal of the proportion of the male population who engage in such activity over a representative length of time. Even with good sampling procedures, a large staff of assistants would be needed to make the observations necessary for an adequate census of this mobile population. All that may be said with some degree of certainty is that the percentage of the male population who participate in tearoom sex in the United States is somewhat less than the 16 percent of the adult white male population Kinsey found to have "at least as much of the homosexual as the heterosexual in their histories."

Participants assure me that it is not uncommon in tearooms for one man to fellate as many as ten others in a day. I have personally watched a fellator

take on three men in succession in a half hour of observation. One respondent, who has cooperated with the researcher in a number of taped interviews, claims to average three men each day during the busy season.

I have seen some waiting turn for this type of service. Leaving one such
scene on a warm September Saturday, I remarked to a man who left close
behind me: "Kind of crowded in there, isn't it?" "Hell, yes," he answered,
"It's getting so you have to take a number and wait in line in these places!"

There are many who frequent the same facility repeatedly. Men will
come to be known as regular, even daily, participants, stopping off at the
same tearoom on the way to or from work. One physician in his late fifties
was so punctual in his appearance at a particular restroom that I began to
look forward to our daily chats. This robust, affable respondent said he had
stopped at this tearoom every evening of the week (except Wednesday, his
day off) for years "for a blow-job." Another respondent, a salesman whose
schedule is flexible, may "make the scene" more than once a day—usually
at his favorite men's room. At the time of our formal interview, this man
claimed to have had four orgasms in the past 24 hours.

According to participants I have interviewed, those who are looking for
impersonal sex in tearooms are relatively certain of finding the sort of partner they want. . . .

> You go into the tearoom. You can pick up some really nice things in there.
> Again, it is a matter of sex real quick; and, if you like this kind, fine—
> you've got it. You get one and he is done; and, before long, you've got
> another one.

. . . and when they want it:

> Well, I go there; and you can always find someone to suck your cock,
> morning, noon, or night. I know lots of guys who stop by there on their way
> to work—and all during the day.

It is this sort of volume and variety that keeps the tearooms viable as
market places of the one-night-stand variety.

Of the bar crowd in gay (homosexual) society, only a small percentage
would be found in park restrooms. But this more overt, gay bar clientele
constitutes a minor part of those in any American city who follow a predomi-
nantly homosexual pattern. The so-called closet queens and other types of
covert deviants make up the vast majority of those who engage in homosexual acts—and these are the persons most attracted to tearoom encounters.

Tearooms are popular, not because they serve as gathering places for
homosexuals, but because they attract a variety of men, a *minority* of whom
are active in the homosexual subculture and a large group of whom have no

homosexual self-identity. For various reasons, they do not want to be seen with those who might be identified as such or to become involved with them on a "social" basis.

Sheltering Silence

There is another aspect of the tearoom encounters that is crucial. I refer to the silence of the interaction.

Throughout most homosexual encounters in public restrooms, nothing is spoken. One may spend many hours in these buildings and witness dozens of sexual acts without hearing a word. Of 50 encounters on which I made extensive notes, only in 15 was any word spoken. Two were encounters in which I sought to ease the strain of legitimizing myself as lookout by saying, "You go ahead—I'll watch." Four were whispered remarks between sexual partners, such as, "Not so hard!" or "Thanks." One was an exchange of greetings between friends.

The other eight verbal exchanges were in full voice and more extensive, but they reflected an attendant circumstance that was exceptional. When a group of us were locked in a restroom and attacked by several youths, we spoke for defense and out of fear. This event ruptured the reserve among us and resulted in a series of conversations among those who shared this adventure for several days afterward. Gradually, this sudden unity subsided, and the encounters drifted back into silence.

Barring such unusual events, an occasionally whispered "thanks" at the conclusion of the act constitutes the bulk of even whispered communication. At first, I presumed that speech was avoided for fear of incrimination. The excuse that intentions have been misunderstood is much weaker when those proposals are expressed in words rather than signaled by body movements. As research progressed, however, it became evident that the privacy of silent interaction accomplishes much more than mere defense against exposure to a hostile world. Even when a careful lookout is maintaining the boundaries of an encounter against intrusion, the sexual participants tend to be silent. The mechanism of silence goes beyond satisfying the demand for privacy. Like all other characteristics of the tearoom setting, it serves to guarantee anonymity, to assure the impersonality of the sexual liaison.

Tearoom sex is distinctly less personal than any other form of sexual activity, with the single exception of solitary masturbation. What I mean by "less personal" is simply that there is less emotional and physical involvement in restroom fellatio—less, even, than in the furtive action that takes place in autos and behind bushes. In those instances, at least, there is generally some verbal involvement. Often, in tearoom stalls, the only portions of the players' bodies that touch are the mouth of the insertee and the penis of the inserter; and the mouths of these partners seldom open for speech.

Only a public place, such as a park restroom, could provide the lack of personal involvement in sex that certain men desire. The setting fosters the necessary turnover in participants by its accessibility and visibility to the "right" men. In these public settings, too, there exists a sort of democracy that is endemic to impersonal sex. Men of all racial, social, educational and physical characteristics meet in these places for sexual union. With the lack of involvement, personal preferences tend to be minimized.

If a person is going to entangle his body with another's in bed—or allow his mind to become involved with another mind—he will have certain standards of appearance, cleanliness, personality, or age that the prospective partner must meet. Age, looks, and other external variables are germane to the sexual action. As the amount of anticipated contact of body and mind in the sex act decreases, so do the standards expected of the partner. As one respondent told me:

> I go to bed with gay people, too. But if I am going to bed with a gay person, I have certain standards that I prefer them to meet. And in the tearooms you don't have to worry about these things—because it is just a purely one-sided affair.

Participants may develop strong attachments to the settings of their adventures in impersonal sex. I have noted more than once that these men seem to acquire stronger sentimental attachments to the buildings in which they meet for sex than to the persons with whom they engage in it. One respondent tells the following story: We had been discussing the relative merits of various facilities, when I asked him: "Do you remember that old tearoom across from the park garage—the one they tore down last winter?"

> Do I ever! That was the greatest place in the park. Do you know what my roommate did last Christmas, after they tore the place down? He took a wreath, sprayed it with black paint, and laid it on top of the snow— right where that corner stall had stood. . . . He was really broken up!

The walls and fixtures of these public facilities are provided by society at large, but much remains for the participants to provide for themselves. Silence in these settings is the product of years of interaction. It is a normative response to the demand for privacy without involvement, a rule that has been developed and taught. Except for solitary masturbation, sex necessitates joint action; but impersonal sex requires that this interaction be as unrevealing as possible.

Tearoom activity attracts a large number of participants—enough to produce the majority of arrests for homosexual offenses in the United States.
Now, employing data gained from both formal and informal interviews, we
shall consider what these men are like away from the scenes of impersonal
sex. "For some people," says Evelyn Hooker, an authority on male homosexuality, "the seeking of sexual contacts with other males is an activity isolated from all other aspects of their lives." Such segregation is apparent
with most men who engage in the homosexual activity of public restrooms;
but the degree and manner in which "deviant" is isolated from "normal"
behavior in their lives will be seen to vary along social dimensions.

For the man who lives next door, the tearoom participant is just another
neighbor—and probably a very good one at that. He may make a little more
money than the next man and work a little harder for it. It is likely that he will
drive a nicer car and maintain a neater yard than do other neighbors in the
block. Maybe, like some tearoom regulars, he will work with Boy Scouts in
the evenings and spend much of his weekend at the church. It may be more
surprising for the outsider to discover that most of these men are married.

Indeed, 54 percent of my research subjects are married and living with
their wives. From the data at hand, there is no evidence that these unions
are particularly unstable; nor does it appear that any of the wives are aware
of their husbands' secret sexual activity. Indeed, the husbands choose public restrooms as sexual settings partly to avoid just such exposure. I see no
reason to dispute the claim of a number of tearoom respondents that their
preference for a form of concerted action that is fast and impersonal is
largely predicated on a desire to protect their family relationships.

Superficial analysis of the data indicates that the maintenance of exemplary marriages—at least in appearance—is very important to the subjects
of this study. In answering questions such as "When it comes to making
decisions in your household, who generally makes them?" the participants
indicate they are more apt to defer to their mates than are those in the control sample. They also indicate that they find it more important to "get along
well" with their wives. In the open-ended questions regarding marital relationships, they tend to speak of them in more glowing terms.

Tom and Myra

This handsome couple live in ranch-style suburbia with their two young
children. Tom is in his early thirties—an aggressive, muscular, and virile-
looking male. He works "about 75 hours a week" at his new job as a

Tearoom Trade: Impersonal Sex in Public Places

chemist. "I am *wild* about my job," he says. "I really love it!" Both of Tom's
"really close" friends he met at work.

He is a Methodist and Myra a Roman Catholic, but each goes to his or her own church. Although he claims to have broad interests in life, they boil down to "games—sports like touch football or baseball."

When I asked him to tell me something about his family, Tom replied only in terms of their "good fortune" that things are not worse: We've been fortunate that a religious problem has not occurred. We're fortunate in having two healthy children. We're fortunate that we decided to leave my last job. Being married has made me more stable.

They have been married for eleven years, and Myra is the older of the two. When asked who makes what kinds of decisions in his family, he said: "She makes most decisions about the family. She keeps the books. But I make the *major* decisions."

Myra does the household work and takes care of the children. Perceiving his main duties as those of "keeping the yard up" and "bringing home the bacon," Tom sees as his wife's only shortcoming "her lack of discipline in organization." He remarked: "She's very attractive . . . has a fair amount of poise. The best thing is that she gets along well and is able to establish close relationships with other women."

Finally, when asked how he thinks his wife feels about him and his behavior in the family, Tom replied: "She'd like to have me around more— would like for me to have a closer relationship with her and the kids." He believes it is "very important" to have the kind of sex life he needs. Reporting that he and Myra have intercourse about twice a month, he feels that his sexual needs are "adequately met" in his relationships with his wife. I also know that, from time to time, Tom has sex in the restrooms of a public park.

As an upwardly mobile man, Tom was added to the sample at a point of transition in his career as a tearoom participant. If Tom is like others who share working-class origins, he may have learned of the tearoom as an economical means of achieving orgasm during his navy years. Of late, he has returned to the restrooms for occasional sexual "relief," since his wife, objecting to the use of birth control devices, has limited his conjugal outlets.

Tom still perceives his sexual needs in the symbolic terms of the class in which he was socialized: "about twice a month" is the frequency of intercourse generally reported by working-class men; and, although they are reticent in reporting it, they do not perceive this frequency as adequate to meet their sexual needs, which they estimate are about the same as those felt by others of their age. My interviews indicate that such perceptions of sexual drive and satisfaction prevail among respondents of the lower-middle to upper-lower classes, whereas they are uncommon for those of the upper-middle and upper classes. Among the latter, the reported perception is of a much higher frequency of intercourse and they estimate their needs to be greater than those of "most other men."

Aging Crisis

Not only is Tom moving into a social position that may cause him to reinterpret his sexual drive, he is also approaching a point of major crisis in his career as a tearoom participant. At the time when I observed him in an act of fellatio, he played the inserter role. Still relatively young and handsome, Tom finds himself sought out as "trade," i.e., those men who make themselves available for acts of fellatio but who, regarding themselves as "straight," refuse to reciprocate in the sexual act. Not only is that the role he expects to play in the tearoom encounters, it is the role others expect of him.

"I'm not toned up anymore," Tom complains. He is gaining weight around the middle and losing hair. As he moves past 35, Tom will face the aging crisis of the tearooms. Less and less frequently will he find himself the one sought out in these meetings. Presuming that he has been sufficiently reinforced to continue this form of sexual operation, he will be forced to seek other men. As trade he was not expected to reciprocate, but he will soon be increasingly expected to serve as insertee for those who have first taken that role for him.

In most cases, fellatio is a service performed by an older man upon a younger. In one encounter, for example, a man appearing to be around 40 was observed as insertee with a man in his twenties as inserter. A few minutes later, the man of 40 was being sucked by one in his fifties. Analyzing the estimated ages of the principal partners in 53 observed acts of fellatio, I arrived at these conclusions: the insertee was judged to be older than the inserter in 40 cases; they were approximately the same age in three; and the inserter was the older in ten instances. The age differences ranged from an insertee estimated to be 25 years older than his partner to an insertee thought to be ten years younger than his inserter.

Strong references to this crisis of aging are found in my interviews with cooperating respondents, one of whom had this to say: "Well, I started off as the straight young thing. Everyone wanted to suck my cock. I wouldn't have been caught dead with one of the things in my mouth! . . . So, here I am at 40—with grown kids—and the biggest cocksucker in [the city]!"

Similar experiences were expressed, in more reserved language, by another man, some 15 years his senior: "I suppose I was around 35—or 36—when I started giving out blow jobs. It just got so I couldn't operate any

other way in the park johns. I'd still rather have a good blow job any day, but
I've gotten so I like it the way it is now."

Perhaps by now there is enough real knowledge abroad to have dispelled
the idea that men who engage in homosexual acts may be typed by any consistency of performance in one or another sexual role. Undoubtedly, there are
preferences: few persons are so adaptable, their conditioning so undifferenti-
ated, that they fail to exercise choice between various sexual roles and positions. Such preferences, however, are learned, and sexual repertories tend to
expand with time and experience. This study of restroom sex indicates that
sexual roles within these encounters are far from stable. They are apt to
change within an encounter, from one encounter to another, with age, and
with the amount of exposure to influences from a sexually deviant subculture.

It is to this last factor that I should like to direct the reader's attention.
The degree of contact with a network of friends who share the actor's sexual
interests takes a central position in mediating not only his preferences for
sex role, but his style of adaptation to—and rationalization of—the deviant
activity in which he participates. There are, however, two reasons why I
have not classified research subjects in terms of their participation in the
homosexual subculture. It is difficult to measure accurately the degree of
such involvement; and such subcultural interaction depends upon other
social variables, two of which are easily measured.

Family status has a definitive effect on the deviant careers of those
whose concern is with controlling information about their sexual behavior.
The married man who engages in homosexual activity must be much more
cautious about his involvement in the subculture than his single counter-
part. As a determinant of life style and sexual activity, marital status is also a
determinant of the patterns of deviant adaptation and rationalization. Only
those in my sample who were divorced or separated from their wives were
difficult to categorize as either married or single. Those who had been married, however, showed a tendency to remain in friendship networks with
married men. Three of the four were still limited in freedom by responsibili-
ties for their children. For these reasons, I have included all men who were
once married in the "married" categories.

The second determining variable is the relative autonomy of the respondent's occupation. A man is "independently" employed when his job allows
him freedom of movement and security from being fired; the most obvious
example is self-employment. Occupational "dependence" leaves a man little freedom for engaging in disreputable activity. The sales manager or
other executive of a business firm has greater freedom than the salesman
or attorney who is employed in the lower echelons of a large industry or by
the federal government. The sales representative whose territory is far

removed from the home office has greater independence, in terms of information control, than the minister of a local congregation. The majority of those placed in both the married and unmarried categories with *dependent* occupations were employed by large industries or the government.

Median education levels and annual family incomes indicate that those with dependent occupations rank lower on the socioeconomic scale. Only in the case of married men, however, is this correlation between social class and occupational autonomy strongly supported by the ratings of these respondents on Warner's Index of Status Characteristics. Nearly all the married men with dependent occupations are of the upper-lower or lower-middle classes, whereas those with independent occupations are of the upper-middle or upper classes. For single men, the social class variable is neither so easily identifiable nor so clearly divided. Nearly all single men in the sample can be classified only as "vaguely middle class."

As occupational autonomy and marital status remain the most important dimensions along which participants may be ranked, we shall consider four general types of tearoom customers: 1) married men with dependent occupations, 2) married men with independent occupations, 3) unmarried men with independent occupations, and 4) unmarried men with dependent occupations. As will become evident with the discussion of each type, I have employed labels from the homosexual argot, along with pseudonyms, to designate each class of participants. This is done not only to facilitate reading but to emphasize that we are describing persons rather than merely "typical" constructs.

Type I: Trade

The first classification, which includes 19 of the participants (38 percent), may be called "trade," since most would earn that appellation from the gay subculture. All of these men are, or have been, married—one was separated from his wife at the time of interviewing and another was divorced.

Most work as truck drivers, machine operators, or clerical workers. There is a member of the armed forces, a carpenter, and the minister of a pentecostal church. Most of their wives work, at least part time, to help raise their median annual family income to $8,000. One in six of these men is black. All are normally masculine in appearance and mannerism. Although 14 have completed high school, there are only three college graduates among them, and five have had less than 12 years of schooling.

George is representative of this largest group of respondents. Born of second-generation German parentage in an ethnic enclave of the midwestern city where he still resides, he was raised as a Lutheran. He feels that his father (like George a truck driver) was quite warm in his relationship with him as a child. His mother he describes as a very nervous, asthmatic woman and thinks that an older sister suffered a nervous breakdown some years ago, although she was never treated for it. Another sister and a brother have evidenced no emotional problems.

At the age of 20 he married a Roman Catholic girl and has since joined her church, although he classifies himself as "lapsed." In the fourteen years of their marriage, they have had seven children, one of whom is less than a year old. George doesn't think they should have more children, but his wife objects to using any type of birth control other than the rhythm method. With his wife working part time as a waitress, they have an income of about $5,000.

"How often do you have intercourse with your wife?" I asked. "Not very much the last few years," he replied. "It's up to when she feels like giving it to me—which ain't very often. I never suggest it."

George was cooking hamburgers on an outdoor grill and enjoying a beer as I interviewed him. "Me, I like to come home." he asserted. "I love to take care of the outside of the house. . . . Like to go places with the children—my wife, she doesn't."

With their mother at work, the children were running in and out of the door, revealing a household interior in gross disarray. George stopped to call one of the smaller youngsters out of the street in front of his modest, suburban home. When he resumed his remarks about his wife, there was more feeling in his description:

> My wife doesn't have much outside interest. She doesn't like to go out or take the kids places. But she's an A-1 mother, I'll say that! I guess you'd say she's very nice to get along with—but don't cross her! She gets aggravated with me—I don't know why. . . . Well, you'd have to know my wife. We fight all the time. Anymore, it seems we just don't get along—except when we're apart. Mostly, we argue about the kids. She's afraid of having more. . . . She's afraid to have sex but doesn't believe in birth control. I'd just rather not be around her! I won't suggest having sex anyway—and she just doesn't want it anymore.

While more open than most in his acknowledgement of marital tension, George's appraisal of sexual relations in the marriage is typical of those respondents classified as Trade. In 63 percent of these marriages, the wife, husband, or both are Roman Catholic. When answering questions about their sexual lives, a story much like George's emerged: at least since the birth of the last child, conjugal relations have been very rare.

These data suggest that, along with providing an excuse for diminishing intercourse with their wives, the religious teachings to which most of these

families adhere may cause the husbands to search for sex in the tearooms.
Whatever the causes that turn them unsatisfied from the marriage bed,
however, the alternate outlet must be quick, inexpensive, and impersonal.
Any personal, ongoing affair—any outlet requiring money or hours away
from home—would threaten a marriage that is already shaky and jeopar-
dize the most important thing these men possess, their standing as father
of their children.

Around the turn of the century, before the vice squads moved in (in their
never-ending process of narrowing the behavioral options of those in the
lower classes), the Georges of this study would probably have made regular
visits to the two-bit bordellos. With a madam watching a clock to limit the
time, these cheap whorehouses provided the same sort of fast, impersonal
service as today's public restrooms. I find no indication that these men seek
homosexual contact as such; rather, they want a form of orgasm-producing
action that is less lonely than masturbation and less involving than a love
relationship. As the forces of social control deprive them of one outlet, they
provide another. The newer form, it should be noted, is more stigmatizing
than the previous one—thus giving "proof" to the adage that "the sinful are
drawn ever deeper into perversity."

George was quite affable when interviewed on his home territory. A year
before, when I first observed him in the tearoom of a park about three miles
from his home, he was a far more cautious man. Situated at the window of
the restroom, I saw him leave his old station wagon and, looking up and
down the street, walk to the facility at a very fast pace. Once inside, he
paced nervously from door to window until satisfied that I would serve as an
adequate lookout. After playing the inserter role with a man who had waited
in the stall farthest from the door, he left quickly, without wiping or washing
his hands, and drove away toward the nearest exit from the park. In the tearoom he was a frightened man, engaging in furtive sex. In his own back-
yard, talking with an observer whom he failed to recognize, he was warm,
open, and apparently at ease.

Weighing 200 pounds or more, George has a protruding gut and tattoos
on both forearms. Although muscular and in his mid-thirties, he would not
be described as a handsome person. For him, no doubt, the aging crisis is
also an identity crisis. Only with reluctance—and perhaps never—will he
turn to the insertee role. The threat of such a role to his masculine self-
image is too great. Like others of his class with whom I have had more
extensive interviews, George may have learned that sexual game as a teen-
age hustler, or else when serving in the army during the Korean war. In
either case, his socialization into homosexual experience took place in a
masculine world where it is permissible to accept money from a "queer" in

return for carefully limited sexual favors. But to use one's own mouth as a substitute for the female organ, or even to express enjoyment of the action, is taboo in the Trade code.

Moreover, for men of George's occupational and marital status, there is no network of friends engaged in tearoom activity to help them adapt to the changes aging will bring. I found no evidence of friendship networks among respondents of this type, who enter and leave the restrooms alone, avoiding conversation while within. Marginal to both the heterosexual and homosexual worlds, these men shun involvement in any form of gay subculture. Type I participants report fewer friends of any sort than do those of other classes. When asked how many close friends he has, George answered: "None. I haven't got time for that."

It is difficult to interview the Trade without becoming depressed over the hopelessness of their situation. They are almost uniformly lonely and isolated: lacking success in either marriage bed or work, unable to discuss their three best friends (because they don't have three); en route from the din of factories to the clamor of children, they slip off the freeways for a few moments of impersonal sex in a toilet stall.

Such unrewarded existence is reflected in the portrait of another marginal man. A jobless Negro, he earns only contempt and sexual rejection from his working wife in return for baby-sitting duties. The paperback books and magazines scattered about his living room supported his comment that he reads a great deal to relieve boredom. (George seldom reads even the newspaper and has no hobbies to report.) No wonder that he urged me to stay for supper when my interview schedule was finished. "I really wish you'd stay awhile," he said. "I haven't talked to anyone about myself in a hell of a long time!"

Type II: Ambisexuals

A very different picture emerges in the case of Dwight. As sales manager for a small manufacturing concern, he is in a position to hire men who share his sexual and other interests. Not only does he have a business associate or two who share his predilection for tearoom sex, he has been able to stretch chance meetings in the tearoom purlieu into long-lasting friendships. Once, after I had gained his confidence through repeated interviews, I asked him to name all the participants he knew. The names of five other Type II men in my sample were found in the list of nearly two dozen names he gave me.

Dwight, then, has social advantages in the public restrooms as well as in society at large. His annual income of $16,000 helps in the achievement of these benefits, as does his marriage into a large and distinguished family and his education at a prestigious local college. From his restroom friends Dwight learns which tearooms in the city are popular and where the police are clamping down. He even knows which officers are looking for payoffs and how much they expect to be paid. It is of even greater importance that his attitudes toward—and perceptions of—the tearoom encounters are shaped and reinforced by the friendship network in which he participates.

It has thus been easier for Dwight to meet the changing demands of the aging crisis. He knows others who lost no self-respect when they began "going down" on their sexual partners, and they have helped him learn to enjoy the involvement of oral membranes in impersonal sex. As Tom, too, moves into this class of participants, he can be expected to learn how to rationalize the switch in sexual roles necessitated by the loss of youthful good looks. He will cease thinking of the insertee role as threatening to his masculinity. His socialization into the Ambisexuals will make the orgasm but one of a number of kicks.

Three-fourths of the married participants with independent occupations were observed, at one time or another, participating as insertees in fellatio, compared to only one-third of the Trade. Not only do the Type II participants tend to switch roles with greater facility, they seem inclined to search beyond the tearooms for more exotic forms of sexual experience. Dwight, along with others in his class, expresses a liking for anal intercourse (both as insertee and inserter), for group activity, and even for mild forms of sado-masochistic sex. A friend of his once invited me to an "orgy" he had planned in an apartment he maintains for sexual purposes. Another friend, a social and commercial leader of the community, told me that he enjoys having men urinate in his mouth between acts of fellatio.

Dwight is in his early forties and has two sons in high school. The school-bound offspring provide him with an excuse to leave his wife at home during frequent business trips across the country. Maintaining a list of gay contacts, Dwight is able to engage wholeheartedly in the life of the homosexual subculture in other cities—the sort of involvement he is careful to avoid at home. In the parks or over cocktails, he amuses his friends with lengthy accounts of these adventures.

Dwight recounts his first sexual relationship with another boy at the age of "nine or ten":

> My parents always sent me off to camp in the summer, and it was there that I had my sexual initiation. This sort of thing usually took the form of rolling around in a bunk together and ended in our jacking each other off. . . . I suppose I started pretty early. God, I was almost in college before I had my first woman! I always had some other guy on the string in

prep school—some real romances there! But I made up for lost time with the girls during my college years. . . . During that time, I only slipped back into my old habits a couple of times—and then it was a once-only occurrence with a roommate after we had been drinking.

Culminating an active heterosexual life at the university, Dwight married the girl he had impregnated. He reports having intercourse three or four times a week with her throughout their 18 married years but also admits to supplementing that activity on occasion: "I had the seven-year-itch and stepped out on her quite a bit then." Dwight also visits the tearooms almost daily:

> I guess you might say I'm pretty highly sexed [he chuckled a little], but I really don't think that's why I go to tearooms. That's really not sex. Sex is something I have with my wife in bed. It's not as if I were committing adultery by getting my rocks off—or going down on some guy—in a tearoom. I get a kick out of it. Some of my friends go out for handball. I'd rather cruise the park. Does that sound perverse to you?

Dwight's openness in dealing with the more sensitive areas of his biography was typical of upper-middle and upper-class respondents of both the participant and control samples. Actual refusals of interviews came almost entirely from lower-class participants; more of the cooperating respondents were of the upper socioeconomic ranks. In the same vein, working-class respondents were most cautious about answering questions pertaining to their income and their social and political views.

Other researchers have encountered a similar response differential along class lines, and I realize that my educational and social characteristics encourage rapport with Dwight more than with George. It may also be assumed that sympathy with survey research increases with education. Two-thirds of the married participants with occupational independence are college graduates.

It has been suggested, however, that another factor may be operative in this instance: although the upper-class deviants may have more to lose from exposure (in the sense that the mighty have farther to fall), they also have more means at their disposal with which to protect their moral histories. Some need only tap their spending money to pay off a member of the vice squad. In other instances, social contacts with police commissioners or newspaper publishers make it possible to squelch either record or publicity of an arrest. One respondent has made substantial contributions to a police charity fund, while another hired private detectives to track down a black-mailer. Not least in their capacity to cover for errors in judgment is the fact that their word has the backing of economic and social influence. Evi-

dence must be strong to prosecute a man who can hire the best attorneys.
Lower-class men are rightfully more suspicious, for they have fewer
resources with which to defend themselves if exposed.

This does not mean that Type II participants are immune to the risks of
the game but simply that they are bidding from strength. To them, the risks
of arrest, exposure, blackmail, or physical assault contribute to the excitement quotient. It is not unusual for them to speak of cruising as an adventure, in contrast with the Trade, who engage in a furtive search for sexual
relief. On the whole, then, the action of Type II respondents is apt to be
somewhat bolder and their search for "kicks" less inhibited than that of
most other types of participants.

Dwight is not fleeing from an unhappy home life or sexless marriage to
the encounters in the parks. He expresses great devotion to his wife and
children: "They're my whole life," he exclaims. All evidence indicates that,
as father, citizen, businessman, and church member, Dwight's behavior
patterns—as viewed by his peers—are exemplary.

Five of the 12 participants in Dwight's class are members of the Episcopal church. Dwight is one of two who were raised in that church, although
he is not as active a churchman as some who became Episcopalians later
in life. In spite of his infrequent attendance to worship, he feels his church
is "just right" for him and needs no changing. Its tradition and ceremony
are intellectually and esthetically pleasing to him. Its liberal outlook on
questions of morality round out a religious orientation that he finds generally supportive.

In an interview witnessed by a friend he had brought to meet me, Dwight
discussed his relationship with his parents: "Father ignored me. He just
never said anything to me. I don't third: he ever knew I existed." [His father
was an attorney, esteemed beyond the city of Dwight's birth, who died while
his only son was yet in his teens.] "I hope I'm a better father to my boys
than he was to me," Dwight added.

"But his mother is a remarkable woman," the friend interjected, "really
one of the most fabulous women I've met! Dwight took me back to meet
her—years ago, when we were lovers of a sort. I still look forward to her
visits."

"She's remarkable just to have put up with me," Dwight added. Just to
give you an idea, one vacation I brought another boy home from school with
me. She walked into the bedroom one morning and caught us bare-assed
in a 69 position. She just excused herself and backed out of the room.
Later, when we were alone, she just looked at me—over the edge of her
glasses—and said: "I'm not going to lecture you, dear, but I do hope you
don't swallow that stuff!"

Although he has never had a nervous breakdown, Dwight takes "an occasional antidepressant" because of his "moodiness." "I'm really quite moody and I go to the tearooms more often when my spirits are low." While his periods of depression may result in increased tearoom activity, his deviant behavior does not seem to produce much tension in his life:

> I don't feel guilty about my little sexual games in the park. I'm not some sort of sick queer. . . . You might think I live two lives; but, if I do, I don't feel split in two by them.

Unlike the Trade, Type II participants recognize their homosexual activity as indicative of their own psychosexual orientations. They think of themselves as bisexual or ambisexual and have intellectualized their deviant tendencies in terms of the pseudopsychology of the popular press. They speak often of the great men of history, as well as of certain movie stars and others of contemporary fame, who are also "AC/DC." Erving Goffman has remarked that stigmatized Americans "tend to live in a literally defined world." This is nowhere truer than of the subculturally oriented participants of this study. Not only do they read a great deal about homosexuality, they discuss it within their network of friends. For the Dwights there is subcultural support that enables them to integrate their deviance with the remainder of their lives, while maintaining control over the information that could discredit their whole being. For these reasons they look upon the gaming encounters in the parks as enjoyable experiences.

Type III: Gay Guys

Like the Ambisexuals, unmarried respondents with independent occupations are locked into a strong subculture, a community that provides them with knowledge about the tearooms and reinforcement in their particular brand of deviant activity. This open participation in the gay community distinguishes these single men from the larger group of unmarrieds with dependent occupations. These men take the homosexual role of our society, and are thus the most truly "gay" of all participant types. Except for Tim, who was recruited as a decoy in the tearooms by the vice squad of a police department, Type III participants learned the strategies of the tearooms through friends already experienced in this branch of the sexual market.

Typical of this group is Ricky, a 24-year-old university student whose older male lover supports him. Ricky stands at the median age of his type, who range from 19 to 50 years. Half of them are college graduates and all but one other are at least part-time students, a characteristic that explains their low median income of $3,000. Because Ricky's lover is a good

provider, he is comfortably situated in a midtown apartment, a more pleas-
ant residence than most of his friends enjoy.

Ricky is a thin, good-looking young man with certain movements and
manners of speech that might be termed effeminate. He is careful of his
appearance, dresses well, and keeps an immaculate apartment, furnished
with an expensive stereo and some tasteful antique pieces. Seated on a
sofa in the midst of the things his lover has provided for their mutual comfort, Ricky is impressively self-assured. He is proud to say that he has
found, at least for the time being, what all those participants in his category
claim to seek: a "permanent" love relationship.

Having met his lover in a park, Ricky returns there only when his mate is
on a business trip or their relationship is strained. Then Ricky becomes, as
he puts it, "horny," and he goes to the park to study, cruise and engage in
tearoom sex:

> The bars are o.k.—but a little too public for a 'married' man like me. . . .
> Tearooms are just another kind of action, and they do quite well when
> nothing better is available.

Like other Type III respondents, he shows little preference in sexual roles.
"It depends on the other guy," Ricky says, "and whether I like his looks or
not. Some men I'd crawl across the street on my knees for—others I would-
n't piss on!" His aging crisis will be shared with all others in the gay world. It
will take the nightmarish form of waning attractiveness and the search for a
permanent lover to fill his later years, but it will have no direct relationship
with the tearoom roles. Because of his socialization in the homosexual society, taking the insertee role is neither traumatic for him nor related to aging.

Ricky's life revolves around his sexual deviance in a way that is not true
of George or even of Dwight. Most of his friends and social contacts are
connected with the homosexual subculture. His attitudes toward and rationalization of his sexual behavior are largely gained from this wide circle of
friends. The gay men claim to have more close friends than do any other
type of control or participant respondents. As frequency of orgasm is
reported, this class also has more sex than any other group sampled, aver-
aging 2.5 acts per week. They seem relatively satisfied with this aspect of
their lives and regard their sexual drive as normal—although Ricky perceives his sexual needs as less than most.

One of his tearoom friends has recently married a woman, but Ricky has
no intention of following his example. Another of his type, asked about marriage, said: "I prefer men, but I would make a good *wife* for the right *man*."

The vocabulary of heterosexual marriage is commonly used by those of
Ricky's type. They speak of "marrying" the men they love and want to "set-

tle down in a nice home." In a surprising number of cases, they take their
lovers "home to meet mother." This act, like the exchange of "pinky rings,"
is intended to provide social strength to the lovers' union.

Three of the seven persons of this type were adopted—Ricky at the age
of six months. Ricky told me that his adoptive father, who died three years
before our interview, was "very warm and loving. He worked hard for a living
and we moved a lot." He is still close to his adoptive mother, who knows of
his sexual deviance and treats his lover "like an older son."

Ricky hopes to be a writer, an occupation that would "allow me the freedom to be myself. I have a religion [Unitarian] which allows me freedom,
and I want a career which will do the same." This, again, is typical: all three
of the Unitarians in the sample are Type III men, although none was raised
in that faith; and their jobs are uniformly of the sort to which their sexual
activity, if exposed, would present little threat.

Although these men correspond most closely to society homosexual
stereotype, they are least representative of the tearoom population, consti-
tuting only 14 percent of the participant sample. More than any other type,
the Rickys seem at ease with their behavior in the sexual market, and their
scarcity in the tearooms is indicative of this. They want personal sex—more
permanent relationships—and the public restrooms are not where this is to
be found.

That any of them patronize the tearooms at all is the result of incidental
factors: they fear that open cruising in the more common homosexual market places of the baths and bars might disrupt a current love affair; or they
drop in at a tearoom while waiting for a friend at one of the "watering
places" where homosexuals congregate in the parks. They find the
anonymity of the tearooms suitable for their purposes, but not inviting
enough to provide the primary setting for sexual activity.

Type IV: Closet Queens

Another dozen of the 50 participants interviewed may be classified as single deviants with dependent occupations, "closet queens" in homosexual
slang. Again, the label may be applied to others who keep their deviance
hidden, whether married or single, but the covert, unmarried men are most
apt to earn this appellation. With them, we have moved full circle in our
classifications, for they parallel the Trade in a number of ways:

1. They have few friends, only a minority of whom are involved in tea-
    room activity.
2. They tend to play the inserter role, at least until they confront the
    crisis of aging.

3. Half of them are Roman Catholic in religion.
4. Their median annual income is $6,000; and they work as teachers, postmen, salesmen, clerks—usually for large corporations or agencies.
5. Most of them have completed only high school, although there are a few exceptionally well-educated men in this group.
6. One in six is black.
7. Not only are they afraid of becoming involved in other forms of the sexual market, they share with the Trade a relatively furtive involvement in the tearoom encounters.

Arnold will be used as the typical case. Only 22, Arnold is well below the median age of this group; but in most other respects he is quite representative, particularly in regard to the psychological problems common to Type IV.

A routine interview with Arnold stretched to nearly three hours in the suburban apartment he shares with another single man. Currently employed as a hospital attendant, he has had trouble with job stability, usually because he finds the job unsatisfactory. He frequently is unoccupied.

> Arnold: I hang around the park a lot when I don't have anything else to do. I guess I've always known about the tearooms . . . so I just started going in there to get my rocks off. But I haven't gone since I caught my lover there in September. You get in the habit of going; but I don't think I'll start in again—unless I get too desperate.
>
> Interviewer: Do you make the bar scene?
>
> Arnold: Very seldom. My roommate and I go out together once in a while, but everybody there seems to think we're lovers. So I don't really operate in the bars. I really don't like gay people. They can be so damned bitchy! I really like women better than men—except for sex. There's a lot of the female in me, and I feel more comfortable with women than with men. I understand women and like to be with them. I'm really very close to my mother. The reason I don't live at home is because there are too many brothers and sisters living there. . . .
>
> Interviewer: Is she still a devout Roman Catholic?
>
> Arnold: Well, yes and no. She still goes to Mass some, but she and I go to seances together with a friend. I am studying astrology and talk it over with her quite a bit. I also analyze handwriting and read a lot about numerology. Mother knows I am gay and doesn't seem to mind. I don't think she really believes it though.

Arnold has a health problem: "heart attacks," which the doctor says are psychological and which take the form of "palpitations, dizziness, chest pain, shortness of breath, and extreme weakness." These attacks, which began soon after his father's death from a coronary two years ago, make him feel as if he were "dying and turning cold." Tranquilizers were pre-scribed for him, "but I threw them out, because I don't like to become dependent on such things." He quoted a book on mental control of health that drugs are "unnecessary, if you have proper control."

He also connects these health problems with his resentment of his father, who was mentally ill.

> Arnold: I don't understand his mental illness and have always blamed him for it. You might say that I have a father complex and, along with that, a security complex. Guess that's why I always run around with older men.

> Interviewer: Were any of your brothers gay?

> Arnold: Not that I know of. I used to have sex with the brother closest to my age when we were little kids. But he's married now, and I don't think he is gay at all. It's just that most of the kids I ran around with always jacked each other off or screwed each other in the ass. I just seemed to grow up with it. I can't remember a time when I didn't find men attractive. . . . I used to have terrible crushes on my gym teachers, but nothing sexual ever came of it. I just worshiped them, and wanted to be around them all the time. I had coitus with a woman when I was 16—she was 22. After it was over, she asked me what I thought of it. I told her I would rather masturbate. Boy, was she pissed off! I've always liked older men. If they are under 30, I just couldn't be less interested. . . . Nearly all my lovers have been between 30 and 50. The trouble is that *they* always want sex—and sex isn't really what I want. I just want to be with them—to have them for friends. I guess it's part of my father complex. I just want to be loved by an older man.

Few of the Type IV participants share Arnold's preference for older men, although they report poorer childhood relationships with their fathers than do those of any other group. As is the case with Arnold's roommate, many closet queens seem to prefer teenage boys as sexual objects. This is one of the features that distinguishes them from all other participant types. Although scarce in tearooms, teenagers make themselves available for sex-ual activity in other places frequented by closet queens. A number of these men regularly cruise the streets where boys thumb rides each afternoon when school is over. One closet queen from my sample has been arrested for luring boys in their early teens to his home.

Interaction between these men and the youths they seek frequently results in the sort of scandal feared by the gay community. Newspaper reports of molestations usually contain clues of the closet queen style of adaptation on the part of such offenders. Those respondents whose lives had been threatened by teen-age toughs were generally of this type. One of the standard rules governing one-night-stand operations cautions against becoming involved with such "chicken." The frequent violation of this rule by closet queens may contribute to their general disrepute among the bar set of the homosexual subculture, where "closet queen" is a pejorative term.

One Type IV respondent, an alcoholic whose intense self-hatred seemed always about to overflow, told me one night over coffee of his loneliness and his endless search for someone to love:

> I don't find it in the tearooms—although I go there because it's handy to my work. But I suppose the [hustler's hangout] is really my meat. I just want to love every one of those kids!

Later, this man was murdered by a teen-ager he had picked up.

Arnold, too, expressed loneliness and the need for someone to talk with. "When I can really sit down and talk to someone else," he said, "I begin to feel real again. I lose that constant fear of mine—that sensation that I'm dying."

Styles of Deviant Adaptation

Social isolation is characteristic of Type IV participants. Generally, it is more severe even than that encountered among the Trade, most of whom enjoy at least a vestigial family life. Although painfully aware of their homosexual orientations, these men find little solace in association with others who share their deviant interests. Fearing exposure, arrest, the stigmatization that might result from a participation in the homosexual subculture, they are driven to a desperate, lone-wolf sort of activity that may prove most dangerous to themselves and the rest of society. Although it is tempting to look for psychological explanations of their apparent preference for chicken, the sociological ones are evident. They resort to the more dangerous game because of a lack of both the normative restraints and adult markets that prevail in the more overt subculture. To them, the costs (financial and otherwise) of operating among street corner youths are more acceptable than those of active participation in the gay subculture. Only the tearooms provide a less expensive alternative for the closet queens.

I have tried to make it impossible for any close associate to recognize the real people behind the disguised composites portrayed in this article. But I have worked equally hard to enable a number of tearoom players to see themselves in the portrait of George, and others to find their own stories in those of Dwight, Ricky, or Arnold. If I am accurate, the real Tom will wonder whether he is trade or ambisexual; and a few others will be able to identify only partly with Arnold or Ricky.

My one certainty is that there is no single composite with whom all may identify. It should now be evident that, like other next door neighbors, the participants in tearoom sex are of no one type. They vary along a number of possible continua of social characteristics. They differ widely in terms of sexual career and activity, and even in terms of what that behavior means to them or what sort of needs it may fulfill. Acting in response to a variety of pressures toward deviance (some of which we may never ascertain), their adaptations follow a number of lines of least resistance.

In delineating styles of adaptation, I do not intend to imply that these men are faced with an array of styles from which they may pick one or even a combination. No man's freedom is that great. They have been able to choose only among the limited options offered them by society. These sets of alternatives, which determine the modes of adaptation to deviant pressures, are defined and allocated in accordance with major sociological variables: occupation, marital status, age, race, amount of education. That is one meaning of social probability.

Epilogue: The Sociologist as Voyeur

The methods employed in this study of men who engage in restroom sex are the outgrowth of three ethical assumptions: first, I do not believe the social scientist should ever ignore or avoid an area of research simply because it is difficult or socially sensitive; second, he should approach any aspect of human behavior with those means that least distort the observed phenomena; third, he must protect respondents from harm—regardless of what such protection may cost the researcher

Because the majority of arrests on homosexual charges in the United States result from encounters in public restrooms, I felt this form of sexual behavior to provide a legitimate, even essential, topic for sociological investigation. In our society the social control forces, not the criminologist, determine what the latter shall study.

Following this decision, the question is one of choosing research methods that permit the investigator to achieve maximum fidelity to the world he is studying. I believe ethnographic methods are the only truly empirical ones for the social scientist. When human behavior is being examined, systematic observation is essential; so I had to become a participant-observer of furtive, felonious acts.

Fortunately, the very fear and suspicion of tearoom participants produces a mechanism that makes such observation possible: a third man (generally one who obtains voyeuristic pleasure from his duties) serves as a lookout, moving back and forth from door to windows. Such a "watchqueen," as he is labeled in the homosexual argot, coughs when a police car stops nearby or when a stranger approaches. He nods affirmatively when he recognizes a man entering as being a "regular." Having been taught the watchqueen role by a cooperating respondent, I played that part faithfully while observing hundreds of acts of fellatio. After developing a systematic observation sheet, I recorded 50 of these encounters (involving 53 sexual acts) in great detail. These records were compared with another 30 made by a cooperating respondent who was himself a sexual participant. The bulk of information presented in *Tearoom Trade* results from these observations.

Although primarily interested in the stigmatized behavior, I also wanted to know about the men who take such risks for a few moments of impersonal sex. I was able to engage a number of participants in conversation outside the restrooms; and, eventually, by revealing the purpose of my study to them, I gained a dozen respondents who contributed hundreds of hours of interview time. This sample I knew to be biased in favor of the more outgoing and better educated of the tearoom population.

To overcome this bias, I cut short a number of my observations of encounters and hurried to my automobile. There, with the help of a tape recorder, I noted a brief description of each participant, his sexual role in the encounter just observed, his license number, and a brief description of his car. I varied such records from park to park and to correspond with previously observed changes in volume at various times of the day. This provided me with a time-and-place-representative sample of 134 participants. With attrition, chiefly of those who had changed address or who drove rented cars, and the addition of two persons who walked to the tearooms, I ended up with a sample of 100 men, each of whom I had actually observed engaging in fellatio.

At this stage, my third ethical concern impinged. I already knew that many of my respondents were married and that all were in a highly discreditable position and fearful of discovery. How could I approach these covert deviants for interviews? By passing as deviant, I had observed their sexual behavior without disturbing it. Now, I was faced with interviewing these men (often in the presence of their wives) without destroying them. Fortunately, I held another research job which placed me in the position of preparing the interview schedule for a social health survey of a random selection of male subjects throughout the community. With permission from the survey's directors, I could add my sample to the larger group (thus enhancing their anonymity) and interview them as part of the social health survey.

To overcome the danger of having a subject recognize me as a watchqueen, I changed my hair style, attire, and automobile. At the risk of losing more transient respondents, I waited a year between the sample-gathering and the interviews, during which time I took notes on their homes and neighborhoods and acquired data on them from the city and county directories.

Having randomized the sample, I completed 50 interviews with tearoom participants and added another 50 interviews from the social health survey sample. The latter control group was matched with the participants on the bases of marital status, race, job classification, and area of residence.

This study, then, results from a confluence of strategies: systematic, firsthand observation, in-depth interviews with available respondents, the use of archival data, and structured interviews of a representative sample and a matched control group. At each level of research, I applied those measures which provided maximum protection for research subjects and the truest measurement of persons and behavior observed.

JOHN HOLLISTER

Topography of Ambiguity and the Collective Private Sphere

I came out of the closet in the early 1980s through the gay student organization on my campus. I understood that homophobia was an oppression
similar to and intersecting with others, and that if all gays would come out
we could support each other in resisting oppression. I came to terms with
my sexuality through reading books on gay life, which were still few. When I
found Humphreys' (1975) study of "tearooms," I had already heard rumors
that such places still existed. Baffled that the majority of gay people did not
seem to find activism to be as necessary and desirable as I did, I saw tearooms as an outcropping of some hidden, alternate gay universe. I
assumed they were a literal manifestation of the closet, where anonymous
men grasped for each others' genitals under toilet stalls without even seeing
each others' faces. There was a very busy tearoom downstairs from the gay
student office (this was before the consolidation of the lesbian, bisexual,
and transgender secessions) but I knew few who admitted to using it.

When I moved to Binghamton, New York, for graduate school, I heard
gossip about friends of friends who were seen at a rest area just outside of
town. It seemed a risky place with queerbashers, abusive police, and fatal
diseases. For a fieldwork class, I took the chance to explore this world and
began an ethnography of the nearby rest area. Although I have not reached
the point where I can confidently declare what the truth of cruising sites is, I
have found that these sites vary too much, both by location and by time of
day, to accommodate any easy generalization.

Since gay studies has been an achievement of the organization-based
gay movement, reflecting the debates and perspectives of organizers concerned with challenging homophobia and securing a future for gay people,
the custom for sexual release among anonymous men often referred to as
public sex poses some puzzles. The notion of gayness marked by the

metaphor of the closet and coming out is often understood in contrast with the homosexuality of the sexual underground. In order to bridge the tension or disparity between the world I came out into with the world I encountered in the course of the research, I increasingly found useful a notion of sites as a unit of analysis for gay history rather than the identities of individuals or the discourses of a culture in a particular era.

The rest area was constructed in 1968 and closed in 1994 and was located along an interstate highway near a city of 250,000. It was lewdly referred to as "Lollipop Heaven" in Bob Damron's Address Book (a guidebook for gay men), although I never heard that name actually used. Different groups of friends had their own nicknames for it. From the highway exit, the road forked, with a sign pointing trucks to the left and cars to the right. A small lodge housing the restrooms and vending machines was located between the parking areas for cars and for trucks. There were three picnic tables on either side of the building on the traffic island. On the other side of the parking lot for cars from the restrooms was a wooded area with six more picnic tables, and behind it a steep slope leading down to a row of trees, and below that a paved trail that followed a river to a point about a quarter mile upstream. According to a sign at the bottom of the slope, the path and park were closed after dark, and that closure was the reason the police would cite in threatening arrest.

Several groups coexisted at the same location but rarely interacted or conflicted with each other: the passing motorists who stopped quickly, used the facilities, and moved on, or slept for the night in their cars; the truck drivers; and the men who sought to get off with each other. A maintenance man would keep guard until 10 P.M., and a police car would come through a few times each night flashing lights and observing each car. On holidays when traffic was heavy, volunteers would set up a stand to serve coffee and donuts.

During daylight hours it was easy to miss the single, mostly older, men sitting alone at the picnic tables, or assume they were tired long-distance drivers, or picnickers from an adjoining park. Late at night, especially after the bars closed, several men would wander among the trees, and many more would sit alone in their cars. A few cars would contain small groups. One or two would sit for lengthy periods in the stalls inside the men's room, or stand at one of the urinals. Often a man would walk slowly and deliberately along the lighted sidewalk looking into each of the cars. Or a man would get out of his car, walk inside, and then back, only to return a few minutes later. A naive observer might assume he had a serious bladder problem.

When he walked in, any sexual activity inside would cease as the participants ascertained whether he was a man looking for sex, and perhaps

interested in anyone there at the moment or just a passing motorist. A man
outside might have noticed him and followed him in. Outside, a cruiser
would stand at a tree, and walk toward someone he was interested in. If
they both moved toward each other, they could assume mutual interest and
consent. Or he could sit for a while at one of the picnic tables waiting for
men to come up and chat—perhaps a friend who was also out for the same
purpose, or someone who was interested in him. If they planned on making
sexual contact, they might move to a picnic table that was out of visual
range of the parking lot, or into the woods behind the rest area, or even
drive off to one of their homes.

I observed the site most intensively, at least twice weekly, in Spring
1990, then periodically afterwards, particularly during summer 1994
shortly before it was closed. For the majority of the 1990 observations, I
stayed in my car. In 1994 I observed from the picnic tables. I also
observed, and confirmed activity at, four men's toilets in the same urban
area, ten rest areas, and two parks within a two-hour radius, and a cruisy
trail along a stream just outside a nearby college town that is most active
on hot summer afternoons. For the sake of comparison with the rural and
small-town sites, I also observed cruising parks in five major North American cities.

I interviewed men who were willing to speak about rest area cruising. I
found eight participants by asking around among men active in local gay
community organizations, and then an additional twelve men from 1995 to
1997 solicited from a notice in the local gay newspaper. All were white,
most in their 40s. All were gay-identified except for two who defined themselves as bisexual and were married to women. For the interviews, the sample was limited to men who took the initiative in contacting me, and so was
not representative. Because of the sensitivity of the topic, I was not willing to
intrude on anyone's privacy. However this method has enabled me to pool
the insights of several participants so as to develop a fuller picture than
what I could have pieced together from my own observations.

I do not keep any records that could incriminate anyone, and I
approached the field site as a potential participant holding out for something better to come along. There is no room for neutral observation without
disrupting the scene. As a gay man, I was enough of an insider to obtain
interviews, but having come out through the world of gay activism I began
as an outsider to that particular scene and became initiated through the
research itself. I had to stop taking notes in the field when a rumor began to
circulate that I was writing down names of people to print in the local gay
newspaper. I interpreted this as an expression of anxiety about activism as
a threat to closeted gays' strategies of survival.

Writing about so-called public sex risks exposing a secret that many of the participants would prefer to remain unexamined. One of the men I interviewed told me how "it is nice that there are such secrets left in the world." Laud Humphreys has already revealed their existence to academic audiences through *Tearoom Trade* (Humphreys 1975) and I trust that queer readers are at least vaguely aware of them. Several websites (most notably http://www.cruisingforsex.com/) provide details on numerous specific locations. But my primary field site was closed down, and others have been increasingly restricted. New sites are not inevitably replacing the old. It is very possible that it is a disappearing custom. Many gays, fearing that so-called public sex may play a role in the AIDS epidemic, actually support its suppression, and are willing to trade in the sexual underground for incorporation into the state-sanctioned kinship system.

I have not specifically researched public toilets because very few actually allow for the niche of an observer such as the "watchqueen role" that Laud Humphreys (1975) found so convenient.[1] I was for a long time skeptical of the reliability of *Tearoom Trade*. Humphreys claimed to have played the part of a "watchqueen"—a voyeur and lookout. I had never observed anyone in such a role until I saw such a convention in place in an urban park men's room in January 1996 and realized the extent of variation in the customs based on location and architecture, although I have not seen a large enough sample of such places to confidently demonstrate that.

As I became more familiar with the scene and got out of my car, it seemed that the men were stepping outside of their lives, retaining only their gender. It seemed anarchic, a wholly different world, like an archaic holdover from some ancient custom. Its apparent outsideness called attention to the nature of the inside, speakable social reality. Just as the men slowly became visible or one's eyes grew used to the dark, I started to see some faint traces of structures and cycles that were parallel to those of any other setting, and were fully meshed with other social processes.

Cruising is not just a repertory of techniques. It cannot be separated from the locations where it takes place. Cruising as an activity may take place anywhere, but men will have a far greater chance of success in a spot where a steady stream of other men expect to find each other, and it is in these spots that men learn the techniques. Communication and consummation take place using the available props. Use of conducive spaces is central to all cruising.

Outdoor noncommercial cruising areas allow for a greater variety in roles and for a more elaborate social structure than a small tearoom where there may be room for only two or three men. In commercial sites, especially gay baths and sex clubs, participants do not need to figure out who is there to cruise and who should not be aware that cruising is going on. They only need to establish who is available and interested. In moments when all the people at a cruising site are part of the game, especially late at night, parks resemble bathhouses more closely with the same order of the orgy, the same etiquette of inviting men or fending them off, the same combinations of bodies.

An organizing feature of cruising sites is a topography of degrees of ambiguity. In some spots it is obvious to initiates why one is there; in others it is much less certain. One's specific location and pattern of movement among areas convey information about one's availability. In outdoor cruising sites, there are two common patterns.

One pattern is dispersed. In two of the large urban parks I looked at, there was a woodsy area with boulders and bushes to hide behind. There are several areas just outside of view of the main paths. Those who were not cruising were either just walking from one side to the other or were obviously naturalists. I assumed that any single man strolling slowly was looking for sex. I found I could convey interest by entering one of the less ambiguous bushes, and convey lack of interest by walking faster and along main paths. One can express interest or availability by moving among these zones.

The second pattern is one where men line the paths. In two other parks, there are certain well-trodden paths with thick brush on either side. Men who may have studiously ignored each other on the trails would follow each other into the bushes. The first, dispersed pattern is closer to what I found in Lollipop Heaven.

Awareness of these zones enables cruisers to separate fellow players from intruders of various kinds. In the woods near a college town, the principle cruising area is at a spot where the stream diverges from the main trail. Most people walking along the trail are tired and too concerned with reaching a waterfall upstream to look carefully through the foliage. The few exceptions are very obvious: naturalists tend to carry such props as binoculars and fieldguides, and fishermen have fishing poles. Even "hetboys" out to look at the "faggots" will walk in a more boisterous, less deliberate manner.

At the rest area, it is ambiguous why any particular man would stop. He could always be a tired long-distance driver. There is enough ambiguity that even an outsider who recognizes one of the cruisers is not likely to suspect his reason for being there, even knowing that it may be a cruising area. Yet at the same time, men who are familiar with the place and its customs will be able to distinguish among the possible purposes of new arrivals based on where they park and how they walk. At Lollipop Heaven, nearly all cars containing a man with a wife and kids will park in a spot close to the toilets.

Most cars with single men park across the lot, facing the picnic tables and bushes, though I have not found the same pattern at all sites and hours. Few noninitiated people will casually walk away from the well-lit parking lot into a dark park with unknown men standing against the trees, especially if they have no prior knowledge as to why they are there.

Once nonparticipants are identified, the same methods separate out who is sexually interested and available. Communication takes place in relation to the space, and the likely possibilities for the use of that space. Participants reach conclusions as to a man's sexual availability based on how he approaches and occupies the space, and they use the space in ways that the other man might recognize. The superficial simplicity means that a viable form that can often be repeated even though the precise meanings for participants may vary considerably. As a form, cruising sites are a possibility that is endlessly rediscovered. Ritualized understandings make it possible to attach meanings to those few gestures in particular sites that convey so a large piece of information as sexual desire and consent. The communication is rarely so obvious or direct as to expose the situation to someone who is there by accident, or who may respond violently.

One's ability to grasp the totality of possible meanings may be more effective than one's physical appearance in finding partners. The question "why else could he be there?" captures the reasoning that several interview subjects expressed. Meaning is drawn from a mutual perception of the totality of likely signals so that the simple act of walking down a path into the woods without even a glance may be an invitation for a nearby man to follow. One man I interviewed spoke about taking the trouble to learn all of the cars of the regulars, and then walking slowly up and down the sidewalks checking each car and accounting for its occupant before taking the risk of seeking contact with someone. The same subject found that car recognition is a common skill: when he deliberately borrowed a different car, other regulars who had always ignored him would treat him as fresh meat and initiate contact.

The topography is defined not only by the problem of separating out purposes for anyone's presence, but also by outside threats, particularly the police. I initially assumed that the rest area was a particularly dangerous place and so was surprised that the men appeared much at ease. But the constant threat of harassment by the police, and violence from queerbashers and other sexual predators produced differences in the degree of safety in using specific spots. Men I interviewed mentioned at most two incidents of queerbashing, and two of abusive sex at the rest area, but they controlled their risk as much as they could. Police were more of a nuisance that forced the scene to remain camouflaged and to limit use of the surrounding woods and park, rather than the overwhelming danger they may be elsewhere.

At Lollipop Heaven, the police would use trespassing laws to arrest men found in the adjoining park, so few ventured down there. I did find piles of used rubbers in places where the bushes were thick enough to conceal men from searchlights, but the overall effect was to limit cruising to the immediate vicinity of the parking lot, with much of the sex taking place elsewhere. It took just long enough for headlights of cars (which could be the police) to appear for men to walk from the bottom of the slope back to the picnic tables where it was at least legal to stand, so some oral sex took place at the row of trees. If the police did arrive, some men would drive away immediately, others would just sit or stand and wait for the police to leave.

Some of the cruisers believed that the bars were far more dangerous, whether for antigay violence or for the risk of being seen walking in. In one's home one takes more of a chance with a complete stranger. The constant presence of a few other men at the rest area, many of whom are regulars and familiar with each other, does provide some safety. One man I interviewed was only half joking when he argued that the Rambles in Central Park was the safest place in New York City at night.

Much interest in the structure of the sexual underground revolves around questions of public health and whether its existence aggravates the AIDS epidemic. Several of my informants reported that sexual activity at the rest area declined significantly after AIDS hit the area in the mid 1980s but picked up again now that it is widely believed that certain sexual practices are safe. Logistically it is difficult to engage in any sexual acts that would take longer than a few seconds to disengage and camouflage oneself. It is probably less risky to engage in sex there on the spot than to take someone home, where one has more room and more freedom to get carried away. The men seemed aware of safer sex and the existence of the AIDS epidemic, but I expect that was because they were reached by generalized media campaigns.

Cruising areas vary considerably in gregariousness and gestural repertory. Silence allows partners to be generous in evaluating each other as desirable, especially when they can barely see each other. Directness and openness of conversation is proportional to the security of the site. In classic tearooms, spoken words may clear the room out as quickly as the arrival of a policeman. In parks and rest areas, some light conversation about the weather may initiate an otherwise silent contact. Only in the most secure sites is conversation likely to be routine, casual, and refer to sexual contact. Since tearoom cruising involves so little spoken language, and is so rarely spoken about by its participants, there is no commonly recognized language to talk about it. The word "tearoom" itself was not recognized by many of my informants and may be passing out of gay slang.

I have found no way to determine if men who cruise tearooms, parks, and rest areas are in any way demographically different from a random sample of men in the area, or even from men in other gay sites. They vary considerably by location. The rest area men are almost all white, as is the surrounding population, while the racial mix was almost random in two of the large urban parks I looked at. In a college town, I found a distinct division between two outdoor cruising areas—in one the men were mostly from the college, in the other they seemed "townie," and probably from the nearby countryside.

The cruisers also vary considerably by time. At Lollipop Heaven there were shifts. The men who cruised in the early evening appeared to be mostly husbands on their way home from work. This was confirmed by two husbands I interviewed. Later in the evening, the men were increasingly gay-identified. After last call at the bars, the shift I observed most frequently, the cruising was the most overt as other traffic was minimized. Many of the men were from the gay bars although their standards for a partner had dropped precipitously.

The pattern of shifts shows the extent to which these places are articulated with work, leisure, and household schedules and so are not entirely set outside other social structures. A full social history would take these into account (Howard 1995 and Chauncey 1994 are two inquiries in this direction). The men had the same aims. Not all reported getting off as a main goal. Many said they hoped to meet a lover there, and a few actually succeeded in finding one. Some just went to see friends, particularly recovering alcoholics in an area where bars are the hegemonic gay meeting site. Some met regularly with the same people and sat at picnic tables watching who was following whom, and occasionally intervening if someone was threatened by a predator. Most went alone. This difference in purpose generated an ongoing tension between individuals who complained about "cliques of queens" whose conversation intimidated them, and those circles of friends who maintained their social lives there.

A contradiction between a hierarchy based on whether there is a seller's or buyer's market for one's body shape and a hierarchy based on familiarity with the scene might be central to its social structure—resulting in the construction of the aggressive troll. In most settings, the regulars set the rules and initiate or deter newcomers. Familiarity with the very subtle games of outdoor cruising, and the possibilities of specific sites, are necessary to succeed. But as in most gay male settings, the young, the muscular, and the unfamiliar are more likely to be sought as partners. This contradiction accounts for the frequency of older men who act as if they own specific sites, or at least that is how younger cruisers often interpret them.

The question of whether the men are gay, closeted, bisexual, or straight is irrelevant to the structure of the rest area but is among the most frequently asked. With the compartmentalization of lives in different settings with different demands, how many people would consistently see themselves as "really" gay or straight in all settings? The metaphor of the closet does not fully cover the problem of presenting oneself in divergent manners in divergent sites. How a man conducts and understands himself in the rest of his life is less important than what strengths he brings to the site in terms of the extent to which he may fit others' profiles of a desirable or safe partner, his ability to socialize with others to the extent that he can rely on their support in a crisis, or on their knowledge to improve his ability to use the space.

Public sex is neither public nor sex. The colloquial "getting off" captures the spirit of the sexual encounters better than "sex." "Getting off" refers to male-centered sexual release and lacks the normative connotations of "sex" which forms a compromise or tension between meanings of sex widely attributed to men and to women and so is effectively heterocentric. The expectations of sex—good sex vs. bad sex, real sex vs. imitation, sex as cement for relationships versus sex as recreation—may obscure the significance that truckstop sex has for most of its participants. Finding a descriptive rather than normative language is closer to impossible for sexuality than just about any other topic.

Likewise, the concepts of "public" and "private" carry implications as to where sexual behavior is appropriate. Rest areas and other settings where cruising takes place are normally and normatively coded as public. Since "public" by definition excludes sexual activity, and "privacy" is by definition the context in which sex is appropriate, referring to rest area cruising and consummation as public sex is ironic or even oxymoronic, even though the shielding bathroom stalls or bushes at night provide are more effective than the walls of many bedrooms. The term in gay-produced writing, "semi-public sex," is a compromise rather than a description. Rest area cruisers take great care in camouflaging themselves. The few who don't are as effective in inducing others to leave as a policeman. Humphreys (1975) documented the self-regulation of tearooms, and the sites I observed were concealed from nonparticipants.

If using the public/private distinction to describe or evaluate the action in tearooms, parks, and rest areas is as compulsory in writing about them as addressing the question of whether the men are really gay or straight, then maybe a phrase like the "collective private sphere" would work. Such a term invites comparison with computer chats where people write as if they are alone, in private, sharing private thoughts with others known only by their handles or screen names. Participants may appear to their spouses or housemates as simply sitting at their terminals, working or conversing with fellow hobbyists, an ambiguity parallel to that of parks where one may simply be going for a walk, in a tearoom using the facilities, at a rest area stopping after a long drive. In fact, they may be making arrangements with strangers to meet.

I initially approached noncommodified outdoor cruising sites as a contrast to the lesbian and gay organizations that structured my own coming out, and much of my life since then. The contrast between them is so stark as to bring out the particular features of each. The worlds of tearooms and of organizations are as separate from each other as either is from other domains of life. It is almost absurd they should be combined and conflated in a single "gay, lesbian, and bisexual history." They are different activities that gay men may take part in at different moments, but they also ride trains, attend schools, hold jobs, and so forth. There is of course some relation; cruising might bring about the critical mass of people and density of networks who know each other that makes bars and then organizations viable, and anecdotes about cruising sites is an occasional topic of conversation among gay people in other settings.

The gay of activism is as evangelical a construction as heterosexuality: anyone who desires a body of the same sex is gay, lesbian, bisexual, or queer and *ought* to come out. The gay of the tearoom is the reverse. While any man may join in the action at a tearoom, I doubt that many cruisers believe that every man *should* participate. In an activist organization, gayness is an almost asexual vocal declaration of one's identity, while in the tearoom it is an unspoken—even unspeakable—mutual recognition that precedes relatively efficient sexual gratification. In the world of gay organizations, where public declarations are privileged, fine distinctions between "gay" and "bisexual" and "queer" can become major points of contention. In a tearoom, such distinctions are absurd except as a possible element of participants' fantasies about each other.

The social reproduction of gay organizations is very easy to trace, as they leave written records of their rhythms through their own functioning: minutes, newsletters, annual reports, by-laws. Organizations assume the existence of motivated volunteers willing to work even if they don't feel like it. They may be formally incorporated by the state, and in a sense function as a state, building and maintaining the infrastructures of a community. While gay organizations require constant inputs of active will, tearooms require only a steady stream of participants, and the very occasional man who is intrepid enough to drill the glory holes and peepholes between stalls.

While the gayness of organizations is often compared to race or ethnicity as the marker of a status group, the unspoken gayness of tearooms more closely resembles such stigmatized or illegal activities as drug use, and often overlaps with them. In one case I found a culture of "tweakers" or crystal methamphetamine users searching for or selling the chemical using a cruising site for camouflage, just as cruising normally depends on other activities for concealment.

Organizations generally value cosexuality, and see male and female homosexuality as parallel. Many have male and female cochairs, and strive to attract equal numbers of members, even if in practice most groups are imbalanced one way or another. Cruising areas are exclusively male domains; any woman is automatically assumed to be an intruder. When a woman walked her dog into the woods at a rest area, men dispersed or camouflaged themselves as bystanders. Truckstop and park cruising are rooted in the old domination of public space by men, and in the gendering of adventure and of rape, which I suspect are the reasons why tearoom sex among women is so rare, rather than because of some innate difference between women's and men's sexuality. Hunting is a common metaphor when cruisers do talk about their experiences.

Organizations are based upon a conception of homosexuality as a plausible basis for forming a group. They are based on the assumption that there is more to being gay than who one wants to make love with. I suspect (but cannot confirm) that most tearoom participants find it as absurd to organize on the basis of homosexuality as might a medieval European or one of the "Sambia" of New Guinea.

Although there is a more extensive folklore about tearooms among gay men than among heterosexuals or lesbians, gay-identified men who use tearooms are as secretive about it, and even the conversations they have at the rest area itself rarely betray the reasons why they are there. Even gay activists will conceal their identities at the tearoom as thoroughly as a Baptist preacher.[2]

The Social Reproduction of Sites

It is only plausible to combine within a single frame the sexual underground, the lesbian and gay social movement, and a variety of other forms for understanding oneself and organizing one's activities in relation to desire for others of similar anatomy because of the extent to which gay and lesbian institutions have projected an "imagined community" in the sense of Benedict Anderson's analysis of nationalism. Imagined communities are fictions that are enabled by the technology of printing and that should be judged by the creativity in which they are imagined rather than the truth or falsity of their construction (Anderson 1983: 15).

The imagined community is sustained by the gay press. The gay press reproduces perspectives which are most plausible in the spatially dense networks of the North American urban gay-identified neighborhoods where that press has its largest market. If we suspend this sense of the gay neighborhood (Levine 1979; Castells 1983; Murray 1996) as the highest form of gay development with hundreds of organizations and bars, and refrain from taking small-town and rural gay life as just impoverished imitations or underdeveloped peripheries, then the centrality of a starkly limited number of socially reproducible sites to gay life becomes very evident. And in returning to those cities, that proliferation of institutions is too easily reduced to variations on a few themes, although a visibly gay neighborhood might be analyzed as a site of its own.

What keeps an organization going is distinct enough from what makes a cruising site viable that their histories are effectively distinct. How homosexuality is understood and organized is not the result of cultural forces that operate on the level of an entire nation in a particular epoch, nor on the level of individual brains, but rather the particularities of the loci of social interaction where individuals identify themselves and feel desire. How this takes place in cruising sites, organizations, bars, and so forth, differ enough that each is best understood separately. Each site has its own impact on sexuality.

It does not seem to make sense simply to categorize different kinds of homosexual people according to class and race and gender along the metaphor of the colors in plaid, with each tone intersecting with another to produce a specific, essential type. These intersections do not exist in the ether: the intersections among them are constituted very differently in each site, and overlapping oppressions can be most effectively challenged at the level of the site where the oppressions do the most damage. It is the differentiation of accessibility and what skills or traits are valuable that accounts for the variation in experiences that are marked by race and class and education and culture, etc. A tearoom can't demand three forms of ID. An intellectual conversation won't pass in a bar. Any conversation won't pass in a tearoom.

Sites are all of the specific scenes we pass through in the course of a day or in the course of our lives. They might include a dinner table, a highway, a combination of TV and viewers, a workplace, a school, a conference. What passes as the "gay, lesbian, and bisexual" community is actually an aggregate of bars, tearooms, computer bulletin boards, activist organizations, support groups, faerie gatherings, music festivals, domestic partnerships, and so forth.

Each site is, in a sense, an organism that draws people in and reshapes them. As one participates, one develops a stake in the game, in one's positioning relative to others within it, whether it be a struggle or more of a dance. One can affect its shape and texture by simply being there and obeying its rules, and even more in influencing how others act in it. In some fields the struggle is more acute, particularly in those that have a strategic place in the larger economy, or which may monopolize a specific need. Each site has its own logic of reproduction—its own means of perpetuating itself, as well as its own conditions of existence. It begins at some point in history, and lasts as long as its participants have a reason to care, and as long as its conditions of existence permit.[3]

Sites are not just locations, or scripts delivered on particular stages: the spatial and cultural aspects of sites are ultimately inseparable. Sites are processes of social reproduction. I could create some nasty neologism such as "situalitizations" but will use the more intuitive but potentially misleading "sites" as a courtesy to the reader. I use "social reproduction" instead of "social construction" because the latter elides and conflates very different social processes, while trapping scholars in a futile debate over whether any given process is constructed or essential. Social reproduction as a focus for conceptualizing continuity in Marxist theory originally referred specifically to those processes that are necessary for the survival and expansion of capitalism, particularly around raising children in homes and schools for their appropriate positions in the distribution of labor. But the phrase is often enough used loosely for any processes of continuity, and that is how I want to appropriate it. Andrew Parker has referred to it as the site of heterosexism within Marxist theory (Warner 1993). Michèle Barrett notes that social reproduction is conflated with biological reproduction, basically a pun (Barrett 1980). Thus, there is some "queering" mischief in using its use here.

Sites are researchable or operationalizable from three aspects, each corresponding to sharp limits on the viability or social reproducibility of any given site, and those limits account for their salience in constructing people:

1. The actual engagement of bodies at specific places and times: physical possibilities of space and time are further limited by such social material conditions as land markets, architecture, rhythms of work and leisure, and patterns of accessibility.

2. Construction of meaning: a) social recognizability in the sense that critical masses of potential participants will recognize compatible possibilities in a particular location—a site only exists *as a site* to the extent that it is socially defined and recognizable; b) communication and structure within the site.

   Each site sustains particular forms of communication, and reproduces distinct but contestable laws for what kinds of statements may circulate, what is imaginable and speakable, and what is silenced or repressed. It presumes particular constructions of the body and the self, and reproduces those constructions in its participants. How people act and what they say is inevitably a performance within specific sites in relation to local power relations and the distribution of strengths, whatever other meanings those gestures may have, though the extent to which one is engaged in the politics of a particular site varies considerably. The boundaries among sites are less clear than they seem. Categorization is a social process, and the very act of defining particular sites is an intervention within them. Each observation and description of a site is an engagement within it. Cultural imaginability is not infinitely polymorphous. There are few sites that critical masses of people will be able to recognize and use.

3. Context: what outside forces shape it and make it possible. In the case of cruising sites, these include the police and queerbashers who force it to take on its camouflaged form. Also, this covers a silent war of architects, some of whom may perhaps deliberately design pubic buildings and parks to make them more conducive for cruising, while others, perhaps following the advice of Delph (1980), attempt to rebuild bathrooms, rest areas and parks so as to deter cruising. On a larger scale is the whole history of public transportation.

If there is anything distinct about sites commonly coded as gay, or even queer, it might be that the closet or the tactical complications of a double life limit the extent to which individuals can willfully contribute to the maintenance of those sites.

My conviction that a site-centered analysis of gay life is theoretically, practically, and politically useful is the result of working for several years building gay and lesbian community organizations in a town where organizing feels like building a fire with wet wood. To what extent do social movements really act on behalf of the people they imagine they represent? Why don't most gay people find activism as compelling as do the activists? Specifically, what is the relationship between gay activism and other, possibly older, social scenes organized around homosexuality.

At my most pessimistic I fear that organizers are not empowering oppressed peoples so much as attempting to colonize them. Building a few new spaces, and coordinating among them through the development of a gay press, is both difficult and important for increasing the means of gays and lesbians to support each other and gain confidence in confronting homophobia in other areas of our lives. In this context, arguments about what gays *really* are, and what words should be used, ring scholastic. It seems

wasteful to fight over imposing utopian standards when it is nearly impossible
to build any kind of gay-positive sites at all. The distinction between radical
and assimilationist politics that is so prominent in 1990s queer political writing seems irrelevant when the most distinctive gay institution—the sexual
underground—is also molded to the prevailing gendered order.

The sites of the university and the activist groups that structure gay
studies or queer theory carry with them some blinders that may limit the
accuracy of the work, and the effectiveness of the politics. They are born of
word-based sites and don't travel well outside of them. Queer theory and
gay studies may be among the most reflexive of academic fields, but do
not take into account how the fields of activism and academia themselves
are situated relative to the people written about. An activism that seeks to
mobilize outside of a few enclaves, and a history that includes and
respects communities as they are rather than how one would like to present them, would be more sensitive to the differences among the sites in
the landscape.

Differences among the kinds of frequently viable settings, largely
defined by the possibility of male-to-male sexual contact, account for at
least some of the permanent instability of sexual categories and the contradictions and ambiguities in the ways that homosexuality is organized and
understood. There is no stable match among sexual practices, identities,
and the words to describe them because they cannot be reduced either to
types of individuals or to particular discourses of an era. Rather, they are
by-products of social processes that take place in particular locations.
Therefore terminological debates cannot be permanently resolved. The literature produced through queer studies may analyze "gay, lesbian, and
bisexual" identities in general, and occasionally observe how they may
intersect with race, gender and even class, but it does little to account for
how jarring the contrasts among their meanings in different settings can
get. The "gay" of a lesbian and gay social movement organization, the
"gay" of a cruising area, and the "gay" of a gay bar are distinct entities.
Indeed, speaking of cruising areas as "gay" at all risks imposing the fantasies of outsiders, whether they be gay or heterosexual-identified. What it
means to be gay is site-specific.

ENDNOTES

Thanks on previous drafts to Terence K. Hopkins, Martin Murray, Evelyn Nakano
Glenn, William Leap, and the audience at the 1994 Inqueery/Intheory/Indeed: 6th
North American Lesbian, Gay, and Bisexual Studies Conference at the University of
Iowa, Iowa City. Thanks to the men I interviewed, who made suggestions as to what
to look for. Errors, misjudgments, and theoretical hubris are my own.

1. For discussion of the ethics of such fieldwork, see Bolton (1995) and the debates appended to Humphreys (1975).

2. For late 1970s examples see Delph (1978:30).

3. My sense of sites has been shaped by the combination of field and habitus in the work of Pierre Bourdieu (1980), though I am using it in a more specific sense than I think Bourdieu intends; Connell's (1987) "settings" as contexts for the enactment of gender; DeCerteau's (1984) "spaces"; Harriet Friedman's (1980) "forms of production" as a strategy for conceptualizing recurring patterns of social organization in terms of both local, especially household, relations and global conditions of existence; and the relation between discipline and discourse in Michel Foucault (esp. 1975).

REFERENCES

Anderson, Benedict. 1983. *Imagined Communities: Reflections on the Origin and Spread of Nationalism.* London: Verso

Barrett, Michèle. 1980. *Women's Oppression Today: Problems in Marxist Feminist Analysis*; London: Verso

Bolton, Ralph. 1995. "Tricks, friends, and lovers: Erotic encounters in the field." In Kulick and Willson, eds., *Taboo: Sex, Identity, and Erotic Subjectivity in Anthropological Fieldwork*, pp. 140–67. New York: Routledge.

Bourdieu, Pierre. 1980. *The Logic of Practice.* Stanford: Stanford University Press.

Castells, Manuel. 1983. *The City and the Grassroots: A Cross-Cultural Theory of Urban Social Movements.* Part 3: City and Culture: The San Francisco Experience. Berkeley: University of California Press.

Chauncey, George. 1994. *Gay New York: Gender, Urban Culture, and the Making of the Gay Male World: 1890–1940.* New York: Basic Books.

Connell, R. W. 1987. *Gender and Power.* Stanford: Stanford University Press.

De Certeau, Michel. 1984. *The Practice of Everyday Life.* Berkeley: University of California Press.

Delph, Edward W. 1978. *The Silent Community: Public Homosexual Encounters.* Beverly Hills: Sage.

Foucault, Michel. 1975. *Surveiller et Punir.* Paris: Gallimard.

Friedmann, Harriet. 1980. "Household Production and the National Economy: Concepts for the Analysis of Agrarian Formations." *Journal of Peasant Studies* 7(2): 158–84.

Howard, John. 1995. "The Library, the Park, and the Pervert: Public Space and Homosexual Encounter in Post-World War II Atlanta." *Radical History Review* 62: 166–87.

Humphreys, Laud. 1975. *Tearoom Trade: Impersonal Sex in Public Places.* New York: Aldine.

Levine, Martin P. 1979. "Gay Ghetto." In Levine, ed., *Gay Men: The Sociology of Male Homosexuality.* New York: Harper and Row.

Murray, Stephen O. 1996. *American Gay.* Chicago: University of Chicago Press.

Warner, Michael. 1993. *Fear of a Queer Planet: Queer Politics and Social Theory.* Minneapolis: University of Minnesota Press.

Speaking to the Gay Bathhouse: Communicating in Sexually Charged Spaces

IRA TATTELMAN

Gay bathhouses are part of the emergence of a gay male community in the latter half of the twentieth century. The baths provide a public place where a wide mix of strangers can come together. Men from vastly different emotional, sexual, and physical worlds arrive at the baths wanting to make connections with other men. Tolerant of difference, open to a diversity of uses, the public territory of the bathhouse gives men the space to define, support, or flaunt their sexual interests. Through voyeurism and exhibitionism, consumption and control, tactility and motion, and authority and inclination, men undergo a public transformation by projecting, acting upon, and maybe even transcending their imaginings and desires. As one factor in the development of a gay identity, the baths offer variety and opportunity, and propose new ways to explore relationships between men. Within the spaces, one can defy conventions through the promise of sexual relations; desire is multiplied and sexual diversity is promoted.

As vital sites of everyday actions and spatial functioning, the baths provide the safety and freedom within which to enjoy a multiple set of interrelations. Those interactions are made possible through a system of codes and behaviors. This paper investigates the network of procedures and practices that govern communication within the baths.

Baths are sites of eroticism and pleasure that try to appear timeless and separate from the world. In this space with water, naked men, and sexually charged situations, behavior is isolated and, as a result, performed with more abandon and candor. The infrastructure of security, the placement of a support staff, and the spatial juxtapositions of activities make this possible; the construction of the baths suggests certain paths and possibilities. The choreography of the spaces, the marks and boundaries that indicate what is seen/scene and not seen/scene are particularly relevant in this culture of looking and touching but also, looking and not touching, or even touching without looking.

In an attempt to break the barriers that separate people, the baths equalize patrons through a uniform dress code: a white towel is distributed at the point of entry, and through the dimness of lights, a theatrically designed lighting scheme favors the other senses over sight. By entering the building, one accepts a position in the performance and rituals of the space.

Communication among patrons often occurs through codes such as body placement, hand gestures, and towel arrangement, rather than words. This should not imply that the baths are silent. The boundaries of the interior spaces, which are clearly articulated and developed in relation to the body, form an exact but incomplete enclosure; the wood panel dividers between cubicles, for example, never reach the ceiling. Even when a room is closed to view, it is never closed to sound. As a result, one's erotic utterances are linked to all others that are happening at the same time.

As a gay man who went to his first bathhouse in 1980, I am interested in the baths because they are places where mainstream society comes under question. Because patrons feel protected, new strategies of exploration and exchange are possible; diverse relations between men happen. By focusing on the rules of interaction, the conditions of operation, and the strategies determined by the movement of a body through the bathhouse, I plan to define these spaces of gay male affiliation.

Gay Male Desire

Men's desire for other men has created a landscape of sex spaces. Sex takes place in parks, alleys, restrooms, and rest stops. Licensed venues also survive, while dependent on legal status, social custom, and local health departments. These commercial sex establishments include adult theaters, video arcades, bookstores, bars, and bathhouses.

Public law officers and health officials, as "protectors" of the general public, seek ways to regulate these sex spaces. They argue that sex, especially between men, is not a private issue. Anti-sodomy laws and AIDS-related closings back them up.

(Studies have suggested that men are likelier to have safer sex in public settings than in private ones. Articles that discuss these studies include "Gay Baths Revisited" [Bolton, Vincke, and Mak 1994], "NYC's War on Sex" [Eigo 1995], and "Why Gay Men Are Having Unsafe Sex Again" [Warner 1995].)

With *Bowers vs Hardwick*, the U.S. Supreme Court decided that an individual does not have the right to engage in certain sexual acts whether in "private" or "public" spaces. And in a recent decision, the Georgia Supreme Court ruled that while citizens have the right to privacy, the state has a more important right to further "the moral welfare of the public" ("Georgia Hangs on to Sodomy Law": 23). Sexuality is legislated and socially controlled.

Homophobia continues to flourish, remaining implicit in much government legislation covering female and male sexuality, and frequently
explicit in the right-wing press, in school playgrounds, at the pulpit, in
men's clubs and in the military.   (Forrest 1994:104)

As a result, the separation between public and private can be described as
an artificial construction.

The homophobia implicit in the denial of a private gay male realm is
often based on fear of objectification and visual desire. The debates center
on the discomfort that a straight man feels when looked upon by a gay man,
the belief that the straight man will be either seduced or forced to protect
himself against the invading gay male. This logic implies that the voyeuristic
gaze or look is available between people of the same gender and has an
overwhelming force. (I use the term "gaze" as theorized in "Visual Pleasure
and Narrative Cinema" (Mulvey 1989) and "look" as theorized in "Fass-
binder and Lacan: A Reconsideration of Gaze, Look, and Image" [Silver-
man 1992].)

In reality, while some homosexual solicitations rely on the language of
the body, that language needs to be learned in order to send a message and
to ascertain whether the other individual is interested. These gestures and
signals guarantee that people who do not want to have sex are not put into
uncomfortable situations and that those who do participate, do so willingly.

While the distinctions between public and private can be arbitrarily
drawn, some argue that responsiveness and consent are a sign of privacy in
the sexual realm. Richard Mohr writes:

> We need to abandon the idea that in order for sex to be considered pri-
> vate, it must be hidden away behind four walls. It is not geography or mere
> physical enclosure that makes sex private. . . . The sex act creates its own
> interpersonal sanctuary which in turn is necessary for its success. . . . If
> the participants are all consenting to be there with each other for the pos-
> sibility of sex polymorphic, then they fulfill the criterion of the private in the
> realm of the sexual.   (Mohr 1996:17–18)

For many, gay liberation was primarily about sexual expression. Gay
men used this freedom to develop erotic environments that celebrated
communal sex options. These spaces offered new social structures, pleasure practices and changing definitions. To make a sexual choice in front of
others, who by their presence were involved contingently and applauded
the ability to make these kinds of decisions, became an impetus for self-
sufficiency, a redefinition of who the gay man is and what he can do. Sex
between men (especially in safe environments) created growing opportunities for resistance, strategic positions from which to construct the "meaning" of one's existence.

As the title of Weinberg and Williams's article "Gay Baths and the Social Organization of Impersonal Sex" implies, the authors believed activities between individuals in the baths were unconnected and detached: "Depersonalization and objectification are salient features of our participants' ideals regarding impersonal sex" (1979:179).

They linked gay male desire to the anonymity of commodification and the mass-production of consumer culture by writing that "gay baths are seen to provide 'easy sex' in the same way that neighborhood shopping centers provide 'easy shopping' " (1979:178). What this and other studies of the time period failed to realize is that sexual expression has the potential to bond men together, a social interaction through physically direct involvement.

(The following books, which began to study and describe gay male desire, also highlight the impersonal nature of gay baths. They include *The Gay World* [Hoffman 1968], *The Homosexual Network* [Rueda 1967], and *Homosexual: Oppression and Liberation* [Altman 1974].)

While participants in 1975 might wish to "conceal the activity or avoid involvements" (Weinberg and Williams 1979:174), by the late 1970s, men were lining up to get into the baths and arriving at the baths in couples. Sexual preferences were openly placed on the street; the intersection of private lives and public personas, commercial property and public opinion, contested the limited experiences and practices that were available to gay men.

> It's difficult to report honestly about what happened at the baths of the East Village in the late seventies. There were so many of us doing things we were embarrassed by, yet we were also finding the expression of dreams we'd dreamt for our entire lives. (Jones 1975:153)

Weinberg and Williams believed that if one does not speak (limiting verbal communication is one of the rules within the bathhouse), any exchange that takes place is impersonal and not very important. This paper argues that the physical honesty and expressiveness of the baths offered both contact and comfort. These meaningful settings involved an array of bodies and actions. These men may have been more open to new experiences and relaxed because membership cards and/or admission fees alleviated some of the anxiety surrounding unexpected visitors and police surveillance. The connections and attachments that were ignored by most studies led to visibility and assertiveness. It is time for the bathhouse to come out.

> Here, you are not wicked for feeling lust. Here, you can look freely at what you desire, get aroused and shoot a load. Most important, here you can bring out into the open a part of you that is completely real, but doesn't usually get to come out and play. (Madison 1995:102)

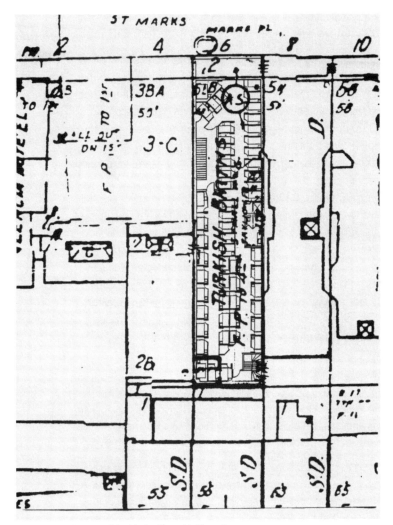

FIGURE 4.1. Collage of St. Marks Site with Floorplan

Welcome to the Baths

My discussion of the baths uses the New St. Marks Baths as its model. This bathhouse on the Lower East Side in New York City was built in 1913 as the Saint Marks Russian and Turkish Baths. In the 1950s, the baths catered to local immigrants in the area during the day and attracted gay men at night. Its survival was dependent on both groups.

> A turkish bath, like the Quaker service, is a place of silent meeting. The silence is shared solely by men, men who come uniquely together not to

speak but to act. More even than the army, the bath is by definition a
male, if not a masculine, domain. (Rorem 1967:188)

In the 1960s, it became exclusively gay, although considered dirty, poorly lit, and uninviting. Bruce Mailman, who bought and refurbished the baths in 1979, wanted to create a space designed for sex; anything that distracted from the sexual activities and satisfactions of its patrons was removed. In 1985, the bathhouse was closed by the city due to HIV and AIDS. The building, which has been boarded up ever since, was recently sold to a video chain that has turned the building into a store, cafe, and studio.

While the New St. Marks Baths is closed, many bathhouses are still open and popular within the United States. (In some cities, gay business-men are designing new ones or trying to reopen those that are closed.) According to *Steam*, there are at least 61 bathhouses currently operating in the United States. These baths are open in eighteen states as well as in Washington D.C. and Puerto Rico ("Listings: Spring 1994"). They distribute condoms, hold HIV awareness sessions, and remain protected environ-ments for male-to-male sexual activity. For these reasons, I have chosen to write about the baths in the present tense.

> We are able to invent safe sex because we have always known that sex is not, in an epidemic or not, limited to penetrative sex. Our promiscuity taught us many things, not only about the pleasure of sex, but about the great multiplicity of those pleasures. It is that psychic preparation, that experimentation, that conscious work on our own sexualities that has allowed many of us to change our sexual behaviors. (Crimp 1988:253)

The building is five stories tall, painted dark gray. Closed off to the street, the building's doors are anonymous and its windows have steel shutters. A bronze plaque on the front, placed by the historical society, reminds visitors that the building was the last city residence of James Fenimore Cooper (1789–1851), best known for writing the Leatherstocking Tales.

> [St. Mark's Place] has cafes and bars for students and unemployed actors and writers. There are boutiques and bookshops, which look tawdry till you draw close and realize many of them are surprisingly expensive. Other shops cater to what New Yorkers think of as punk. . . . At one end of this short street is a gay bathhouse, a blank facade with only a discreet plaque on the door to identify it. (Brook 1985:55)

One enters the building by pushing open a solid door and climbing up a marble staircase with dark-tile walls to the first level. Because mainstream society often tries to exclude gay men, to render them invisible, the baths create a desirable, associational space, removed from the rest of the world.

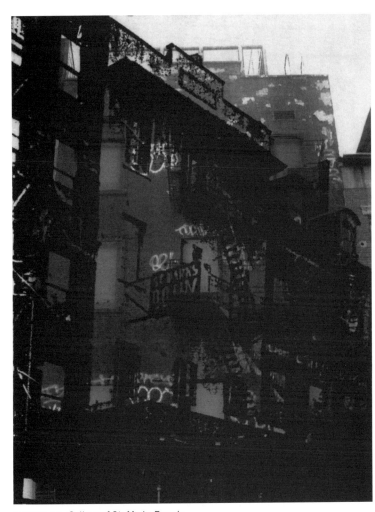

FIGURE 4.2. Collage of St. Marks Facade

Inside, men search for love, community, release, and human touch; they are free to congregate with others who like what they like, or want what they want. Through spatial exclusivity, the baths establish an order and organization that automatically links otherwise unrelated bodies. As spaces of mostly unrestricted activity, the interactions within begin to dispel notions of isolation, alienation, self-control, and loneliness.

Issues of class, age, race, and sexual orientation create a dilemma for social interaction on the street. The baths try to offer something else. While one can argue that they inevitably define, exclude, and limit their inhabitants (for a discussion about the structures of power in the baths, see Bersani 1988), many different kinds of men pass through the door

FIGURE 4.3. Photo of Cafe Countertop

and derive sexual pleasure from the activities of the bathhouse. The married, gay, straight, questioning, experimenting, and enjoying men (ideally, a heterogeneous cross-section of men) are able to participate in the baths without having to question their role within homophobia, racism, classicism, agism, and the other phobias and isms found outside the bathhouse. As a result, the baths sustain contradictory notions of reality and desire.

At the landing there is an admissions desk and to the right, a cafe. If there is a line of men waiting to get inside or if all the rooms are taken, one can wait in the cafe. On this side of the counter, everyone is fully dressed, wearing their street clothes. Coffee, tea and sandwiches are available. Directly across the counter are men eating and drinking in their towels or nude. The interaction and sense of ease between these two groups at this particularly fragile boundary, basically a three foot counter, define the baths as much as the sexual contact that takes place elsewhere. No one crosses the counter to get to the other side and no one on the clothed side even considers undressing.

At the brass-caged cashier's desk (retrieved from a dismantled bank), the choices include a single room, double room, or locker. Choosing a room gives one a space to call one's own. A locker provides a space to hang ones clothing; no other private space is guaranteed.

The bathhouse generally costs more than a movie but less than a hotel room. Its rates are fairly comparable to amusement parks, major museums, and aquariums. In addition to money, the bath asks for two signa-

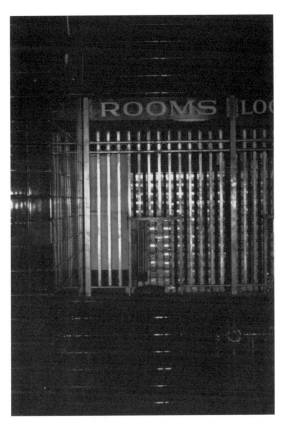

FIGURE 4.4. Photo of Cashier's Window

tures, one for registration and one for valuables, which are put into a locked safety deposit box. The attendant then hands over a towel, key, and condom.

> The steam baths are not free, and for this reason alone they are beyond the means of many who know what they offer. Most of them, also have some minimum safeguards of decorum, refusing, for example, to admit customers who are obviously drunk. Age may also inhibit some people who might otherwise patronize them—the demeaning possibility of being cast as a lecherous and "dirty old man" if you are past forty-five. Nudity, too, is distasteful to many men, particularly to those who are sensitive about the "manliness" of their physiques and are embarrassed even in the approved asexual atmosphere of the locker room.   (Read 1980:37)

A buzzer unlocks the heavy inner security door that separates the space outside from the space inside. One can begin to appreciate the sights, sounds, smells, and tastes that are available. Off to the left is a long row of

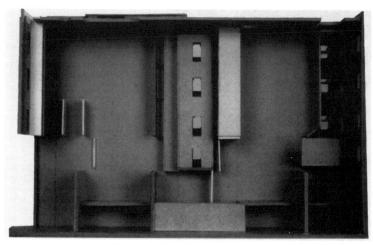

FIGURE 4.5. Model of East Wall, the Plumbing Wall

FIGURE 4.6. Model of West Wall, the Circulation Wall

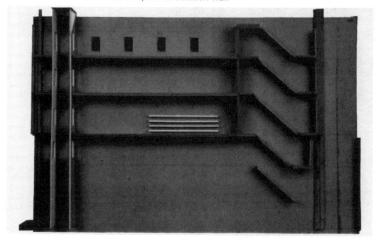

double lockers with very little space in between. To the right is the cafe. Around the corner is an orgy room and straight ahead is a black steel staircase leading upstairs.

The materials and colors of the bathhouse are masculine: fake pine paneling, brown carpet, gray paint, and maroon vinyl. Materials are durable and easy to maintain; they must age gracefully. Sensitivity to light is important to the ambiance of the baths. Illumination is fairly low, the hallways are bathed in shades of pink and red to help everyone look healthy and inviting. The imagination of the space is connected to the style and tastes that inhabit and sustain the space.

In the St. Marks one finds pointed spatial relations in the building construction. The east wall compares the tight individual rooms of the upper floors to the large collective spaces of the lower floors through the placement of plumbing and interior "walls"; one can contrast and relate the water of the sink and toilet to the water in the swimming pool or whirlpool, or the space of a 4' x 6.5' cubicle to the space of a 16' x 26' orgy room.

The west wall describes the circulation spaces, a circuit for cruising. The bathhouse invites a continuous flow of traffic repeatedly passing each room, sometimes finding a door open and inviting, sometimes closed to view.

The baths create a theatrical experience. Figures materialize out of the shadows, steam, and long halls. One's eyes begin to adjust to the blur, distinguishing body outlines and facial profiles. Obstacles, things that come between, accentuate the sensuous and suggestive. Mirrors emphasize indirect contact with the body and flatter the physical culture of urban life; in order to participate, one is required to be on public display. Screens, surfaces, and windows delay direct interaction while piquing one's interest, coyly adding uncertainty and flirtation to the mix. The relationship between stage, props and actors transforms the qualities of camouflage, surveillance and narcissism that have become stereotypes of gay life. Theater and fantasy offer a multiplicity of interests, a complex set of relationships and an interchangeability of roles.

> Tonight's top is tomorrow's bottom. We're all more interested that the ritual
> be enacted than concerned about which particular role we assume.
>
> (White 1980:268)

Walking Through the Baths

On the second, third, and fourth floors, a narrow doorway leads into the red-toned corridors that separate the long array of numbered rooms. The passageways are as cramped and constricted as the cubicles.

> The main thing we see are doors. Doors and doors and doors. Each door
> has a number. Outside all these doors are corridors. Lots and lots of corri-
> dors. Filling these corridors are men. Lots and lots of men. They are prowl-
> ing the corridors.   (McNally 1976:6)

There are about fifty rooms per floor, a small digital clock, and two loudspeakers which play music tapes continuously. The music is generally what one hears at a disco, loud and with a strong beat. Each room has a door with a large black number on it. These repetitive units mimic the size and safety of closets. Inside, the room lights are on dimmer switches that allow

Ira Tattelman

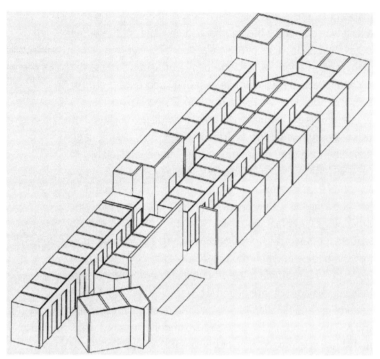

FIGURE 4.7. Computer Drawing of Room Arrangements

one to adjust the light to an appropriate brightness or darkness. The furnishings include a hard, raised, minimal platform bed, small table, bit of floor space, sheet and pillow, and hook for hanging street clothes or a towel. Some baths incorporate strategically placed mirrors, peep and glory holes, windows, or video monitors. Specialty rooms might include leather swings, which offer the opportunity to play theatrical as well as sexual roles. In the St. Marks, the rooms are exactly alike. It is the bodies that individualize the space.

Sexual opportunities, which are embedded in the rituals of the baths, are often formalized and silent. Behavior and meaning are coded by location, posture, and dress with sufficient distinctions between one and another. These standing rules, symbols, and expressions are generally followed, understood, and respected. They create a common understanding, giving coherence and clarity to the activities.

Although propositions may be defined, even the most blatant advances can be misinterpreted, especially when one is unfamiliar with the context. In an exchange through the eyes and body, there can be an ambiguity and uncertainty in the transmission of messages. A hand motion, a set of eyes

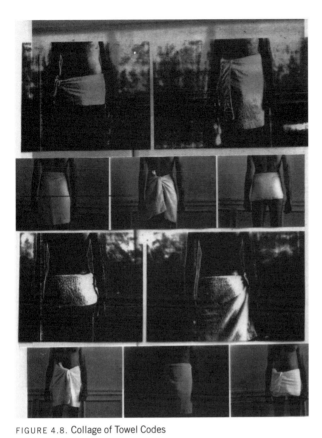

FIGURE 4.8. Collage of Towel Codes

staring, or an encounter on the stairs, while compelling, are occasionally misunderstood.

In the baths, men are everywhere, their towels knotted with intent. Towels can be draped long and tight or over the shoulder, folded once or twice to highlight the thighs, knotted at the front so that it opens like a curtain or at the back exposing the buttocks. Men tend to highlight the area to which they want the most attention paid. They walk around the labyrinth, circling aimlessly, trying to master the organization of corridors as if trapped in a maze. Where the layout is more complex, rambling and confusing, the traffic flow is more interesting and titillating. Men stand against the walls, watching the parade as well as the sequence of opening and closing doors. Others rest in their rooms, looking, lying, or smoking.

> We all rushed to the Baths at that time of year: the halls were filled with circuit queens and out-of-towners . . . rude old men whose attitude of contempt always chilled me as I slipped the money across the counter . . . the

> hot moans and hisses from the rooms you passed, the distant sound of
> someone being patiently spanked with steady rhythms of a metronome,
> the leather queens standing in their red-lighted doorways in cowboy hats,
> dangling handcuffs.   (Holleran 1978:152–54)

When rooms are kept dim, the patrons are hardly perceivable in the shadows; they are mere forms waiting. When a room is bright, the person inside has something he wants to show off. For the men in the room, those who want anal intercourse will lie on their stomach, displaying their ass. A desire to receive fellatio involves lying on one's back, spreading one's legs and, possibly, fondling one's penis. To convert interests into involvements, one can arrange oneself so that what one wants is what is shown. The non-verbal language of the body is one's guide to the adventures of the baths. If one looks long and hard enough, one can locate patrons in search of any imaginable sex act or fetish. While house rules legislate bathhouse etiquette, the conventional rules and regulations of sexual "normality" are removed. Assumptions and beliefs are questioned by the disparate mix one can find and the experience of multiple encounters with a variety of partners.

The activities of the baths shape the act of cruising, a constant search which takes the form of an oblique glance, a suggestive nod, a long stare, or a quick feel.

> You give it a little look, pretending not to look, but being able to see, out of
> the corner of your eye only, if anyone else is pretending not to look back at
> you. If you see someone else pretending not to look, you look the other
> way. Only after a few moments do you look back, to see if he's still looking.
> And if your eyes look, at the same moment, you'll only let it happen for a
> second, and then you'll look away again.   (Kramer 1978:261)

In cruising, who becomes the subject and who the object? In the exchanges between the man in the hall and the man in the room, surely one is dependent for definition upon the desires of the other. By waiting in the room, displaying oneself, one offers oneself up as a spectacle to the men in the hall. While some consider this subordination, there are transgressive ways to perform it.

The man in the hallway assembles the repeating frame of doorways and believes he has access to every body behind every frame but he chooses, making a visible statement by blocking traffic in the hallway while waiting for a signal or invitation. An approach might include suggestive positioning, the display of one's genitals, or a tightened towel drawing attention to the outline of one's penis. This man indicates his interest to a potential partner by pausing in the hall near the opening to the room, waiting permission to enter.

FIGURE 4.9. "A Corridor in the Baths"© Douglas Blair Turnbaugh
from *Strip Show: Paintings by Patrick Angus*

The man in the room takes charge of his domain, setting the stage with lighting, door position, and body placement while waiting for someone to advance, to break the rhythm of bodies passing. Once someone approaches the door, the man in the room maintains the right to accept, reject, invite, or refuse access to the room and to himself. The contacts are verified with an exchange of eye signals.

Once an invitation is accepted, the men quickly disappear behind the door. The closed door signals the room is for occupants only, providing a degree of privacy and exclusivity to their activities. On occasion, the men in the room will leave the door slightly ajar, attracting others to watch over the activity or join in.

> I never had occasion to go to the baths till I was in my 40s. Some of my most memorable sexual experiences took place there. . . . A man was sucking my cock and somehow the door of our cubicle was open. I didn't

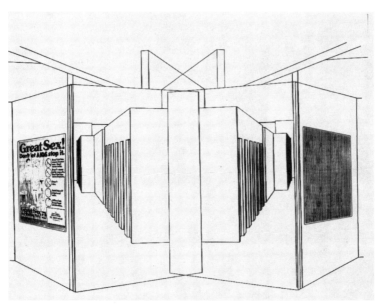

FIGURE 4.10. Collage of Bathhouse Corridors

see anyone enter the room, but suddenly I was aware of lips and tongue and fingers all over my body. Six or eight men were contributing to my pleasure. . . . Hands caressed me all over. When I came, I came in surges. It felt like a tidal wave. While it was happening I was scarcely aware of who these men were or what they looked like or what they were doing. When it was over I sat up on the bed. I thanked the men. We chatted idly.

("New Hope for the Heteros" 1984: 214–15)

Getting Together

Downstairs, just below ground level, are the brightest rooms in the building, the wet area which includes communal shower, sauna, steam room, and an open area containing plunge pool and hot tub. Wooden benches line the wall where one can rest, start up a conversation, or take in the view of manly traffic. This floor invites a variety of people to congregate, to comfort hints of rejection, and exchange a few words. Men can quietly laugh or talk without disturbing the mood of the place. While the conversation is generally light, without much information being exchanged, small talk can be engaging.

[At the Mount Morris Baths in Harlem] I found that the incidence of anonymous sex was not as pronounced as I'd expected. Men asked each other's names, what they did for a living, what their interests were, far

FIGURE 4.11. "The Mysterious Baths"© Douglas Blair Turnbaugh from *Strip Show:
Paintings by Patrick Angus*

more often than one would presume . . . .It seemed, in fact, that there was
more social bonding taking place than physical bonding.

(Harris 1990:174)

Across from the pool are large mirrors lining the wood-planked wall. The
visual character of the mirrors allows one to look and be looked at. The
splash of water, the flexing of muscles, and the sensation of toweling dry are
enervating, helping one feel sensual. There is a never-ending display of
fronts and backs, couplings and uncouplings, and the sometimes hard-to-
decipher rules of attraction. In this space, the barriers between people
seem to break down; the spectator and spectacle merge.

In the steam room, tiled benches are enshrouded by moisture clouds.
Above is a pitched metal ceiling and on the wall is a shower head, cold
water only. When the room gets too hazy to see, the bathhouse conflates
looking and touching. Inhabitants believe that everything seen can be
touched, but sometimes, in the steam or orgy rooms, one can only see by
touching. In the darkened spaces, with bodies made slick by the mist, the
imagination is enhanced. Propositions are often more direct; body contact
might proceed from light touching to genital groping.

In these communal spaces, the nature of desire can also become rude
and demeaning. Young men can be ruthless in their rejection of older men.
At the same time, those less attractive can persistently grab at the more
attractive to the point of humiliation. Issues of race and class are often

FIGURE 4.12. Collage of Steam Room

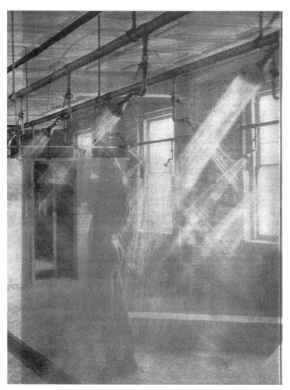

FIGURE 4.13. Collage of Shower Room

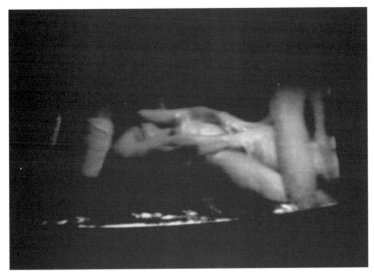

FIGURE 4.14. Photograph of Orgy

reproduced inside the baths and exaggerated or campy mannerisms are discouraged.

> In my imaginings about the bathhouses, the big factor I'd left out was rejection. My visions had been boisterous, rowdy, scenes of convivial abandon. But men were constantly being rejected, not chosen, which is why the place was so silent, so thick with longing and dread.
>
> (Weiss 1985:12)

The dormitory or orgy room is on the first floor of the St. Marks. While the lack of lighting makes the bodies indistinct, the contours of the room slowly come into view. It is furnished with an expanse of mattresses on two levels, like bunk beds. One can make out all combinations of fucking and sucking; one can touch any body one chooses or rub one's body against another; one hears familiar and unfamiliar noises, endless music, urgent moans, ecstatic murmuring, and the jangling of keys against their numbered brass disks.

> In the fifties, homosexuality was a solitary perversion. Before and above all, it isolated you. . . . But what this [the orgy at the baths] experience said was that there was a population not of hundreds, not of thousands, but rather of millions of gay men, and that history had, actively and already, created for us whole galleries of institutions, good and bad, to accommo-
> date our sex. (Delany 1988:174)

In the orgy room, the focused couplings of men is not so much negotiated as adaptable and continuous. The security of male affinity creates and operates a space of intimate physical relations that dissolves one to another, sometimes offering more than one can imagine. A body part reaches out. One may not know who is doing the touching, licking, or sucking, but one feels adoration. One can reach out in wonder to pass this feeling onto someone else.

> While I was sucking on it guys gathered around until I could feel a hand searching my ass, then a moist cock filling that hole, until I knew the fantastic feeling of being entered from both ends, filled with cock, thrilling at every plunge. The room was filled with the sounds of cocks fucking moistened assholes and the sucking sounds of cocks slipping in and out of many mouths. ("Sweet Ass at the Baths":145)

The surprise is the willingness one finds, a willingness to be touched, to be connected, to be put into a position one would not normally be in. In the orgy room, one finds people standing and sitting as well as kneeling, lying down, leaning, and crouching.

If the baths have a hierarchical organization, then the water area is the life-giving force at the base. The rooms are the limbs stretching up to the top. The orgy room, however, is at the center. Here, the nude body is inscribed exclusively with sexual desire.

> Jim surrenders for only moments to the hands, limbs, mouths, bodies. Only for moments. Here, it doesn't seem to matter whose cock, whose ass, whose body. (Rechy 1977:265)

This desire for another is also a desire for oneself. If the body creates the baths, then the baths create the body. The bathhouse brings people into contact with themselves and puts them into the position of the other.

Finishing Up

Also on the first floor is a darkened lounge. Black vinyl cushioned banquettes line three walls with a table at the center. The men in the lounge are tired, relaxed, spent. They have retreated into this den for a rest.

While one's presence in baths indicates an availability, displays of sexual expression are not permitted everywhere. Sex generally does not occur in the open hallways or TV lounges, which are places for recuperation. To have an erection in the lounge is unusual and unwanted. Sometimes, these common areas include publications, local literature, and vending machines. At the St. Marks, little square footage is devoted to this unprofitable space.

While the baths have links to the outside, through music, condoms, commercial products such as toiletries and dildos, and traces on the body

FIGURE 4.15. Photograph of Locker Area

such as tattoos and jewelry, it is the clothing "that makes the man," which helps one flaunt, tempt, and distract. When it is time to get dressed, one feels constricted; one's "street" identity returns all too quickly.

At the door, one leaves one's towel and signs the receipt for one's valuables. Glancing back, the building looks deserted, even though it never closes. Upstairs, moving through the hallway, an attendant picks up used towels, cleans an ashtray, changes a bed sheet. The laundry room is constantly in motion, cleaning the uniform for another visitor. Over the loudspeaker, a voice announces the room numbers for those whose time is up.

Over the past ten years, many baths have been dismantled or discredited. While my intent is not to idealize these spaces, I do hope to allow them an important place in the development of gay male community.

Men have always checked each other out. Society, however, teaches us that seduction is a form of losing control; dominant culture preaches caution. Men originally felt the need for a rationale to enter the baths, for partic-

FIGURE 4.16. Photograph of Keys in the Office

ipating in the activities. Issues of paranoia, social silence, and personal shame were reproduced inside.

In time, however, the baths helped gay men accept their difference from society while creating a place for themselves in society. The baths helped multiply the collection of spatial forms and physical advances in which and through which gay men make connections. Because people feel safe, they are able to take risks, to experiment. This self-discovery is an important part of the development of an "identity."

In the bathhouse, desire does not have to be curbed or eliminated. Eye contact can happen anywhere. What follows the eye contact is what matters. In this place of abandon, there is no fear of arousal. One finds a secure place in which to diverge from a "proper" or "mainstream" course of action. This liberation challenges a heterosexually biased culture, redefining basic concepts and values, and bringing change to oneself and to society. The authority of desire, which can be fluid and varied, is celebrated and with it, very specific forms of language, contact, and consumption develop.

These rituals and behaviors are part of a language that only the initiated can understand. While they are not indecipherable to people who are not part of this subculture, they are specific to the men who inhabit the baths. My research details the construction of these encounters and systems within this very particular space. These rules permit everyone to make a general assessment of the motives of others. They help shape the bathhouse, providing a set of directions for accomplishing many different ends.

ENDNOTES

I would like to thank Sheila Kennedy, Norman Bryson, and Brett Abrams, who each provided a great deal of support and encouragement during the formation of this paper. I would also like to thank Robert Rindler and Deborah Willis, curators of the exhibition "Techno-Seduction" at The Cooper Union, where some of the images included with this text were publicly displayed.

All of the collages, models, and photographs are by Ira Tattelman unless noted otherwise.

REFERENCES

Altman, Dennis. 1974. *Homosexual: Oppression and Liberation*. London: Allen Lane.

Bersani, Leo. 1988. "Is the Rectum a Grave?" In Douglas Crimp, ed., *AIDS: Cultural Analysis, Cultural Activism*, pp. 197–222. Cambridge: MIT Press.

Bolton, Ralph, John Vincke, and Rudolf Mak. 1994. "Gay Baths Revisited." *GLQ* 1(3): 255–73.

Brook, Stephen. 1985. *New York Days, New York Nights*. New York: Atheneum.

Crimp, Douglas. 1988. "How to Have Promiscuity in an Epidemic." In Crimp, ed., *AIDS: Cultural Analysis, Cultural Activism*, pp. 237–71. Cambridge: MIT Press.

Delany, Samuel R. 1988. *The Motion of Light in Water*. New York: New American Library.

Eigo, Jim. 1995. "NYC's War on Sex." *Steam: A Quarterly Journal for Men* 3(4): 414–23.

Forrest, David. 1994. "We're Here, We're Queer, and We're Not Going Shopping." In Andrea Cornwall and Nancy Lindisfarne, eds., *Dislocating Masculinity*, pp. 97–110. London: Routledge.

Gay 1–4 (1970–1973). Collected at National Museum and Archive of Lesbian and Gay History, The Center, New York.

"Georgia Hangs on to Sodomy Law." March 15, 1996. *Washington Blade* 27(11): 23.

Harris, Craig G. 1990. "Coming Together in the Baths." In Franklin Abbott, ed., *Men and Intimacy*, pp. 173–76. Freedom, Calif.: Crossing Press.

Hoffman, Martin. 1968. *The Gay World*. New York: Basic Books.

Holleran, Andrew. 1978. *Dancer from the Dance*. New York: William Morrow.

Jones, Bill T. 1995. *Last Night on Earth*. New York: Pantheon Books.

Kramer, Larry. 1978. *Faggots*. New York: New American Library.

"Listings: Spring '94." *Steam: A Quarterly Journal for Men* 2(1) (Spring 1994): 111–20.

Madison, Kyle. 1995. "An Introduction to the Baths." *Steam: A Quarterly Journal for Men* 3(1): 100–2.

McNally, Terrence. 1976. *The Ritz*. Copyright c 1976 Terence McNally.

Mohr, Richard C. 1996. "Parks, Privacy, and the Police." *The Guide* 16(1) (January 1996): 16–19.

Mulvey, Laura. 1989. *Visual and Other Pleasures*. Bloomington: Indiana University Press.

"New Hope for the Heteros." 1984. In Reverend Boyd McDonald, ed., *Smut*, pp. 214–18. New York: Gay Presses of New York.

Rechy, John. 1977. *The Sexual Outlaw*. New York: Grove Press.

Read, Kenneth E. 1980. *Other Voices*. Novato, Calif.: Chandler and Sharp.

Rorem, Ned. 1967. *The New York Diary of Ned Rorem*. New York: George Braziller.

Rueda, Enrique. 1982. *The Homosexual Network*. Old Greenwich, Conn.: Devin Adair.

Silverman, Kaja. 1992. *Male Subjectivity at the Margins*. New York: Routledge.

"Sweet Ass at the Baths." 1982. In Boyd McDonald ed., *Flesh*, pp. 145. San Francisco: Gay Sunshine Press.

Warner, Michael. 1995. "Why Gay Men Are Having Unsafe Sex Again." *Village Voice* 40(5) (January 31, 1995).

Weinberg, Martin S. and Colin J. Williams. 1979. "Gay Baths and the Social Organization of Impersonal Sex." In Martin P. Levine, ed., *Gay Men: The Sociology of Male Homosexuality*, pp. 164–81. New York: Harper and Row.

White, Edmund. 1980. *States of Desire*. New York: Dutton.

Young, Perry Deane. 1973. "So You're Planning to Spend a Night at the Tubs." *Rolling Stone* 128 (February 15, 1973): 48–50.

Weiss, Philip. 1985. "Inside a Bathhouse." *The New Republic* 193 (December 2, 1985): 12.

DAVID BERGMAN

Gay geography is divided between urban areas like the Castro and Christopher Street and resort areas like Provincetown and Key West. South Beach in Miami or Venice in Los Angeles straddle those two worlds. But the oldest area known for its gay and lesbian inhabitants that continues to draw lesbian and gay vacationers is Cherry Grove and Fire Island Pines, adjourning communities on Fire Island. From their beginning as gay resorts, they have attracted artists, especially writers, who have depicted Fire Island in various books. As I hope to show, these representations of Fire Island, which include some of the more famous works of gay literature, were not merely mirrors of gay life on the island, but ways of projecting the image of the liberated gay man, a personage newly minted and never before circulated, and of critiquing that life and image as it was developing. The terms of that critique varied from one writer to the next, although there was surprising unanimity about the defects of the hedonistic and aestheticized ethos of the island. Representations of Fire Island are particularly valuable in gauging the response to the visibility of homosexuality in its most overt form— public sex. No gay man of my generation was unaffected either by the image of what it meant to be a liberated gay man or the drawbacks of that representation. Yet as time has passed, it has become a historical task to delineate the terms that constructed these representation, but all the more important to take that journey back to Fire Island.

The boat slips from the dock into the green, murky canal, and until the ferry makes its way into the Great South Bay, I can hear the grating sound of winches lifting or hauling, the squeal of metal on metal mixed with the high pitched yowl of a Yorkie squeezed beneath the arm of one of the passengers. Soon all that is left behind. The waters open up and change color; the blotches of oil disappear, and the only sounds are the grumble of the ferry's motor and the swish of spray against the vessel. A woman in front of me is traveling with her two sons, ten- and twelve-year-olds I'd guess, and they sit

quietly together, pointing at the gulls and at some buildings on the Sayville
shore. They are the only two children on the boat, and they seem to know
how to behave among adults. They are unfazed by the two older gray-haired
men with their arms around each other or the lean college student with long
dark hair resting his head on the shoulder of his body-builder boy friend.

I grew up in Queens, and on the way out, the train from Manhattan
passed by my old neighborhood; yet in all the time I lived in New York, I
never ventured to Cherry Grove or The Pines, the two gay communities on
Fire Island, which seemed to me as a child as remote and exotic as Zanzibar. Even in the '70s, when I was in my twenties and many of my friends
were making the trip out to The Pines, I held back. Only now that I'm middle-aged and living in Baltimore am I going for the first time.

The day is hazy, and from the Long Island shore, I cannot see Fire
Island, which is only a short trip from the mainland. The rather anxious narrator of Edmund White's first novel, *Forgetting Elena* (1974), set on an allegorized version of Fire Island, obsesses about "the gauze" that seems to
hover in the sky, fearful that it will "drift silently to earth and smother [him]
in its intricate mesh" (38), but to me it looks more like a theatrical scrim
that will rise on cue. It is part of the theatrical unreality of the place, one reason I never before ventured out to Fire Island and why it still fills me with a
certain anxiety. And I realize as I look at my fellow passengers, there is
another reason I haven't been out here before: the men, all of them, are
exceptionally beautiful, quite out of my league.

I am not the only person whom Fire Island has made anxious. The Pines
has always been a daunting place for those unprepared for its spectacle of
beauty. One of the great documents in the history of recent homophobia is
Midge Decter's twisted little essay, "The Boys on the Beach," her account
of living in The Pines before Stonewall, that is, before its heyday. Even then
the body beautiful was the salient feature of gay life in which "flesh [was
never] permitted to betray any of the ordinary signs of encroaching mortality, such as excess fat or flabbiness or on the other hand the kind of muscularity that suggests some activity whose end is not beauty" (38). Decter is so
unsettled by this display of male beauty that she imagines it as an active
attempt to insult, to "mock" and "diminish" the heterosexuals, and particularly the heterosexual men, who are there and witness it: "Naked or covered, then, the homosexuals offered their straight neighbors an insistent
reminder of the ravages to their person wrought by heterosexual existence"
(38).

In one of the more bizarre turns in this studied piece of resentment and
condescension, Decter blames gays for their apparent healthiness, as if
being beautiful were a sin and heterosexuality a chronic and virtually incur-

able disease that leads from childbirth to the grave in one steady, unalterable descent. But if Decter's response is more than a little over the top, there can be no doubt that later on The Pines could be intimidating even to the average run of gay men.

Fred Lemish, the protagonist of Larry Kramer's novel *Faggots* (1978), recalls that he "had first come to Fire Island Pines when he was thirty. He wasn't ready for such beauty, such potential, such unlimited choice. The place scared him half to death" (224). Richard Bronstein, another character in *Faggots* feels a similar Prufrockian trepidation:

> When he'd finally summoned the courage to pick himself up and off the beach and have a look around this Forbidden Island, he'd found all his worst fears transmogrified into flesh. Oh, so much flesh! Everywhere! Everyone was Mr. America. And he hadn't been able to be a Mr. Soho Loft. His workouts hadn't worked out at all. . . . He couldn't look anybody in the eye. They can see I'm a loser. They can see I've got the smallest cock in captivity. They can just see it! (242)

Of course, all of Kramer's Jewish characters suffer from a similar sense of angst, and one could write this insecurity off as an ethnic trait, but writing just a few years later, Edmund White admits in *States of Desire* just how intimidated Fire Island makes him feel. "As a person of average looks and average income," he confesses, the place "fill[s] me with insecurity" since it had become "unrivaled" as "a spectacle of gay affluence and gay male beauty" (294). Fire Island intimidated gay men on three fronts: the aesthetic, the economic, and the sexual. Clearly these aren't separate—in fact, what is most frightening is how they converge—and no place epitomized their convergence like Fire Island, and no place problemized these issues so much as the Meat Rack, the strip of National Park between Fire Island Pines and Cherry Grove, which is the place where outdoor sex has traditionally occurred.

No wonder Fire Island was a setting that attracted novelists of the first generation of gay writers to emerge after Stonewall, particularly the writers who have been collectively known as the Violet Quill, the short-lived group that emerged in 1979, which included Edmund White, Andrew Holleran, Felice Picano, George Whitmore, Robert Ferro, Michael Grumley, and Christopher Cox. The island became a focus for their most pressing concerns: the cultivation of beauty, and particularly the beauty of men; the redefining of the social structure to include gay men; and the exploration of gay sexuality and gay relations.

Although Larry Kramer wasn't a member of the group, he is an author whose work derives from the same historical and cultural moment, and he

was as well a friend of several members of the Violet Quill. He helped
Andrew Holleran find a publisher for *Dancer from the Dance*, and he invited Edmund White to that fateful meeting in Kramer's apartment that led to
the formation of the Gay Men's Health Crisis, the oldest AIDS organization
in the world. Kramer's *Faggots*, which appeared in the same year as
Edmund White's *Nocturnes for the King of Naples*, Andrew Holleran's
Dancer from the Dance and Felice Picano's *The Lure*, helped establish gay
fiction as a regular part of commercial publishing. Yet despite his close connection to the Violet Quill, his work differs from it in several ways. The orgy
at the Meat Rack, which serves as the climax to *Faggots* highlighted public
sex as a particular concern, something the Violet Quill never did. The difference between Kramer's representations of the Meat Rack and the Violet
Quill's relative silence on the matter is a sign of the conflicts in gay representation which will emerge more significantly after the AIDS pandemic
appears.

Fire Island's importance for Kramer as well as for the writers of the Violet
Quill is that it represented a way of life for certain gay men in which they
were free from the most overt forms of surveillance and policing from
straight people. More than any place else, Fire Island was a world made by
gay men and lesbians for gay men and lesbians. Although under the jurisdiction of Suffolk County police, the Meat Rack was free of police raids from
the end of the '60s on; indeed, as related by Esther Newton, getting the
police out of the Meat Rack was one of the most successful campaigns of
the Mattachine Society. Even before Stonewall, lesbian and gay men had
enough clout in the area to free themselves of police surveillance and
arrest. The letters that Dick Leitsch, the president of the New York Mattachine Society, wrote to Suffolk County officials are an excellent gauge of
how sex out-of-doors was part of that assertion of gay sovereignty. He
claimed that "these 'raids' are gross violations of civil liberties, mockeries of
justice, and a blot on the conscience of Suffolk County" (quoted in Newton
197). Benedict P. Vuturo, the straight lawyer hired to defend the men taken
in raids is reported to have said, "It's the cops who are disturbing the
peace" (quoted in Newton 200). That on Fire Island the first gay political
activity organized by a homophile organization should be to protect men
having sex in public indicates the early link between such activities and the
way gay men wanted to use the space that they saw as their own. In short,
the issue of public sex, at least on Fire Island, was viewed as a significant
part of the entire issue of how to define gay space.

Space is very much an issue on Fire Island. The scale of Cherry Grove
and to a lesser extent The Pines is very small. Although Fire Island in its

entirety is 30 miles long, it is only a half mile wide at its thickest. Cherry
Grove and The Pines—at the island's midpoint—are about a quarter of a
mile wide. Moreover the absence of cars in the Grove or The Pines keeps
everything within walking distance, or rather strolling distance, for nothing
could be less in the spirit of these resorts than hiking.

Consequently, the two communities are shallow stages better suited for
comedy than tragedy, small intrigues rather than epic battles. When Willem
De Kooning, who is so closely associated with the Hamptons, another Long
Island resort down the coast, came to paint Fire Island (1946), his homage
to the neighboring community, he employed his usual palette of dazzling
orange, teal green, shocking pink, and white. He also included his usual
Amazonian women (perhaps given more point in this context); a headless
female leans over another female, bodiless but for her breasts. A third
woman with limbs like tentacles appears to be swimming at the top of the
painting. The colors, the shapes, the light are all similar to the work he did
in the Hamptons. What distinguishes Fire Island from those other De Kooning's paintings is the size (48.3 X 67.3 cm): the arabesque of women is
pressed tightly together—the pleasures dense with incident.

Similarly, the works that the Violet Quill wrote about the island—White's
brief novel *Forgetting Elena*, Felice Picano's novella *Late in the Season*,
George Whitmore's short stories series *Out There* and his play "The
Rights"—tend to be chamber works, where each detail is careful wrought.
Andrew Holleran's *Dancer from the Dance*, whose climax is set on the
island alone aspires to the tragic, the epic, although its ironic shimmering
tone keeps deflating such aspirations. Like Holleran, Larry Kramer ends
Faggots on the grand scale. But Kramer's excesses, although meant to be
satiric, do not quite succeed in their Swiftian intentions. The characters
cannot pull themselves completely away from the spectacle they
denounce. Fire Island resists large-scale representation, preferring the
small, lapidary style.

Coupled with the smallness of Fire Island's scale is the density of the living accommodations. In Cherry Grove, particularly, people are tightly
packed in little houses, sharing common areas and sometimes bedrooms.
And because Fire Island is essentially a summer resort, the houses are
designed to open outward into gardens, pools, and terraces. The result of
the smallness of scale, the density of living, and the architectural style is
that the distinction between private and public space is not just blurred, but
often completely erased. In fact, The Pines and Cherry Grove confound the
public/private dichotomy in yet another way—the communities by being set
off from the mainland and accessible only by ferry are removed from the
larger public sphere. Many of the arguments against public sex, particularly

its deleterious effect on children, do not obtain in Fire Island's case since no child (or adult, for that matter) would simply wander into the community unaware of its ethos. The Pines and Cherry Grove could become so public a space for gay life including gay sex because it was so private, that is, so removed from other communities.

Sex and particularly sex in public must be viewed as occupying only space on the wide spectrum of activities gay people felt free to perform on Fire Island and nowhere else. Esther Newton writes about the long tradition of street drag—that is, drag outside of a performance—that flourished in Cherry Grove since the '50s. Coming to Fire Island served for many as a kind of revelation of what gay life could be without the repression of straight society. Larry, one of the central characters in George Whitmore's comedy "The Rights" (1980) describes his entrance into the harbor of The Pines in ecstatic terms:

"I'll never forget that entrance into the harbor," he tells his ex-lover, who has invited him out for the first time,

> the yachts bobbing into view, a wide crescent of yachts skirting the bay. Enchanted older couples perched in the afterdecks drinking—oh, something long and cool. Pennants snapping in the wind. . . . That extraordinary press of people, That great mass lining the quay. Waving, welcoming us, all us outlanders to their island. Lithesome boys in little T-shirts and little white shorts. Stalwart gentlemen in abbreviated ensembles laced with leather and chains. Statuesque sirens in the flimsiest of shifts. . . . and the dancers! The dancers and the music! The steady thump-thump-thump of the engines and our hearts and the music! It was like Bora-Bora or something! It was like crossing the bar. It was like Disneyland and Cleopatra's barge all rolled up into one.   (17)

Men dancing together in public, kissing in public, holding hands in public, these are many of the activities unselfconsciously performed on Fire Island, which are highly policed outside of the Island. Sex in public is only an extension of these other forbidden activities given visibility—indeed, it becomes the test of exactly how much visibility these less proscribed activities are actually permitted.

Whitmore's references to Bora-Bora, Disneyland, and Cleopatra's barge allude to several aspects of the community ethos that representations of The Pines always ascribe to the community: a primitive ritualism crossed with theatricalized entertainment. Public sex is part of both. By emphasizing ritual as one of the ways gay writers represented Fire Island, I do not want to suggest that these works partake of the carnivalesque in the way that Mikhail Bakhtin uses the term. The seeming breakdown of order—and particularly of sexual order—is really an attempt to establish a different hierarchy, a different order. None of the writers under discussion represents Fire Island as a place of anarchy, no matter how free it might appear. To the contrary, it imposes a ritualized or aesthetic order on what might seem to be the least suitable of objects. In *Forgetting Elena*, a house catches fire. Those attending a dance—one of the most ritualized activities represented in all the works about Fire Island—watch the blaze admiringly from a distance. A "man in the centipede costume" remarks like an art critic, "pity there isn't a touch more blue in the flames. Blue, being a recessive color, would give more depth, more plasticity to the whole *swirl* and make it much more impressive, I think" (italics in the original, 23). This fire on Fire Island is judged against an aesthetic order and found wanting.

Drugs, too, are not allowed to blaze in a disorderly fashion in Islanders' minds. The epitome of the gay need to aestheticize experience by turning it into a ritualized performance was the "contoured" drug trip, a rigorous and exhausting spiritual discipline if there ever was one. Here's how Roger Sansarc, the narrator of Felice Picano's novel *Like People in History* describes drug taking on Fire Island:

> [We took] a hit of window-pane acid, softened with a few joints of good grass before we left the house and on the way to the Pines harbor, where we would catch one of the small water taxis to flit us across the black bay waters. Upon disembarking at Cherry Grove, we'd cosmetically inhale a hit of coke for that "Entrance Buzz," into the Ice Palace, a sort of last-minute blush-on. During the remainder of the night, we'd pick ourselves up with poppers whenever appropriate. As a rule with eschewed angel dust and ethyl chloride, two popular "enhancers" among our set. But we always carried a light hypnotic—Quaalude or Dormidina—to ease our way off the acid, which could at times become speedy and teeth-clenching.
>
> The trick to taking one's down was to do so at the exact point when one was about to be physically and mentally exhausted, but before one actually was. . . . Those who didn't contour their drugs, who took too many ups or downs, or took them too early were "pigs." Tales of extreme piggishness were gossiped about —"She was found facedown on the edge in the Grove Meat Rack, out like a light! Not even the deer would fuck him!"— and laughed at all the following week. (337)

Picano's porcine metaphor suggests the polarities that serve as the aesthetic limits on Fire Island. One the one hand, there is the smooth "contoured" drug experience—something beautifully proportioned, classically heightened, and sensitively controlled. The "pigs" are rough, crude, demeaned, insensitive, and wild. Picano allows no middleground—and in the absence of such a middleground rests the great anxiety of failing to perform to the

Island's standards. You might arrive thinking you were beauty, only to discover through some miscalculation that you had turned into a beast "not even the deer would fuck."

I also want to point out the casual way that activity at the Meat Rack is alluded to in the passage. It is not foregrounded, but rather presented as the predetermined end of an evening of drugs and dancing, the final movement in the contoured drug experience properly wrung to its last drop. The scandal is not that one is seen in the Meat Rack having public sex, but rather that one could not contour the evening skillfully enough to finish it off with the proper sexual release. Public sex is viewed as the appropriate aesthetic conclusion to an artistically contoured experience. Picano does not divide sex from the ritualized aesthetic of the Island's ethos, rather he makes it the ultimate test of a person's ability to meet its esthetic imperative. To burn out before the night is done is to be like the fire in *Forgetting Elena* that lacks the right recessive tints.

When the Violet Quill speaks about Fire Island, it always speaks about beauty—natural, human, and man-made. The beauty of the beach is what has made The Pines and Cherry Grove attractive to the original vacationers. Malone, the hero of Holleran's *Dancer from the Dance* "felt he had found Paradise his first visit to Fire Island; and it took him three or four summers to even admit it was anything else. . . . because nowhere else on earth was natural and human beauty fused; and because nowhere else on earth could you dance in quite the same atmosphere" (207). Larry in "The Rights" calls it an "enchanted isle" out of Shakespeare's *The Tempest*. The importance of being aesthetic was established early in the history of representations of Fire Island. John Mosher, a *New Yorker* writer, penned a series of sketches set on Fire Island. Collected as *Celibate at Twilight* (1940), they contain a character, Mr. Opal, a semiprecious gem of a man, who regards the cottage he has built after the Hurricane of the Century devastated the island in 1938.

> Mr. Opal's house was finished, his small and perfect jewel of a house was done at last. So he himself thought as he sank back in one of the big rattan chairs in his living room and appraised the sailcloth curtains with immense satisfaction. For the moment, he was alone and might indulge himself to the full, unobserved, in a gratification that was frankly smug, at a work accomplished, at a creation of his own at last complete. The curtains gave the final needed refinement to the establishment. They hung stiffly from the wooden poles in glowing melon masses, and had in this place, Mr. Opal concluded, almost a kind of elegance. "A gentleman's house," Mr. Opal thought in a sudden spasm of self-appreciation. "I can live here on this island for decades, for the rest of my life." (122)

Moser was gay, and according to Esther Newton, one of the first gay home-owners in Cherry Grove. His parties were the first to bring large numbers designers and artists out to the Island for the weekend (Newton 32).

The work of the Violet Quill that epitomizes the aesthetic of exquisite, luminous detail is Edmund White's brief but lapidary first novel *Forgetting Elena*. All its characters are acolytes in "a cult of beauty" (172) and their bible is a purple book which includes a chapter on "Aesthetics as Ethics" (167).

> One bush, or tree, particularly interests me because it has three different leaf shapes, one that looks like an elm's, another with three lobes and a third that looks like a mitten. This plant has arched over to touch a holly bush, creating a dark tunnel of waxy greenery and a grill of shadows. Our house, like the others I've seen, stands on stilts above marshy ground. The decks and walks, built of rough-cut withered planks, are raised. Long strands of grass have grown up between the slats. Constantly bruised by passing feet, the strands have withered, turned brown, and now lie list-lessly across the wood, like tiny whips in tatters. The immediate vicinity is hillier than the area around the harbor and in one direction I see a black cottage, timidly ostentatious, perched high above us, flying four purple pennants. (29)

As readers of *Forgetting Elena* will recognize, the medievalism of this pic-ture of Fire Island is intentional (at one point Elena is described as having "stepped out of a medieval book of hours" (71)). We should recognize the dark tower from which fly four purple pennants—purple, the color of royal-ty and homosexuality—as though it were a detail in a Bayeaux tapestry. But the castle is only a cottage, and although by contrast it may appear to be perched high above him, its elevation is "timidly ostentatious." This exquisiteness of detail cannot fully mask the summer resort on which it is overlaid.

What complicates the efforts of the anonymous narrator of *Forgetting Elena*—and for us initiates into the gay world—is that the rituals of the soci-ety are not static, indeed they seem constantly to be shifting and subject to revolutionary change. The narrator may hope to find some unifying system, but he discovers instead a society "mad for novelty" in which language is "inexact, experimental, an amoeba possessing mobility but sluggish and perfectly adjustable" (72). This is a society that prefers things "original and complex and elusive" (76), unaware even that it speaks "a peculiar, unfath-omable dialect" to the outside world (75). The sensibility cultivated on Fire Island is one that favors subtlety (although with a decidedly theatrical flair) and fluidity, and thus requires a sense of tradition with a desire for originali-ty and freshness.

To a greater or lesser extent all the beauty on Fire Island is ingrown and claustrophobic. The lushness of the island is all artificial, since as an extended sandbar it could boast nothing more fertile than various grasses—and even these have had to be meticulously planted and maintained. The wild, overgrown feel of the place is the work of decades of dedicated homeowners and well-paid gardeners who have made a kind of faux-tropics east of New York. Moreover, the Meat Rack is an excellent example of the anxiously oxymoronic aesthetic that dominates the Violet Quill representations of Fire Island. Technically it is part of the National Park System, and so respectful are the residents of the preserve—portions of scrub brush are roped off like old furniture in a museum—that the "naturalness" is completely artificial. For example, sand dunes are geographical features that move quite easily up and down an unpopulated coast. They ought to be a fluid part of the landscape, but on Fire Island, where the shoreline is particularly fragile, every effort is made to glue them to the spot with the adhesive of sawgrass. To the naturalness which is artificially maintained is added a fixed fluidity. Sex in the dunes is no spontaneous expression of passion, but the highly respectful use of fragile terrain. People in the throes of sex carefully did not stray into the roped off areas.

I have called *Forgetting Elena* a novel set on Fire Island, but it never mentions the name, and White wrote me that the setting "was only very approximately Fire Island."

The setting is imported from the world of comic operetta, *The Student Prince*, for example. But because the setting is so unconcerned with reality, so pleased to be viewed through the Vaseline lens of the imagination, *Forgetting Elena* is, I would argue, a better representation of Fire Island—a community, after all, dedicated to fantasy—than any "realistic" treatment would be. For in this ambiance of Lords and Ministers, ladies-in-waiting and servants in livery, White can capture simultaneously the unreality of the resort, its strange and magical beauty, its seemingly carefree hedonism, as well as satirize those very qualities. In the same letter that he distanced the novel's island setting from the actual Fire Island, White describes The Pines as "always a poetic melancholy place that combined a heart-rendingly beautiful landscape and seascape with an intense social life reminiscent of high school and an abundant sexuality." By invoking the intensity, fantasy, and cruelty of adolescence, when passionate friendships are as ephemeral as they are life-changing, he has characterized the very ethos of *Forgetting Elena*.

In *Dancer from the Dance*, Andrew Holleran strives for a similar effect. Through his heightened lyricism, he spreads across the island a kind of fairy tale magic that he paradoxically hopes will capture the more salient reality of Fire Island in the '70s.

> Down at the beach, in both directions, people faced the sea in the lotus position, meditating. The sky behind us was a tumult of gold- and salmon-colored clouds in the west, and before us the day had already died, unwitnessed, to give birth to the primal dream of this particular place, the musical, glittering, erotic night.
>
> Everyone—everyone except us, and the people meditating on the ridge of sand facing the sea—was preparing now for that magical night, showering, dressing, locating the pills they would take at nine o'clock after a light supper so that by midnight the night would be even more illusive.
>
> (212)

Holleran's and White's strategies are similar. White's allegorical dreamscape develops the magical, illusionary atmosphere while Holleran evokes and discards—or almost discards—the detritus of the everyday world. But for both men, Fire Island is a "primal dream," musical, glittering, and erotic, dotted by men as beautiful as flowers and engaged in a spiritual exercise that makes them only more beautiful. The sex that would close the night of illusions is merely hinted at as part of the aesthetic magic of the place.

The authors of the Violet Quill believed, however, that the aesthetic that ruled Fire Island was superficial and self-destructive, a remnant of the self-hating attitudes that prevailed a decade earlier, attitudes exemplified in Alexander Goodman's part-pornographic, pseudo-sociological study, *A Summer on Fire Island* (1966). Bill, an executive from IBM, removes the Barbra Streisand albums that have been playing continuously on the stereo so that he might think. His housemate, Charles, shrieks in horror:

> Think!!! Then you really don't belong here. Get thee back to IBM! Thinking is much, much worse that Bartok. There are strict Fire Island rules against it.
>
> Frankly, Bill, just between us girls, what is an intelligent, cultured "thinking" person like yourself doing at Cherry Grove in the first place? Why would any self-respecting "thinker" spend a whole summer among these very sweet, very amusing, but generally bird-brained queens and faggots? (43)

Charles suggests that Bill "hand over [his] tube of K-Y and [his] beaded bag" and "leave Cherry Grove this minute." The reference to K-Y suggests the sex, which is quite public even in the mid-'60s.

In Whitmore's "The Rights," Buddy, a young man whose sole artistic achievements are his body and the composition of a disco song, is not stupid; to the contrary, he shows himself at the conclusion to be quite savvy, but he represents a common figure of Fire Island gay literature: the young man caught up in the superficialities of the Island, its absence of historical awareness, its mindless hedonism. Buddy's ignorance of politics is one of the ways that the powerful exercise their power. In *Forgetting Elena*, The Minister of the Left, who is a friend of the Valentines, announces rather brusquely about Elena, "Let's be honest. . . . all these fads and styles are so desperately important; it keeps them busy and makes them feel they count. But we know it's money and power that keeps the first families first" (82). The power of the beautiful is nothing compared to the power that keeps the beautiful as a diversion. In *Dancer from the Dance*, Malone, who is present- ed as the gay ideal of beauty and placid good manners and gives up a suc- cessful career as a lawyer to dedicate himself to the pursuit of love and beauty, becomes in the end a person stripped of both the love and beauty he desired. "In a country where one is no more than what one does (a country of workers) or the money one possessed, Malone had ceased, like us, to have an identity at all. He was simply a smile now, a set of perfect manners, a wistful promise, as insubstantial as the breeze blowing the hair across his forehead," and consequently the narrator wonders "why Malone had fascinated us so" (219).

The criticism of Buddy (and Malone) as beautiful looking, emotionally placid, and intellectually vacuous is a criticism that has been traditionally leveled at Fire Island. And Malone—who did not start out as empty-head- ed—warns the young intellectual John Schaeffer, who has fallen in love with him, of the moral and spiritual risks that the beauty of Fire Island and its inhabitants holds.

> Never forget that all these people are primarily a visual people. They are designers, window dressers, models, photographers, graphic artists. . . . They are visual people, and they value the eye, and their sins, as Saint Augustine said, are the sins of the eye. And being people who live on the surface of the eye, they cannot be expected to have minds or hearts. It sounds absurd but it's that simple.
>
> Everything is beautiful here, and that is all it is: beautiful. Do not expect anything else, do not expect nourishment for anything but your eye—and you will handle it beautifully. You will know exactly what you are dealing with. (228)

David Leavitt, in his downright stupid introduction to *The Penguin Book of Gay Short Fiction* wrote, "According to *Dancer from the Dance* . . . only the most exceptionally beautiful among gay men were entitled to erotic ful- fillment" (xviii). But Holleran's point is just the opposite: those entranced by their own beauty, or just beauty itself, will never find erotic fulfillment, or any other kind of fulfillment at all because living "on the surface of the eye, they cannot be expected to have minds or hearts." For while it is true that Holleran, White, and Whitmore respond to the physical beauty both of the Island and of the men who vacation there, they are terrified of the Medusa-like effect of such beauty—that it will hollow out the heart and the mind, and turn the spirit to stone.

Dancer from the Dance is suffused with an elegiac longing for a lost world in which beauty and innocence are combined with emotional warmth and an intellectual stimulation, but it is a cautionary tale about mistaking Fire Island or the disco circuit for such an idyllic place. The sex, both public and private—indeed, no distinction is made between the two—which is part of the aesthetic of the island, is not separated from the other aesthetic limits. It has become a "sin of the eye" (but not of the body), and as such, it will not satisfy.

Larry Kramer's *Faggots* extends this critique of the Fire Island aesthetic by explicitly linking it to public sexual performance. Kramer satirizes the contention that public sex is beautiful and seeks to reveal it as base, vulgar, exhibitionism. Leather Louie "with his hand on the rubied swastika so smartly medalioned over his black leather chest" intones in the original Italian of Michelangelo's dictum: "One doesn't achieve inner discipline until one reaches the extremes of art and life" (274). But it is not clear whether it is art or life whose extreme he is pompously and pretentiously entertaining at the moment. Later in the episode, in a scene that is a haunting reminder of Malone's speech to John Schaefer, Tim Dildough, the new male supermodel, refuses to have sex. "I want to be looked at by everybody and to pass around my beauty so the world can appreciate my handsomeness," he explains to one admirer, who tries to engage him in conversation, "But I don't want to have to talk. You would make me talk. I just want to be seen. And to be worshiped for my beauty" (278). Kramer, too, is concerned about the sins of the eye.

Unlike White, Holleran, or Picano, Kramer mocks the very landscape that the Violet Quill finds so unassailably beautiful and emphasizes the tawdry, grotesque abjectness of public sex on Fire Island. In the mock-voice of a Victorian narrator, Kramer sets the scene:

> So, picture if you will, a particularly scenic nook, slightly off the beaten path, just to one side of the main highway through these woods, in this veil of myth and story, equidistant from The Pines and Grove, an open patch, trod down by years of Indian braves, deer, then men, surrounded by tall evergreens and ringed with low ones. The moon was just able to kleig it into atmospheric cofraternal welcomeness. . . . And was there not much finery everywhere! iron crosses and swastikas and military marching boots with soles like heavy slabs of darkest bread, Visors and helmets and caps

and hoods and bayonets and swords and rifles and holsters and bullet belts plugged full with poppers. And on [the host's] belt, the smart executioner's mask he'd borrowed . . . to later case his head. Very smart. Very sinister. As [the host] wished for it to be.   (270)

The sarcasm of the passage is sufficiently marked that the concluding evaluation of the scene, "Very smart. Very sinister," is thoroughly ironized. The string of copulas suggests just how stagily overblown the scene has become, and the split infinitive, "to later case his head," is just the right touch to make the paragraph's conclusion awkward and ungainly, the very opposite of smart and sinister. This passage is followed by Dr. Ike Bulb, an honored guest, observing, "I notice some of our boys over there contemplating playing with their feces. . . . Nice to see it. I think I'll go and join them." Such banal expressions of politeness—more fitting for a matron at a Bar Mitzvah than for a sadist at an orgy—makes this public sexual display silly rather than sinister, dull rather than smart.

Yet the orgy episode in *Faggots* does reach a kind of grotesque climax that pushes past its satirical intentions when Dinky Adams, the object of Fred Lemish's amorous longing, is subjected to the punishing ministrations of Jack Humpstone. Tied on a sling lashed to four trees, Dinky is fist-fucked before an admiring crowd. "Look at those doors open," they cry in amazement, "That guy can really take it," and in a kind of ecstasy, with Jack Humpstone's arm completely in him, Dinky mumbles: "I can feel!" But that is not the end of the scene. Kramer continues:

> Dinky just continued to jerk up in pleasure and smile at heaven. The elusive heaven. Now so close. Now almost here. He tried to say a few more words to Jack. "I . . . I . . . I . . . want . . . your . . . other . . . arm!"
>
> (283, ellipses Kramer)

I am entirely unsure how Kramer wishes us to respond to this passage, but it is certain not with unallied humor or with a sense of beauty. I can imagine disgust, or pathos, or horror, or clinical detachment. There is a kind of sublimity at work here, but it is hard to know what response it warrants.

Like the authors who formed the Violet Quill, Kramer is attracted to the sexual sublime, which they ally with public sex on Fire Island; but unlike the VQ writers, Kramer holds above the sexual sublime his own vision of a domestic ideal. According to Kramer, for sex to be a part of the gay sublime, it had to be removed not from love—for there is the lieberstode—but from domestic affection. Kramer's vision—for all its insistence on gay pride—is drawn from a deeply Jewish origin, a sublime that is also domestic. In *Faggots*, Abe, a fabulously rich Jewish businessman, is permitted, despite his highly questionable heterosexual morals, to assume the moral high road by

wrestling with his son, whom he catches performing various public scato-
logical acts at the orgy at the Meat Rack. "And God gives now his answer to
Abe, who takes his younger son and hurls him to the ground. . . . And the
son knees back in protest and suffocation and not quite so experienced
heft. And together they toss and they turn, like some biblical nightmare"
(287–88). Kramer's paratactic style imitates the biblical nightmare of not
only Jacob wrestling with the angel, but Abraham's sacrifice of Isaac. Not
that Kramer wishes to reinscribe the heterosexual imperative that motivates
Abe, but to energize a Patriarchal bonding that has been lost in modern
domestic life: "The pop has said I love you to the son, the scene and dream
of every son who's backed away beneath these sheltering trees. He's said
he loves me. The sheltering veil now shelters. God has forbidden a fantasy
might come true! That would be too scary!" (289). Public sex, those "sheltering trees," is a substitute for, and a reaction formation against, the protective arm of the father to his son. Man has come to believe that God has
forbidden such protective and nurturing love between men because
mankind would find such love and all its intensity too scary. But it is just the
awesomeness of male affection brought within the bonds of family—such
domestic sublimity— that Kramer believes is what gay men need to offset
the destructive appeal of the sexual sublime.

But Kramer is a Jeremiah, not a Pollyanna. Even before AIDS he held up
little hope that gay men would choose domesticity over the sexual sublime.
Fred Lemish, the novel's protagonist and Kramer's quasi-alter-ego, meets
up with Dinky Adams one more time before the novel closes. They retire to
Fairyland, the garden Dinky has established for Ike Bulb, and they lie down
"among some sand and scrub pines, [where] nestles is growing, a huge
symphony of flowers and planters and weeping tubs of willows and man-
made stars of light a cupolas and gazebos and cozy swings for two and tiny
benches for intimate picnics and breezy lanterns swinging out to say
Hello," in short the *Better Homes and Gardens* version of Eden (298). Fred
is there with Dinky, the latest in a long line of Adams. But it is a dinky sort of
Adam that Fred is left with, and he realizes that once again he has bought
into a fantasy. "If I'd chosen a real person," he tells himself, "I would have
had to face up to a real relationship. Too scary. Too full of Mom and Pop"
(300). For Kramer, sex outdoors is associated with a kind of prelapsarian
love that is impossible to aspire to; it is the trap that has seduced everyone
from Kubla Khan down.

Public sex in the Meat Rack is sex in nature. The fantasy of having sex
out-of-doors is, I think, particularly strong for gay men because for so long
sex had to be confined to rooms and behind the closet door. The most popular pre-Stonewall pornographic books were the *Song of Loon Trilogy,*

which celebrated outdoor sex between a Euro-American woodsman and his Native American lovers. If Kramer rejects sex in the open, it is because he maintains a different way of conceptualizing nature than the Violet Quill. Haunted by the Old Testament Prophets, Kramer wants to avoid acting contra naturum; he maintains, it seems, a belief in the rightness of "natural law" and its set of norms. His caveat with the Bible and its laws is his belief that for some men, same-sex love is not contra naturum, that gay men are following their natural law. In contrast, the VQ writers understand nature as a force of diversity and variety.

There isn't one tree, but thousands of different trees. Not a single apple, but dozens of varieties of apples. Nature avoids uniformity particularly in small matters—fingerprints, snowflakes, the wings of may flies—where it goes wild with possibilities. Nature, however, is not wasteful; its prodigality is part of its survival. Felice Picano articulates the tension between these two ways of conceptualizing Nature in *Like People in History* when the narrator/hero, Roger Sansarc explains to his young lover how shocking AIDS is in a metaphysical sense to the habitués of Fire Island:

> "Nature is usually so tightfisted with what it provides. So very prudent how it husbands its resources. Why would Nature go to all the trouble to create such much luxuriance in what after all was a group of nonreproductive creatures? Why create such an extraordinary generation of beautiful, talented, quirkily intelligent men, and then why let them die so rapidly, one after another? It doesn't make the least bit of sense. It's not natural. It's not the way Nature behaves. (416)

Picano can reconcile the tightfisted nature of strict norms with the luxuriant nature of gay creativity only by believing that these extraordinarily beautiful and "quirkily intelligent men" were produced for some special mission. But he can't reconcile either way of conceiving of Nature with the wastefulness of AIDS which seems to mock both the economy and the extravagance of Nature.

These two competing notions of nature—nature as normative and nature as floridly inventive—play themselves out in the various gay utopias imagined by the Violet Quill. Fire Island is at once an escape to the natural world from the concrete, steel, and glass environment of Manhattan and an entrance into the otherworldly—a metaphysical dream. In Fire Island the most beautiful and symmetrical forms of the male anatomy expose themselves against a nature where the pines are grotesquely twisted and stunted like overgrown bonzais. The island is remarkably lush, not because it has been left untouched, but because its inhabitants have so carefully fertilized the barren sands to create their gardens. In short Fire Island is one example of the denatured nature of the pastoral tradition. It is a tableau out of Edward Hicks's Peaceable Kingdom paintings.

Yet across this idyll runs a shadow. Giovanni Francesco Guercino sometime in the 1620s painted a picture, now in the Galaria Corsini, which is described by Joshua Reynolds's biographers as showing "gay frolickers stumbling over a death's head" sitting atop a moldering piece of masonry (309). Beneath the skull carved into the brick or stone are the words, ET IN ARCADIA EGO, the voice of Death telling the inhabitants of a pastoral retreat, "Even in Arcadia, there am I." Guercino meant by the phrase that death can be found even in the ideal pastoral landscape. Panofsky shows that Nicholas Poussin altered the notion. In Poussin, "Arcadians are not so much warned of an implacable future as they are immersed in a mellow meditation on a beautiful past" (313). Both interpretation apply to Fire Island as a pastoral setting where death stalks and a place to be recalled as part of an idealized past. At the end of *Dancer from the Dance*, for example, Malone and his friends scan the crowd at a party, "looking at the new faces with an odd sensation of death, for they had all been new faces once" (226). This "odd sensation of death" is both the elegiac recollection of the golden past and the proleptic vision of everyone's—even the youngest and most beautiful person's—impending demise. Malone warns Schaeffer that he "no longer live[s] in the magic world that is yours for ten more years. Adolescence in America ends at thirty" (227). *Et in Arcadia ego.*

Death in Arcadia—its chilling effect is the contrast between the seeming immortality of youth and beauty and the austere, unyielding figure of the skull. Even the earliest gay accounts of Fire Island trade on this contrast. Alexander Goodman retells this tale of public sex:

> A slim, good-looking boy was being screwed by a big Negro. Just as the Negro was about to come, he snapped a popper. He first inhaled it, then he passed it to the boy, then he inhaled it again.
>
> The tremendous stimulation from the sexual act and the drug tore at his heart and broke it. At the height of orgasm, the man died.
>
> For several minutes the boy lay there, not realizing that the body above and in him was that of a dead man. (96–97)

Elsewhere love and death remain distinct, what is above and within stay separate, the ecstatic and the fatal unfused. But on Fire Island they are indistinct, inseparable, commingled especially in the Meat Rack.

Once the AIDS epidemic began the Violet Quill writers turned their backs on Fire Island as a scene for their stories, plays, and novels. The site, which had been such a staging point for their raids on the, if not inarticulate, at least unspoken, life of certain gay men, became after AIDS a location of less strategic value. In a sketch he published in his 1987 collection *I've a Feeling We're Not in Kansas Anymore*, Ethan Mordden depicts a character clearly modeled on Andrew Holleran on the beach adjacent to the Meat Rack, "ensconced with friends between Pines and Grove. Between: as if respecting fashion but resenting it." The character has been "hiding from both the swank and the drab, hiding between, as if instituting a new sort of gay in which neither praise nor blame will be freely given" (106). For Mordden, Holleran is trying to use resentment and resistance as a means of finding a middleground between the swank and the drab—those extremes of gay life. But that middleground—no matter how life preserving it may be in the Age of AIDS—cannot be built on the shifting sands of Fire Island regardless of how much beach grass is sown in the dunes or how deeply the foundations of the houses have been sunk.

The most damning and most powerful portrait of Fire Island gay life to emerge since AIDS is Allen Barnett's "The *Times* as It Knows Us," a work modeled on Joyce's "The Dead." Before his own death from AIDS, Barnett interviewed the remaining members of the Violet Quill for an article he never wrote, and his work quite self-consciously continues the line of their work. Noah, Perry, Stark, Enzo, Horst, and the narrator, Robert, all share a house for the summer. Robert's lover, Samuel, has died of AIDS. Perry has spoken to a reporter from the *New York Times* for an article, "New Rituals Ease Grief as AIDS Toll Increases," a story that features these friends and their cold response to the pain of others. Yet "The *Times* as It Knows Us" does not repudiate the article—Enzo's attack of fever is ignored by nearly everyone, including Enzo's lover, an AIDS activist. Only Robert and Stark spend the night trying to lower Enzo's temperature until he can be transported to a hospital. "Since the deaths began," Robert comments, "the certified social workers have quoted Shakespeare at us: 'Give sorrow words.' But the words we used now reek of old air in churches, taste of the dust that has gathered in the crevices of the Nativity and the Passion" (105). The old words do not help, and the old places where those words were spoken do not help either. Some new style is required—some new mode of speech, or living, some new community must be constructed now that Death is not merely to be found there, but has taken over the place, dominating every vista, flitting through all the rooms.

Yet for Barnett, this new language will come not by denying or erasing what came before, but by transforming what was most valuable from the past: "Think of him, the one you loved," Robert asks us to imagine, "on his knees, on his elbows, his face turned up to look back in yours, his mouth dark in his dark beard."

He was smiling because of you. . . . You had brought him, and he you, to that point where you are most your mind and most your body. His prostate pulsed against your fingers like a heart in a cave, mind, body, body, mind, over and over.

Looking down at him, he who is dead and gone, then lying across the broken bridge of his spine, the beachhead of his back, you would gladly change places with him. *Let your weeping be bitter and your wailing fervent; then be comforted for your sorrow.* Find in grief the abandon you used to find in love; grieve the way you used to fuck.   (106)

The sexual is not for Barnett a denial of our deepest humanity, but the portal to it, the passage to that new language, that new style of being which we must create in the wake of AIDS. In the phrase "the beaches of his back," indeed in the entire way he turns anatomy into geography, Barnett makes clear that sex is not confined to a single space but is part of the larger, and public, environment. It is in the public visibility of gay sexuality that his characters begin to learn the lessons that will serve them in their communal grief.

Nights on Fire Island are dark. Only the heart of a forest is darker. The ocean stretches out, cloaked in its thick mist richer than blood. On Fire Island no cars prowl the street, shooting headlights into the far ends of the room, like two hands feeling for the wall or fingering the furniture. On clear night stars might, the foam on the crest of the waves might glimmer. But the natural light of stars and moon is the perfect lighting for sex out of doors, showering the bodies of lovers with its cool, caressing, silvery light.

It gives even the driest lips fullness and moistness. In the moonlight, the eyes grow wide, still, sensitive. Men pass alert to every gesture, every sound, not for fear of being discovered, but in hopes that they may be found. They are attuned to the dark because they know that darkness is also a door inscribed with a final verdict. *Et in Arcadia ego.*

Even in Arcadia, I am.

REFERENCES

Barnett, Allen. *The Body and Its Dangers and Other Stories.* New York: St. Martin's Press, 1990.

Bergman, David. *Gaiety Transfigured: Gay Self-Representation in American Literature.* Madison: University of Wisconsin Press, 1991.

Decter, Midge. "The Boys on the Beach." *Commentary,* September 1980: 35–48.

De Kooning. Willem. *Fire Island.* Oil on paper. c. 1946. Margulies Family Collection.

Goodman, Alexander. *A Summer on Fire Island.* Washington, D.C.: Guild Press, 1966.

Holleran, Andrew. *Dancer from the Dance.* New York: Morrow, 1978.

Kramer, Larry. *Faggots*. New York: Random House, 1978.

Leavitt, David. Introduction to *The Penguin Book of Gay Short Fiction*, edited by Mark Mitchell and David Leavitt. New York: Viking Penguin, 1994.

Mordden, Ethan. *I've a Feeling We're Not in Kansas Anymore*. New York: St. Martin's Press, 1985.

Mosher, John. *Celibate at Twilight*. New York: Random House, 1940.

Newton, Esther. *Cherry Grove, Fire Island*. Boston: Beacon Press, 1993.

Panofsky, Irwin. *Meaning in the Visual Arts*. Chicago: University of Chicago Press, 1955.

Picano, Felice. *Like People in History*. New York: Viking Press, 1995.

White, Edmund. *Forgelling Elena*. New York: Penguin, 1981

White, Edmund. *Nocturnes for the King of Naples*. New York: St. Martin's Press, 1978.

White, Edmund. *States of Desire*. New York: Dutton, 1980.

Whitmore, George. "The Rights." Manuscript. Collection of Victor Bumbalo, New York.

WILLIAM L. LEAP

In this chapter I discuss two different types of "public places"—the locker room and sauna of a commercial health club and the backroom of an adult bookstore. Each place becomes constructed as a space where men have sex with other men, though each does so in somewhat different ways. How men go about constructing male-centered erotic space at these sites is of interest to the discussion, and so is why men consider backrooms and saunas as appropriate sites for erotic engagement.

In that sense, the chapter joins the preceding discussions by Tattelman, Hollister, Bergman, and others in exploring connections between landscape (that is, following Cosgrove 1985, a "way of seeing" and interpreting a particular terrain) and male-centered erotic practice. Raymond Williams (1973: 9–12 passim) reminds us, however, that landscape is a product of class position and other components linking human agency to opportunity structure. Accordingly, any discussion of *erotic site* must also be a discussion of *erotic actor(s)*. I address the issue in several ways, but primarily by asking how forms of social action within the erotic moment mesh with the actors' claims to gendered identity.

These intersections of local terrain, erotic practices, and identity are of interest to the anthropology of gender and to the rapidly expanding field of cultural geography. For example, Butler's suggestion (1990: 13–25, passim) that gender has a performative rather than a prediscursive status in human experience closely parallels the insistence by Ingold (1994: 738) and others (see discussion in Hirsch 1995, especially page 5 and note 6) that landscape is not a static formation, but a form of cultural process. This parallel suggests that landscape might be performative (that is, a product of social conditions, not an antecedent of it); and that gender itself might be "a way of seeing" relevant to a particular terrain.[1]

More important, these intersections of terrain, erotics, and identity have cutting-edge relevance for HIV education. We are now entering the fourth decade of the AIDS pandemic; and while HIV infection rates in the United States may not be expanding exponentially, as researchers had once feared, HIV infection rates are certainly not declining. Because sexual safe- ty continues to compete with risk-taking within the erotic moment, some authorities propose lowering infection rates by eliminating the sites where men regularly engage in at-risk erotic activity, e.g., close the gay bathhouses, prohibit male sex clubs, police the highway rest-stops, monitor the department store bathrooms. Such proposals assume that the physical location itself creates incentives for sexual risk-taking.

I will argue here that the source of sexual risk-taking lies not in the physicality (or availability) of the sexual site, but in the sense of *sexual landscape* that grows out of participation in male-centered erotic activities in previous locales, foregrounds erotic possibilities at particular sites, and structures site-specific erotic memories. Understanding how sexual landscape promotes sexual risk is the first step toward understanding what sexual landscapes might contain if they were constructed independently of risk-taking, and the first step toward developing AIDS education/prevention efforts which will actually promote such constructions.

Two "Private" Sites: Some Preliminary Contrasts

To develop these issues, I focus specifically on two sites of male-centered erotic exchange in the Washington D.C. area: the sauna and associated areas in the men's locker room of an "(officially) heterosexual" health club and the backroom of a "gay"-oriented, adult bookstore.[2] Let me begin by explaining why I am using these particular sites as the data-base for a discussion of landscape, erotic practices, and identity.

First, I have become familiar with these sites through previous research activities, and have been drawing comparisons between their details for quite some time.

The health club in question here was an important research site during my earlier study of *Gay Men's English*.[3] While the health club does not advertise itself as a gay-friendly site, and does not actively solicit a gay clientele, health club patrons include gay men and straight men, and the logistics of the locker room, the aerobics studio, and the weight-room floor provide ample opportunities for conversation and other forms of communication within and across gendered boundaries. By studying "language use" at this health club, I was able to observe instances where gay men and straight men used English in similar as well as different ways, and the points of similarity and difference helped sharpen my sense of distinctiveness and authenticity in gay English grammar and discourse.

The bookstore backroom has become an equally valuable research environment, now that my gay English research has begun to explore the *language of gay city*. Events and activities at this second site figure prominently in the narratives and anecdotal comments I have collected from several informants in the project. And, as was the case in the health club sauna, the backroom has also become a site for my own participant-observation.

Second, the bookstore and the health club are located in different areas of the District of Columbia, and "surroundings" contribute to the construction of each site in rather different ways.

The health club occupies three floors of an office building in an upscale area (upper northwest) of Washington D.C. Adjacent to the health club are the administrative offices for several federal agencies and several private commercial firms, whose staffs are eligible for a variety of health club membership packages and discounted membership fees. Even with those discounts, the costs of maintaining a monthly membership at the health club is higher than for any other commercial health club facility in the city. "The fee structure is deliberate," one staff member told me when I first visited the club, "to ensure that certain types of people will not apply for membership." I asked what she meant by "certain types of people," and she replied: "You know, college students, people who cannot afford what we have to offer, people who would not be comfortable here, who wouldn't fit in."

One result of this policy is particularly striking: while there are African Americans, Asians, and Hispanics on the club's membership roles, the membership's predominant racial/ethnic category is Euro-American. In fact, by my estimate, no more than two or three of the fifty or sixty persons on the weight room floor at any given time will be persons of color. Moreover, and further submerging any sense of ethnic/racial differences at this site, club members share certain similarities in occupational status and job description, e.g., middle-level managers, upper-level administrators, university professors, broadcast journalists, health professionals, lawyers in corporate or private practice, and (occasionally) congressmen.

I cannot say that the club caters to an *elite* clientele, because only a handful of the club's members (by my estimate) are from high income or high status backgrounds. But I can report that management tries to create an *impression* of privilege. Certainly club furnishings and amenities speak directly to that image, e.g., high-back leather chairs in the waiting area, lockers made of real wood, not veneered particle board; complimentary coffee, tea, and mineral water at the refreshment bar; and the assortments of soaps, shampoos, and other toiletries in the men's shower area. And so do the club's selection of top-of-the-line, high-tech fitness equipment and the range of personal training services, which club staff will provide to individual members for additional fees.

The club's physical separation from the outside world contributes richly to this impression. The club is underground, and the patron's only access is through a security-guarded elevator. Just by entering the club, the patron leaves the mundane world behind. There are no windows or exterior vistas. The walls of the workout areas and locker rooms are filled with mirrors, reflecting the viewer's gaze back onto the details of interior spaces. Once entering the club, there is no "outside" to be seen, and the continuous thumping of disco music ensures that outside noises cannot be heard.[4]

No such pretense of privilege has influenced the construction of facilities at the bookstore or its backroom, or directed the managers' efforts to attract and retain a clientele. Bookstore customers come to the bookstore from across the city and from the surrounding Maryland and Virginia suburbs; unlike the health club, their income-levels, employment status, and racial/ethnic backgrounds are quite diverse. Moreover, the bookstore is located in a part of the metropolitan area which gay men (and other D.C. residents) describe as "low income," "warehouse district," "run down," "dangerous," and "this is where I go when I go slumming."[5] The surrounding neighborhood is industrial, not residential; it has, however, been home for several of D.C.'s more popular gay clubs in recent years.

Third, activities that take place at these sites present rather different intersections of erotics and spatial practice.

The health club's advertising positions this facility as a gymnasium, not as a male-centered sex-club and, each time I have raised the issue with staff members, they insist that on-site sexual activity between men does not occur here. Of course the forms of erotic display usually associated with all-male sports facilities can regularly be found in the men's locker room behavior—the parade of partially exposed or undraped male bodies, flexing of muscles, competitive teasing, and continual sexual innuendo. And, unstated but powerful restrictions which limit close physical contact and other forms of spatialized intimacy obligate men to "keep their distance" in the sauna, in the locker room, just as they do in the workout areas and on the weight room floor. So when sex between men occurs at this site—and, staff assertions to the contrary, sex between men *does* occur here, as I will explain below—the male-centered erotic activities violate on-site norms in multiple ways.

Sex between men in the bookstore backroom, in contrast, explicitly affirms the social norms maintained within that locale. The backroom contains a complex arrangement of dimly lit chambers, enclosed cubicles for one-on-one erotic exchange, and open areas for group sex and other visible erotic displays. All of these features help make this a site *marked* for sex between men, and the front area of the bookstore anticipates this message through its assortment of sexually explicit all-male videos, its racks of "jerk-off" magazines and books, and its displays of dildos, cockrings, "poppers" (marketed as "room deodorizers" or "video head cleaners"), and other sex toys.

Finally, as the label implies, the "backroom" location of this bookstore is very much intended as a private space and not as a public location. To gain access to this area, the customer pays an entrance fee ($14.00 per visit, during the summers of 1995 and 1996 when I conducted my interviews and the on-site research), then passes through a turnstile and through thick black curtains into the darkened area beyond. The further into this area the customer goes, the greater the opportunities for male-centered erotic exchange—and the greater the restrictions on using verbal statements as a means for facilitating such exchange; panting and groaning in the heat of passion are, however, entirely appropriate within this context.

The backroom is not a cruising area, or a site for preliminary sexual negotiation; this is an area where people go "to take care of business," as one of my informants pointedly explained. And the seclusion, the darkness, the avoidance of verbal communication—all of which signify *private* erotic spaces in many segments of modern day America—work together to underscore this point.

The health club sauna, interestingly enough, shares many of the features of "private space" which are commonly associated with male-centered sexual practices (and which are richly illustrated by the bookstore's backroom, as I explain below). The sauna is located at the furthest point from the entrance to the health club. To reach the sauna, a club member must check in at the entry desk, walk past the aerobic studios, enter the men's locker room, walk past the television room, disrobe and store clothing in a locker, go through the room with the lavatories and toilets, pass the whirlpool, walk up three steps, and turn left: only then does the club member face the sauna room door. There is a panel of clear, tinted glass in the center of the sauna door, but the sauna itself has a single lightbulb of low wattage, and otherwise provides a darkened interior. Subdued conversation between sauna users is acceptable, but such conversations should not be loud enough to disturb other occupants' enjoyment of the facility, and occupants will direct pointedly ferocious glances at the offending parties if a conversation is boisterous or prolonged.

But, structural and situational privacy notwithstanding, the sauna is still very much a *public* location. At least, that is the position of health club management and staff, who have reacted quite negatively when individual club members violate the rules of decorum central to the institutional culture at this site, e.g., loud, boisterous conduct in the locker room or on the workout floor, use of profanity or obscene language, unsanctioned appropriation of another's personal property, or on-site erotic activity. "The real problem here," one staff member told me, "is visibility." He continued: "Acting like a bully, talking dirty, stealing—these are events which are difficult to ignore. Whatever people do on their own time here is their own business, and none of my concern. But when what you do starts affecting other people's use of the club, hey, we gotta put a stop to that."

"So," I asked, "if you found out that two guys were 'fooling around' in the showers or in the sauna . . .?" "We'd have to stop 'em," he replied. "People'd object to that. This isn't what they want to see when they come here for their workout." And sure enough, soon after "people" began complaining about men having sex with men in the sauna room, one of the janitors began walking up the stairs to the sauna at irregular intervals, so he could peer through the tinted panel and ensure that the club members were not making personal use out of the areas designated as "public spaces" within the health club's "official" geography.

Erotics, "Public Space," and Privacy: The Health Club

Studying Sex-on-Site

But the fact is, management's assumptions about public space notwithstanding, some club members *were* actively using the sauna and other areas of the locker room as sites for erotic activities. Other club members began to tell me about these activities as soon as I started working out at this club (fall 1991), and—continuing a line of research which I had begun during my gay English research at similar sites in the D.C. area—I was curious to understand why some of my fellow club members found on-site sexual exchange to be so attractive. Were these incidents merely a product of pragmatic, if unplanned, opportunism—two horny guys, feeling the heat of mutual attraction, spontaneously acting on their impulses? Did they reflect the idea (see discussions in Pronger 1990: 125–36; Klein 1993: 221–33) that athletes can do anything they want and never compromise their masculinity? Did they suggest the emergence of a new type of gay male erotic oasis, given the negative sanctions that the AIDS pandemic has imposed on impersonal sex at other locales?

To answer these questions, I began making three visits a week to the club, and except for interruptions due to out-of-town trips or illness, I maintained that schedule over the period October 1991 to February 1993. Two of these visits were always in the early evening; the third was

either in the evening, a mid-week afternoon, or a late afternoon on Saturday or Sunday. Each visit lasted two hours, and included a warm-up period on the stationary bicycles, a sixty minute workout on the weight room
floor, and thirty minutes (or longer) in the locker room, the sauna, and in
the showers.

This schedule gave me ample opportunity to observe fellow health club
patrons in a variety of on-site settings. As I reported in Leap (1996b:
109–24), these observations offered abundant examples of gay English
usage, both in the presence of straight men and in conversations exclusively between gay men. They also gave me opportunity to continue my study of
gender diversity in nonverbal message-making, work which I had begun at
other health club sites. Because I was now coming to the club on a regular
basis, I was also able to get to know other men who used the club facilities
at similar times. Conversations with these men elicited their perspectives on
a range of topics relevant to the social organization of the site.

Some of these men self-identified as "gay," either during the opening
moments of our first conversation or as friendship began to develop. Two of
them introduced me to other gay men who regularly used the club facilities,
and soon I had access to a small network of gay companions whose
insights into on-site sexual practices soon became invaluable. I talked with
them frequently, in one-on-one conversations and in small groups, and
began to look forward to these discussions each time I visited the health
club. I was also able to hold more detailed discussions with several of the
men, both over the telephone and at locations away from the health club;
their comments helped me flesh out my observations about the undercur-
rents of erotic activity present at the site.

Other men either offered no identification of their gender-identity, or
quickly made their claims to heterosexuality explicitly clear. I found it difficult to talk informally with men in this "unidentified" category; I noticed that
they used the gym facilities on their own and rarely spoke to anyone else
under any circumstances. On the other hand, I became friends with several
of the self-identified straight men, a few of whom also became valuable
sources of information as the research progressed.

Earlier research at other health clubs made it easy to identify the verbal
phrases and nonverbal cues which signaled that male-centered erotic
negotiations was occurring on the weight room floor or in the locker rooms,
showers, and saunas (see discussion in Leap 1996b: 47–48, 63–66). Once
I identified the beginning stages of such a negotiation, I tried to monitor the
exchange discreetly and to make verbatim notes on the dialogue, if paper
and pencil were available; my workout sheets were especially useful for this
purpose.

In some cases, I observed the transition from initial expressions of inter- est to the beginnings of the erotic exchange; and in others, I was able to fol-low these negotiations from beginning to conclusion.

Locations for on-site erotic activities included the partially enclosed alcoves in the changing rooms, which were created by the cul-de-sac placements of the lockers; the shower stalls, which were protected from outside viewing by heavy cotton shower curtains; the steam room, the rooms used for suntanning, massage, and physical therapy (when those rooms were not otherwise engaged), and the sauna—which, by other men's reports and my own observation, was the on-site location most fre-quently employed for this purpose.

The erotic activities that took place in these locations included hand-jobs (self-administered, administered to another man, or administered in tandem), blow jobs, and (though occurring much less frequently, by all reports) frottage and butt-fucking. Using hands, fingers, and/or tongues to feel, probe, caress, and massage one's partner or one's own body could precede and/or accompany any of those activities. Usually, all such physi-cal contact ended as soon as one or both participants reached orgasm.

Individual exchanges could have one, two, or more participants, and could also occur in the presence of other men who might, on their part, ignore the exchange entirely, feign indifference to its detail, agree to provide "look-out" services and warn of the approach of others, or join the other participants in the exchange.

Importantly, while verbal commentary usually signaled help to structure the beginning stages of these negotiations, verbal communication during erotic activity was largely limited to programmatic or performative phrases. Often, the exchanges took place almost entirely in silence.

Finally, while I cannot specify the frequency with which male-centered erotic activities occur at this site, I can offer several informal indications of frequency. For example, comments in my field notes show that I found men engaged in same-sex erotic activity at least twice a month during the eigh-teen-month period I was on site. My field notes also show that, at least three times per month, I observed initial phases of erotic exchange, even if I was not able to determine the specifics of the outcome.

Anecdotal comments from the club patrons (gay and straight) I inter-viewed suggested that their observations of other men's on-site erotics occurred at similar frequencies. Some of these men also reported that, "as often as once a week" (to cite one respondent's phrasing), they found evi-dence of completed erotic activities (puddles of semen on the sauna seats and locker room floors, on workout or locker room towels that had not been placed in the laundry baskets, or on the furniture in the physical therapy rooms. And most of them had at least one story to tell about sex-between-men on-site. These stories may have been derived from their own club experiences or based on experiences reported to them by other patrons. But either way, these stories helped them summarize, in a single narrative, what they knew about male same-sex erotics, and men who had such stories to tell insisted that I include these narratives in my data base.

To be sure, this health club was not functioning as a thinly disguised bathhouse, but sex-between-men was frequent enough to have become integrated into the social practices and the cultural narratives patrons associated with this site, whatever their own sexual or erotic interests. The prominence of these practices and narratives raised questions in my mind regarding the participants: who were the men-having-sex-with-men at this site?

Erotics, Landscape, and Identity

As I got to know some of the gay members of the health club, I asked them to talk about occurrences of sex-between-men at this site and, where possible, I tried to get them to give me descriptions of their own on-site erotic experiences. Initially, the men spoke of locker-room- and sauna-sex in generalized terms, as an enactment of fuck-film imaginaries or a fulfillment of hot erotic fantasies. Consistently, however, these boisterous, carefree claims soon gave way to one or more of the following reflexive pronouncements:

1. *Locker room sex is risky sex*, particularly since (according to informant commentary and my own observations) participants are unlikely to wear condoms and may disregard safer sex practices in other ways.

2. *Locker room sex leads to discovery* by health club staff or other club members; discovery will reinforce images of gay men as sexual predators, and may also endanger the participants' continuing membership in the health club.

3. *Locker rooms are not appropriate places for men to have sex* with other men; sex is something to do "at home," not "in public."[6]

The third point is of particular interest here. Certainly, self-identified gay men have no problems initiating negotiations that may lead into erotic exchange. But, by my observation and according to participants' self-reports, once both parties begin to express serious interest in erotic activity, they either exchange telephone numbers, arrange to continue the negotiations off-site once their workouts are ended, or agree to continue their conversation the next time they see each other at the gym. Much less frequently, again by my observation and participants' self-reports, self-identified gay men continue the negotiations to an on-site, erotic conclusion.

Self-identified gay men spoke candidly about their experiences with on-site sex when I asked questions about it during informal conversations and interviews. They insisted that they only pursue these options under special circumstances, usually in instances where the object of desire satisfies their fantasized expectations about the "ideal" sex-partner in some extraordinary way. And they always acknowledged the need for self-restraint in the health club setting (paraphrasing points 1 and 2, above), even while they explained why they could not ignore the appeal of the particular erotic moment.

Consistent with this argument, self-identified gay men claim that the men who regularly participate in on-site erotic activities, who are most likely to initiate and pursue these exchanges, and who are key figures in the anecdotes and narratives about "locker room sex" which circulate among the members of this health club—these men are not "gay men" but (as one gay friend put it) simply "guys who like having sex with other guys."

At first, I thought there was a political distinction hidden in this typology: "gay men" heed one set of rules and constraints appropriate to this site (a sort-of "situated gay culture," perhaps) and violate those rules only under special circumstances; while "guys who like having sex with other guys" do not recognize the importance of those rules and model their behaviors around other, more permissive standards. But after observing one instance of on-site sex between men, I began talking to the (50+-year-old Euro-American) man who (I later learned) had started the exchange.[7] He, too, insisted that he was "straight," not "gay," and that the mutual masturbation/blow-jobs which he and his sex-partner had just enjoyed did not constitute "gay sex." He went on to describe himself as "bisexual," said he was involved in a long-term, live-in relationship with a women, but also enjoyed sex with men—"especially," he explained, "when there are no strings attached."

Of all those I interviewed, there were twelve men who regularly had sex with other men on-site, but who refused to self-identify as "gay" and insisted that they were "straight." As the discussions continued, two men in addition to the 50-year-old mentioned earlier also went on to identify themselves as "bisexual." The other nine men offered other forms of self-description: a 38-year-old government administrator exclaimed: "I'm a married man with kids, for crissake!"; an attorney in private practice said: "I'm a Mormon"; a college student announced, quite simply, "I'm horny, and if another guy wants to do it, I'll do it."

It is tempting to consider these men's use of identifiers like "married," "Mormon" and "horny" as instances of sublimation and self-denial, and to conclude that *all* of these men are really "bisexual" (or, perhaps, latently homosexual), even if most are unwilling (or unable) to recognize their connection to that gendered stance. There are, however, some more substantial (and less self-evident) interpretations to be made of these claims to identity.

For one thing, "men having sex with other men" has a wider occurrence in U.S. society than many people commonly recognize, and the activities observed and reported at the health club site may be nothing more than a localized reflection of this larger trend.[8] Moreover, both Pronger (1990) and Klein (1993) have shown how men's participation in competitive athletics can coincide with expressions of hypermasculinity, as well as claims to free-ranging sexual license. Willing participation in same-sex erotic activities combined with an avoidance of homosexual labeling is entirely consistent with this construction of male ideology—particularly when the activities (and discussions) take place in an all-male environment like a health club locker room.

Additionally, all of the self-identified straight men I interviewed occupy prominent, and often prestigious, positions in D.C.'s business/professional community, and I wonder how greatly issues of male-centered privilege contribute to the enactments of sexual desire here. Indeed, judging by the comments recorded in my field notes, the self-identified straight men's descriptions of their on-site sexual pursuits resemble the "I see it, I want it, I take it" perspectives which underlies the sexual harassment of women in the workplace. If a predatory sexuality also underlies these men's pursuit of male-centered on-site erotics, then the close ties between power and pleasure which these men are addressing through such pursuits need to be highlighted, not obscured.

Particularly relevant to this point is the unified description of the health club's landscape that all of the straight men gave me during our on-site conversations. While the men identify themselves and their erotic interests in multiple ways, they agree that the health club offers them forms of shelter, retreat, and secluded relaxation unavailable in other, more "public" settings. The 38-year-old government administrator (the man who told me he was "married with two kids, for crissakes") developed this point more fully during an off-site interview:

> After a full day of in-your-face federal regulations, with the paperwork grind and a boss who wins national awards for being a jerk, I like to come to the club, do some exercises, work out a while, have a leisurely sauna, see who walks through the door [three-second pause], then take my shower and drive home to the kids.

Similar interpretations of the health club as a *private* locale, something separated and protected from the ordinary locations of daily life, show up in other comments made during these interviews. Frequently, the health club sauna or other specific locations became the focal point for these discussion of privacy. Straight men insist that erotic encounters in the sauna always happen spontaneously, without the kind of elaborate preluding usually associated with "pick up" activities in places like bars, parties at friends' houses, or at social events at work. And because they never know whether they are going to have sex in the sauna, straight men do not have access to condoms or other safe-sex paraphernalia within the erotic moment, and either avoid penetrative sexual practice or pursue penetration without using any form of protection.[9] Encounters which begin in less secluded settings have more time for planning, and protected penetration can become much more feasible.

So differences in *lead-time* and in the use of *safe-sex practices* are two of the signifiers which prompt straight men to identify the health club, and particularly, the sauna, as a *private* space. *Discovery* is another such signifier. The straight men I have interviewed tell me that they would never go to a park, a "gay beach," or other outdoors location to meet and have sex with another man. Such places are too visible, too open, too unprotected, too dangerous, these men told me; anyone can see what you are doing when you are there. The health club is more enclosed, more protected, and more secure, so there is no reason to worry about discovery: people respect each other's privacy, and they leave each other alone.

Finally, the constraints of family life, live-in girl friends, and the like, make it impossible for these men to have sex with other men in their homes, and their insistence that they are not gay makes the bathhouses, sex clubs, and other explicitly gay locations less than appealing locations for such encounters. The health club is not identified with any of these constraints, and its distance from family *and* from gay life make it a highly *appropriate* site for male-centered sexual exchange.

These interpretations of the health club landscape may not explain why self-identified straight men could also be interested in having sex with other men (and do not help me resolve the questions of category and labeling I mentioned above). But they do help me understand why these straight men choose locations like a health club sauna as the site for male-centered sexual activity. Additionally, the characterization that straight men give to this location—health club as *private* space—is quite different from that given by the self-identified gay men I interviewed, and with whom I regularly socialized during my visits to the club. Gay men consider the club to be *public* space, not a private locale; in fact, they consider it *too* public for anything more than preliminary erotic pursuit. For the straight men, the health club extends conditions of privacy which (they claim) they do not usually find at other locations. For gay men, however, the health club is public in its internal detail, and sources of private space lie elsewhere.

Erotics, "Public Space," and Privacy: An Adult Bookstore's Backroom

Backrooms provide one of the settings for privacy. Whether the surrounding location is a bar, a movie theater, a bookstore, or a sex shop, backrooms offer opportunities for men to have sex with men which are not available in quite the same way in other locales. The important characteristics here are several: the site is marked, explicitly, for erotic activity, and persons who enter the site may freely assume that they share similar erotic interests with persons already on-site. Of course, some people may be there simply to observe the sexual activities of others, and not to participate in them. But even a detached observer is likely to become the target of another person's erotic interests at some point during his visit; and he is equally likely to become a target of negative sanction and ridicule if he continues to rebuff those overtures.

Studying Sex-on-Site

"Backrooms are for serious sex; they're not for children," said Charlie, a 41-year-old accountant from Miami who recently had been transferred to the D.C. area. "The only limits," he continued, "are the limits that you impose on your partner." The descriptions of backroom activities I have collected from other informants support Charlie's claim. Any kind of erotic exchange may occur during a person's visit to a backroom, and no one is patrolling the area to regulate behavior. ("No sex police," Charlie noted.) In fact, informants always refer to the open-endedness and unpredictability of the backroom's erotic opportunities when they discuss the attractiveness of such sites.

I became interested in backrooms as a by-product of my current research, a study of the cultural construction of gay space(s) in urban areas. As part of the data-gathering for this project, I have been collecting life-story narratives from gay men who live in the Washington D.C. area, as well as their descriptions of the landmarks, locations, and activities that define Washington D.C. as a "gay city." Some of the men I have interviewed said nothing about backrooms and backroom sex, and have made clear from their comments that they have nothing good to say about such locations and the sexual practices that go on there. Others have included backrooms as part of the terrain of gay city as they know it from their own experiences. And for several of these men, backrooms are especially prominent features of the urban gay landscape. Their comments resemble the descriptions of anonymous sex between men presented by Delph (1978) and, more recently, in the essays in Dangerous Bedfellows (1996), and they bring back memories of my visits to the gay baths in the 1970s and early 1980s.

But these narratives offer more than mere details of erotic chronology. They provide glimpses into personal desire, of "want of being" (to use a Lacanian paraphrase of that term); they show the close connections between desire and nostalgia, probing a "hunger of memory" that cannot be satisfied through simple recollections of the past; and—important to my purposes here—they position backrooms, and backroom experiences, as public *and* as private spaces.

Collecting these narratives has prompted me to visit several of the backrooms so I could observe at firsthand the range of erotic negotiations that take place there. It was difficult fieldwork for me to undertake. Because sexual activities are intended to be anonymous at these sites, follow-up conversation was difficult to arrange, and usually conveyed signals of erotic interest even though I did not intend my questions to do so. Moreover, I found myself reluctant to respond to any of the sexual invitations that other men in the backroom directed at me. By maintaining a "distanced" stance, I was violating one of the basic assumptions that defines the backroom as a sexualized terrain: men who go into the backroom do so because they want to have sex with other men. Much in the way that Styles reports for his earliest visits to the gay baths (1979), I felt very much as if I had pushed myself, uninvited, into some exotic location in search of some exotic "other." I felt the same way when I was working with language renewal projects on American Indian settings (see discussion in Leap 1996a: 129–31). I did not like placing myself in that stance while in Indian country, and I remain equally uncomfortable about doing so in "gay city."

Accordingly, while I use my own observations to focus my discussion of backrooms as erotic locales, the primary data for this discussion come from my off-site conversations with several D.C.-area gay men who have visited D.C.-area backrooms on various occasions; and, to narrow the focus of this section, I concentrate here on their discussions of the adult bookstore I described earlier. I draw heavily here on the comments of one of these men, Mark, a 40-year-old college-educated businessman of Euro-American background. It was Mark's frequent visits to this site and his detailed descriptions of experiences in the backroom which led me to give serious attention to the backroom, and the particular meanings of "public" and "private" that apply.

Sex, Space, and Identity

All the descriptions of the bookstore's backroom, which I have collected, begin with references to movement, displacement, and transition. The bookstore itself is located in an area of Washington D.C. that is at distance from the federal monuments and the city's major shopping areas. There is little tourist traffic in this area, and commercial activity is largely confined to the neighborhood's warehouses and automotive/electrical repair shops. For all of the men I interviewed, African American as well as white, going to the bookstore means venturing into a part of the city with which they are not ordinarily familiar. Repeated visits may help the customer find a more convenient place to park his car (see comments below), but does not otherwise increase his knowledge of the local terrain.

Intensifying the unfamiliarity of the neighborhood, most bookstore visits occur at night, when street lights and passing automobiles offer only partial disruption to the surrounding darkness. And because street-parking in front of the bookstore is quite limited, customers often park their cars two or more blocks away, then rush from their cars, through the darkness, to the bookstore. Anyone they meet on the street is likely to be in the area for similar reasons, but no one stops to inquire. If street-cruising occurs at all, it happens only in the well-lit area in front of the bookstore; and, even in that setting, street cruising is rare. Erotic negotiations take place "inside"—inside the bookstore, or inside the other gay businesses on this block—not in any external domain.

Going "inside" the bookstore does not give the customer instant access to erotic opportunity, however. Entering the bookstore brings him into an area with displays of gay magazines, videos, sex toys, and other paraphernalia. Off to one side are a set of one-person sized cubicles with coin-operated video screens. The visual fare includes gay as well as some straight fuck-films. Mark calls them "peep shows" and he adds: "Each of those cubicles has a glory hole in it, um, and I have only gone there once. I've seen men back there, but I don't see much happening back there."

At the other side of the room is the cashier's desk, whose attendant also mediates entrance into the backroom. Mark and other gay men refer to the front part of the bookstore as the "outside area," because it is open to everyone who comes into the store. Entrance into the backroom requires payment to the cashier of a $14 fee (at the time of my research), but the size of the payment is reduced substantially if the customer has already purchased an annual membership and displays his membership card. (Informants disagree on the amount of the reduction, and I wonder whether the amount may be negotiated on an individual basis.)

The attendant's gatekeeper functions as well as the fee/membership requirements underscore the backroom's status as "private" space, and Mark and other informants use the term "private" throughout our conversations to identify and describe this space. Importantly, "private" in this refer-

ence denotes "restriction of access," not a seclusion—which was the
meaning signaled by the term in the health club setting.

So, fee arrangements completed, the customer "is buzzed through"
(Mark's wording) a locked doorway and enters a small movie theater. Mark
continues the description of the terrain:

> There are about three benches [in the theater], um, rather uncomfortable
> things. They had theater seats and they just put wood benches there. And
> uh a screen with porno flicks on it.
>
> That's the first room that you go into. And then the next room is a
> series of wooden cubicles with mesh wire on the top and you can lock
> them, and there are glory holes: wherever there is another cubicle there is
> a glory hole. Some of them are bigger glory holes; some of them are little.
>
> There are two cubicles where there are beds. And then they added a
> side section with more cubicles and there is another cubicle with just
> video games and pin ball and drink machines.
>
> And then there's a backroom with a freestanding, a back room with
> freestanding blocks that can be moved however you want to move them.
> And that tends to be more group stuff that happens back there, group sex
> that happens back there. Not as well lit, much darker. The other place is
> fairly well lit; you can pretty much see everyone.

So there are actually four different locations within the "backroom"—the
movie theater with the wooden benches, the room with the wooden cubicles, the room with the freestanding movable blocks, and the side area with
drink machines and video games. (The entrance to the washroom, offering
bar soap, paper towels, a toilet, and a water cooler filled with mouthwash, is
also located in this area of the backroom.) Each area has its own physical
composition, and each area is associated with a different type of erotic
activity and participation "style."

The small movie theater is a site for individualized fantasy and for masturbation. Men are seated, not standing, while they are in this area. Men
may sit next to each other, or signal sexual interests in other ways. If those
signals are acknowledged, the men move away from the theater area and
go into one of the cubicles or elsewhere in the backroom to complete the
erotic exchange. Otherwise, men who begin their evening in the theater
area tend to spend most of their evening in that location.

Men are much more mobile in the second area of the backroom, and
the erotic activities call into play a wider variety of roles and stances:

> People just walk around, and cruise. They go into the booths and then
> most of it—I, I only do oral sex, but uh some, uh I have seen people do uh
> anal sex uh on occasion. It's not, it's not very, I don't think it is very com-
> mon. I see it occasionally. It's usually two people who are in a booth

together. Like you know, like sometimes people will be in a booth and they
say, "will you come over here?" so then two people will get in one cubicle.
And other people may look on, through the glory holes. But two people will
do their thing, whatever they want to do in the booth.

The third area of the backroom, the open area with movable, freestanding blocks, is also the darkest part of the backroom, and the darkness substitutes for the symbolic seclusion created by the cubicle walls
(and disrupted by the glory holes) in the backroom's central area. Men
move about in this area, just as they do in the area adjacent to the cubicles. But here, the whole of the erotic event remains in plain view; there
are dark corners, but no enclosures into which sex partners can retreat.
Men can use the freestanding blocks to partition this area in various ways,
but those divisions still cover a large amount of territory and are in no
sense personalized spaces. In fact, there is enough space in this part of
the backroom for several groups of men to be participating in "group sex"
activities at the same time. Some of the groups are random formations;
other form around shared physical features or cultural attributes. Mark
explains:

> Like pretty boys will get into a group or hunks will get in a group, too.
> That's just about the only grouping. Sort of hunk types. And then there are
> leather types. Any anyone who wants to join in will join in. It's not exclu-
> sive; but the pretty boys and hunks will tend to get exclusive.

Other informants have made the same point about the relative inclusive-
ness of these groupings: "pretty boys" and "hunks" aside (whose entrance
criteria are more demanding), anyone who wants to become a part of an
ongoing erotic exchange is free to do so. Informants describe groups of as
many as ten or twelve men enjoying forms of group sex in this setting.

The fourth area of the backroom, with soft drink machines, video
games, and the washroom, is a neutral terrain. One informant has told me
stories of men having sex there, but Mark and my other informants do not
find his stories to be credible. They admit that some cruising occurs in this
area, but they usually see men moving into other backroom areas to complete the erotic exchange. Mark himself describes the washroom as a place
where he can "come down" after an especially intense erotic exchange;
having sex in that environment would be "totally out of place," he says,
"and quite unthinkable."

Who are the men who are having sex in the backroom? Mark answered
this question by noting:

> There are all sorts of people. Very young kids, they don't look eighteen
> years old to me, but you know I don't know if they check ID's or whatever.

But all the way up to you know very elderly men. It's uh, no one type of
person that goes there.

[I ask:] What about your ethnic mixture?

[Mark:] Absolutely. A lot of blacks, um, Hispanics, Latinos are probably the smallest group, but it is absolutely mixed, absolutely mixed, and once you, and according to the rest of the population, there is a significant number of blacks. Half the people there are black.

[I ask:] And they are having sex with each other and with non-blacks?

[Mark:] Yes. Once you are there, there is no distinction except what you like, but there is no color distinction.

[I ask:] And most of these men are gay, in your estimation?

[Mark:] Gay, yes, but some guys, straight guys, also come there to get off. Straight guys will go there to get a blow job and cum. But most people are there just to enjoy the raw sexuality of it, having different people suck you off, having different dicks in your mouth. That's really what it is.

And what are the sexual activities that take place between men in this setting, which constitute this "raw sexuality" of the backroom erotic experience?

Mark's comments place oral sex at the centerpiece of the erotic practices occurring here. Earlier, he reported that anal sex occurs much less frequently, at least in his experience, in this setting. Other informants agree, but note that masturbation, either as a solitary activity or something occurring while one or more partners caress and/or manipulates another participant's body, also takes place quite frequently, and so does mutual masturbation.

One constraint influencing choice of sexual activities in any single erotic moment is the number of persons who are present at, and who may be participating in, the erotic exchange. The layout of the backroom includes areas for single-person sex, for sex-in-pairs, and for group-sex, as I have just described. The movement between these areas increases a man's prospects of finding the kind of erotic activity he is looking for during that particular part of his visit. While some men choose to remain seated on the movie theater benches, most men divide their time among several of the backroom's locations.

Clothing is another constraint influencing choice of erotic practices at this site. Men are fully dressed when they enter the backroom and, while lockers are available for storage of clothing, they are rarely used. Accordingly, erotic activity always includes negotiations around t-shirts, jeans, and sneakers (the participants' usual attire). The most accessible, and hence most convenient, erotic activities are those which do not require removal of shoes and pants.

All informants agree, and my observations support this claim, that men are not using condoms during oral or anal sex while they are in the backroom; and management does not provide condoms either at the entry desk, in the washroom, or in any of the backroom areas. The *absence* of con- doms imposes a third set of constraints on backroom erotic activity, as Mark explains:

> Every once in a while, people use condoms for oral sex. That's very rare. Almost all oral sex is unprotected.
>
> [I ask:] So your partner cums in your mouth?)
>
> [Mark:] N-no. It's sort of etiquette. If someone is going to cum, they tell you. And uh, my experience is that people always pull out before they come. So there is sort of an etiquette about that. If they want you to take their load, they'll ask you. And either you agree or not agree.
>
> [I ask:] You mean, "Can I cum in your mouth?"
>
> [Mark:] Yes, "Can I cum in your mouth?," they'll ask you. Or they'll say, "I'm coming" and you know to pull out.
>
> [I ask:] And if the answer is no?
>
> [Mark:] Shake your head, or you just pull out, and then he comes. Now that doesn't happen all the time, and sometimes I have gotten surprised; but, but it's pretty rare. It's all very consensual. You do what you want to do with whom you want to do it.

Absence of condoms affects erotic exchange somewhat differently, when anal sex is the activity under negotiation. Robert, a 38-year-old government attorney, developed this theme:

> Ass, ass stuff is really rare. It really is. There are people who will ask you if they want to fuck you, "Will you let me fuck you?" And the next question from one or the other is, "I have a condom, do you have a condom?" And if you say, "I don't have a condom," that's as far as the conversation goes. I mean, I don't do that anyway, so I always say, "I don't have a condom."

Mark had more to say about the persons who pursue anal sex in the backroom without using condoms:

> [Mark: I am fairly sure that there are people there who are HIV positive, that do let themselves get fucked without a condom. And just do it. I have seen that a couple of times.
>
> [I ask:] Why do you assume they are HIV positive?
>
> [Mark:] Umm [pause]. I suppose my assumption, well, they tend to be younger people. As a matter of fact, I am sort of surprised that the

unsafest sex is between younger people. The younger they are, the more unsafe they are. Um, my feeling is that the way they have sex, the way they have absolutely no concern for any kind of protection, my assumption is they are HIV-positive.

[I ask:] Could it be the other extreme? Could it be people just don't believe that they are ever going to get . . .

[Mark interrupts:] It could be, but obviously I have never had a conversation about it.

Mark's and Robert's comments speak to an additional set of constraints structuring erotic practices in the backroom. All of the men I have interviewed refer to the various forms of consensual "etiquette" (Mark's term) which, for example, prompts some men to seek their partner's permission before cuming in the partner's mouth, or to propose anal sex when assessing the availability of condoms; and which prompt them to comply with their partner's preferences, once each partner indicates what they are.[10] These comments suggest the partner-centered, cooperative erotic exchange that Mark and Robert have occasionally found in this setting, and they would *like* to find more frequently there.

Elsewhere during their interviews, Mark and Robert each told me that they are very dissatisfied with the impersonality of gay life in Washington, and are constantly looking for new ways to meet gay men both for sexual purposes and for friendship. One of the appeals of the backroom, in this sense, is its directness. Men are there to have sex with other men, and there is no reason to waste time with unnecessary preliminaries. Mark explains:

> If you don't want to do it with someone, you just put your hand in their hand or you push them away. That feels awful when that happens to you, but it's very consensual.

Robert made a similar comment:

> There's no joking around here. Men are here for one reason only. They want to have sex, or they don't. There's no wishy-washy games playing, no waste of time. You come here, meet someone, take care of business, and go home.
>
> [I ask:] Like at the baths?
>
> [Robert:] Yeah, like at the baths.

Moreover, if the sexual experiences are satisfying to both partners, there is always the chance that the men will exchange telephone numbers and arrange for follow-up meetings in other locations. Robert continues the point:

I'm not saying that the backroom is a social club or anything. But I have
met some very nice men there, and we've gone out on some lovely dates.

[I ask:] Did anything ever come out of this ? Anything more lasting?

[Robert:] Well, no—but I still call a few of them, or they call me, and when
we see each other occasionally [at the bookstore] we always speak. We're
not exactly strangers.

The safety of the backroom also adds to its appeal, both as a site for
"raw sexuality" and as a space for meeting other men. All of the men interviewed during this project agree that the bookstore's backroom is prefer-
able to other sites of male-centered erotic opportunity in the D.C. area. The
backroom provides an enclosed, regulated, sex-positive environment,
where men are able to pursue male-centered erotic interests without fears
of discovery, harassment, or retaliation. Public parks, department store
restrooms, and highway rest stops do not offer the same amount of protection, and invite interference from unwanted spectators, from the police, and
from queer-bashers,

Mark spoke directly to the issue of interference, when I asked him why
he no longer frequented the LBJ Grove, one of D.C.'s well-known cruising
sites. His immediate answer was: "Oh, I wouldn't want to be arrested."
Then he continued:

Um, it's also outside and there is no bathroom. One of the things I do, it's
obsessive of me and probably's done a little good, but, they've got this
thing of mouthwash [at the backroom bathroom], they've got this gallon
jug of mouthwash, so after sex, I gargle and wash my mouth out and
wash my hands. You can't do that at LBJ Grove. That kind of public, outdoor sex, the titillation of perhaps being found, that doesn't excite me in
particular.

And also, it's the [pause] wanting to feel safe, and about knowing who
is in there is, you know, a gay man. You go to the LBJ Grove, maybe
there's some fag-bashers there, maybe they're married men—not that
there aren't going to be married men at the backroom, but there are *lots*
[his emphasis] of married men out there.

[I ask:] Going to the backroom, you are not going to run into fag-bashers?

[Mark:] Well, they have to pay money [to get inside].

Implications

Mark is not the only man I have interviewed who associated the bookstore
backroom with *restriction*, *privacy*, and *safety*. Men who frequent the backroom consistently described this location as "private space," in contrast to

the more accessible, more visible and more "public" areas on the "outside." Similar features informed the description of the health club's landscape offered by self-identified "straight men" who pursue sex with other
men at that location. These features did not show up in gay men's descriptions of that landscape; for them, health club was a public location, and
they looked elsewhere for sites of gay-centered privacy.

These examples bring me back my opening discussion of the performative nature of *landscape* and its implications for male-centered sexual practices. To say that landscape is performative is to suggest that "ways of seeing" cannot exist independently of particular experiences with local terrain.
Certainly, the regulatory authority of the state can designate any location as
public space and enforce that designation through various means. But
such regulations cannot prevent interpretations of public space in completely nonregulatory terms—which is what gay men were doing at the
health club; nor can they prevent assertions of privacy within such locations—which is what the "straight" men were doing at the health club, and
gay men (and possible other men as well) were doing in the backroom.

Accordingly, rather than assuming that interpretations of *public* or *private* space are locations, fixed within local terrain, it seems more appropriate to treat *public* and *private* as attributes of landscape which are assigned
to particular sites by particular social actors and for particular reasons. As
far as the sites discussed here, "straight" versus "gay" identities have
proven to be a significant influence in that regard. Moreover, as shown in
the case of the health club, "straight" identity may reflect a stance of privilege which extends beyond the conventional boundaries of sexual orientation and associates "object of desire" with vulnerability and power.

Finally, this discussion speaks directly to the intersections of *landscape
and sexual risk*. Building on an idea first developed by Paul Farmer (1992),
geography has always been a central element in Western thinking about
AIDS. Public health authorities began establishing their symbolic control
over AIDS by locating the pandemic within particular locations—in areas of
dire poverty (Africa, Haiti, Southeast Asia), in the gay baths, in the IV drug
users' dirty needles, in the "tainted blood" of "innocent victims." What
resulted were particular geographies of blame whose internal terrain could
be adequately described through labels like "erotic oasis," "sex in public
places," and "risk-taking" and did not require any additional exploration.[11]

This essay has examined two sites within this AIDS-related geography of
blame and, at these sites, the relevant characteristics of the local terrain are
far from self-evident. The participants in "gay sex" are not limited to self-
identified "gay men." Their involvement in "sexual risk-taking" is sub-
merged by the pursuit of privileged desire, by attention to personal comfort,

or by responses to sexual directness. And most importantly, perhaps, erotic
practices themselves are closely entwined with assertions of privacy,
regardless of the seemingly "public" nature of the surroundings.

"Private space" also gains a new meaning as a result of its connections
to erotic practices at these sites. In ordinary reference, a private space is
something that is sheltered from outside scrutiny, something concealed, or
something protected. When applied to the locker room and the bookstore
backroom, however, "private space" highlights the *detachment* of the particular site from the outside context, not just its promises of concealment
and protection.

Detachment was what "straight" men find attractive about the locker
room as a site for erotic activity. The locker room lies "between" the office
and the home. It allows participants to pursue erotic activities unavailable to
them in other locations. It avoids any pretense of long-term obligations. And
(unlike a visit to a bathhouse or public cruising area) it does not force the
participants to question their claims to "straight" identity.

Similarly, detachment was what led gay men like Mark to prefer the
bookstore backroom over public parks and other outside locales. The location of the bookstore, the self-selection of the clientele, and the darkness of
the backroom help segregate the site from threats of danger and discovery.
Clientele share similar interests in erotic activity, so (unlike the case at a gay
bar) there is no need to disguise sexual intentions. And (unlike having sex
in public parks and restrooms) shared rules of "consensual etiquette" and
other on-site practices ensure that the sex, while certainly anonymous, is
not entirely mechanical and inhuman.

Moreover, by freeing the "private" site from the constraints of everyday
experience, detachment opens the door to the unpredictable, the unexpected, and even the dangerous. And once those features become part of
the local landscape, private space becomes a suitable space for sexual
risk-taking.

Consistent with this point, I understand why the straight health club
patrons are much more likely than gay patrons men to participate in on-site
erotics; and why the straight patrons are willing to disregard safe-sex practices when they did so. The privacy of the health club locker room provides
the straight patrons with a site of detachment within which familiar (e.g.,
heterosexual) constraints on erotic activities could be suspended. Gay
men, in contrast, are not so dependent on the health club as a site of sexual
opportunity or as a source of sexual detachment; moreover, and remembering here Mark's and Robert's comments about consensual etiquette in
the backroom, the conditions of detachment available to gay men at those
other locations are likely to be constructed quite differently, as well.

My thanks to Michael Clatts, Douglas Feldman, Ralph Bolton, and Liz Sheehan, who made helpful comments on various drafts of this chapter; and to the men at the health club and the bookstore, whose ideas and experiences provide the data-base for this analysis.

1. Important to note, "landscape" is not a stable or inflexible construction. While "ways of seeing" are imposed on a site by participants, "ways of seeing" are also (re)shaped by erotic activities and other experiences that take place within that setting. Moreover, because experiences are not identical, "ways of seeing" the local terrain may not be the same for all participants, In other words, landscape, like gender, is pluralized as well as performative.

2. I label these sites "private" because this is how the men who participate in erotic activities at these sites characterized these locations during on-site conversations and follow-up interviews.

3. See discussion in Leap 1996b: 109–24, 159–63.

4. The physical separation and related enclosures provide an additional function—reproduction of the closet — for some of the men who pursue same-sex erotic opportunities within these walls.

5. African American and white D.C. gay men offered similar descriptions of this part of the city during their interviews. They also rarely had anything to say about the individuals and families who live in the area adjacent to the bookstore, or the handful of (nongay-oriented) businesses providing services to these residents.

6. These three categories summarize comments give to me during informal discussions with gay members of the health club. Because these discussions occurred on-site, and usually were unplanned, I was not always able to take notes during the exchange, and I cannot provide extensive, verbatim illustrations for each category. However, comments from more structured interviewing, cited below, expand on these themes in various ways. The same three categories summarize the comments I have collected on this issue from gay men at other health clubs in the D.C. area.

7. This man and his partner were deeply involved in the erotic exchange when I entered the sauna that evening. They invited me to join them; I declined, but agreed to stand by the glass panel in the sauna room door and to alert them if the custodian or other staff member began to come up the stairs. After both men climaxed, one left the sauna and entered the showers, and I began talking with the remaining participant.

8. See for example the statistics on male-centered sexual practices disclosed in Janus and Janus (1992) and Laumann et al. (1994).

9. I have asked whether these men are worried about HIV infection. From their replies, most men seem unconcerned by this possibility. One man told me that he was not at risk from HIV because "AIDS is a gay disease," but "I'm not gay and what we're doing isn't gay sex."

10. As other comments in their interviews make clear, Mark and Robert are not suggesting that all men having sex at this site follow these conventions to the letter. Both men have had personal experiences with men who have done otherwise; see, for example, Mark's comment, p. 133. And other men's comments, as well as my

own observations, suggest that condom use may never become an issue in the negotiations leading up to erotic exchange in this setting, e.g., most participants are there (repeating Mark's words, p. 132) "just to enjoy the raw sexuality of it"; and outside of the statements of invitation (see Mark's example, p. 131) backroom erotic negotiations take place almost entirely in silence.

11. The phrase "geography of blame" is Paul Farmer's (1992), and grows out of his front-line experiences with the pandemic in rural Haiti. My usage expands the scope of Farmer's metaphor, but at the same time it strengthens, rather than weakens, his claims.

REFERENCES

Butler, J. 1990. *Gender Trouble: Feminism and the Subversion of Identity*. New York: Routledge.

Cosgrove, D. E. 1984. *Social Formation and Symbolic Landscape*. London: Croom Helm.

Dangerous Bedfellows, eds. 1996. *Policing Public Sex*. Boston: South End Press.

Delph, E. W. 1978. *The Silent Community: Public Homosexual Encounters*. Beverly Hills: Sage.

Farmer, P. 1992. *AIDS and Accusation: AIDS and the Geography of Blame*. Berkeley: University of California Press.

Hirsch, E. 1995. Introduction: Landscape: Between place and space. In E. Hirsch and M. O'Hanlon, eds. *The Anthropology of Landscape*, 1–30.

Hirsch, E. and M. O'Hanlon, eds. 1995. *The Anthropology of Landscape*. London: Oxford University Press.

Ingold, T. 1994. Introduction to Social Life. In *Companion Encyclopedia of Anthropology: Humanity, Culture and Social Life*. London: Routledge.

Janus, C. and S. Janus. 1993. *The Janus Report on Sexual Behavior*. New York: Wiley.

Klein, A. M. 1993. *Little Big Men: Bodybuilding Subculture and Gender Construction*. Albany: State University of New York Press.

Laumann, E., R. Michael, and J. Gagnon, eds. 1994. *Sex in America*. Chicago: University of Chicago Press.

Leap, W. L. 1996a Studying Gay English: How I Got Here from There. In E. Lewin and W. Leap, eds., *Out in the Field*, 128–47.

——. 1996b. *Word's Out: Gay Men's English*. Minneapolis: University of Minnesota Press.

Lewin, Ellen and W. L. Leap, eds. 1996. *Out in the Field*. Urbana: University of Illinois Press.

Pronger, B. 1990. *The Arena of Masculinity: Sports, Homosexuality, and the Meaning of Sex*. New York: St. Martin's Press.

Styles, J. 1979. Outsider/Insider: Researching Gay Baths. *Urban Life* 8: 135–52.

Williams, R. 1973. *The Country and the City*. London: Chatto and Windus.

Ethnographic Observations of Men Who Have Sex with Men in Public: Toward an Ecology of Sexual Action

MICHAEL C. CLATTS

. . . And these men who would come here to cruise and connect for sex, instead keep raising the volume of their radios as if to throttle the sound of their own bruised laughter, and in the lot off Santa Monica Boulevard, in the darkest hours of the night and early morning, they drink and smoke grass and they dance, clap, and twist their bodies.

– John Rechy (1983: 35)

There was a time, not long ago, when Rechy's vivid descriptions of men engaged in public sex evoked a powerful sense of communion among gay men–giving voice to the silent acts of individual rebellion that for many were part and parcel of being and becoming "gay." For better or worse, AIDS has changed all that. Once a gesture of communion for many gay men, unrestricted sex, particularly public sex, has become increasingly resignified as evil and deployed as a symbol of sanction even within the gay community itself. Indeed, in virtually all American discourses on the subject, promiscuity has been singled out as the primary behavioral vector of the spread of AIDS. Unregulated sex has been medicalized as "sexual addiction," identified with a personality "type" that is clinically termed "compulsive," "out of control," and "maladjusted." Similar diagnostic images attend the contexts in which some men find male sexual partners—bars, bathhouses, bookstores, public parks, and bathroom "tearooms"—places represented as conducive to "impersonal sex"—a term that is itself loaded with cultural meanings denoting something "strange," "deviant," and "dangerous" (Weinberg 1974; see also Hoffman 1968; Humphreys 1970).

Self-appointed leaders within the gay community have been among the most avid critics of public sex and some have been among the first to argue for measures such as closing the baths and other establishments said to "accommodate" promiscuous sex and the spread of AIDS. This despite the

fact that there is no epidemiological basis for such a response and no guarantee that such a response would have the desired outcome of reducing
the spread of HIV (Bolton et al. 1993). The forces that have fed the inherent
contradictions in this policing of desire from within the gay community are
complex. In part they have arisen as a response to the profound experience
of loss with which many gay men are suffering and the need to do something—anything—to try to stop the spread of the HIV. It is also perhaps a
response to overwhelming feelings of fear and anger with which many gay
men live in the face of AIDS—feelings that serve to exacerbate internalized
self-hatred and self-blame. Finally, it must also be acknowledged that a
dominant factor that some of the "worried well" may see as an opportunity
to advance larger political concerns aimed at legitimating gay and Lesbian
issues in mainstream American politics and culture by exploiting the sheer
visibility of AIDS as a political issue.

It is beyond the scope of this essay to fully examine these complex questions. The aim here is to be primarily descriptive rather than analytical.
Based upon informal ethnographic research of public sex among a diverse
group of gay-identified men in a Greenwich Village neighborhood, this
paper problemitizes the assumption that public sex is unsafe sex, or more
precisely that public sex is unsafe because it is public. Social and economic
differences in observed public sex exchanges are described, including their
association with use or nonuse of safe-sex precautions. I then consider,
albeit briefly, three interrelated policy questions related to public sex: Is
public sex inherently risky? If so, for whom, and why? Finally, I consider
some problems with the way in which sexual risk has been researched, particularly in relation to drug and alcohol use.

The Setting

The scene where these observations took place is in the heart of Greenwich Village, in and around a bar called The Stonewall, so named because
it was once the site of an earlier establishment where the "Stonewall
Riots" occurred in 1969–an event that many gay men and women mark
as pivotal event in the emergence of the modern gay liberation movement
(Katz 1992). The bar has two rooms, a large front room and a smaller
back room. The large front room has the main bar, which stretches along
one wall, as well as several small tables, and a pool table. The backroom
has a small bar as well as a variety of video game machines and a lotto
game.

On the evening in which the activities that will be described here
occurred, the bar is crowded, the music thunderous, the air filled with

smoke and the collective din of a multitude of conversations. Unlike many of the bars in the area that are oriented primarily to older gay men, the Stonewall attracts a fairly diverse crowd, including men of different age groups and some women. As usual, older men are usually seated at the bar itself, either the main bar in the central room or at the backbar with its close proximity to video games, lotto screen, and gambling machine. Most of these men have relatively stable employment and several are reasonably affluent. Many go back and forth between two or more bars in the immediate area over the course of an evening, visiting other bars that they also frequent on a routine basis depending on their mood, the night of the week, or where their friends happen to be on a given night.

A second group in the mix involves a number of relatively young males who are clearly young urban professionals, wearing jeans and sneakers but with businesslike haircuts that suggest employment in the mainstream economy. On week nights some come from work for "Happy Hour," still clad in business suits and carrying briefcases. Many work on Wall Street, in law firms, or in similar kinds of upwardly mobile occupations. A third group, also composed of relatively young men, are characteristically East Village—long hair, tattoos, faded Dead-Head t-shirts. Many of these young men work within the service economy that thrives in the East Village, which is full of dance bars, ethnic restaurants, leather boutiques, tattoo parlors, record stores, and Head shops. There are relatively few women in the bar and most are in some way associated with this particular group of young men. A fourth group of young men—commonly referred to as "hustlers"—are discernibly engaged in a variety of illegal economic activities ("hustles") that are centered in the bar itself or in the surrounding streets.

Thus the bar serves as a nexus for a wide variety of people. It also serves as a nexus of a wide variety of activities, including complex sets of relationships that, in both space and time, extend beyond the intersections that occur in the bar itself. Notably, these activities include a variety of activities related to drug distribution, including selling drugs directly, marketing or carrying drugs for a drug dealer, "steering" someone who wants to buy drugs to a dealer, and various kinds of sex work.

Although less apparent from looking at the makeup of the bar clientele itself, there is also a fifth group of young men who participate in the social and economic activities described above. These young men are typically found not in the bar itself, but in the surrounding streets. Some are too young to be able to get into the bar. Others have been in the bar in the past but have been banished for some reason, typically one related to selling sex or drugs. Still others are barred at the door, based on the doorman's assessment of their appearance or demeanor and any overt association with sell-

ing drugs or being under the influence of them. These youth work the
streets, sometimes also selling drugs but primarily trading in survival
sex–sex for money (less than $20), sex for a share in someone else's drugs,
or even sex for something to eat and a place to sleep

Although there are a few instances of youth in these latter two groups
who are able to sustain specialized economic roles in this setting, most are
simultaneously engaged in multiple economic "hustles," including carrying
drugs (largely powder cocaine), and selling drugs to/buying drugs for individuals (usually other gay men in the bar) with whom they are also trading
sex (for money and/drugs). Almost all are engaged in sex work and most
derive the majority of their income from it. Drugs are an important part of
sex work in this context for a number of interrelated reasons. First, many of
these youth are chronically drug dependent and having the "john" buy the
"party" saves the youth from having to buy the drugs they would otherwise
have to purchase on their own, typically from the cash they receive for sex
work. As many of the youth see it, getting the "john" to buy the drugs in
effect increases the total remuneration that they receive for exchanging sex
since most will receive some amount of cash in addition to drugs. Second,
youth who are able to serve as a connection to drugs enhance their mar-
ketability," particularly to upscale "johns" who do not want to risk buying
drugs themselves. Third, "johns" who are high on drugs are thought to be
easier to control and hence in some sense "safer." Some are unable to perform sexually because of drug use but will pay the youth without requiring
actual sex work. Others become so inebriated and high that they fall asleep
before sex and are then easy to rob.

Drugs also have importance from the perspective of the "johns." Many
of the "johns" use drugs as disinhibitors, both for themselves as well as for
youth. Others recognize that many of street youth are acutely drug dependent. Some "johns" exploit this dependency, using it to bargain for a lesser
price in the sex trade and as a lure for particular sexual acts to which youth
would not otherwise submit.

The Context of Public Sex

There are two small restrooms in the back of the bar, and on busy nights
such as this there is a long waiting line outside both. One restroom, used
exclusively by males has a large trough-like urinal where, under a pretext of
urinating, men make a "show" of demonstrating the size of their penises to
other men. As in any drama, there are different roles to be played (Turner
1974). Some pretend not to be looking, an action that is not without meaning and consequence in terms of a potential sexual liaison. Others linger,

sometimes "showing" their own penises in response and initiating conversation and sometimes a sexual liaison.

The second restroom is ostensibly for female patrons since it has a private toilet. Although there are relatively few women in the bar, the line outside the second restroom is always the longest and although it accommodates only one person at a time, many patrons enter and exit in groups of two or three. New comers to the bar often assume that the room is being used for the purposes of sex. The restroom is utilized for the sale and use of cocaine. Indeed, except for the occasional couple making out in the back of the bar, there is remarkably little actual sexual exchange in the bar itself. Rather the bar serves as a semi-controlled, norm-governed environment in which desire is made public and where potential partners meet and the terms of a sexual exchange are tentatively explored.

This is not to say that there are not abiding social relationships among some of the patrons. On the contrary, there is a fairly large number of regulars, many of whom circulate among a handful of similar neighborhood bars in the area, sometimes in search of a potential sex partner, but often as not simply looking for a place to have a drink and talk. To the extent that sexual liaisons are established, often as not they are among individuals who are known and who have exchanged sex on previous occasions. Thus, although much of this kind of sexual exchange occurs in the privacy of someone's apartment, and hence is not in and of itself public, there is a running commentary at the bar regarding the configuration of each night's circulation (pairing) of sex partners. Indeed, there is considerable effort to bring these exchanges into a public domain, including fanciful descriptions of past sexual exchanges with a partner with whom another patron is seen leaving, descriptions of body types, penis sizes, and details of preferred sexual acts.

In addition to public talk about sex, there are two public areas within a block or so of the bar where men from the bar gather for sexual exchanges that have been arranged in the bar. The first is in the entrance hallway of a brownstone apartment building, between the outer door (which is usually unlocked) and the inner door (which requires a residents' key). The spot is considered ideal because of its close proximity to the bar, the fact that most of the residents in the building are elderly and not likely to be up late at night where they might interrupt activities in the hallway, and because the front door has a one-way mirror allowing those inside to see who is entering. The second location is in an alley that leads down an incline to an underground garage of an apartment building. Along the alley is a wide concrete ledge, shielding those on the ledge from the view of pedestrians on the sidewalk. Although neither of these public sex areas are physically located within the confines of the bar itself, many of the liaisons that occur in these scenes are nevertheless founded in, and tied to, relations that are established in the bar–an explicitly defined gay space–in effect extending the social "boundaries" of the bar itself.

Men can be found engaging in various sexual acts in both locations. Both scenes become somewhat more crowded as the night progresses until around 3 A.M. when the bar closes and those who are still out go to one of the after-hours clubs, many of which also feature places for public sexual contact. Both locations are strewn with condom wrappers, used condoms, cigarette butts, empty popper bottles, and abandoned crack vials. Some men stop at these locations on their way to the bar, later reporting that they took the presence of activity in these locations as a sign that the bar would be busy and that the prospects for a sexual encounter that night were good. A few men go to these locations without any connection to the bar but most are regular patrons and newcomers are viewed with palpable caution, albeit sometimes with interest.

Unlike the public sex which sometimes occurs in backrooms and bathhouses, there is remarkably little multiperson sex in either of these locations. Often, in fact, there is considerable antagonism expressed toward those who attempt to intrude on two men who are engaged sexually. Thus, paradoxically, while the sexual exchange that occurs in this location is explicitly public, and indeed is in part "for show," the sexual exchange is at the same time infused with its own kind of proprietary meanings and rules, features that are in fact remarkably like sex in private space. Individuals who attempt to join an ongoing sexual exchange are sometimes brushed away with a hand or scornful looks denoting intrusion. If persistent, they are subject to verbal and even physical abuse, also reflective of a violation of norms governing private space.

Around midnight I leave the bar and duck into the alley to see what is happening there. It is empty, perhaps due to the light rain that is falling and the fact that it is still a little early for a Saturday night. There are several young male hustlers milling about the streets but they appear to be soliciting men in cars that are circling the block. Exiting the alley, I see James, a homeless youth with whom I have conducted life history research over the preceding couple of months.

James is a 23-year-old gay youth who has been homeless for the past nine years. Following repeated physical and sexual abuse from his stepfather, James made his way to the streets of Portland at the age of fourteen where he learned quickly that he had something that other people wanted, or, as he described it, that he was a commodity. Since then he has traveled across the country, supporting himself through prostitution. Now in advanced stages of HIV disease, he lives on the streets of New York, begging for food, and selling sex when he can.

We talk about how things have been going since I last saw him, his latest struggles with the NYC Department of AIDS Services and his efforts to find housing. He explains that D.A.S. placed him in a S.R.O. in the South Bronx, that he was attacked on the streets in front of the building as well as by other residents, and that consequently he is back to sleeping on the West Side piers. He has not eaten in two days, in part because he is worried about having diarrhea and the fact that he does not have access to a bathroom, shower, or clean clothing. I urge him to try a nearby outreach project that will provide him with clothing, a shower, emergency food assistance, and free medical care. I write the address and phone number on one of my business cards and tell him to use my name to cut through the agency red tape.

He complains about the weather and its negative impact on the street prostitution market, noting that most people would probably stay home that night rather than come out in the rain. He is worried because he is a heroin user and if he is not able to get enough money soon to buy a fix he will begin to feel the pains of heroin withdrawal. I give him a few dollars, encouraging him to get something to eat, suggesting that soup might keep him warm. I leave him knowing full well that it is more likely that he will use the money to buy drugs, probably crack, to keep him awake and alert while he "works" the streets, hustling sex to earn enough money to pay for a hotel room, some food, and enough drugs to get him "straight" (i.e., not in pain from drug withdrawal) the next morning so that he can begin the vicious and deadly circle all over again the next night. James spots a familiar car among those that are circling the block looking to pick up a hustler, often for sex in the car in exchange for a few dollars. James follows the car down the block, trying to establish eye contact with the occupant–a prelude to negotiating sex trade.

I leave James to his work on the streets and enter the foyer of a three-story brick building that is also used for public sex. There are several men in the hallway. Two in the back of the room are engaged in deep kissing, one pressing his groin into the groin of the other while at the same time massaging his buttocks. Several new people enter behind me, all of whom are regular customers at the bar. They move to the wall and stand alone for a moment, evaluating the scene both for interest and safety.

Ed, an older gay male, is standing with his back against the wall. He is a familiar figure in the area and in this particular scene. He is intensely disliked by many in the scene and has been banned from several of the bars. Tim, a seventeen-year-old street youth, is crouched down in front of Ed,

performing oral sex. Tim moves in and out of this street scene quite mysteri-
ously, appearing almost every night for weeks at a time and then suddenly
disappearing for months without any warning. Part of the reason for the
mystery surrounding his movements is that he does not have close social
ties with anyone else in the scene, not even other street youth. Tim is very
heavy crack user and consequently it is likely that some of this "disappear-
ance" is due to frequent arrests. However, it is also rumored that he is
sometimes "kept" by a man in the East Village who has a reputation for
using desperate, drug -dependent street youth for sex in exchange for shelter and drugs. Himself a heavy cocaine user, he is reputed to be extremely
violent. Youth flee his apartment having been beaten, taking their chances
back on the streets, often only to return again when they are desperate for
drugs or a place to sleep. The physical and emotional condition in which
youth return to the streets seems to confirm the rumor, as I observe that Tim
has grown thinner and has a bad bruise on his face.

I prepare to leave the scene because it is unappealing. On previous
occasions I have overheard Ed negotiate the terms of the sexual exchange
with Tim and with other street youth like Tim. I know that Ed will take advantage of Tim's acute addiction to crack and the poor social and cognitive
skills that make it especially difficult for Tim to manage in the street economy. He will pay Tim only two or three dollars for sex, well below the going
rate but enough for Tim to purchase a single hit bottle of crack–an overwhelming temptation for Tim–to get him through the next two-dollar blow
job.

Tim takes Ed's penis out of his mouth and reminds him to pull out before
he "cums" (ejaculates). Ed thrusts his penis back in Tim's mouth and
begins thrusting his hips into Tim's face again. Tim suddenly jumps to his
feet in obvious but silent protest, spitting cum on the floor, and scowling at
Ed. He is clearly angry at Ed for having cum in his mouth. However, he is
hesitant to raise too much of a protest because he is afraid that Ed will
refuse to pay him at all–a likely prospect given Ed's reputation in the area.
Ed massages his penis, closes the zipper on this pants, and throws a couple of one dollar bills on the floor, leaving without a word.

Tim grabs the bills, and also leaves, heading a few blocks away to a drug
dealer that markets drugs specifically for street youth, selling in the small
quantities that they can afford, sometimes allowing youth to buy a bottle on
credit at the start of the night–also an overwhelming temptation for these
youth. Essentially, the dealer has adapted the product and marketing strategy to this particular niche in the street economy, and the fact that many
street youth only have a couple of dollars to spend at a time. The dealer is
successful in the peddling of poor quality drugs because few other dealers

in the area will sell to street youth or are willing to sell in the very small quantities that street youth can afford at any one time.

The couple in the back of the room have ignored the episode with Tim and Ed, and have progressed to exchanging alternating fellatio. I see one inhale poppers while the other slips a condom on his own erect penis. The individual who has inhaled the poppers turns his back, bends over and, reaching behind him, he inserts the other man's penis into his rectum. Several of the other men in the hallway inch closer to watch. One of the onlookers approaches the man who is bent over, trying to position his groin near the man's face, solilciting oral sex. The attempt is coarse and is abruptly rebuffed. The other onlooker begins to masturbate but does not intrude. After several moments, one of the men groans, pulls his penis out of the other's rectum, makes several more groaning sounds suggesting climax, and slips off the condom—throwing it on the floor. The two men kiss while the other "jerks off," and then leave together. Soon after, one of the other onlookers finishes masturbating and leaves as well. Leaving the building and returning to the streets, I see that both James and Tim are back hustling on the corner. Their eyes trace the movement of men in passing cars and men walking past them on the streets, searching for eye contact, signaling interest in commercial sex trade.

Discussion

There are a number of limitations to the analysis presented here. Some are a function of the preliminary nature of the data presented. First, I acknowledge that there are many different kinds of public places in New York City in which men engage in sex. The scenes described here do not exhaust the wide range of forms and settings used for sexual exchange. Second, I note that these descriptions primarily involved relations among men who self-identify as gay and that none of the events involved men from ethnic minority groups. Third, in as much as the data are derived from an urban setting that includes a large and highly organized gay community, these data may not be representative of rural settings or even other urban settings with less elaborated gay institutions. Fourth, although the data is derived from long-term and ongoing ethnographic research in this setting, a number of important issues are not examined here. I do not, for example, consider the issue of social and behavioral change, either in terms of changes in sexual behavior specifically or in terms of the foundation of more generalized social and sexual relations over time. There is a dire need for careful study of the construction and maintenance of social groups in these and other public sex settings, particularly in relation to sexual identification and sexual risk. Finally, these descriptions only begin to explore the role of social and monetary "capital" in the context of sex exchange–a topic that also bears further investigation and is especially important for targeting prevention messages among men who have sex with men.

These limitations notwithstanding, there are a number of features of sex in this public setting that bear comment. First, it is important to point out that none of the sexual behaviors described here were risky simply as a consequence of the fact that they were public. Tim would have been no less at risk, and no more able to negotiate safer sex, if the event had occurred in Ed's bedroom rather than in a dim hallway. Risk in this sexual exchange was predicated upon Tim's economic dependence upon Ed, not the setting in which the exchange (behavior) occurred. Conversely, the sexual exchange that occurred between the two unnamed men would not have been significantly "safer," at least in terms of condom use, if it had occurred in a private setting such as their bedrooms rather than in a public setting.

Second, although public sex is often represented as "anonymous," all of the men who participated in these events knew each other on some level and most had some form of ongoing social interaction. Thus, while early research on public sex among men suggested that anonymity is a dominant feature of sex in these settings, these data suggest that this anonymity is by no means universal and indeed may not be representative of the social relations that typify men who have sex with men in public settings. The issue of anonymity has importance for rethinking some of the political ground on which debate over public sex has been forged. Perhaps even more importantly, it may have great significance for the development of targeted prevention strategies. If indeed there is a significant social foundation to public sex interactions, this suggests that these social groupings may provide key "windows" in and through which to funnel prevention resources, much as gay saunas have in places where they have not been closed for homophobic political expediency (Bolton and Vinke n.d.). At a minimum, the data suggest that prevention strategies that are antagonistic to these social groupings, contexts, and meanings are likely to have very limited efficacy and may do more harm than good.

Implications for Research

There are a number of striking features about these observations that bear further analytical investigation. However, given limitations in space I would like to focus on one particular issue because of its importance in understanding the nature of sexual risk, and that is the omnipresence of drugs and alcohol in these settings. It is increasingly acknowledged that the construction of "risk group categories" early in the AIDS pandemic perhaps had more to do with the intellectual and political biases of the time than with any empirically defensible rational. Indeed, it is hard to escape the conclusion that, at their core, these categories were ultimately grounded in ideologies that served to obscure the role and confluence of inequities based upon race, class, gender, and sexual orientation and their implications for risk for poor health outcomes such as AIDS (Clatts and Mutchler 1989; Glick 1992). These categories persist in contemporary AIDS research in part because this was the political "turf" in which AIDS research was initially founded but also because it is in researchers' interest to sustain and reproduce them. The vast majority of epidemiological and behavioral research on AIDS continues to be focused on high-risk behavior within high prevalence and incidence exposure groups, dominantly "men who have sex with men" on the one hand and drug users on the other, as if these so-called risk groups did not overlap both behaviorally and epidemiologically. Whatever the utility of the notion of "risk group" may once have had, if any, the cost of this obfuscation is now becoming clear. While I do not wish to overgeneralize the role of drugs and alcohol among "men who have sex with men," or to suggest that drug and alcohol are necessarily the root cause of sexual risk, recent epidemiological research on the spread of HIV infection among drug users who report sexual behavior with same-sex partners suggests that achieving a better understanding of the relationship between sex and drugs is critical to preventing the spread of HIV infection.

For example, although the incidence of new HIV infections has leveled off and in some areas even declined for men who report having same-sex partners as their only risk factor, the incidence of men who have sex with men and who use drugs, particularly those who inject drugs or use crack cocaine, is growing rapidly, particularly within ethnic minority and younger age cohorts (CDC 1995). Similarly, in a national sample of out-of-treatment drug injectors and crack smokers in which there was an overall seroprevalence of 8.4 percent, Deren et al. found that gay and bisexual identified men had seroprevalence rates of 57 percent and 25 percent, respectively (Deren n.d.).

It is noteworthy that these patterns are not limited to men who have same-sex partners. Similar findings are emerging in epidemiological data of women drug users who have sex with women. For example, Ehrhardt et al. (1995) studied a sample of women IDUs recruited through a methadone clinic and infectious disease clinic: 28 percent of their sample of IDU women reported gay/lesbian or bisexual orientation, and 48 percent reported having had sex with a woman at some point in their lives. Similarly, a 1992 survey of drug-using women held in New York City's central correctional facility found that over 45 percent reported female sex partners during the previous ten years, and nearly a quarter reported at least one female sex partner who injected drugs (Schilling et al. 1994).

Recent studies of high-risk youth populations also demonstrate these patterns. For example, in a recent study of high-risk youth in New York City, both drug and sex-related risk behavior are common throughout the sample but are distributed differently across -sub groups within it (Clatts et al. 1995). Of particular concern, multiple partner unprotected sex (deriving largely from economic dependency on commercial sex work) was significantly associated with gender (male), sexual orientation (gay/bisexual), homelessness, and the use of a wide range of drugs (including a history of having injected drugs, current use of injected drugs and current use of crack). These patterns are of particular concern because these youth are known to interact behaviorally with two "risk groups" that evidence high background seroprevalence–adult gay men in the context of commercial sex work and adult IV drug injectors in the context of drug injection–forming an epidemiological bridge between these "exposure populations" (Clatts 1994; see also Battjes et al. 1989; Chu et al. 1992; Edlin et al. 1994; and Marmor et al. 1987).

It is noteworthy that these three populations–men who have sex with men, women who have sex with women and use drugs, and high-risk youth–are among the subgroups that evidence the highest incidence of AIDS and the highest numbers of new cases in the United States.

The ethnographic descriptions presented in this chapter demonstrate that drugs and alcohol are prevalent in many of the social settings and sexual environments in which men gather to socialize and sometimes "connect" with other men for sex, a fact that is supported by the behavioral and epidemiological data cited above. Inasmuch as many of these same settings and environments are also among the primary social institutions in and through which many homosexual men establish a sexual identity–albeit one that is highly stigmatized and typically fraught with acute conflict and self-doubt–we should not be surprised to find that men who have sex with men are at high risk for drug and alcohol abuse. Having said this, however, it must also be acknowledged that nearly a decade into the AIDS pandemic, there is relatively little high-quality data available about the structure and function of drug and alcohol use among men who have sex with men or conversely about the exchange of sex among same-sex partners in drug-using populations.

With notable exceptions (see Bolton and Vinke 1992; Gorman 1996), much of the available behavioral data is based upon simplistic statistical associations of self-reported high-risk sexual practices among persons who also report use of alcohol and drugs. Most of these data are drawn from

highly biased sampling frames which are expedient in experimental
research paradigms but which often serve to guarantee confirmation of the
predicted outcomes. Few of these studies pay any attention at all to differences in how and why drugs and alcohol are used in the context of sex,
including their beneficial properties (perceived or "real"), or to alternative
explanations for a statistical association between drug and alcohol use and
high-risk sexual behavior among homosexual men. There has been little or
no consideration of the management and transformation of sexual identity
in relation to alcohol and drug use or to the way in which socialization into
same-sex identity has changed historically (particularly in relation to alcohol
and drugs). Where is the attention to the role of pleasure and play? What
are to we to make of the misappropriation of the concept of culture in which
some alleged cultural trait such as sexual identity or ethnicity is said to produce a given behavior? What utter nonsense! And, why is it that there has
been little or no attention to the role of economic exchange in these settings
and relations—indeed that systematic economic predation and its relationship to sexual risk is widely suppressed in AIDS research (Clatts 1994).
Could it be that we just do not like this particular image of ourselves?

If we are ever to begin to understand associations between sexual and
drug risk—as opposed to simply documenting their prevalence and infer-
ring cause from statistical correlation—we need to examine the way in
which risk behavior is connected in the real world. We need to understand
the influence of the physical contexts and social groupings in which risk
behaviors occur, and the relationship that these behaviors have to the larger social and economic institutions in which they are embedded and from
which they emerge. In short, we need to forge an ecological model for the
study of sexual risk, including and perhaps particularly the diverse,
dynamic, and interacting sets of social and economic factors that govern
sexual action and which give rise to sexual cognition and sexual meaning
(sexuality). This will require that we move the discourse beyond individualistic lines of inquiry, beyond static conceptualizations of politically constructed behavioral groups, and perhaps most of all beyond self-serving
reifications of an idealized "gay community." If nothing else, the experience of AIDS has taught us much about the discontinuities which our
research models must account for . . . the fact that our lives are ultimately
solitary and alone . . . that our interactions with one another are fragmented
and sometimes divisive . . . that our illusions of communion are betrayed
by inequity and inevitably by loss . . . and that our knowledge of ourselves
and one another, in every sense of the word, is only partial. As perhaps
Rechy (1983: 35) understood, maybe this is why we "drink, and smoke
grass, and clap, and dance, and twist our bodies."

ACKNOWLEDGMENTS

This chapter is dedicated to the memory of James Powell, a brave young man who struggled to find his way out of the crack-ridden sex economy of New York City, and who before his own death from AIDS worked to help others to find a way out as well.

I would also like to acknowledge Ralph Bolton, for his pioneering work in human sexuality and AIDS, as well as for the many thoughtful conversations that we have had about some of the ideas developed in this paper.

REFERENCES

Baltjes, R. N., R. W. Pickens, and Z. Amsel. 1989. Introduction of HIV Injection Among Intravenous Drug Abusers in Low Seroprevalence Areas. *J. Acq Imm Defic. Syndrome* 2: 533–39.

Bolton, R., J. Vincke, G. Mak, and E. Dennebhy. 1992. Alcohol and Risky Sex: In Search for an Elusive Connection. In *Rethinking AIDS Prevention*, edited by R. Bolton and M. Singer. Philadelphia: Gordon and Breach Science Publishers, pp. 323–64.

Bolton, R., J. Vincke, and R. Mak. 1993. Gay Baths Revisited: An Empirical Analysis. GLQ 1(3): 255–74.

Bolton, R. and J. Vincke. n.d. Risky Sex and Sexual Cognition: The Cartography of Eros among Flemish Gay Men. *Journal of Quantitative Anthropology* (in press).

Centers for Disease Control and Prevention. 1995. HIV/AIDS Surveillance Report. Vol. 7 (no. 1).

Chu, S. Y., T. A. Peterman, L. S. Doll, et al. 1992. AIDS in Bisexual Men in the United States: Epidemiology and Transmission to Women. *American Journal of Public Health* 82: 220–24.

Clatts, M. C., J. L. Sotheran, W. R. Davis. 1996. Patterns of Sexual Risk Among NYC Street Youth: Implications for Community-Based Public Health Initiatives.

Clatts, M. C., W. R. Davis, and J. L. Sotheran. 1994. At the Cross-Roads of HIV Infection: A Demographic and Behavioral Profile of Street Youth in New York City. Paper at the Second Annual Symposium on Drug Abuse, Sexual Risk, and AIDS: Prevention Research 1995–2000, Flagstaff, Arizona.

Clatts, M. C. 1994. "All the Kings Horses and All the Kings Men: Some Personal Reflections on Ten Years of AIDS Ethnography." *Human Organization* 53(1): 93–95.

Clatts, M. C. and K. M. Mutchler. 1989. AIDS and the Dangerous Other: Metaphors of Sex and Deviance in the Representation of a Disease. *Medical Anthropology* 10, no. 2(3): 105–14.

Deren, S., A. Estrada, M. Stark, R. Needle, M. Williams, and M. Goldstein. n.d. *American Journal of Public Health*, in press.

Donoghoe, M. C. 1992. Sex, HIV, and the Injecting Drug User. *British Journal of Addiction* 87: 405–16.

Edlin, B. R., K. L. Irwin, S. Faraque, et al. 1994. Intersecting Epidemics-Crack Cocaine Use and HIV Infection Among Inner-City Youth. *New England Journal of Medicine* 331(21): 1422–27.

Ehrhardt, A. A., C. NostInger, H. L. Meyer-Buhlburg, R. S. Gruen, Exner, T., B. Ortiz-
Torres, S. Yingling, and R. Zawadzki. 1995. Gender-specific risk and strategy
for behavior change among women. Presented at HIV infection in Women
Conference, Washington D.C.

Gorman, E. M. 1996. Methamphetamine abuse among gay men in Seattle. Paper
presented at a NIDA Technical Review, San Francisco, CA.

Glick Schiller, N. 1992. What's wrong with this picture? The hegemonic construction
of culture in AIDS research in the United States. *Medical Anthropology Quarterly* 6: 237–54.

Hoffman, M. 1968. *The Gay World.* New York: Bantam Books.

Humphreys, L. 1970. *Tearoom Trade: Impersonal Sex in Public Places.* Chicago:
Aldine.

Karon, J. M. and R. L. Berkelman. 1991. The Geographic and Ethnic Diversity of
AIDS Incidence Trends in Homosexual/Bisexual Men in the United States.
Journal of Acquired Immune Deficiency Syndrome 4: 1179–89.

Katz, J. 1992. *Gay American History: Lesbians and Gay Men in the U.S.A.* New York:
Meridian Books.

Marmor, M. D. Des Jarlais, H. Cohen, et al. 1987. Risk Factors for Infection with
Human Immunodeficiency Virus Among Intravenous Drug Users in New York
City. *AIDS* 1(1): 118–23.

Penkower, L. M. A. Dew, L. Kingsley. 1991. Behavioral, Health, and Psychological
Factors and Risk for HIV Infection Among Sexually Active Homosexual Men:
The Multicenter AIDS Cohort Study. *American Journal of Public Health* 81:
194–96.

Rechy, J. 1983. AIDS Mysteries and Hidden Dangers. *The Advocate* 27 December.

Schilling, R., N. El-Bassel, A. Ivanoff, et al. 1994. Sexual Risk Behavior of Incarcerated Drug-Using Women, 1992. *Public Health Reports* 109 (4):539547.

Turner, V. 1974. *Dramas, Fields, and Metaphors: Symbolic Action in Human Society.*
Ithaca: Cornell University Press.

Vinke, J. and R. Bolton. 1995. Social Stress and Risky Sex Among Gay Men: An
Additional Explanation for the Persistence of Unsafe Sex. In *Culture and Sex-
ual Risk: Anthropological Perspectives on AIDS.* Philadelphia: Gordon and
Breach Science Publishers.

Weinberg, M. 1974. *Male Homosexuals: Their Problems and Adaptations.* New York:
Oxford University Press.

STEPHEN O. MURRAY

Sociologists Edward Laumann and John Gagnon (1995:196) assert that "actual sexual performances are expected to occur in private."[1] In claiming that it is a human universal to keep sexual intercourse "invisible to all but the participants (and not always visible to them)," anthropologist Ernestine Friedl (1994:833) explicitly includes homosexual intercourse, although mentioning bathhouses as a place "where the rule is suspended." In defending park sex, the individualistic gay philosopher Richard Mohr (1996:18) similarly contends that "sex is inherently private. The sex act creates its own impersonal sanctuary which in turn is necessary for its success. The whole process and nature of sex is interrupted and destroyed if penetrated by the glance of an intruder."[2]

Having spent times in places (Mesoamerica, Taiwan, Thailand) where display of genitals is shocking, shameful,[3] and anxiety-provoking, and knowing of many other such places, at first I was ready to accept Friedl's claim that display of intercourse is universally tabooed. It is quite plausible that humans are among the species that hide sexual activity from those who might object and try to stop a particular sexual liaison. Even where evidence of defloration must be made public as part of establishing approved heterosexual liaisons, the audience does not witness the actual deed. That is, the groom copulates with the bride in private even where bloodstained bedclothes must afterward be displayed.

Friedl sweeps the reader along on an evolutionary just-so story relating invisible estrous signals, female capacity for orgasm, the unlinking of copulation from periods of fertility, and increased consciousness of self, whereas Laumann and Gagnon (1995:188–89) dismiss any biological explanations whatsoever. They nonetheless converge with Friedl's views in treating sex being out of sight of nonparticipants as necessary to participants' sense of self. Laumann and Gagnon (1995:213) go so far as to suggest that sexual " 'turn-on/turn-off' is probably interactive with the felt state of 'aloneness';

being without an audience facilitates arousal while arousal facilitates the sense of aloneness."

Insofar as the self results from taking the view of (real or imagined) oth- ers—i.e., self-objectification as discussed by George Herbert Mead (1934) and his followers—feedback might enhance not only pleasure but also the sense of self (as an adult, as a desired sexual being, as part of the procreative chain, etc.). By exciting one's partner in a way one imagines (or knows) that the other wants to be excited, one receives in imagination the excitement one gives "in the flesh": "alternately looking at the partner through one's own eyes and at oneself through the partner's eyes. (One can also look at both through the imagined eyes of some observing third party. Mirrors facilitate this last, omniscient view)," as sociologist Murray Davis (1983:130) puts it. Although not always the case, excitement can be "contagious," so that one partner's excitement excites the other, which may further intensify the first one's excitement. A combination of observing and imagining both self and/or partners while "having sex" seems to me common—with or without a physically present "partner" or nonparticipant observers.

Moreover, many see sex as a means of transcending the self, of breaking down ego walls, false pride, and/or everyday consciousness to attain union with another—or at least some focus on another human being—not the "self-absorption" Friedl (p. 838) asserts is central to sex. In addition to what Davis (1983) calls the Jehovanist perspective on "sex," in which being seen to have sex shames and lessens the sense of self, are at least two other Western ones. In what he calls the gnostic (or sex radical) tradition, "sexuality remains one of the demonic forces in human consciousness," including (at least on occasion) a "voluptuous yearning for the extinction of one's consciousness" (Sontag 1970:57), not just a diminuition but a cessation of self. From the naturalist (or sex liberal) view, in contrast to both of the others, the self is not fundamentally involved in sex and/or "self" is a loose, open system, mutable and neither contaminated nor exalted by "sex" (Davis 1983:188–89),[4] so that being seen having sex neither increases nor decreases a sense of self.

While noting that "sex" is not a transparent term and that different people include different behaviors and meanings within that category (see Bolton 1992), I think that, in general, good sex requires focusing on what one is doing, on synchronizing this with what one's partner is doing, and on attending to the partner's responses or lack of responses. I do not think that sex in private leads to *self*-absorption,[5] or that the identity involved in sexual intercourse is only that of a "coconspirator."[6] For many people, sex involves absorption in the other partner. I am even more skeptical that lack of privacy "diminishes the self," as Friedl (1994:838) contended. Neither she nor Laumann and Gagnon found it necessary to allude to even one human being's experiences of either hidden or observed sex in drawing sweeping conclusions about how it affects self-regard.

This chapter will include instances in which being observed had no effect on sense of self and self-esteem, and others in which being observed enhanced the sense of self and the amount of self-esteem. Before relating them, however, it is necessary to consider factors having nothing to do with sense of self (worth/size) that make "hiding" sex prudent (and therefore common).

Genuine External Dangers

Someone who is doing what s/he considers shameful feels diminished, whereas someone who is doing what s/he takes pride in being known to do generally also takes pride in being seen to do this, so long as there are not dangers of being interrupted or punished by others. These are real and recurrent dangers, though pragmatic precautions should not be mistaken for a species-wide human drive or universal need to "hide" sex. One very significant constraint on observed sex is fear of reprisals—for "poaching" on someone else's sexual partner, for "straying" from one's own prescribed partner or category of legitimate partners, or for "outraging public morals," i.e., the heteronormative social order (enforced by both self-appointed and paid police). Another constraint is the set of consequences of a reputation for having sex with proscribed partners. A reputation for sexual receptivity outside marriage makes males as well as females fair game for importuning by others (see Murray 1995:56–57, 1996c). Generally, women's sexual contacts are more regulated, their violations of the rules are more severely punished, and subsequent importunings of them are more coercive. Men in many cultures are encouraged to take whomever they can (not least by the assumption that they will), while women generally are discouraged from giving themselves—and are encouraged to manage sexual access to attain other goods (power, in particular). Insofar as there are double standards of male and female fidelity, women have a greater interest than men in keeping their sexual behavior from being observed and reported.

Anglo North America is far from being the only place where being known to be having sex enhances masculine reputations, while a female thought to be engaging in sexual intercourse (even with only one steady partner) may be labeled a "slut." Recalling the sexual culture in which I grew up in rural Midwestern United States during the mid-1960s I feel that it was girls who did not want to be observed having sex; boys were discreet more to protect their sexual partners' reputations (to "get further" with them or, once they "went all the way," to keep the girls "putting out") than to keep their own "success" secret. Many more boys than girls wanted to show off sexual conquests. The most extreme example, so-called "pulling a train," involved one girl and a line of boys.[7] Having to take all comers is a risk wherever there is a shortage of sexual outlets in contrast to the numbers ready, willing, and able to try them. The corresponding risk to the male of being shown unready or unable may diminish self-esteem, though he can often get away with claiming distaste and unwillingness (thereby denying inability, or even unreadiness). Similarly the risks of pregnancy and the time involved in it are disproportionately greater for women. In a number of ways the consequences of sexual intercourse are greater for women, and women's greater carefulness in choosing sexual partners does not seem just to be a product of socialization.

Unashamed Insertees

One of the interesting facets of examining what gay men do is interpreting gay male patterns as male patterns undeterred by the demands women are able to make on those to whom they provide sexual access. Men, in the United States and elsewhere, are socialized by women, and I do not mean to suggest that gay male sexual patterns are uninfluenced by women or by the readily available models of heterosexual sexual access negotiated between women and men. I only want to take some gay men's unconcern about whether the sex in which they engage is observed (at least that is observed by those who are not going to interfere with its completion or take reprisals against those observed) as providing some support for the hypothesis that hiding sex is not a universal human goal and as evidence against Friedl's contention that being observed while having sex diminishes the self.

I want to distinguish "observed" from "public" in the sense of occurring where a variety of kinds of persons are likely to be. As should be clear from the examples below, what I am calling "observed sex" occurs in places in which those co-present are males known or believed to be interested in having sex with males and/or in seeing males have sex with males. Most of what has been called "public sex" either is foreplay that isn't labeled "public sex" if it involves two sexes (e.g., holding hands, kissing), or is "public" in a formal but not a substantive sense (the sections of beaches and parks that are not frequented except by males seeking male sex partners). The anecdotal evidence on observed sex that I am going to discuss should suffice to undercut the equation of being observed with damaging or shrinking the sense of self. It is clearly not sufficient to do more than suggest that there are male/female differences in commitment to hiding sex from the view of others. It shows that (at least for some men) the difference is not between being seen to penetrate or being seen to be penetrated (subject honor versus object shame), though such a contrast may matter to others (in the United States or elsewhere).[8] The pattern of not feeling diminished by being observed having sex may not be general. It is not unique to San Francisco, however. Four of the six men who describe instances below recount experiences from smaller cities in southern California and Arizona, and another recounts an Asian-Asian encounter in Thailand.[9]

Someone who sets store on being a top does not want to risk his reputation, so being observed being topped may diminish his self-esteem, as might being revealed to be impotent or to ejaculate very quickly. Disparity between any part of self-presentation and one's actual behavior makes knowledge of the disparity potentially costly.[10] That one's sexual partner might say something to others probably deters a lot of behavior, and engaging in sexual behavior that is contrary to someone's public posturing is especially unlikely to be performed before audiences, even those that are expected to be sympathetic. Various kinds of male reputations (including those for celibacy, monogamy, or sexual prowess) are vulnerable (see Murray 1995:61–62).

Excitement versus Lack of Access to Private Locales

Many people (especially men) without residences or vehicles of their own, and without the means to rent rooms in hotels or bathhouses (or to travel to cities with such amenities), can find partners and have sex in relatively secluded parts of "public space."[11] As Johnston and Valentine (1995:100) wrote, "The privacy of a place is not necessarily the same as having privacy in a place. . . . Although the home may be a more or less private place for 'the family' it doesn't necessarily guarantee freedom for individuals from the watchful gaze of other household members." More explicitly, Scott Tucker (1990:17) observed, "Gay people often have no freedom to be gay in the privacy of their own homes, due to family and neighborly pressures. . . . Lacking a secure privacy, they may find an insecure privacy and a selective publicity among similar seekers" of sexual partners. Even in metropolises with venues for male-male sex, many men who have sex with men seek to keep their desires from being known (i.e., as part of their public persona) and do not reveal their names to sexual partners. Anonymous sex can be seen as more private than sex in bedrooms shared by people in ongoing relationships in that most everything about the self remains unknown to sexual partners in anonymous encounters.

However, anonymous sex in "public" locales is not entirely nor always a desperate remedy for those lacking alternatives. While some would prefer to have real privacy and not to have to run such risks in order to have sex, at least some others find the risk of being caught exciting (Humphreys 1975:151–52). Still, it is important to remember that totally secure privacy for lovemaking is a luxury for most people. I would guess that most of the heterosexual sex and a lot of the homosexual sex that is observed involves couples who sought not to be observed but were unable to wait or to find a place where they could be certain that no one else could see (or hear) what they were doing. No research of which I am aware attempts to assess the relative magnitudes of such preferences among those who (sometimes) have sex with men in public spaces.

I think that crosscutting the distinction between those excited by danger and those who are not is another distinction between those who are excited by being observed having sex by men who are interested in men and by those who are not. That is, not all those who seek "privacy" from hostile observers also want "privacy" from excited observers. I would guess that few of those who are excited by the risk of being caught by agents of repression mind being observed by excited observers, but would not hazard a guess on the relative size of the other three cells of a two-by-two table (± excited by risks of hostile observers, ± excited by sympathetic observers).

I would guess that men more commonly *risk* being observed than *seek* to be observed. In the following instance I elicited, Bill sought to expand his erotic experience, both in locale and in partner. He acquiesced to one observer, but not to another who was not at all the kind of observer Bill would knowingly have risked performing before. It is Bill speaking; my questions or comments are in italics.

How I Became a Registered Sex Offender: Bill

[Bill:] It was really stupid. I had a lover, but, unlike him, I had very little sexual experience. I thought I should have more, get more. So I went to this notorious beach—it had to be very notorious for me to have heard about it!—and met this attractive man. I mean, he was my type, *you* wouldn't have liked him! He was one of those brainless surfer types that think that catching a wave makes them a stud. I'd never had sex outdoors, and I wanted to try it. . . . We went back into the bushes between the beach and the cliff. Someone followed us, which made me nervous, but he jacked off maybe five yards away while I went down on Mr. Surfer Stud and jacked off at his feet.

I didn't think that anyone else could see us. My field of vision was Mr. Surfer's washboard stomach and maybe the trees behind him, but he

could see anyone coming up the one path which we'd taken in. I didn't
scan the top of the cliff to make sure no one could see us from there. And
I'm not convinced that I could have seen the one who was. A policeman
was lurking on top of the cliff in something like a duck blind. There is no
reason other than monitoring sex in the bushes for anyone to be there.[12]
There is no trail nearby and there are much better ocean vistas elsewhere.
I consider that three men were having consensual sex in private, even
though I don't know why I consented! I guess I wanted to find out what it
was like to suck off someone I didn't know, to find out what anonymous
outdoor sex felt like. Now that sounds really childish to me, but, you know,
we have to find out these things for ourselves after we're supposed to be
grown up. It would have been better if I'd tried this out when I reached
puberty instead of when I was legally an adult, you know? It was conse-
quential in a way that it wouldn't have been if I was a teenager (though it
would have been worse for the surfer, whose name I've repressed).

Unfortunately, the three of us enjoying the two of us having sex were
not as alone as we thought. A fourth man was in hiding to catch fags. The
idea simply had not occurred to me, but when I got to the parking lot I was
arrested. In most of the photographs I was not recognizable. At least I don't
recognize the top of my head, but the one with his head in another man's
crotch was clearly the same person as in a couple of pictures, before and
after, in which both of us were recognizable. I wanted to argue that this was
in no ways "public," but my lawyer convinced me to plead guilty to "gross
indecency" and be put on probation, especially since Mr. Surfer did.

This not particularly good sex with this dolt led to my being a registered
sex offender. I was asked for an alibi when someone was stabbed to death
at another park, and anywhere I move in California, I have to notify the
local police department, so they can round me up among their usual suspects for any murders related to "public sex." I can imagine worse things.
I suppose that Mr. Surfer or Mr. Masturbator could conceivably have killed
me, but to me the crime is police surveillance. I was naive, sure. I had sex
in a public park and I knew that another man was watching. I suppose he
could have been a cop—even Mr. Surfer could have been one. I also
knew that rather than being horrified by what we were doing, our voyeur
was getting off on it. He was an uninvited guest, an unwelcome gate-
crasher (to me; Mr. Surfer liked to show off), but it was still a *private* party,
sexual conduct secluded from any reasonable prospect of shocking the
public. And "the forces of public order" were not shocked either, having
prepared their little nest and stocked it with a telephoto lens. For all I
know, the policeman who smirked and called me "cocksucker" was jacking off just like the guy closer to us.

[SM:] You reject applying "public sex" to that horror story. Have you
engaged in other instances that others would label "public sex"?

[Bill:] Not outside in California! Inside in clubs within view of other gay men, a segment of the public, a segment who is there to watch and/or engage in gay sex.

[SM:] Do you like to watch other men have sex?

[Bill:] Yeah.

[SM:] Do you identify with the tops or the bottoms?

[Bill:] The bottoms, usually, doing what I'd be doing if I was doing instead of watching.

[SM:] Do you like to be watched while you're having sex?

[Bill:] Sometimes. I prefer not to have any distractions from the one I'm with, but there is something exciting about being watched.

[SM:] Is it any more exciting to be watched while you're taking it than while you're giving it?

[Bill:] I'm a little embarrassed to have men watching me suck cock. Maybe the arrest trauma, though I was a little embarrassed by the voyeur seeing me go down on the surfer, too. I don't mind men watching someone go down on me. I don't think it's a top/bottom thing, though, because I like to wiggle my butt a little extra for an audience watching me get fucked and also to exaggerate my thrusts if people are watching me fuck someone.

[SM:] You don't think sex should be done in private?

[Bill:] It shouldn't be done only in front of those who are upset by it—or who have the power to arrest you for it and pretend to be "shocked, shocked." Otherwise, I think it's fine. I enjoy watching other species do it on TV nature shows—though I should probably consider that the animals have not given informed consent and that the photographers are lurking like the policeman was, but if he'd developed the pictures to beat off to instead of to prosecute me, I wouldn't particularly have minded, so maybe that's OK.

[SM:] You masturbate to "Wild America"?

[Bill:] No, no. To "Nature." Just kidding—not to that either. Sometimes watching one animal mount another makes my cock hard, though, as watching barnyard animals surely must excite farm children—and adults. Doesn't everyone love to watch this?

[SM:] Some people are embarrassed by it.

[Bill:] Yeah: those who like to get fucked, but think they shouldn't like it. Fucking is natural. Maybe at some level I feel that sucking cock isn't nat-

ural, but mounting and pushing it in sure is. Well, of course, fellatio is part
of nature for humans, but all mammals fuck—so why not me? If someone
enjoys watching, and my partner isn't nervous about being watched, I
enjoy being enjoyed. By my partner, of course, but also it's exciting that
what I'm doing is exciting to someone who chooses to watch me, whether
they want to have me or be me while I'm doing whatever I'm doing. I feel
like I'm sharing and increasing excitement, and that excitement is good as
long as it doesn't lead to anyone getting hurt. But, I'm a registered sex
offender, so I must be a real pervert, right?

Bill's foray into the bushes illustrates two of the dangers of semi-open
sexual behavior (police interference and unwelcome additional participants). Bill was not seeking to be observed, and did not want to be
observed. He was not excited by being observed, even by the man masturbating at some distance. He lived where there were no private sex clubs in
which to explore other kinds of homosexuality than the ongoing relationship
he had (and still has).

Gay sex clubs are "open to the public" but provide a space more protected from bashers, thieves, and Vice Squad quota-fillers than the bushes
of gay beaches and parks.[13] Gatekeepers collect money, so that anyone
who is present is not only conscious of what kind of place he is in, but has
paid to be in a place where men meet men for sex, most of which occurs on
the premises, albeit in varying degrees of seclusion. Nick, my recurrent
prime explicator of gay norms,[14] gave me his views of seeking a modicum
of privacy in so-called "public sex," and then recounted the two instances
in which he had been anally penetrated "in public." The first instance fits
the "nowhere to go" pattern. The second involved conscious (albeit
unplanned) display.

The Thrill of Being Watched: Nick

> [Nick:] I would guess that most sex between gay men is done in private.
> And much of what is called "public sex" takes place in secluded places,
> where only those who are seeking sex go. I have no experience of "tea-
> rooms," but from what friends have told me, they "show hard" and per-
> haps grope in the open space of the urinals, but that the sex—the pene-
> trations—occurs in stalls. Similarly, in the parks, men generally pair off
> and go deeper into the bushes to get it on.
>
> [SM:] So as not to be observed by others?
>
> [Nick:] You want to get where you are not going to be interrupted, espe-
> cially not by hostile others.
>
> [SM:] Do you mean bashers or rivals?

[Nick:] I meant bashers. They know of and hunt in the same territories as the fags they want to bash or rob.[15] You don't want to be visible to attackers, especially when you have your pants down, or even just when your head is down. But rivals? You might *want* to be seen by rivals, to rub their faces in it: "You wanted him? Well *I* got him!" That sort of mentality. It seems to me that a lot of men want to show off their conquests, whether it's a woman on their arm, or a man skewered on their cock, or, for some, a hard cock planted in them. Whatever one man thinks some other man wants but he has or is getting, including being plowed. I think that many straight men would be quite happy to have other men watch them screw pretty much any attractive woman.

[SM:] Do you think that this is tied into shame at being penetrated in contrast to glory for penetrating?

[Nick:] It's more blessed to give than to receive? Maybe that's part of it. Clearly a lot of straight men are horrified at the idea of a cock in their mouth or ass, but don't mind mixing their sperm with their buddy's inside a woman—or inside a man. Among men with some sexual experience, those who aren't concerned about impotence or premature ejaculations, there's often an interest in taking turns on the same orifice, watching your buddy stick it in and then sticking it in the same place while he watches and then watching him stick it in again, and so on. I think this is a substitute for getting it on with each other. I'd like to know if they fantasize at least momentarily that they are taking their friend's dick or putting theirs into him, but I don't suppose they'd admit it, even to themselves—or especially to themselves.

[SM:] Do you think that gay men are more willing to be seen with their cocks in another man than to be seen with a man's cock in them?

[Nick:] Like I said before, I think that the main thing is showing you have what your audience wants to have. I guess the really perverse thing is to fuck someone really butch or really hung who your friend or your rival wants to be fucked by, but, generally, getting what you want is more important than what other people think about the value of what you want.

[SM:] Do you find an audience exciting?

[Nick:] Yes. I like watching men having sex, and back when I had sex [before AIDS] I liked to be watched. I don't ever recall the "Nyah, nyah, nyah, I've got him and you don't!" feeling about anyone I connected with in parks or bathhouses. I'm not denying that I ever had such unworthy feelings of competitiveness, just not in anonymous sex that I knew others were watching.

[SM:] So what was the excitement for you?

[Nick:] The vicarious enjoyment of the spectators, knowing that they were excited by what I was doing, that they were fantasizing participating, that I was part of their fantasy.

[SM:] Did it matter which part?

[Nick:] You mean top or bottom?

[SM:] Yeah.

[Nick:] No. I remember the occasions I was a bottom more, so maybe I was more excited about being taken, or maybe it's just that they were so rare. At Land's End [in the woods above a gay nude beach in San Francisco] I was sucked off with other men watching many times, and even more times fucking or being sucked in the baths and backrooms of bars, sometimes really in the middle of crowds—the small crowds that would fit in small places, I mean. As you surely remember, there was a tendency for some of "the audience" to do more than watch: to rub my tits or my balls or my ass while my cock was in a man's orifice. This pawing really bothered some men, especially if it interfered with "the main event"—as it sometimes did. Some of my sexual partners wanted to have me to themselves. They didn't want to be part of an orgy, even in an orgy room. I brushed off hands at various times, many times, actually. The only time someone really pissed me off was this man who seemed to want to feel my cock while it was in another man's ass. He didn't just feel around the outside, but tried to go in with me. Maybe he wanted to pull my cock out and put it in him, I'm not sure. We did not have a polite conversation about what he wanted. We were not interested! The man I was fucking pushed this intruder roughly away before I did. It was his ass and he already had what he wanted in it, you know? On other occasions, other partners retreated to more protected places, if only to a corner so that walls cut off access from two directions.

I didn't feel degraded. Maybe if I'd grown up as a sex object I'd have been tired of it but, like a lot of gay men, I grew up feeling that no one would ever want me—and that, most certainly, no one would ever want to *be* me. That others were turned on by watching me was very validating—of something important.

[SM:] That you were desirable?

[Nick:] That's too abstract: that I was desired. That was an astounding revelation after a typically horrible adolescence filled with self-loathing that I wasn't like other boys and that no one *ever* would want me or find me the least bit sexually interesting. The constantly hard cock that embarrassed me in high school—that I was terrified of being seen with!—was transformed into being a major asset. I must have been remarkably stupid as a teenager not to know that what I was hiding was something that both boys and girls like, and that men and women want.

[SM:] So it was pride in having a big cock that was validated . . .

[Nick:] Not the size. I don't think it's all that big. But there seemed to be a shortage of hard cocks relative to the number of eager consumers. You know: "A hard man is good to find"? Like a reversal of adolescence, when cocks are standing at attention desperately pleading for a wet warm orifice and there's no place to put them, to all these limp dicks and eager, frustrated orifices hoping to be filled. I felt that most of the audience identified with my partners, not with me. I mean that they wanted to have a hard dick in them, not that they wanted to have particularly *my* dick in them, but they imagined themselves getting an adequate cock, a generic hard cock. One of the things any "hot man" has to offer. This sounds really conceited, but I don't think the desire had anything to do with who I am or was any credit to me personally. I like to fuck, and if doing it brings pleasure and excitement to more people than the one I'm fucking [that] is a bonus.

[SM:] You weren't ashamed to be seen putting your cock in this or that man?

[Nick:] No. And I wasn't ashamed when it was the other way. When I had sex with strangers it was almost exclusively as a top, regardless of how many men were in the space where I was having sex—which was usually no others. Even in the wild days of the late 1970s, I didn't take in strange dicks, I mean strangers' dicks, even though I did and do like to be taken from behind without any "by your leave." The fantasy is that someone wants me so bad that he just takes me. Mostly this has happened in private with my lover, but there were two occasions in public, in so-called public, both involving black men—but let's not get into whether I objectify black men, OK?

One was late at night. The first one, I was waiting for a bus after leaving a gay disco. A short black man asked me where I'd been. The short is important. If he'd been bigger I probably would have just said "Dancing," but I named the place. He asked me, "Do you give good head?" and I honestly answered "No." He continued, "It looks like you got a nice booty, do you like to take it up the ass?" I must have been a little, umm high, because I continued to answer honestly: "Sometimes." He took out his semi-hard, not insubstantial drill, and asked "Would you like to take this up your ass?" I was amused by his forthrightness, and wondered if he fucked as good as he talked. We didn't have any place we could go to bed together. (I never took tricks home—but then I didn't usually bend over for men I met in the street, either, or for strangers I met anywhere.) Anyhow, we ended up in a schoolyard. He shoved it in, rooted around a little, got off quickly, and hurried away. As far as I know there was no audience. . .

The other occasion was more thrilling to me, because it was wordless and because it was witnessed. It was the only time that I know of that I was fucked while others watched. There was a large window between the video room and the maze at the old Ritch Street baths [in a nocturnally deserted warehouse district in San Francisco]. I'd just cum and while, you could say, my batteries were recharging, I was standing in front of the win- dow between the maze and the video room, watching a fuck film. A very lithe black man, very much my type, not super-hung but definitely endowed, came up behind me and reached under my towel to finger my butthole. I hardly ever got fucked at the baths and never (before or after) in front of others, but here was my fantasy man doing what I fantasized about: being stripped, bent over, and fucked without any "by your leave." Having seen what he looked like and made up my mind to let him "have his way with me," I turned back to watching the film. He unknotted my towel and draped it around my neck, lubricated me (I have no idea where he was carrying the lubricant!). I braced myself and got fucked in front of a growing audience.

[SM:] How do you know it grew?

[Nick:] There were murmurs and some were in my peripheral vision. Somewhat unusually, no one approached. We were performing in the light. They were in the semidarkness, and they stayed there. Is transfixed the word? I was transfixed by this gorgeous man who came up and started fucking me and I thought that everyone else present shared my awe. I now doubt that that was it, but there must have been something about the lighting and the light (me) and dark (him) that was so visually arresting that the audience stayed back. I found it thrilling. I find it still exciting to remember it. It was my brief stint as a porn star.

[SM:] Did you cum?

[Nick:] You have an impoverished sense of what excitement is! I don't think I could have! I'd probably cum three times in the previous hour or so. I must have gotten hard despite that, but my cock was not involved. No one, including me, touched it. I forgot that it existed. For once I was the hole being filled, not the filler.

[SM:] Did anyone say anything about it to you afterwards?

You probably would have conducted an audience survey and would be able to tell how many identified with the one being fucked, how many with the one fucking . . .

[SM:] I wish I were that bold!

[Nick:] I feel that most of the audience identified with me being taken, but no one told me so. Maybe they thought I had a hot hole and fantasized being the one drilling it, being the Stud instead of fantasizing the Stud taking them . . .

[SM:] So you didn't talk about it. What did you do then?

[Nick:] Probably wiped my ass, showered, sat in the jacuzzi awhile, then returned to being a top.

[SM:] You didn't talk to the man who fucked you?

[Nick:] Not a word. He wanted me, I wanted him to have me, he had me, people watched. We didn't get married. We didn't live happily ever after. But at least one person retains a memory of that fuck. It was better than several of my so-called "lover" relationships. I hope that he is well and he remembers it. And maybe some of the audience was moved. They enhanced the experience for me and I hope that some of them have a good memory of it, too.

[SM:] But you don't know . . .

[Nick:] No. I was doing sex, not scientifically studying it. I didn't do any follow-up interviews!

In contrast to Nick's remembrance of one special occasion, Rufus, an African-American "preacher's kid," recalled a regularly scheduled ensemble performance. When he was a junior and senior in high school in a San Bernardino County (southern California) town, he recalled "servicing the [church] baseball team in batting order, every Wednesday."

A Part of the Team: Rufus

[SM:] They lined up and took their turns?

[Rufus:] They sure did. Just like at the plate. Everyone got a hit; no one struck out and there was no other team to interrupt them. Of course, none had to wait very long for their turn. One of them would shoot in my mouth, then the next one, then the next one. Teenagers can't hold it back very well—if at all, so my jaw still wasn't sore when the ninth one finished, when I went down the ninth time.

[SM:] And the others watched?

[Rufus:] Oh, yes. They loved watching each other, some of them more than being done. They could see their friends' dicks hard and not have to figure out what to do with it. No one left after his turn. They all wanted to watch everybody else get done.

[SM:] No one wanted to compete with you? Do what you were doing?

[Rufus]: I don't know if any wanted to. There probably wasn't anyone else in the school that was ready to suck nine[16] cocks one after the other, plus whoever wanted a second at-bat. Someone might have wanted to try one, but what if he didn't like it and had eight more to do? No. It was like my monopoly. I was happy, my team was happy.

[SM:] Did you get off on their watching?

[Rufus:] I got off later, remembering it. While I was doing them, I'd be hard, but I wouldn't jack off or anything.

[SM:] They were interested in each other's cocks, but not in yours?

[Rufus:] That's what I thought. Maybe I was wrong, but I thought that I supplied the mouth and they supplied the cocks, and that was just fine with me.

[SM:] Can you separate your enjoyment from sucking their cocks from your enjoyment of eight watching while you did one of them?

[Rufus]: That'd be difficult. I think it was better that everyone saw and they all did it together as a team. One of them also came to me by himself other times, but on Wednesdays, he took his turn—he batted third.

[SM:] They didn't call you names or beat you up?

[Rufus:] No. They should have called me "the cocksucker," and maybe they called me that to each other when I wasn't around, but they were grateful and they protected me if any of the other boys started to give me a hard time. I was in a way part of the team, like the equipment manager or the coach.

[SM:] Did the coach know you were going down on his whole team?

[Rufus:] He must have, but he chose not to know, like my dad chose not to notice I was a fag.

Both Bill and Nick explicitly deny that being penetrated or penetrator mattered to their willingness to "perform" before an appreciative "audience." For Bill, a performance captured in photos led to an unwelcome labeling (albeit one he does not accept and has evaded by moving out of California). An important part of Nick's self-esteem was, he says, enhanced rather than diminished by being watched—with the most memorable instance being one in which he was anally receptive. Similarly, Robert Glück (1985:54–55) recalled feeling that he was the focus of feelings of awe being fucked in the San Francisco Club Baths, c. 1981:

> We watch the pleasure rather than the men, feeling the potential inter-changeability. One of them masturbates me, others tended me respectfully because the one who is fucked induces awe by his extreme exposure. . . . Their collective mind said "he's doing it" which my finite mind repeated. Although they masturbated themselves to obtain immediate knowledge of

my excitement, it was as spectators that they solemnly shared in what my
pleasure revealed. In the first place I was naked, their eyes and hands on
my body confirmed that. In the second place I was desired. In the third
place I was penetrated, which put me in a class by myself.

Rufus recalled his performances with palpable excitement; Nick still had
a keen esthetic appreciation of the scene he staged (quite consciously willing a sexual role he did not generally enact). Receptivity, even being seen to
be receptive, did not bother them. The novelty was part of the excitement
for Bill (the novelty of anonymous, outdoor sex) and for Nick (being taken
by a stranger). For Rufus, the least sexually versatile of the three (i.e., the
one who generally —perhaps always—was sexually receptive), being
watched was a routine part of the scene. In that I saw him many times
through open bathhouse cubicle doors lying on his stomach or at the bottom of tangles of men in the orgy rooms, his public availability continued.

I am well aware that some people (even some gay men) disapprove of
such goings-on as I've discussed.[17] "Shameless" is not a positive label anywhere, though it may be applied with some ambivalent awe. I hope that
exploring the excitement of simultaneously transgressing both normative
heterosexuality and normative privacy is not taken as showing how dis-
solute and/or perverted gay men are. Nick and Rufus and Bill are proud of
being gay, proud of their bodies, and not threatened by other gay men
knowing that they are penetrable.

Nonetheless, I should add that a number of my friends either denied
ever having had sex within the view of those not directly involved or did not
want to talk about instances. Some recalled being mortified by lovers or
family members walking in on them. Although he was embarrassed by one,
Felix remembered some excitement in the instances he recalled, and rev-
eled in the points he thought were made to specific others.

Caught in the Act: Felix

> [Felix:] My ex-lover Bruce and my replacement Juan were staying with us.
> They had gone out shopping, but Juan changed his mind. I was sitting on
> the couch in the living room sucking what Jim, this young black man,
> called his "joystick," when Juan came in. Jim leapt back, pulled up his
> pants and stuffed this dick back in his pants. And, let me tell you, there
> was a lot to stuff! Juan just smiled and went to the guest room. Later he
> commented, "You had quite a mouthful. I didn't mean to interrupt you."
> In a sick way I was glad that Bruce would hear that I had moved on to a
> bigger dick than his. Not that I'm a size queen, just that I hoped he would
> feel small. Or maybe just know that I didn't need him, that he wasn't the
> only man in the world that would ever want me.

[SM:] You weren't embarrassed because you were the receptive one?

[Felix:] Not at all. I'm not even sure I was embarrassed at all. It was Jim who was afraid that Bruce was going to beat him up, because I still belonged to him. A totally ludicrous notion, but probably Jim got off in his own way in fantasizing about taking another man's man. . . .

[SM:] Was your own "joystick" out?

[Felix:] No. I'd just taken his big dick out and made it hard when Juan walked in. I'm sure I was hard—just being around Jim made me hard most all the time—but I wasn't doing myself while I was doing him. We probably would have gotten naked and gone to my bedroom . . .

[SM:] In that order?

[Felix:] Probably Jim wouldn't have taken my clothes off in the living room and might have suggested moving if I stopped to try to strip him.

The other time was years earlier, when I was married [to a woman] and just realizing I was really gay, that it wasn't a phase I'd grown out of, but was serious. It's when I found out what "passion" is. I was madly in love with Luis, and he was frightened by how gone on him I was. He liked to fuck me and suck my cock but he didn't want to be boxed in—and he was right: I really did want to monopolize him. He was avoiding me, but I saw his car at his grandmother's. He let me watch him take a shower. After he got out I begged him to let me suck his cock, which I'd like never done before. Normally he'd suck me and fuck me and I'd be in heaven. This, unfortunately, was different. I don't think he could cum from being sucked. I was working hard and neither of us heard his grandmother come home. The door opened and Argh!—an Olympic-scale jump backward. In fact, he bumped into his bed, so he was sitting there naked trying to cover up this immense hard-on wet with my saliva.[18] Well, I felt really bad that I'd gotten him in trouble (though if he'd just come over in the morning and fucked me like he was supposed to, I wouldn't have had to hunt him down there!), but at the same time I was perversely happy to be linked with him in someone's eyes. I mean we were (I thought) carrying on this very secret affair and were protecting my marriage (I can't remember why!), but part of me wanted to be seen as a couple—me and this astonishingly beautiful and very obviously hung man. The way he dressed—tight pants and no underwear—left no doubt about that! I selfishly didn't mind his grandmother being upset that Luis was fucking my mouth. Even though it wasn't what we did or had ever done before! Since my jaw was sore, I didn't even mind that her seeing us interrupted it. If he'd been fucking me—Oh! I forgot, that happened, too!

Later, Luis moved in with this straight coworker and there was a time when I was on my back and Luis was fucking me. Joe came in his room supposedly to get something, but I think really to see who was fucking whom. Luis told him "We're busy" and kept screwing me. I didn't care. I just pulled him tighter against me. Like I said, I wanted people to know that we were together. I wanted us to be together, to be a couple. I'd have been relieved if he told my wife that this very effeminate Chicano queen was fucking her precious husband's eager asshole and sucking his cock, but he didn't. I don't know if Joe wondered what it would be like to have that hot chile up his butt. Maybe I'm projecting. But, then again, maybe he found out . . .

[SM:] You didn't mind a straight man seeing you get fucked?

[Felix:] He definitely knew that Luis was a fag before they got the place together. Everyone knew that. Joe probably assumed that Luis took dicks—which he did, in his mouth—maybe [he took] Joe's, too. He also had to know that Luis had a lot between his legs. The way Luis dressed, you'd have to be blind not to see he was well-endowed, but maybe Joe thought that was just an ornament. I don't know what he thought, but I know that if he didn't want to see two men getting it on, he shouldn't have come in, so I think he *wanted* to see what we were doing. Like with the grandmother, as I said, I was pleased that someone saw us as a couple. I wasn't particular who it was or what they saw us doing. That he had his cock in me both times didn't bother me in the least. Since I was married to a woman and Luis was pretty flamboyant it may have educated Joe that the seemingly butch, supposedly straight one may be the one who takes the dick of the apparently femme one.

As Friedl noted (albeit only in relation to children's ignorance), lack of direct observation leads to misconceptions about what people do sexually. Felix and Luis were not trying to educate Luis's grandmother or straight roommate, but their invasion of what was going on behind closed doors inadvertently showed them something of what men can do with each other and that insertive/receptive roles do not necessarily map to gender appearances. Hard-core gay films from Europe and the United States more systematically show men around the world that masculine men can be sexually receptive, which undermines gender-stratified organization of male homosexuality.[19]

Some men (even among those who are gay-identified) are not "versatile," and, among those who are, some are more reluctant to be observed being penetrated than to be observed penetrating, e.g., Ken.

On and Off the Beach: Ken

[Ken:] The first time I went to a gay nude beach, I didn't really know how one is supposed to behave. I had some experiences in parks, where I was more discreet. You cruise there with your clothes on, you know? This was

like the first time I was naked and a naked man came on to me, so it
seemed natural just to go ahead and fuck him right there. That can't be
entirely true, else I'd have put on a condom and just gone at it exactly
where we were.

All of us were on top of the dunes, and if I'd fucked him there, people
jogging on the beach could have seen us. We went down the other side of
the dunes, away from the beach, but not into the woods that were further
back. We could be seen by the gay boys on top of the dunes, but not by
bypassers going along the beach, understand?

I wanted to face the ocean—not for the scenic view, but to see if anyone was coming toward us. That meant that those on the dune could see
my new friend jacking off while I fucked him. Gay missionary position, you
know? with his legs against my chest and his ankles locked around my
neck. So his cock was sort of on display. Mine of course was burrowing
out of sight.

[SM:] So his body mostly blocked the view of yours?

[Ken:] Right. What I was doing was obvious to anyone who was looking.
They could see my head between his ankles, but the lower half of his body
was up in the air, blocking any view of me.

[SM:] Did that matter to you?

[Ken:] Not really. Like I said, I wanted to be able to see anyone approaching. As far as being watched, I wouldn't care if those on the dunes saw my
back and ass while I plowed his ass.

[SM:] How about if you were getting fucked?

[Ken:] I wouldn't get fucked that openly.

[SM:] Why not?

[Ken:] I guess I'd be a little embarrassed for everyone to see me taking it
up the ass. Not that I think there's anything wrong with that or that I don't
like taking it sometimes. Indeed, even later that same afternoon, I took a
black sailor into the bushes and he fucked the shit out of me.

[SM:] Away from any viewers?

[Ken:] Not in the plain view of everyone, like when I fucked that man earlier, but someone either followed us or happened upon us and was watching me get mounted.

[SM:] Were you embarrassed then?

[Ken:] No, I was really into it. I motioned the other one over and sucked
his cock while the naval artillery was getting ready to shoot up my
behind.

[SM:] Would you have been embarrassed if the third person had just continued to watch you get fucked?

[Ken:] I don't think so. Behind the dunes was really public, in-your-face even. This one was clearly there because he wanted to be, whether he came in his own hand or in my mouth. I mean, he sought us out. The boys on the beach weren't there to see my sexcapade, this one was.

[SM:] So it's not that you didn't want anyone to see you get fucked.

[Ken:] I didn't want *everyone* to see it, but interested parties, sure. If there had been more? Well, while I was on vacation from being a top, maybe I'd have taken them in turn, or an orgy might have started, though I preferred being the center of attention . . . .

[SM:] Was there any other time you got fucked where others could see?

[Ken:] No. I know that I was sucked off with circles of onlookers many times, but I remember the two incidents at the beach that day more vividly. They are still very exciting to think about, but I never again fucked anyone so publicly, and never got fucked again either by a stranger or where anyone else could watch it.

[SM:] So, it did matter whether you were seen fucking or being fucked?

[Ken:] Yes. I was willing for anyone and everyone to see me being a top, but slunk away into the bushes when I agreed to be topped.

[SM:] Did his being black matter for this?

[Ken:] No. I would have wanted a more sheltered place to get fucked regardless of what color dick was going in me.

[SM:] What do you think the gay men on the dunes were thinking?

[Ken:] At the time I thought they either didn't care or envied our boldness. Now I think that some were probably appalled by our vulgarity and indiscretion, endangering acceptance of a nude beach, while others wished that they were the ones with their legs up and a hard dick pounding in their asses.

[SM:] You mean identifying with your partner, not with you?

[Ken:] Right—most would rather have me [inside them] than to be me and do what I was doing.

In the final instance, Krishna, a top of South Asian origin who was visiting a Bangkok sex palace, details an encounter in which the excitement was enhanced by discovering during it that he and the young Thai man he was penetrating were being watched by an appreciative audience, although they had thought they were having sex in private.

[Krishna:] In my experience Asians (whether East, Southeast, South, or Southwest and whether or not interested in sex with members of the same sex) are prudish about anyone seeing their genitals or even bulges through clothing,[20] let alone seeing dicks in action. In the most luxurious bathhouse in the world, the Babylon and the Obelisk in Bangkok, men generally wear not only a towel but also a robe. Unlike European and American bathhouses, men do not have sex in the well-lit parts of Bangkok bathhouses and they are usually very covered-up even while searching for sexual partners. Once contact is made, pairs go to a cubicle and close the door before removing their towels and robes.

On the night in question I saw a beautiful twenty-something Thai boy sitting on the platform in a room on the third floor of Babylon. The light was on. He had on a towel, tied below his navel, emphasizing his washboard stomach and wasp waist. After holding eye contact from the doorway, I entered the cubicle, shutting the door behind me. He rose, I took off my robe and pressed his body to mine. We each still had a towel on. I took his face in my hand, gently caressed it, and covered it with little kisses. This had an easily discernible effect on his large organ, which was firmly sandwiched between our bodies. We fondled each other under our towels. It was only after we were horizontal that the towels very naturally came off. Gradually his caresses became warmer, his breath quicker. I lightly ran my fingers down to his firm buttocks, and gently stroked the crack between them, implicitly requesting permission to visit (waiting in another doorway, as it were). He clenched the opening shut and shook his head. "We can suck, but not there," he said, pointing to what Thais usually call their back-door. I instantly desisted without any complaint and focused on his earlobes and neck and nibbles, while my hands roamed affectionately over his body.

I could feel him relax. Suddenly, he whispered, "OK, you can go in" and turned on his side to give me easy entry . . .

After I was inside his back-door, I suddenly realized that the room's door was open. I had not latched it, and it had come open—or been opened by someone. Several people were gazing intently at us. The young Thai closest to the door seemed transfixed by the sight of our joined brown bodies and was stroking his own erect cock. Probably because I froze for an instant, my partner looked at the door. I believe that he also thought about disconnecting long enough to get up and close the door, but when I pushed in as far as I could, he wiggled back, confirming that he, too, wanted to continue.

Unknowingly, we had been watched fucking. Now we knew, and the boys at the door knew that we knew. I found the experience electrifying. The audience, politely staying offstage (that is, outside the door), somehow thrilled me. My partner who had initially resisted being fucked

Self Size and Observable Sex

seemed to have lost his inhibitions. . . . He went into fairly acrobatic heat. I think that the fact that the two of us were already comfortable in "private" (or at least what we thought was "in private") before we knew that we were being watched gave us a "special" relationship with each other, which we "shared" with the watching group. I think that it would have been different if we had started sex in full public view, but we had already been through establishing trust, negotiating with each other, and through several minutes of sex before the others saw or before we knew that we were being watched.

There was no indication that being observed bothered him: he did not lose his erection (visible only to me, the bed, and the wall). In fact, he seemed to become randier, showing the audience that he was enjoying what was happening by gyrating and moaning more, and then swiveling onto his back. With his knees touching his shoulders, I thrust very visibly into him. With his legs straight up, his large erection audibly slapped against his belly. Doggy-style, my pubic bone slammed against his firm bumpers. He sat, wriggling and moaning, on my pole.

I felt that those outside the room were also participating. The intensity of the gaze from the boy in the door made him also a part of the action. He was panting and vigorously masturbating. A major component of the thrill for me was the aura of debauched abandon that transcends just the two people. The unsought, unexpected audience boosted both of our energies.

Finally, my partner shot his load on my chest while mine fired deep inside him. He collapsed onto the pool of his cum. The crowd drifted away. I extricated myself to shut the door. We snuggled awhile. When we left the room, no one was in the vicinity of the doorway. Later, in the terrace bar, I saw the boy who had been jerking off in the doorway. "Next time" his smile told me.

[SM:] You thought he identified with the one being fucked . . .

[Krishna:] Right.

[SM:] So if there had been a next time, you would have expected to fuck him?

[Krishna:] Right. He'd seen that that was what I wanted to do. If he didn't want me to fuck him he'd know not to get together with me.

[SM:] Which in fact he didn't . . .

[Krishna:] That's right, too. It is possible that he was fantasizing being jerked off by me rather than getting fucked, though my feeling is that he wished he was exactly in my partner's place. If we'd gotten together, I would have knocked at the back door. I think it would have opened, but if not, I'd respect that, as I in fact did with his countryman.

[SM:] Would it have mattered to you—in deciding not to stop, get up and close the door—if you were the one getting fucked?

[Krishna:]It probably would have made no difference if hypothetically the positions had been reversed—it was the thrill of performing for a crowd, not that I was on top. Whether the position was important to the young Thai man's excitement about being watched, I don't know.

By no means is being seen having sex with a man a necessary rite of passage to gay male identity. Involuntarily being seen might inhibit the process, but, as even these few instances show, having sex in front of others (inadvertently or advertently) may be a part of gay affirmation and self-acceptance. Not a necessary part. Not a sufficient part. But also not *necessarily* a diminution of sense of self or of self-worth. Rather than self-absorption being how sex increases the sense of self (Friedl 1994:838) or being essential to arousal (Laumann and Gagnon 1995:213), seeing oneself having sex with a man as one imagines those who are viewing it (or those whom one imagines viewing it) see and understand it might build self and increase gay men's self-confidence and self-esteem.

The extent to which fantasy has enhanced the memories elicited in this chapter—an extent difficult to gauge, though several readers have opined that it is substantial in Rufus's example—bolsters the case that being observed is exciting (for some men sometimes). In the symbolic interactionist tradition of George Herbert Mead, a self is an internalization of (what one believes are) the views of significant others.[21] Sometimes males choose to be seen in order to show that they are gay, as does the adolescent Clifford in Greg Johnson's (1992) story "The Valentine," weary of fending off a female admirer. He decides not to pull away when he hears a nun approaching and thereby ensures that he will be labeled. Less drastically, Felix above recalled that, despite embarrassment, he was glad to have his secret relationship with Luis discovered by straight people happening upon the scene—and also to have the sexual aspect of his relationship with Jim seen by his ex-lover's current lover. In the instances Felix recalled, as in the one recalled by Krishna, consciousness of being seen only momentarily interrupted "engrossment" in sex. Krishna, Rufus, and Nick all reported that awareness of audiences increased their excitement/enjoyment. When sex involved only men, they accepted the presence of male observers who were not expected to interrupt the sex they observed.

Sex often asserts an identity and a relationship—to one's self and to one's partner(s), along with those who see or are told about it. The actual or unimagined view of others may enhance sexual self-affirmation and a range of self-identities. That is, an unimagined empathetic viewer may facilitate

rather than inhibit sexual self-confidence. Viewing of homosexual behavior
by those who wish they were in one's place, or who one imagines wanting to
be there, may strengthen commitment to and enhance valuation of a gay
self and of gay sex both for viewers and for those who know they are being
viewed.[22] In that having sex is a marker of adulthood in U.S. (and other)
societies, the presence of observers may ratify one's maturity as well as
desirability and sexual ability—all of which increase self-esteem.

At least for five of the six in the unrandom sample of gay-identified men
(from diverse cultural backgrounds) quoted herein, the excitement or pride
in being observed having sex, or the indifference to it, were not dependent
on whether they were insertive or receptive. I have been told (recurrently)
that straight-identified men who are married to women and who also have
sex with men in public parks and toilets frequently take receptive roles with
little concern about whether other denizens of those locales see them "taking it," i.e., that men married to women and publicly heterosexual are frequently sexually receptive when they have sexual encounters with men,
even with particularly effeminate ones. Felix recalls exemplification of this
both times someone walked in on him with Luis inside him (although married to a woman, Felix considered himself gay by the time these instances
occurred). I have not attempted to interview straight-identified American
men who have sex with men, so do not know if this is queen folklore or an
empirical phenomenon.[23] Whatever the mix of fantasy and attested examples on which this belief about what "straight" men do is based, it provides
further evidence that which sexual role one is observed to be playing is not
crucial for some men.

Afterword: "Private" and "Public" Spaces

The focus of this chapter has been not on "private" versus "public," but
rather on observed by others in contrast to not observed by others. Some of
each kind occurred in what was supposed by the participants to be "private
space" (including bedrooms), as well as in other known "gay spaces," and
a public space (a deserted after-midnight schoolyard) that was borrowed
for a brief sexual encounter. The instances discussed vary from anonymous
encounters to ongoing relationships and in the ethnicity of participants.
While the sexual orientation of the narrators is in all instances gay, that of
some of their sexual partners (especially a number of young African-American insertors) likely was not.

When they began, all the men felt safe in engaging in sex where they
did. Several were surprised to be "caught in the act," including one of the
two bathhouse encounters recounted in this chapter. Bill felt he was in a

"gay space," albeit one with which he was not familiar, but he was mistaken in thinking that a remote space was safe from hostile official surveillance. He was, in fact, in a space known to police as somewhere men went to have sex with each other and could therefore easily be caught (when they left by the trail from a parking lot to the beach). After engaging (as a top) in the only instance in this chapter that I would characterize as "public sex," when he was himself topped, Ken went to a spot less observable from far away, but one that was often used by men having sex.

Neither Nick nor I ever saw anyone else "performing" where he did within the Ritch Street Baths (although we both saw a lot of sex in which we were not directly involved there, and in similar venues, though usually in semidark or in total darkness). The particularities of lighting and audience enhanced his excitement in what was for him an especially exciting (but never repeated) encounter. Gay bathhouses like Ritch Street and Babylon are places where those who stop to watch are presumed to be voyeurs, not agents of social control seeking to stop such goings-on. Although not everyone in such places is gay-identified, no one wanders into such out-of-the way places without knowing that men have sex with men in them.

Although they are suffused with homoeroticism, suburban school locker rooms are not gay spaces,[24] and it seems likely that the young males Rufus "serviced" did not consider themselves gay. They probably did not acknowledge any excitement of seeing their teammates' members being sucked off or in being seen to be potent by their teammates. Of the sites for observed sex discussed in this chapter, this one seems to me the one most fraught with the potential for roughing up the "queer," but Rufus's personality and/or oral skills and/or stamina sufficed to avoid that potential being realized.

Nick and his schoolyard partner seem to me to have seized a nocturnally deserted public space for private sex, while Felix was in the privacy of his home in the first instance (though in the living room rather than a bedroom), and in Luis's bedroom in the other two instances. In all three, no one else was at home when they began sex "in private." (Felix told me that Jim was more inhibited than Felix, so that it was the difference between them, not that one "intruder" was gay and the other was not that explains stopping or continuing.) The "gay space" of Luis's bedroom were breached by curious straight people entering it without knocking. Neither Felix nor I know whether what they saw surprised them or confirmed their conceptions about Felix and Luis. What Juan saw did not surprise him.

The narratives reproduced in this chapter evidence that some men are unashamed and unembarrassed to be seen having sex, whether they are being receptive or insertive. Some are proud and/or excited to be observed, although none seem to have been excited by having sex in what they con- ceived as "public places" or in front of any but appreciative audiences.

ENDNOTES

I would like to thank Bill Leap for cajoling me into writing about what I don't think should be considered "public sex" by (more or less) forcing me to read Friedl (1994). This prompted me to draw again on some friends' experiences and views. I would like to thank the six men who told their stories and answered intrusively personal questions. All of the names have been changed, as is conventional. I would also like to thank Ralph Bolton, Peter T. Daniels, Badruddin Khan, John Alan Lee, Douglas Mitchell, Frank Proschan, and one of the two anonymous referees for encouraging comments and helpful suggestions, not all of which I took.

1. I interpret specifying the scope to "contemporary Western societies" later on to mean that they intend earlier statements, including the one quoted, to apply universally and that they aim to circumscribe only when they specify their scope. As I know from my own experience of being trained as a sociologist, sociologists generally regard the burden of proof that their assertions apply only to limited times or spaces to be on others, i.e., a contemporary American pattern is universal until proved otherwise. Anthropologists generally add "the culture where I did fieldwork" to "my natal culture" before generalizing, though I do not see any data on what people anywhere feel about sex being observed in Friedl (1994), nor any combing of the Human Relations Area Files to test her claims.

2. Mohr rightly stresses that more than two people can be involved in a sex act, but categorically states, "There is no such thing as casual observation of people fucking" (p. 18). He might not be able to imagine this, but I have seen counterexamples. Indeed, I have been a counterexample!

3. Shame at uncovered genitals is by no means uniquely Christian. For the ancient Greeks, for instance, shame was "straightforwardly connected with nakedness, particular in sexual connections. The word *aidoia*, a derivative of *aidos*, 'shame,' is a standard Greek word for the genitals" (Williams 1993:78; also see p. 220 on a wider equation of exposure with vulnerability).

4. The naturalist view has been predominant in Islam, and the gnostic view is akin to Tantric Buddhism, while the Jehovanist view has been predominant in Christendom. Davis (1983:231–33) suggests that in the West the gnostic views is most prominent before social crises, the Jehovanist view after them, and the naturalist view during tranquil interludes (though he does little to suggest how to identify any of these kinds of social times).

5. "Engrossment," the label suggested by Laumann and Gagnon (1995:213) is better in being less individualistic.

6. I get no sense of one "partner" seeking to imagine the other's pleasure and to enhance it from Friedl's article. Even solo masturbation does not always instance absorption in the masturbator's self insofar as s/he is imagining the responses of a fantasized partner and/or gazes at representations of bodies or of sexual connec-

tions. Perhaps it is easier and more common for same-sex sexual partners imaginatively to take the role of their partner and to enjoy what they feel their partner is feeling from more directly comparable experience. "Co-conspirator" is certainly sometimes a part of lesbian and gay copulation, as well as of heterosexual copulation, and the everyday identity may be transcended, but "reduced to that of coconspirator" (Friedl 1994:840)? I think not. Nor would I accept Davis's (1983:63–64) contention that "the physical concentration of the self in the genitals is a necessary prerequisite for the ultimate psychological interchange of identity, for the genitals are the point at which that interchange occurs." Despite his discerning recognition of the multiplicity of sexual ideologies and his refusal to regard everyday work as everyone's paramount reality, Davis's phenomenology of "erotic reality" (including the sections, pp. 13–16 on sexy/unsexy spaces and times) is clearly that of a straight man with an oversocialized and excessive (functionalist?) confidence in shared norms and evaluations (of who or what is desirable when and where).

7. In the one instance I directly observed as an adolescent, the line extended from a hallway to the bedside. Some others I have heard of involved one male at a time going into a room, so that the intercourse was not directly observed, though everyone present knew both who was in the "train" and who was "pulling" it.

8. See Murray (1995: 49–70; 1996c, 1997) and Taylor (1978) on Latin America; Allyn (1995, 1997) and Jackson (1995:24, 44, 183, 273) on contemporary Thailand; Leupp (1995:178–82) on Tokugawa Japan; and Murray (1998) on contemporary Kenya.

9. Most of the encounters recollected are from the era before AIDS was recognized. This accounts for the lack of mention of condoms.

10. See Goffman (1963) on the costs of being discredited in contrast to the costs of being discreditable.

11. Age and economic barriers to finding and entering gay clubs and friendship cliques exist, especially for rural youths.

12. In the classic review of public indecency cases in Los Angeles, Gallo et al. (1966:804) found that the arresting officer presented the testimony of "offense" in 459 felony cases and 475 misdemeanor cases. Independent observers testified in only twelve of the felony cases and 28 of the misdemeanor cases. I consider that anyone seeking out an area where he knows that what is called "public sex" occurs cannot credibly be offended. Like the others there, he is present for what he expects and hopes is going on. He may be titillated, but not shocked. Frank Proschan pointed out to me that the nineteenth-century German jurist Karl Ulrichs made a similar argument that the policeman's job is to *pretend* to be offended on behalf of society.

13. The range of urban niches in which North American men cruise men and how men seeking sex with men behave in them are discussed in Lee (1978, 1979). See Kramer (1995:207–9) for an account of a place (Minot, North Dakota) with even fewer options for men to meet and have sex with men, and the necessity of having a car to reach any. On socialization, i.e., learning how to behave in such settings to attain one's goals, see Bolton et al. (1994), Brodsky (1993), Lee (1978), Murray (n.d.), Rubin (1991), and Styles (1979).

14. He provided the lengthy discourse about what *gay community* means to gay San Franciscans in Murray (1992:118–19; 1996a:200–201), and a personal document entitled *Cloning* which led to the dialog with him in Murray (n.d.), and his views of sex differences in quest for privacy and his rejection of "public" shaped the argument I make in this chapter.

15. See Myslik 1996.

16. Exactly nine seems a reconstruction (from the knowledge of how many positions comprise a team) rather than a memory. In that this was a black church team, however, it is possible that the team consisted only of one starting roster. Several readers regard this account as a fantasy rather than a memory. My observation of Rufus taking on a series of sexual partners in rapid succession makes me less skeptical of his self-reported adolescent experience.

17. But like the policeman lurking near the cruising grounds, those who read this book are seeking to see what some find shocking.

18. Despite Nick's slap at my impoverished sense of what excitement is, I also asked Felix if he was masturbating while fellating Luis. He said that he was hoping that Luis would go down on him in turn, especially since Luis usually sucked him off after fucking him, so that he "never had to do myself" with Luis. Therefore, his genitals were covered.

19. Eric Allyn long ago suggested this to me in regards to Thailand; Luiz Mott more recently in regards to Brazil. More generally, Friedl (1994:840) noted that having sex unobserved hides the extent of variability from prescribed norms and inhibits learning about sex.

20. This was not the case in Cambodia in the late thirteenth century, when the Yüan (Mongol-dynasty) envoy Zhou Daguan was shocked/titillated by Khmer casualness about nudity (see Murray 1996b:36–37).

21. See Williams's (1993:77–85, 102) compelling argument for internalization of standards even in a "shame culture" seemingly preoccupied with appearances of honor (focusing on Ajax's suicide late in the *Illiad*).

22. From the Jehovanist worldview, the voyeur is changed more than the voyee (Davis 1983:130), though both are degraded. From the gnostic view, the knowingly observed one is changed (positively) more, though both benefit from transgressing taboos. From the naturalist view, neither is changed, though the voyeur might learn something to try later.

23. For reasons discussed in Murray (1996c), I generalize little about usual patterns from my own sexual experiences in Latin America. I would also distinguish "said they are married" from "married to a woman," and did not independently verify the marriages of any of my Mesoamerican sexual partners who told me they were married.

24. In the view of the ostensibly straight males, locker rooms are not "public" space either (see the analysis of one locale in Leap 1996:109–24 and also this volume).

REFERENCES

Allyn, Eric. 1995. *The Dove Coos, II*. Bangkok: Bua Luang.

——. 1997. *The Men of Thailand*. 6th ed. Bangkok: Bua Luang.

Bolton, Ralph. 1992. AIDS and Promiscuity: Muddles in the Models of HIV Prevention. *Medical Anthropology* 14:145–223.

Bolton, Ralph, John Vincke, and Rudolf Mak. 1994. Gay Baths Revisited: An Empirical Analysis. *GLQ* 1:255–73.

Brodsky, Joel I. 1993. The Mineshaft: A Retrospective Ethnography. *Journal of Homosexuality* 24:233–51.

Davis, Murray S. 1983. *Smut: Erotic Reality/ Obscene Ideology.* Chicago: University of Chicago Press.

Friedl, Ernestine. 1994. Sex the Invisible. *American Anthropologist* 96:833–44.

Gallo, John J. et al. 1966. The Consenting Adult Homosexual and the Law: An Empirical Analysis of Enforcement and Administration in Los Angeles County. *UCLA Law Review* 13:643–842.

Glück, Robert. 1985. *Jack the Modernist,* New York: Gay Presses of New York.

Goffman, Erving. 1963. *Stigma.* Toronto: Prentice-Hall.

Humphreys, Laud. 1975. *Tearoom Trade: Impersonal Sex in Public Places.* Chicago: Aldine. (2d ed.)

Jackson, Peter A. 1995. *Dear Uncle Go: Male Homosexuality in Thailand.* Bangkok: Bua Luang.

Johnson, Greg. 1992. The Valentine. In G. Stambolian, ed., *Men on Men* 4, pp. 202–15. New York: Plume.

Johnston, Lynda and Gill Valentine. 1995. Wherever I Lay My Girlfriend, That's Home: The Performance and Surveillance of Lesbian Identities in Domestic Environments. In D. Bell and G. Valentine, eds., *Mapping Desire*, pp. 99–113. London: Routledge.

Kramer, Jerry Lee. 1995. Bachelor Farmers and Spinsters: Gay and Lesbian Identities and Communities in Rural North Dakota. In D. Bell and G. Valentine, eds., *Mapping Desire*, pp. 200–213. London: Routledge.

Laumann, Edward O. and John H. Gagnon. 1995. A Sociological Perspective on Sexual Action. In R. Parker and J. Gagnon, eds., *Conceiving Sexuality*, pp. 183–213. New York: Routledge.

Leap, William L. 1996. *Word's Out: Gay Men's English.* Minneapolis: University of Minnesota Press.

Lee, John Alan. 1978. *Getting Sex.* Toronto: General.

——. 1979. The gay connection. *Urban Life* 8:175–98.

Leupp, Gary P. 1995. *Male Colors: The Construction of Homosexuality in Tokugawa Japan.* Berkeley: University of California Press.

Mead, George Herbert. 1934. *Mind, Self, and Society.* Chicago: University of Chicago Press.

Mohr, Richard D. 1996. Parks, Privacy, and the Police. *The Guide* (January): 16–19.

Murray, Stephen O. n.d. *Cloning.* Manuscript.

——. 1992. Components of *Gay Community* in San Francisco. In G. Herdt, ed., *Gay Culture in America*, pp. 107–246. Boston: Beacon Press. (Revised version in Murray 1996a, pp. 182–214.)

——. 1995. *Latin American Male Homosexualities*. Albuquerque: University of New Mexico Press.

——. 1996a. *American Gay*. Chicago: University of Chicago Press.

——. 1996b. *Angkor Life*. Bangkok: Bua Luang.

——. 1996c. Male Homosexuality in Guatemala: Possible Insights and Certain Confusions from Obtaining Data by Sleeping with the Natives. In E. Lewin and W. Leap, eds., *Lesbian and Gay Ethnography*, pp. 236–60. Urbana: University of Illinois Press.

——. 1997. The Will Not to Know: Islamic Accommodations of Male Homosexualities. In S. Murray and W. Roscoe, *Islamic Homosexualities*, pp. 14–54. New York: New York University Press.

——. 1998. Kamau, a 26-year-old Kikuyu. To appear in S. Murray and W. Roscoe, *Boy Wives and Female Husbands: African Homosexualities*. New York: St. Martin's Press.

Myslik, Wayne D. 1996. Renegotiating the Social/Sexual Identities of Places: Gay Communities as Safe Havens or Sites of Resistance. In N. Duncan, ed., *Body Space: Destablishing Geographies of Gender and Sexuality*, pp. 156–69. London: Routledge.

Rubin, Gayle . 1991. The Catacombs: A Temple of the Butthole. In Mark Thompson, ed., *Leatherfolks*, pp. 119–41. Boston: Alyson.

Sontag, Susan. 1970. *Styles of Radical Will*. New York: Dell.

Styles, Joseph. 1979. Insider/Outsider: Researching the Gay Baths. *Urban Life* 8:135–52.

Taylor, Clark L. 1978. *El Ambiente*. Ph.D. dissertation, University of California, Berkeley.

Tucker, Scott. 1990. Gender, Fucking, and Utopia. *Social Text* 27:3–34.

Williams, Bernard. 1993. *Shame and Necessity*. Berkeley: University of California Press.

Baths, Bushes, and Belonging: Public Sex and Gay Community in Pre-Stonewall Montreal

ROSS HIGGINS

In the "they walk in shadows" world before the Stonewall Riots kicked off the gay liberation movement in New York in 1969, only Liberace was gay, and he denied it.[1] But many men, whether gay-identified or not, engaged in public sexual encounters in parks, saunas baths, cheap movie houses, locker rooms, public toilets, highway rest stops, and other such places in and around major cities. For centuries (if not millennia), places where men took their clothes off, and quite a few where they were not supposed to, were (and are) potential venues for public sex. Though most gay men rarely participate in casual sexual encounters in public places, those who do integrate that experience with their overall participation in the gay world. It is not a separate compartment of experience as it would be for a nongay participant, for instance a suburban husband and father who makes occasional trips to downtown washrooms for sex. Such a man would not have (and would avoid acquiring) a social framework in which to anchor his experiences there, would see fewer familiar faces and share less "common knowledge" with a participating member of the gay world.[2]

In this paper I want to look at the bridge between these two extremes, one that could sometimes form in the arenas of public sex. Though many of the men who engage in public sex never identify as gay, in the days before gay newspapers, community centers, and gay situation comedy characters, some found in the sexual arena a point of entry to the hidden worlds of bars and private gay sociability of the pre-Stonewall era.

Most participants were content, beyond achieving sexual outlet, as Dr. Kinsey would have put it,[3] to limit their symbolic investment in sex to learning just enough of the rituals and codes so that they could function safely and efficiently as public eroticists. The symbolic side of public sex has been described in Laud Humphreys' (1970) widely noted study of public sex in park toilets and in Edward Delph's (1978) participant observation of sex in the washrooms of the New York subways and other locations. Though I find

Delph's rich ethnographic description of this "silent community" very useful, his interpretation of it leaves me dissatisfied. Delph is so committed to
the idea that the community he finds in the toilets is silent that he disregards his own data on speech, ignoring instances of friendships formed in
sexual venues.[4] Of course a lack of verbal communication is the usual pattern in public sex settings, but it is not the only one, and the relations
between the codes he details so well and the broader symbolic structures
they were part of also needs to be investigated.

In researching the development of a sense of community among gay
men from the two major cultural groups in Montreal, I gathered accounts of
public sex from a minority of the men interviewed. This was a nonrandom
sample, selected for their knowledge of a variety of times, places, and social
patterns of gay life in mid twentieth-century Montreal. Thus it cannot be
taken to indicate how prevalent gay involvement in public sex actually was.
Narrators controlled the content of the interviews to a large extent, and it is
possible that some others would have added stories to those gathered from
the men who talked at length about such experiences.

The relatively small number of particularly situated individual accounts,
reflecting a range of class and generational points of view, is not generaliz-
able in a statistical sense, but exemplifies the social and discursive practices of Montreal francophone and anglophone gay men in the 1950s and
1960s. Stories of escapades and arrests in public sex venues reflect the
values and expectations of the specific ethnic, class, and generational
milieux of the tellers and their audiences. Thus members of ethnic and
racial minorities face a different horizon of meanings that influences their
experience of public erotic activity. They employ intersecting, yet different,
community-maintained discursive forms for expressing them. But the variation in point of view does not obscure the fact that some public sex participants were men who identified as gay.[5]

How then did gay men who engaged in sex in sauna baths, parks, movie
theaters, and public washrooms articulate that experience to other aspects
of their gay lives? The experiences of public sex, rendered as narrative and
description in the interview situation, constitute a body of data that illustrates not only the factual backdrop of what went on where, but also the role
they had in the development of a sense of community. They became topics
for meaningful elaboration in gay social and political discourse, in which a
specifically gay point of view was expressed. By enlarging the set of stories
to include a broader range of narrative forms and topical emphases, we can
compare local forms of identification with gay discourse and action concerning public sex (as one of many aspects of gay experience) with the
development of situated points in the discourse of other minority communi-

ties in Montreal, and with the discursive aspects of the formation of gay communities throughout North America.

Defining Gay Community

But what do I mean by "gay community"? I do not find it useful to consider "community" simply as a label for a well-defined standard social entity against which gay social patterns can be measured. Before 1970, any such measurement could only find the gay community wanting, as Murray (1980) suggested in his insightful attempt to apply the criterion of "institutional completeness" to the gay world as a "quasi-ethnic community." Rather, I think that in highly differentiated mass societies, like those in which we know organized gay life has developed in the past two centuries or so, we need to view it as a political objective, an ideal nurtured by conscious community builders in the gay world[6] which they used as a focal topic in developing a new, specifically gay rhetoric. I will argue that such people saw the development of communal consciousness as a means of protecting a valued way of life for a population subject to stringent social opprobrium. To grasp the particularities of gay experience, it is not helpful to conceive of community as a social fact, waiting to be apprehended, as anthropologists have tended to assume in approaching the traditional small-scale societies. In the urban culture of late twentieth-century industrial societies, community is more usefully understood as what Singer (1991:125) termed a "call to action," a project for groups to engage in, a process that requires constant work to construct and maintain. No one opposes community. Raymond Williams (1983:76) observed that the word "community" is never used in a pejorative sense. It is always positive, something we want to be part of. Ethnographies show that even bikers and outlaws have it. As a folk category, it was a natural concept for gay men to apply to the social totality in which they had membership as they came to perceive bonds extending beyond their immediate circle of friends and acquaintances. Yet despite its emphasis on the positive, the concept rests on a series of exclusions, of decisions and discursive enactments of who is and who is not "one of us."[7] In this paper I will look at some aspects of gay men's perception of and action toward nongay others in terms of public erotic activities as part of a larger analysis of collective identity formation.

Sex and Community

Can we retrospectively trace the processes that led at least some men to move from mapping desire onto body parts in the obscurity of the under-

brush to conceiving of themselves as members of a social group too large to
see directly? Samuel Delaney (1988) describes how he experienced this
new perception in New York in the late 1950s. He describes his fear at seeing a raid on the famous "Trucks," a public sex site at the end of Christopher Street, and on visiting a gay bathhouse for the first time:

> What frightened oddly, was not the raid itself, but rather the sheer number
> of men who suddenly began to appear, most of them running, here and
> there from between the vans. . . . (In the 1950s) homosexuality was a soli-
> tary perversion. Before and above all, it isolated you. . . . That there was a
> "gay bar society" was, itself, conceived of in terms of that isolation, and
> was marginal to it. . . . What the exodus from the trucks made graphically
> clear, what the orgy at the baths pictured with frightening range and inten-
> sity, was a fact that flew in the face of that whole fifties image.
>
> (1988: 173–74).

These experiences forced Delaney (perhaps reflecting the impact of the
Kinsey statistics on the prevalence of homosexuality as well) to reconceptu-
alize the social patterns involved with homosexuality on a larger scale. He
had caught a sudden glimpse of the larger gay community.

Among the Montreal narrators I have interviewed, only Patrick had had
such a vision of gays as a social group, but unlike Delaney, his experience
had no connection with public sex. Patrick remembered that this perception suddenly came to him after reading Ed Sullivan's newspaper account
of the Broadway production of Tennessee Williams's *The Milk Train Doesn't
Stop Here Any More* in 1963. Sullivan, as Patrick recalled, had reported,
"We haven't seen so many lavender lads out together since the last time the
Ballets-Russes de Monte-Carlo played New York." Reading this, Patrick
saw all at once the social scope of the gay world, the possibility of gay
crowds dominating public spaces, and caught a glimpse too of the possibilities of community.

But none of the Montreal narrators articulated a link between their experiences of public sex and their perception that there was a large-scale collectivity, a community to which they belonged. Some of the incidents related in the interviews did, however, point to links between the experience of
public sex and the development of a sense of community. I will discuss
three types of links: first, those relating to social networks; second, those
relating to the larger society, which I will call political links; and third, those
of a symbolic nature, relating to the growing awareness among gay men in
urban North America after 1945 that they belonged to a large social group
which shared common language, symbolic systems, interests, and values
distinct from those of the surrounding society.

The most obvious type of link between involvement in public sex and other social relationships is that of acquaintanceship. Thus I am using the term "network link" to refer to encounters in public sex arenas that led to the establishment of social links beyond those venues. There are three kinds of connection to consider: those that provided newcomers with access to the clandestine gay world, those that led to new friendships or other social relationships, and those with people who were already acquaintances.

Gay World Access

For many men, public sex was a continuation of relationships with fellow students in adolescence. One narrator (whom I call Pierre) had extensive experience with other boys, but began a new phase in his sex life when he discovered park sex.

> The first time [he recounted] was completely by accident when I was 17 or 18. I had no idea what went on there. I was studying at the library and went for a walk in the park to take a break . . . It was around 5 or 6 o'clock. In the early 1960s, the park wasn't very busy at that time. It happened in the bushes, where a guy who obviously knew about the place led me. After that, I went back to meet people to have sex with.

But this experience did not connect Pierre to the gay world in general; his coming out into the social scene would not happen until a few years later, when he fell in love with a fellow university student who took him to the bars and introduced him to his friends.

However, some narrators did find their way into the bar world through park sex. Len, for example, had had a number of sexual encounters in suburban parks in his late teens. It did not occur to him that this could lead to a social life organized around sexual orientation until one of his partners told him about the Tropical Room, Montreal's leading downtown gay bar in the 1950s.[8] It took him several preparatory drinks in a nearby nongay bar to get up the courage to climb the stairs to the Tropical. Once there, however, he soon became a regular, and formed a circle of bar-going friends with whom he not only had sexual contact, but established a complex web of social relations that continue to the present.

Another narrator, Trevor, bragged of having organized circle jerks with older boys in the small school he went to when he was only in grade 6. Some time later he discovered sex on the "Mountain" (the usual name for Mount Royal Park) and then progressed to cinemas near where he lived. By his mid-teens he had begun cruising in Dominion Square downtown, and this resulted in an invitation to have a beer at a gay bar when he was six-teen. He said he was amazed and then a little disappointed. It was Friday night, and the place packed, but "nobody looked at me twice."

Meeting New Friends

Both Len and Trevor started building new gay social networks as a result of park contacts. Other venues could produce network links as well. Though toilet sex is generally regarded as being much more anonymous and alien-ated[9] than activity that occurs in other venues, or than the purely social interaction of bars, even such stigmatized activity could sometimes lead to the formation of friendships. For example one of Donald's most entertaining anecdotes revealed a friendship he had made while studying accounting. At Sir George Williams University, he explained, the "interesting" wash-rooms were unfortunately on the same floor as the library. (The interjections in this group interview excerpt are by John, a British friend of Donald's, whose contributions were added in a hilarious mock-Cockney accent, as the two men performed in an uproarious moment of a gay after-dinner con-versation with three other gay men, including myself.)

> [Donald:] [It was] hard to be gay and go to Sir George so much. I would go to the library with best of intentions. . .
>
> [John:] It took the poor cow years to . . .
>
> [Donald:] . . . took me forever to get that fucking degree! But my friend-ships are long-lasting. I met Tim Elton—from one of my classes there. He was married. Still is. We spent many an enjoyable study period there. One night he wore my shorts home by mistake.
>
> [John] (*flatly*): She noticed.
>
> [Donald:] We had to say we'd been exercising at the Y and somehow mixed them up.

In a tone that indicated juicy detail yet to be told, John continued the story by getting Donald to talk about another friendship formed in a toilet:

> [John:] Then he met someone else we all know.
>
> [Donald:] Who?
>
> [John:] Walter.
>
> [Donald:] No, I met him at the washroom of the grocery store in the base-ment of Morgan's Department Store. Very kicky[10] at lunch time. You could get your rocks off at noon. What straight guy could do that so easily?
>
> [John] (*laughing*): And still have time for a deli sandwich!

This sense that gays in the 1950s, as a collectivity, had advantages over heterosexuals was probably not just due to nostalgia, looking back fondly at those days from decades later. Gay men like those in this cohesive group of close friends were aware of it at the time. Thus I think their stories can be taken as clear indicators of how the micropolitics of discourse, even in light-hearted banter, builds of a sense of community.

I have already mentioned parks as places where gay men could meet new friends. Surprisingly, for one narrator, public sex could even lead to business relationships as well. Percy and his lover Walter, who celebrated their sixtieth anniversary in 1993, moved to Montreal soon after they met in Toronto. They had such an open relationship that when Percy met a man he liked on Mount Royal, he brought him home, much to Walter's good fortune. It turned out that the man was one of Montreal's most prominent couturiers. At that time Walter was working on his own, making leather goods in a studio in their apartment. As a result of Percy's little infidelity on the mountain, Walter got a series of contracts to make purses and other accessories to match the shoes of the couturier's wealthy customers. He moved his studio into the basement of the couturier's shop, and continued to do this work until he joined the army when war broke out in 1939. Though the couturier was a married man with a son, the link was social as well as commercial. Walter and Percy were often invited to the family's country place on weekends, and their relationship continued until the couturier moved to California after the war. It's hard to say how much this represented a link to "community," though one assumes the man's wife was aware of what was going on and complicit in her husband's bisexual involvement.

Meeting Old Friends

Public sex venues, in Montreal at least, were places where one could meet old friends as well as new, sometimes with embarrassing results. In the 1950s Donald and his lover Evan were both fond of visiting the back toilets ("cans") of Morgan's Department Store one floor after the other. Apparently all of them could be "interesting." Donald related a funny experience his lover had:

> Once Evan was doing the back cans. On one floor, he ran into someone he did business with. He was very circumspect—made a show of combing his hair, and a comment about seeing the ball game, etc. Fifteen minutes later, they ran into each other on another floor. Evan felt embarrassed, but the other guy said, "Oh, so what! We both have weak bladders."

Even more dramatically, Donald explained how his relationship with Evan changed one day.

We had a policy that wanting to do it [with someone else] was just as bad as doing it. Just cruising someone was as bad as sex. But then one day, I was fed up with my job. I wanted a new one. I had been for an interview and stopped for quick turn at the Kiltie [Lounge] washroom. I was standing at the middle urinal, so whoever came, I was bound to have good view of. And who should come in but Evan. I recognized it! He said, "We'd better talk at home." From then on we both started having serious extracurricular activities.

So sexual relations in public, while they were supposed to be anonymous, silent, and quick, could sometimes be quite otherwise.

Political Links

It is often in relation to outsiders, in their perception of the group, that a collectivity becomes a community (Murray 1980:40). For gay men, relations with outsiders were often traumatic. Several narrators spoke of problems with the police. The consequences of an arrest could devastate an individual, as the suicide of a Montreal doctor after being arrested for inviting a police decoy to a tourist room in 1956 dramatizes.[11]

One anglophone narrator, Ralph, entered gay life in an unusual way thanks to the police. A deeply religious man, Ralph came to Montreal from a small Ottawa valley town in the 1950s to attend a fashion school, much against the wishes of his father. He spent a decade suppressing his desire for other men, immersing himself in his studies and then his job, and filling his spare time with Catholic charities and parish work. By the spring of 1969, he was beginning to feel that it was time to do something about his attraction to men, so after an evening of shopping, he allowed himself to be tempted by two handsome men who cruised him on Ste. Catherine Street. He followed them down into an underground public toilet, but as soon as he went and stood at the urinal between them, even before he had time to unzip, they flashed their badges and took him back up to the street. But the officers were not finished their work for the evening, so they simply handcuffed Ralph to the outside door handle of the police cruiser, leaving him to face down the stares of strolling shoppers on a busy downtown street while they went to entrap others. Later that night, in custody at police headquarters, he told himself that if he could survive this experience, coming out as a homosexual could surely not be that bad. Within a few months Ralph found his way to the bars and became part of a circle of regulars with whom he has maintained friendships ever since.

One francophone narrator told a tale of overt gay resistance. Eugène knew a man who got arrested by a railway policeman in the washroom at Central Station, a well-known cruising spot. However the man was a lot big- ger than the arresting officer, and managed to grab the handcuffs from him, lock the policeman to the washbasin, and make his getaway. One can easily imagine the triumphant tellings and retellings of this tale of outsmarting the authorities, a favorite theme in the discourse of oppressed groups. This story contains within it its own "call to action," the moral that action is sometimes effective.

As well as having effects for the individual, an arrest for public sex could have consequences for a man's friends and acquaintances, and ultimately, for the gay community. When Donald's friend Leo was picked up on the Mountain, their whole group of close friends was deeply concerned over the problem of keeping the secret from his wife and mother-in-law, and helping him cover up absences for his court appearances. In the 1950s, this was dealt with as a purely individual matter, but after 1960, the idea of gay resis-tance or gay action presented by the homophile movement and others became better known, even though Montreal had no group of its own. In inspiring political action, an arrest could have consequences that would eventually extend well beyond the immediate friendship group, and which were surely not intended by the police.

In one such case, Étienne was among fourteen men caught in a raid on the Colonial Steam Bath in the spring of 1962. He had been there with a friend, and said that the police had completely and arbitrarily fabricated an accusation that he had been committing gross indecency with his friend, the very last person in the place he was likely to have sex with.[12] But the friend was the son of a prominent court official, and his name quietly disap-peared from the roster of the accused, whereupon Étienne found himself suddenly accused of indecency with someone else. This lesson in class politics was not the only radicalizing aspect of the experience. Étienne was lucky enough to have an older French friend who had some familiarity with both the group Arcadie in Paris and the American homophile movement. As a result he understood what had happened to him not simply as a per-sonal tragedy, which it was, even though he eventually got off, but as an act of injustice against homosexuals.

In the years that followed, Étienne, in company with his friend Eugène, became increasingly interested in and aware of gay thinking in the United States through their annual trips to the baths of New York. When gay libera-tion hit Montreal in the winter of 1970/71, it was not surprising to find the two friends among the leaders of the "Front de libération homosexuel" that

was created, and other friends of Étienne's, with his arrest story looming
large in their thinking, were there too.

Symbolic Links

Public sex intersects with several orders of symbolic links to collective identity. These range from practical knowledge to the narration of sexual conquests as a group entertainment, to the more abstract symbolization of the group's existence through its assertion of control over the definition of place.

Practical Knowledge

In practical terms, engaging in public sex requires knowledge of where to go and how to act. These aspects are very well documented in Delph's ethnography, and constitute the essential evidence for his "silent" community. In Montreal the places are different, but as Delph points out, the codes are shared internationally. Several narrators were able to produce a long list of toilets, outdoor cruising spots, and saunas that they had been to or heard about.

Narrators not only carried in their heads this factual data, but had access to a prototypical set of conditions and categories that would help them identify likely public sex venues, even in an unfamiliar city. For example, toilet cruising was known to be common in any movie house (not just those where sex took place in the theater but ordinary ones as well), in train and bus stations, hotels and shopping concourses. Parks where sex occurs have certain features concerning access and possible egress in case of police or other forms of attack (well documented by Delph 1978:96–105). Other than the steam room at the Y, a likely venue in any city, finding the cruisiest sports facilities requires local knowledge. Only Montrealers were likely to know about the men-only swimming club on the river that was ostensibly a charitable venture to give impoverished boys a chance to exercise during the summer.

Shared knowledge structures (or schemata) of where to go are supplemented by schemata for what to do and how to act. One narrator described how at fourteen he had learned a technique for toilet sex at the public library in Ottawa:

> I must have gone there because of the movies, I don't think I knew it was gay, and ended up going down and having sex in the washrooms in the basement. Somebody had a shopping bag and told me to stand in the shopping bag so we could have sex in the cubicle. . . . And the second time that happened was at the theater beside Morgan's. There again it was the old shopping bag routine . . .

This technique for disguising the compromising sight of two sets of legs and feet in the washroom cubicle was well known in the gay world, as attested by the vivid description in *Dancer from the Dance* (Holleran 1978), a novel about New York and Fire Island gay life with a character who used the shopping bag technique at Grand Central Station and rode the Long Island Railroad at rush hour for quickies in the toilets. In Montreal, the only man who related using a technique like the second one was Donald, who rode the streetcars after work, going far out of his way if he happened onto a car packed with workmen, hot and sweaty and ready for a little stand-up action on the way home.

Stories

Narrating personal sexual adventures was described by Leznoff (1954:124) as serving a different purpose than simple amusement or knowledge sharing: it determined the relative prestige rankings of members of the gay friendship group in terms of their ability to make sexual conquests.

> The content of conversation within the Overt Participating Homosexual Group[13] was predominantly sexual, while the group itself served as a type of forum where the homosexual came to relate his sexual experiences. . . . Those who were considered physically attractive and easily procured sexual partners held high status, while the individual who was sexually unsuccessful held a correspondingly lower status. The capacities of homosexual to "get sex" were openly discussed, commented upon, and joked about. (1954:124–25)

Donald and his friends may have competed in this way, but they also liked stories just for fun, since they delighted in telling the adventures of their friends as well as their own. Donald knew someone who had a regular rendezvous near the Mountain for some period of time:

> We had a friend who lived near Mount Royal [Avenue] and Park who went for early morning walks and regularly met and blew a milkman several times a week in the tunnel under Park Ave.

He gained no prestige from recounting this story, except in being regarded as an amusing talker and connoisseur of gay lore. Respect for discursive skills and the cultivation of collective memories is surely as important as prowess in the hunt for sex as a basis for prestige in the group. Donald also recounted a story that seems to stem more from the realm of urban folklore than from anecdote:

> There was one awful glory hole in Morgan's in front. Gruesome story. Two-seater can. Some enterprising person had cut through the steel. Some guy's cock was chopped in there. We avoided it like the plague.

Donald could not say how he and his friends knew about this particular story, but it matches too well for coincidence the two variants of a slightly less violent glory hole legend reported by Goodwin (1989:105–6). The elaboration of gay voices in such stories as these, whatever the speaker's purpose or the sociologist's understanding of their social "function," is also, I argue, an expression of community action through discourse. It puts into practice the heritage of social ethics and knowledge of the gay world.

Place And Identity

Alain Sanzio, an early theorist of gay space, writing in the French gay magazine *Masques* in 1980, offers the term "*ghetto sauvage*" for public sex venues. Echoing John's derisive comment that straights couldn't hope to have lunchtime sex, Sanzio sees these gay territories as an enormous advantage that gay men have over heterosexuals. He asserts that they give gays access to space where ordinary social norms do not apply, and are replaced by limited, function-oriented codes (much like those described by Delph). In these spaces, gays not only escape from social control, but also from loneliness and isolation while enjoying the physical presence of our "brothers." Speaking of both the commercial ghetto and the "ghetto sauvage," Sanzio concludes: "The strength I get from the presence of this collective life is what makes it possible to face the rest, knowing that I will be able to return later" (1980:109–10; my translation). Gay space, he says, favors self-acceptance; it is a territory of desire, not necessarily sexual, a desire for life, for social contact.

Though this early text has a polemic ring, I think it points to the important role which spatial mastery played in developing a sense of collective worth among gays in the urban landscape. While little of this type of feeling may be evoked by toilets, dominance over other venues was easily visible for Montreal gays. No one could miss the fact that on bright summer afternoons they controlled two of the city's most dramatic and desirable pieces of real estate. High on the eastern face of Mount Royal, at some times of the day at least, only gays were present to enjoy the splendid panorama of the city and the Saint Lawrence valley beyond. At water level, gays commanded another spectacular view down the river from the Montreal Swimming Club at the eastern tip of Saint Helen's Island, just opposite the harbor. There, according to Len and Henri, nearly 100 percent of the men lounging on the grass or swimming were gay. They were enjoying one of the most visible public spots in the urban landscape, right at the foot of a major bridge. Together with the bars and restaurants to which gay sociability was confined in the winter months, these outdoor spaces made up a set of gay "places," urban space created in word and deed as meaningful locations in the gay city. Maintaining knowledge about them, and using them as themes in gay conversation provided a major anchor of collective self-consciousness in the pre-movement era.

This discussion of the relationship between public sex and the rise in a sense of gay community in Montreal after 1945 has led me to reformulate my understanding of the notion of community. If, as Murray (1980) says, by the 1970s there were gay men who were willing to openly represent gay communal interests by setting up political groups or making cultural statements, this willingness should be seen, I think, as the end result of a long process of self-conceptualization on the collective level. "Communalization," as Weber (1990:91) called it,[14] had been going on since the late nineteenth century (the earliest date for which there is evidence in Montreal is a group of news items from 1869). The stages by which the gays moved toward self-awareness paralleled in some ways the process of identification that individuals go through in accepting themselves as gay.

Individuals respond to the culturally offered schema of what Escoffier (1992) terms the "authentic self." Following this imperative, we experience out sexual orientation as something that we discover in ourselves, our true natures, which then must be expressed socially so that we do not violate the strong cultural rules against dishonesty and hypocrisy. Once many individuals have thought their way through this chain of reasoning, it becomes likely that a sense of community will follow if they find each other. A growing number of authentic individual selves with one particularly salient trait—a tabooed sexual orientation—leads to the formation of an authentic collective self based on that trait. This does not simply happen. It is the result of a conscious effort to develop a collective point of view.

When some members come to perceive that their identity connects them to a wide range of others, they naturally draw on culturally defined concepts of social groups to interpret their experience. From the limited range of folk categories for groups that we are members of, the never negative term "community" is sure to be selected in references that opinion leaders make to the collectivity. The "call to action" that Singer sees in community is a result, then, of an imperative of Euroamerican culture. There should be no surprise that even some of the men who took part in anonymous public sex, presumably those without commitments to family, religious values, or work-related fears that overpowered the impulse to authenticity, would feel its call as strongly as those in other venues, and would act to attach community sentiment to the relationships formed there.

1. I have borrowed the title of a biological, medical, and legal summary by Mercer (1959); Liberace was targeted as gay in the Montreal yellow newspapers and other tabloids of the day.

2. Leznoff (1954:73–80) bases a typology of gay men on the individual's relationship to secrecy concerning his sexual orientation (overt versus covert), and participation in gay life (participating, solitary participating, restricted, or nonparticipating).

3. Kinsey's influence on the realization among gays that they shared a collective identity has not been systematically investigated, though many witnesses report that it had considerable weight in the hostile climate of McCarthy's attacks on communists, and his assumption that "gay" was merely a synonym for "communist."

4. One man Delph knew had met a young friend in a subway toilet (1978:76–77), but this did not enter into his conception of a community completely divorced from verbal discourse.

5. "Gay" was not the term they used at the time, but is used here for convenience, since there is no consensus on what they did call themselves in the 1950s and 1960s.

6. Singer (1991:124–25) reminds us of the Christian ideology of community, and its importance in Christian culture as an orientation to the social world. She also emphasizes the liberal conception of the social contract and the rights of citizens. Similarly, the ethical impetus toward community in liberal ideals of citizenship is stressed by Mouffe (1991). Both authors were members of a collective seminar on community organized at Miami University, which produced a stimulating collection of reflections on the topic (Miami Theory Collective 1991).

7. Elias (1991:157) uses the terms "we-identity" or "we-group" in his framework for the analysis of "established-outsider" relationships which can readily be applied to homosexuals in Euroamerican societies. See Elias and Scotson (1964) for an early formulation of the theory and Mennell's (1994) summary of Elias's conceptual framework.

8. For gay and straight establishments alike, the Montreal bar scene centers on two poles: the more respectable and, in the 1950s, more English-speaking "downtown" scene, and the "Main" (the nickname used in both languages for the Boulevard Saint-Laurent), the French-speaking "East," centered in the old "red light" district. There were also outlying bars in other parts of the city and in surrounding towns and resort areas.

9. There is a sharp distinction in gay taxonomies of place between those where "sex on the spot" is expected, and those where courtship and seduction lead to retiring to some private space for consummation. For many nonparticipants in public sex, it can be a strongly devalued activity.

10. This usage of "kicky" was traced by Rodgers (1972) to the jazz slang "kicks."

11. This incident is discussed in my article (Higgins 1995) on a gay murder in Montreal, which the police followed up with a wave of arrests of gay men, including Dr. Horst Kohl.

12. Leznoff (1954:76) was one of the first to comment on the systematic avoidance of sex between friends, and more recently Weston (1991:119–21) has outlined the history of gay ideological positions on the "friend/more than friend" dichotomy.

13. One of the categories in his typology of gay men mentioned above.

14. Weber even mentions (p. 92) the possibility of an erotic relationship as the basis for developing solidarity, though he did not have gay public sex in mind.

REFERENCES

Delaney, Samuel R. 1988. *The Motion of Light in Water: Sex and Science Fiction in the East Village, 1957–1965*. New York: New American Library.

Delph, Edward William. 1978. *The Silent Community: Public Homosexual Encounters*. Beverly Hills/London: Sage.

Elias, Norbert. 1991. "Changes in the I-We Balance" In Elias, *The Society of Individuals*, pp. 153–237. Oxford: Basil Blackburn.

Elias, Norbert and J. L. Scotson. 1965. *The Established and the Outsiders: A Sociological Enquiry into Community Problems*. London: Frank Cass.

Escoffier, Jeffrey. 1992. "Generations and Paradigms: Mainstreams in Lesbian and Gay Studies" In Henry L. Minton, ed., *Gay and Lesbian Studies*, pp. 7–26. New York: Harrington Park Press.

Goodwin, Joseph P.. 1989. *More Man Than You'll Ever Be*. Bloomington: Indiana University Press.

Higgins, Ross. 1995. "Murder Will Out: Gay Identity and Media Discourse in Montreal." In William L. Leap, ed., *Beyond the Lavender Lexicon: Authenticity, Imagination, and Appropriation in Lesbian and Gay Languages*, pp. 107–32. New York: Gordon and Breach.

Holleran, Andrew. 1978. *Dancer from the Dance*. New York: Morrow.

Humphreys, Laud. 1970. *Tearoom Trade: Impersonal Sex in Public Places*. Chicago and New York: Aldine-Atherton. 2d ed. "Enlarged Edition with a Retrospect on Ethical Issues." New York: Aldine, 1975.

Leznoff, Maurice. 1954. "The Homosexual in Urban Society." Masters thesis, McGill University, Montreal.

Mennell, Stephen. 1994. "The Formation of We-Images: A Process Theory." In Craig Calhoun, ed., *Social Theory and the Politics of Identity*. Oxford: Blackwell.

Mercer, J. D. 1959. *They Walk in Shadow*. New York: Comet Press.

Miami Theory Collective. 1991. *Community at Loose Ends*. Minneapolis: University of Minnesota Press.

Mouffe, Chantal. 1991. "Democratic Citizenship and the Political Community." In Miami Theory Collective, eds., *Community at Loose Ends*, pp. 70–82. Minneapolis: University of Minnesota Press.

Murray, Stephen O. 1980. The Institutional Elaboration of a Quasi-Ethnic Community in Canada." In Joseph Harry and Man Singh Das, eds., *Homosexuality in International Perspective*, pp. 31–43. New Delhi: Vikas. First published 1979, *International Review of Modern Sociology* 9(2): 165–77.

Rodgers, Bruce. 1972. *The Queens' Vernacular: A Gay Lexicon*. San Francisco: Straight Arrow Press. Reissued as *Gay Talk: A (Sometimes Outrageous) Dictionary of Gay Slang*. New York: Paragon Books, 1972.

Sanzio, Alain. 1980. "Les espaces du désir." *Masques: Revue des homosexualités* 6:105–13.

Singer, Linda. 1991. "Recalling a Community at Loose Ends." In Miami Theory Collective, eds., *Community at Loose Ends*, pp. 121–30. Minneapolis: University of Minnesota Press.

Weber, Max. 1962 (1990). *Basic Concepts in Sociology*. New York: Citadel Press.

Weston, Kath. 1991. *Families We Choose: Lesbians, Gays, Kinship*. New York: Columbia University Press.

Williams, Raymond. 1983. *Keywords: A Vocabulary of Culture and Society*. London: Fontana, 2d ed.

Homosex in Hanoi? Sex, the Public Sphere, and Public Sex   **10**

JACOB ARONSON

My friend enters the hotel room excitedly that spring morning in 1990: "They've arrested someone like you," he reports, "It's in the *People's Army Daily* here: yesterday in Lenin Park they arrested one homosexual man like you." "A foreigner?" I ask. "No, no, a Vietnamese man. He was arrested in the park." "For having sex with foreigners?" I continue. "No, it was because he would beat up his Vietnamese partners and rob them after they finished having sex," my friend explains. He shows me the article in *Quan Doi Nhan Dan,* the *People's Army Daily,* a widely read newspaper that curiously juxtaposes the latest ideological pronouncements of the Vietnamese military with true-crime reports and scandal-mongering reminiscent of the *National Enquirer.* The arrest, I later learn, was part of a nationwide crackdown on vice and corruption initiated in response to the global crumbling of communism, a police effort to improve both the quality and the image of party members and government officials while at the same time reminding those who might be inclined toward lawlessness that the government remained capable of asserting its authority (cf. Voice of Vietnam 1990).

So what was the intended message of the arrest and its attendant publicity: that homosexuality was forbidden, or that the police were ever-vigilant to protect tricks from dishonest hustlers? I could only speculate, since I could certainly not go to the police to inquire. But I was led to speculate further: how was it that my friend was so certain about what the police really intended with their arrest, when the newspaper did not specify so? Was he a police informer, perhaps compelled to cooperate in the entrapment of foreign men so as to avoid punishment for himself being homosexual? Had his contacts with me over the past few weeks—contacts that were sexually charged but physically unconsummated—been encouraged or even ordered by police seeking to gather incriminating evidence against me? Or were his intentions honorable?

The Italian explorer Cristoforo Borri rejoices in 1631 that the
Cochinchinese[1] "do not lie under that great impediment to receiving the
grace of the gospel, that is, the sin of sodomy, and others contrary to
nature, which is frequent in all the other eastern countries, the very name of
which the Cochin-Chinese naturally abhor" (1811 [1631]: 828). Samuel
Baron, a half-century later, emphasizes that "with no less disdain [the
Tonkinese] reject that law of their neighbours which encourageth the most
execrable and abominable vice not fit to be nam'd" (1732 [1685]: 23). In
1778, missionary Jérome Richard notes that "One cannot reproach any of
them for the abominable vices, outraging Nature, and which are only too
common, in climates as hot as Tonquin" (Richard 1778, 2:282). By the
account of Baron Antoine de Montyon,[2] writing in 1812, "violation of the
laws of nature and the shameful perversions of love, common and often
indecently public in the hot countries, are unknown in [Tonkin]" (in "La
Bissachère" 1812, 2:47–48).[3] In the waning days of the French empire,
one visitor to the penal colony at Poulo Condore was pleased to hear
"Another remark favorable to the Annamite . . . [i.e.,] that he does not, by
taste, submit to the games that flourished at Sodom and Gomorrah"
(Demariaux 1956:249–50). A Vietnamese and an American psychiatrist
writing together in 1975 (in the waning days of the American empire) note
that "homosexual activity is clearly condemned in Vietnam . . . the Vietnamese consider homosexuality shameful . . . [and] have no socially established role for the homosexual or transsexual" (Heiman and Cao Van Le
1975:91). One recurrent tendency of commentators for several centuries,
then, has been to displace homosexuality from the Vietnamese public
realm entirely, to deny even the possibility of its existence.

This displacement has also long been institutionalized in official silence:
the ancient legal codes of the Le Dynasty (1428–1787) and the Nguyen
Dynasty (1802–1945) detail the penalties for crimes such as heterosexual
rape, assault, adultery, and incest, but leave homosexuality unmentioned
(Nguyen Ngoc Huy and Ta Van Tai 1987; Philastre 1909). The only provisions in the codes that *may* refer to homosexuality (and at that, only
ambiguously) are one prohibition against "men who wear weird or sorcer-
ous garments" (Le Code, article 640 in Huy and Tai 1987, 1:269) and
another article prohibiting castration and autocastration (Le Code, article
305 in Huy and Tai 1987, 1:183; Nguyen Code, article 344 in Philastre
1909, 2:552). Huy and Tai note that both of these provisions are not found
in earlier Chinese codes, but were Vietnamese innovations (1987, 2:174;
1987, 2:326). Vietnamese legal codes were typically influenced by then-
contemporary Chinese codes, but when in 1740 the Ching Dynasty in
China elaborated, "for the first time in Chinese history, punishment for

sodomy between consenting adults" (Ng 1989:76; cf. Meijer 1985), the
Vietnamese did not follow suit, once again omitting any such prohibitions in
the Nguyen Code that was promulgated soon after.

In the colonial and postcolonial era this legal silence on homosexuality
was maintained. The French colonials never instituted explicit prohibitions
against sodomy or pederasty in their colonies, since under the Code
Napoléon such vices did not fall under the explicit purview of the legal system (Sol and Haranger 1930:2)—although in France the silence in legal
codes did not inhibit police persecution of men-who-loved-men, under
more general prohibitions against disorderly conduct or offenses against
decency (Copley 1989). The situation is similar today: although homosexuality or sodomy is not specifically referred to anywhere in modern Vietnamese criminal law, "sex buying and selling in any form" are prohibited
(Voice of Vietnam 1993), as are more general and diffuse crimes such as
"undermining public morality" (the prohibitions against "weird garments"
have disappeared). As Dao Xuan Dung and Le Thi Nham Tuyet point out in
1996, "The Vietnamese State has not yet had legal documents about
homosexuality. Even in the latest Law on Marriage and Family (1986), there
is not an article mentioning the State attitude or even any guidelines for
public opinion about this problem. The Penal Code doesn't mention homosexuality while it has articles on incest, rape, prostitution, sexual assault,
child marriage" (Dung and Tuyet 1996:30). When two Vietnamese men
held a marriage ceremony in Ho Chi Minh City in March 1997, authorities
acknowledged the lack of controlling legal authority: " 'If we'd known about
[the wedding] we would have stopped it,' a police official was quoted by the
Nguoi Lao Dong paper as saying. 'But we can't fine them because we don't
have any laws to punish them' " (Reuters 1997).

A second tendency of commentators has been to dislocate homosexuality's origins away from a golden space-time of Vietnamese tradition, conceiving it as a polluting force from outside, imported to Vietnam by intruding
foreigners. In the early days of European empire, the tendency was that if
pederastic practices were acknowledged, foreigners—sometimes Chinese,
sometimes Europeans—were blamed for introducing them to Vietnam.[4] De
Montyon insists that "if they take place, as shown by the rarity and obscurity of these vices, they cannot be considered native" (in "La Bissachère"
1812, 2:48). (Almost two centuries after de Montyon, a Vietnamese ethnologist tells me that, "In the traditional village, there was no homosexuality.
That was something the French and Americans introduced. It's not part of
Vietnamese culture.") Military physician Matignon contrasts the situation in
Indochina with the pervasive pederasty he encountered in China, since
"the Annamite, who in so many ways recalls the Chinese, had no acquain-

tance with pederasty, which was surely imported to Tonkin by the European" (1900:189). He continues that "pederasty is very much practiced in
Tonkin by our [French] nationals: this sad habit, combined with the even
more frequent opium smoking, is not likely to give the Annamites a very
high idea of their protectors" (1900:192).

While some observers portrayed the French colonials themselves as
innocent victims of the hot tropical climate, isolation, temptation, and the
corrupting morals of the Vietnamese, physician Roux concurs with de Montyon and Matignon in seeing the Vietnamese as students in vice of the colo-
nizing French: "The licentious mores of certain of our compatriots make it
difficult [for the Vietnamese] to maintain a virtuous path" (Roux 1905:345).
The blame was sometimes shared, or the Vietnamese damned with faint
praise, as by the "old colonial" Kobiet:

> One could affirm that the responsibility for these [homosexual] disorders
> falls more onto the Europeans than the Annamites; the latter debase
> themselves for a few piasters, so as to satisfy their other vices such as
> gambling and opium, but, in my acquaintance, Annamites do not have
> the habit to degrade themselves with one another, even if their morals are
> far from being exemplary. (1953:9)

In this second tendency, then, pederasty is deemed possible, but it is
translocated to some exotic foreign place outside of Vietnam—it is once
again displaced from the public space of Vietnamese culture and conceived as a polluting or corrupting influence of external origins.[5] The emergent colonial cities of Hanoi and Saigon, Haiphong and Danang, came to
represent hotbeds of cosmopolitan degeneracy, contrasted with the idyllic
and timeless countryside of the traditional peasantry. Thus novelist Farrère
describes Saigon as Sodom (1905), and physician Roux, like my anthropologist friend today, considers pederasty to be an urban phenomenon: "We
even think that pederasty is rare in the countryside. In the town it becomes,
as in our cities, the prize of senile passions or of degenerate sexual
appetites" (Roux 1905:347). Cities were the home of large Chinese immi-
grant populations, who were stereotyped in Vietnam and elsewhere as the
ambassadors of sodomy and the sources of prostitution, opium, and
crime.[6] Thus, journalist Jammes writes of the Cholon district of Saigon that
"Sodom, Gomorra, and Stamboul have nothing to envy in the Chinese city,
in whose plutocratic interiors license flourishes without obstacles, without
the law being able to show its power" (Jammes 1900:65).

Cities, as the loci where colonial and colonized interacted most intimate-
ly, were also the home of dangerously marginal people who were seen by
the colonials as deracinated (Pujarniscle 1931:91) and deculturated—no

longer Vietnamese, but never to become French. These interpreters, mis-
tresses, houseboys, métis, and métisses were condemned as "those who
have been deformed, morally, in the cities that they inhabited after leaving
their villages" (Roux 1905:345). Geographer Joleaud-Barral notes that "the
peasant, the 'nhaque,' has kept the qualities of his race, but the Annamite
of the cities—he who has drawn near us, who has become interpreter,
orderly in our quarters, the Annamite who becomes the domestic of the
Europeans—has taken all of our defects, without taking any of our qualities" (Joleaud-Barral 1899:13). Importantly, these notions of urban degeneracy—of "*acculturation manqué*" ("failed acculturation") among city residents and the nouveaux riches (Nguyen Van Phong 1971:256; cf. pp.
229–30, 271)—were not possessed by the French colonials alone: they
were interiorized by indigenous Vietnamese authors, whether writing in
French (Yeager 1987:63–90) or in Vietnamese (Hoang Ngoc Thanh
1991:144–67).

Vietnamese socialist ideology calls for three revolutions: the revolution in
the relations of production, the scientific and technological revolution, and
the ideological and cultural revolution; the goal and intended outcome of
the latter are to create a new, socialist culture and a New Socialist Man
(see, e.g., Le Duan 1976; Truong Chinh 1977). The New Socialist Man is
distinguished most sharply from those persons shaped under the "enslav-
ing, mongrel, decadent, and utterly reactionary 'culture' " created by the
United States in South Vietnam, in which people led "an individualistic,
egoistic life of depravation" and were induced to indulge the "basest
instincts and the most vulgar tastes." By Le Duan's account, "The evil
intention of U.S. imperialism was to destroy all traditional moral values and
the wholesome way of life of our people, to debauch young people and
make hoodlums out of them" (1976:190). While female prostitution and
drug addiction are explicitly listed as examples of this depraved debauch-
ery, homosexuality remains both invisible and unuttered.[7] Within the public
image of the New Socialist Man, there is little room for sexuality, let alone
homosexuality. What Stephen O. Murray has described as "the will not to
know" (ms., 1994) permeates contemporary Vietnamese society, allowing
cadres, for example, to eat in sumptuary fashion in a ministry-owned
restaurant in Hanoi, under the shadow of television screens pumping out
(heterosexual) pornographic videos, in an ostensible state of pure unknowing. It is then hardly more difficult to unknow that homosexuality exists, to
ensure that it remains unacknowledged and inexplicit in the public
sphere.[8]

But it would be wrong to blame this complicity of silence solely on the socialist revolution. In the traditional Vietnamese worldview, strongly pervaded by neo-Confucian ideologies of family and filiation, it is virtually unimaginable that one might live life exclusively as a homosexual, because that would constitute a grave and unpardonable breach of filial obligations: "The Annamite loathes dying without being assured of male dependants. One can say that there exists a veritable obligation, of the religious or at least mystical order, to give birth as early as possible to the cult's heir" (Khèrian 1937:29). To eschew marriage in favor of an exclusively homosexual life is a choice that hardly needs to be suppressed by civil authorities, because the authority of tradition itself has sufficient force to ensure virtually total compliance. Ethnologist Nguyen Van Huyen noted in 1939 that "male celibacy is always in complete disfavor. It continues to be considered as an act of filial impiety. In certain villages the celibate are not allowed to attend the communal fetes. . . . In everyday life they are the object of mistrust and mockery from their families" (Nguyen Van Huyen 1944 [1939]:41).

The tenacity of this traditional stricture is evident from current census data: of Vietnamese males over age 40, both nationwide and in the city of Hanoi, barely 1% have never married. In rural areas the percentage is .9%, and even in Saigon, the urban area with the highest proportion of unmarried men, those over 40 who never married constitute only 3.6% of the population (Vietnam Population Census, 1989), and many of these are likely to be demobilized soldiers of the former regime and consequently not very desirable marriage partners. In the United States, by comparison, fully 6.4% of all males over 40 have never married, and in San Francisco the proportion is as high as 28.9% of males over age 35 (U.S. Population Census, 1990).[9]

But even if homosexuality has little place in the Vietnamese public sphere, the invisible is sometimes seen, the unutterable sometimes spoken. At a Comedy Revue in 1990 in the Soviet-Vietnamese Palace of Culture (the name has since changed), my friend translates the dialogue to me as we watch a sketch: "Look, look, there's someone like you," he says, pointing to the young man being scolded on stage by his father. Indeed, I begin to notice, the son is somewhat effete and seems to be the target of admonition for his indolence or ineptitude, to the delighted amusement of the audience. A moment later, his sister arrives on stage with her handsome boyfriend, who contrasts strikingly with the increasingly effeminate brother. The brother virtually swoons, enraptured with the handsome young man who stands a head taller than he, posing robustly, almost in a parody of the stage hero of an agitprop drama. As the sibling rivalry over the suitor is made manifest, the audience howls with laughter and my friend need not translate the remaining dialogue.

For those who know where and how to look, though, there is often much more to see. In 1990 my friend had spotted me while I was changing money at the bank, tipped off, he explained, by my maroon pants. By the time we'd finished a walk around the Lake of the Redeemed Sword in the center of old Hanoi, we'd determined, through that elegant verbal ballet familiar to gay men everywhere, that we could speak openly about things usually left unsaid.

Hoan Kiem Lake, the Lake of the Redeemed Sword, turns out to have many interesting sights for those not committed to unknowing. In 1993, I stroll out on a misty evening and take a seat on a lakeside bench. Young couples, with little prospect of privacy in their family's tiny apartments, come here to snuggle together in a curiously public intimacy; groups of children bicycle past on their way to buy ice cream; and Western tourists—business executives, well-dressed retirees, or backpackers alike—stride purposefully past. In their midst are a few solitary young men, slowly walking their bicycles around the lake's edge or sitting, like me, alone at a bench. When I first visited Hanoi in 1985, Vietnamese were not supposed to talk to foreigners, barely even to make eye contact with them. Now there are many eager to try out their English, even if it extends no further than "Hello, what is your name?" One night I strike up a conversation with a university student, studying English at the Foreign Languages University. He insists on inviting me to be his guest at one of the nearby cafes, where we have tea and ice cream while speakers blare out disco songs and the video screen shows images of scantily clad women doing aerobic dances. The loud music makes conversation difficult, so the student says little until the screen images change to those of a musclebound male bodybuilder on a beach. "He is very handsome, yes?" my friend asks, but soon it is time for him to go home to study and we part, after an overly long handshake.

By Matignon's 1900 account, we are hardly the first to have engaged in a little cruising beside the lake:

> In Hanoi, it is not rare to be snagged in the evening, on the main promenade around the lake, by little gamins speaking French—and what French, my god!—"M'sieur cap'taine! Come with me—me is a very nasty boy," that is the invitation. The governors general are rightfully upset, and have taken severe police measures, but their efforts have not been entirely crowned with success. (Matignon 1900:192)

And Briton Michael Davidson describes meeting around 1950 a "small and vivacious Tonkinese who became my companion" while he was visiting "an elegant and diminutive pagoda" (i.e., Ngoc Son pagoda) alongside "a small, curling, carefully drawn lake [Hoan Kiem] with a stone bridge at one end, green parkland around it, and pleasantly eccentric trees bending from its banks over the water" (Davidson 1988:142–43). Elsewhere he describes "being charmingly enticed into the little island temple on the edge of the lake . . . by an acolyte and shown delights which can't, I'm sure, have been liturgical" (Davidson 1962:285). Around the same lake today there are gamins to be sure, as economic reform shreds the social welfare safety net that was once part of the socialist social contract, and Vietnam joins the United States in seeing homeless mendicants on the streets of every city. For some young men, a shoeshine kit provides not only a paltry living but also a pretext to converse with a foreigner—a conversation that might finally lead back to the visitor's hotel.

But my eye catches those not of street-kids or shoeshine boys but of neatly dressed young men. "Hello, what is your name?" one says to me as I walk by a few nights later. As I sit down, the familiar litany proceeds: "How long have you been in Vietnam? Are you a businessman? What hotel are you staying at?" We chat for a while, trying to guess from a distance the nationality of foreign tourists as they approach on the sidewalk—"German? Or Polish?"—speculating until they are close enough that we can hear what language they speak. The French are always unmistakable, the Australians and Americans hard to distinguish from one another. Soon come the important—if ostensibly innocuous—questions: "How old are you? Are you married?" If it is a sociolinguistic truism that Southeast Asians tend to speak indirectly about things, it is even more true that Vietnamese and their foreign friends have developed exquisite skills of circumlocution, of elaborate paralipsis, in which the topic of conversation never gets spoken but is nonetheless certainly understood for being unsaid. Indeed, "don't ask, don't tell" could well serve as the national motto, whether it is sex or politics we are not talking about.

So for me to identify myself as a forty-year-old unmarried man to a Vietnamese man of similar age and marital status is enough for both of us to understand we also likely share other attributes, especially when that conversation takes place in what we both know to be a sexually charged setting. And so it may be that we never use the words that would explicitly define ourselves or our shared interests, nor do we have to. While there may be little doubt about this man's sexual identity, there are other aspects of his identity that give me greater pause. For one cannot forget the reason for our verbal ballet: the affinity we share is one that might not easily survive public scrutiny. Just as the French authorities a century earlier, the police in Hanoi today have the discretion to arrest my friend, or myself, for homosexuality

(or undermining public morality, or assaults against decency) should they
so wish.

Indeed, I can only assume that the police must know what I am up to, if it is not in fact a police agent or informer with whom I am chatting. Jammes, writing in 1898, remarks on "the sometimes criminal benevolence of the morals police" charged with controlling vice: "Aren't the brothel *boys* often precious informers for the local police? We are led to say that these interested scoundrels pay a monthly fee to certain unscrupulous Annamite agents" (Jammes 1898:233).[10] In an authoritarian state, citizen or visitor alike must assume that one's actions are well-known to security officials, and yet we each draw lines beyond which we will not stray, often a line that separates "identity" from "behavior," "sexuality" from "sex." Not only have my contacts with Vietnamese men always stopped well short of overtly sexual behavior, my friends and I have engineered our conversations to allow plausible deniability should the need arise. We have each willed ourselves not to know too much about the other. Yet in the end, is this anything other than convenient self-deception? Can I be sure that Vietnamese authorities, any more than those in Georgia or the U.S. military, will really be satisfied with my careful sophistries distinguishing between who I am and what I do?

In North America in the late 1990s, we gay men assume that we will not generally be subject to arrest simply because of our identities or our orientations, and we feel secure engaging in (almost) all kinds of sexual behavior within private settings. Our notion (accurate or not) is that we risk incurring judicial attention only when our actions somehow violate the carefully inscribed threshold demarcating public and private realms and separating those behaviors deemed "appropriate" for each. So "public sex," with its attendant risks of criminal sanctions, is seen to involve actions out of place: sexual acts and activities that are performed in settings accessible to non-participants, rather than being confined to their notionally proper place, the private realm. Because they are potentially visible by others, thus intruding into the public sphere, the acts are consequently considered to be of greater concern to "the public" and thus to its designated guardians, the police. For most of us, then, most of the time, "public sex" entails sex *acts*, not simply "talking dirty"—indeed, much of the attraction that public sex holds for many men involves the manipulation of silence rather than speech, as literary renditions of public sex make clear. And "sex acts" are most often understood to be those defined in legal, psychological, or clinical discourses that speak of physical contacts between bodily parts in prohibited combinations and configurations.

Whether we do high theory or low praxis (and whether we do it in ivory towers or public parks), we tend to replicate in diverse ways this notion that behavior and identity are severable. Thus certain theorists assert an analytical difference between behavior and identity, an analytical distinction that reflects some empirically verifiable social reality (at least, for those theorists who admit the possible existence of a social reality). Some propose, for example, a historical threshold in the Western cultural tradition that separates prior conceptions centered on specific behaviors from emergent conceptions of roles and identities. The threshold may also be geographic or cultural rather than chronological: comparativists insist that culture-specific bundlings of behaviors and identities should not be applied heedlessly to cultures that potentially bundle things differently. Politically, gay and lesbian conservatives reacting to progressive or liberationist gay and lesbian political movements insist that "good gays" can earn "a place at the table" if heterosexual others would simply separate behaviors (especially stigmatized ones) from identities (which would thus somehow magically lose their stigma). Pragmatically, people are accustomed to acting and interacting as if behaviors are not automatically and perfectly predictive of identities, as if one may engage in transgressive sex acts while never self-identifying as a sexual transgressor. Indeed, the folk knowledge of the gay culture embodies in countless ways the experience that someone engaging in homosexual acts may indeed have a very unexpected identity, for instance that of a policeman engaged in entrapment or a queerbasher engaged in erotic foreplay to his intended violence.

When queer theorists on the one hand, or just plain queers on the other, carefully distinguish "identity" from "behavior," we think we speak a common tongue and operate with stable understandings of those terms—understandings that we share even with those who find our identities objectionable and our behaviors improper. It is not just theorists or intellectuals who propose analytical distinctions like these: they are also embodied in public consciousness and legal institutions. Indeed, the severability of "identity" and "behavior" is the rhetorical keystone of many of the most repressive and retrograde laws, policies, and ideologies that threaten our existence as gay folk. Fundamentalist Christians "love the sinner, but hate the sin"; the U.S. military pretends only to prosecute behavior and promises not to persecute identity; politicians piously profess their tolerance of "what they do in the privacy of their bedrooms." But their intolerance depends upon *our* self-victimizing complicity in *their* rhetorical distinction between actions and essences—complicity which has the unintended effect of licensing and legitimating their acts of repression (repression which is, of course, visited—often violently—both upon our minds and identities as well as upon our bodies and behaviors).

Public sex is one of several transgressions that throw that specious distinction into question or confusion, by juxtaposing and recombining "behavior" and "identity" in novel ways—ways that threaten received notions of both. As Leap has pointed out (essay 6) for men engaging in male-to-male sexual acts in health clubs, one may practice the behaviors quite publicly yet disclaim—even repudiate—the identity, both publicly and privately. The same has long been noted for sexual contacts in parks or other public settings that are accessible to all without regard to self-identification. But public sex also exposes unmistakably the tenuousness of the distinction at the moment it is repressed: typically, identity and behavior are conflated or collapsed and people face legal or extralegal sanctions *not* for their erotic interactions or genital contacts but simply for their speech—for "soliciting" an illegal act, for example, or for "using obscene language" (Higgins 1995:116; Rubin 1985:269)—or even for "looking funny" at a homophobe.[11]

The convenient fictions that encourage us to pretend we live in a tolerant society are punctured and deflated when "public sex" is punished, especially as is usually the case where that "sex" amounts to nothing more than "soliciting" or "loitering" or "frequenting a public nuisance." The acts that are ostensibly punished here are not defined by their practitioners or by the law as sexual acts, and indeed it is clearly our homosexual identity itself that is criminalized rather than any sexual behavior. This is nowhere more apparent than in the U.S. military regulations that purport to concern themselves only with behavior, yet rest upon the virtually unrebuttable presumption that those who simply identify themselves as homosexual possess a "predilection" for prohibited acts. The public speech act of self-identification is criminalized just as surely as the private sex acts that it may refer to. Indeed, the sign "homosexual" may not refer to *any* sex acts, if we accept as we must the possibility that one may identify fully and publicly as homosexual (and be so identified by others) without ever having engaged in the behaviors "constitutive" of that identity (cf. Murray 1996:202ff.). And by consequence, "public sex" when applied to gay people may simply mean any kind of public displays of affection or public affirmations of one's orientation, identity, or desires—behaviors that would never be identified as sex acts if practiced by those identified as heterosexual.

The Tet holidays in February 1996 coincide with a campaign by the Vietnamese forces of public order to increase enforcement of laws regulating "social evils" such as prostitution and gambling. The campaign is characterized by international journalists as a repressive anti-Western, anticapitalist effort to root out cultural pollution and contaminating influences from abroad and to preserve the ever-diminishing authority of the party and state (see, for example, Chalmers 1996a, 1996b, 1996c; Richburg 1996). Yet the only chill that the visitor perceives is in the weather, as the new year is greeted by temperatures colder than they have been anytime in the past twenty years. International guidebooks for gay travelers are still silent about Vietnam, but Internet users can be advised that Hoan Kiem Lake is the place to go in Hanoi for cruising, and a half-dozen cafes, bars, and discos are recommended as meeting places in Ho Chi Minh City.

At Hoan Kiem Lake, the shoeshine boys are more insistent than ever, even if their English vocabulary still goes hardly further than a few words. And maybe it is the cold weather that impels some young men to speak more directly than they would have in previous years: "Let me invite you to a very special bar I know about, where men go with women," one tells me, "or men go with men." Another man moves in quick succession from asking the innocuous questions, "What is your name? Where do you come from?" to the straightforward, yet still exceedingly polite, "Pardon me, I am gay. Do you want to sleep with me?" Some, though, take on a hectoring tone: "I know what you want, you want a boy. Why are you talking to that one? Why don't you take my friend here? What's the matter, don't you think he is handsome? I know a hotel you can go to." Or, stung by my lack of interest, one man rails at me: "I know what you want. You should be on Nguyen Dinh Chieu street [adjoining Lenin Park]; that's where the [male] prostitutes are."

The visitor's apprehensions are not necessarily assuaged by the greater explicitness of speech. Police around the lake seem to be far more numerous than previously—there to target criminals such as pickpockets and petty thieves, according to news accounts, and during the Tet holiday itself, to enforce the recent national ban on firecrackers. Most encounters are still shrouded in ambiguity and deniability, leaving the interlocutors free to disclaim criminal actions or even intent. Yet the ambiguity also creates substantial sexual excitement, in the highly charged context combining risk and recklessness, exposure and concealment, knowing and unknowing, public and private.

So, what should be my response when my Vietnamese colleague and friend of long standing tells me, "In the traditional village, there was no homosexuality. That was something the French and Americans introduced." Do I join in the playful banter when Vietnamese friends—people I met when they were studying in the United States—are teasing another friend because his name sounds to them like "gay?" When a translator, formerly a tourist guide, tells me about an American male tourist who invited him to his room one evening, with intentions that were unanticipated by the guide, do I ask the myriad questions I would like to ask, or do I let the subject drop? In Vietnam, where homosexuality's place in the public sphere is vastly different from its place in the United States, and where the consequences of identifying as homosexual—whether publicly or privately—remain uncertain to foreigners and indigenes alike, what does a visiting ethnographer decide to publicize about himself to colleagues, friends, and villagers?

Recent years have seen increasing attention to the question of how an ethnographer's sexuality and his or her ethnographic fieldwork are interimplicated (see, e.g., Lewin and Leap 1996; Kulick and Willson 1995; Seizer 1995; Williams 1993; Bolton 1992; Proschan 1990; Warren 1988; Whitehead and Conaway 1986; Hamabata 1986). We have often been inclined to leave vitally important elements of our personhood back home when we depart for the field, obscuring signs not only of our gender but especially of our sexuality, adopting new, asexualized professional identities. We constrain to the realm of the private things we are otherwise accustomed to saying or doing in public; we surrender, at least temporarily, our fierce attachments to individualism and to subjectivity.

Partaking as ethnologists in the conjoined roles of tourists and colonials, we curiously forsake the sexual license that both roles afford—or at least we disavow it by our professional silence, even if we may perhaps indulge it secretly (perhaps donning the robes of a third role, that of missionaries).[12] In this case we are like those we study: we, like they, operate through a series of displacements. Vietnamese society today offers little space within the public sphere of sociopolitical discourse even to discuss homosexuality—although Vietnamese men-who-love-men report that the situation is ever improving. For good or bad, AIDS prevention efforts ignore the possibility of homosexual transmission, demonizing drug injectors and female prostitutes alone as the vectors of infection. Happily, gay men are not similarly demonized; unhappily, gay men and their health risks are virtually ignored. If homosexuality *can* be talked about, it is most often translocated to places beyond the frontiers of nation and tradition, conceived as a problem imported to Vietnam by the Other. Like the Vietnamese, we as anthropologists similarly situate sexual activity in some neverwhere, neverwhen: either we do it but don't talk about it, or we talk about it but don't do it, or we don't do it and don't talk about it.

Working in Vietnam I have been inclined toward the latter strategy, while at the same time carving out areas in which, I tell myself, I can maintain some greater degree of integrity as a sexually sentient being. I keep private from my closest friends some of the most important aspects of my self-identity, while sharing in public with virtual strangers our shared identity as men-who-love-men. But to what extent can we even talk about "public" and "private" when they are delineated in ways quite different from our own understandings, and when they interpenetrate in ways that are literally unknowable?

Young couples seeking a venue for intimacy flee the overbearing privacy of their homes in favor of the most public of settings, where darkness confers some small shield of anonymity. A whole slew of "garden cafes" provide tree-shaded places for young lovers to meet; those who cannot afford the cafes eagerly seek out empty park benches, especially those hidden in obscurity under drooping branches. In a city where indoor plumbing is far from universally available, public curbs become the site of private acts that range from bathing to shitting, while the passing public un-sees those so engaged. The protectors of *public* morality are concerned more than anything else with *private* acts, and the "secret" police are no secret to anyone. And surely they must be no less adept than I at finding those public places where men come together for those glances that last a moment too long, those synchronized head-turnings and innocuous greetings, those handshakes that are an infinitesimal instant overlong or an infinitesimal degree overtender—those public places that hold out the promises of private pleasures.

ENDNOTES

1. Older sources use the names Tonkin, Annam, and Cochinchina for territories that are now part of Vietnam, and Tonkinese, Annamite, and Cochinchinese respectively for the inhabitants of those areas whose descendants are now known as Vietnamese. In citing older sources, I repeat the then-current usage.

2. By Maybon's account, the 1812 edition attributed to La Bissachère is indeed heavily revised by de Montyon; the cited passages cannot be found in La Bissachère's original notes (Maybon 1920).

3. Insofar as the early travelers based their accounts on short visits where they had little opportunity for direct contact with Vietnamese people, they necessarily depended on local informants and thus are reporting societal norms and public ideologies of behavior rather than actual social life or observed behaviors. Their pious denials, necessarily based on negative evidence, cannot by consequence be considered evidence that homosexuality did not in fact exist in precolonial Vietnam. It remains to be seen whether these early travelers who were almost completely dependent on indigenous informants might have more accurately communicated local attitudes and ideologies than later writers who relied more upon their own "field research" and direct observations, presenting their own perceptions rather than the opinions of local people.

4. My discussion here necessarily relies on colonial sources that typically inform us more about interethnic sexuality than they do about indigenous Vietnamese

behaviors and identities. With a few exceptions, e.g., the Vietnamese legal codes discussed above, we have no documents that would inform us about local attitudes and
perceptions, and must rely on outsiders' accounts.

5. This is of course a well-established pattern, expressed in language, literature,
and political rhetoric: in French, homosexuality is known as *"le vice allemand"* and *"le
vice italien"*; the English word "bugger" derives from "Bulgar"; the expressions "Greek
love" or *"l'amour grec"* have their counterparts in many languages. In modern African
fiction, according to Cobham, "first the Arab, then the European colonizers are presented as the sources of all evil and corruption in sub-Saharan Africa, as evidenced by
their decadent sodomite practices" (Cobham 1992:46). See also Goldberg's discussion of Spanish colonial accounts of an Inca story where "sodomy is something that
comes from the outside, and is not native at all" (1991:50). The tendency has crucial
implications today, when AIDS is regularly conceived as originating elsewhere and
imported to a given country by female prostitutes and male homosexuals.

6. See, among others, Bleys (1995), Hyam (1990), Junod (1912–13).

7. Female prostitution in South Vietnam during the American period is discussed
in Bergman (1975), Mai Thi Tu and Le Thi Nham Tuyet (1978), and Eisen (1984).
Recent initiatives of the Vietnamese government include a "Resolution on Prostitu-
tion Control" of January 29, 1993 (Voice of Vietnam 1993) and an article in the
Party's theoretical journal (Bui Thien Ngo 1993). For drugs see, e.g., *The Struggle
Against Drugs* (1982).

8. I use "public sphere" here in a way suggestive of but not intending to implicate
in its strictest sense Habermas's idealization of the bourgeois Western European
public sphere of "private people come together as a public" to engage as equals in
"critical-rational discourse" (1989). As I use the term, it encompasses the realm of
public discourse (without presupposing that interlocutors are equal or that they are
ensured of the right to speak freely), the realm of public behavior of all sorts, the
realm of public media, and the realm of public spaces and sites.

9. Clearly, the set "those who have engaged in male-to-male sexuality" and the
set "those who have never married" are overlapping but not identical. But the behavioral option of exclusive homosexuality cannot *exceed* the number of those who
remain unmarried, even if homosexual acts may be more widespread and even if not
every bachelor is homosexual. On the question of U.S. urbanization and the emergence of specific configurations of male homosexuality, see among others Rubin
(1985), Chauncey (1994), Murray (1996).

10. The English loan word *"boy"* was used by French colonials to refer to young
male servants, regardless of their sexuality. For Jammes, all *boys* were presumed to
be thieves and blackguards; for some such as Jacobus X., the presumption was that
they were all sodomites. The quote is ambiguous as "bambou" has two senses:
Jammes refers to *"boys familiers aux bambous,"* which could refer to those familiar
with the opium pipe (i.e., "bambou"; cf. Abadie [1913]:642 and thus habitués of
opium dens, or those familiar with the brothels, whether as attendants or as prostitutes themselves (i.e., "bambou"; cf. Jacobus X. [1893]:33).

11. Copley points out similarly that although prostitution, like homosexual activity,
was not criminalized under French law, "It took no more than an 'oeillade' (a

provocative look) or a 'geste lascif' (a lewd gesture) to find oneself hauled before the Tribune de Simple Police" (Copley 1989:88).

12. On gay tourism, see the discussion by Bleys (1993); on colonial era explorers' Jacob Aronson visions of sexual sin, see Poirier (1993) and Bleys (1995); for the place of homosexuality in the British colonial adventure see Hyam (1990); for discussions of sexuality and French and Dutch colonialism, see Stoler (1989a, 1989b, 1991). To my knowledge the study of missionary sexuality remains to be undertaken.

REFERENCES

Abadie, Jean. 1913. Les fumeurs d'opium. *Archives d'anthropologie criminelle, de médecine légale, et de psychologie normale et pathologique* 28:639–64.

Baron, S[amuel]. 1732 [1685]. *A Description of the Kingdom of Tonqueen.* In Awnsham Churchill and John Churchill, eds., *A Collection of Voyages and Travels*, 6:1–40. London: Awnsham Churchill and John Churchill.

Bergman, Arlene Eisen. 1975. *Women of Viet Nam.* San Francisco: Peoples Press.

Bleys, Rudi. 1993. Homosexual Exile: The Textuality of the Imaginary Paradise, 1800–1980. *Journal of Homosexuality* 25:165–82.

Bleys, Rudi. 1995. *The Geography of Perversion : Male-To-Male Sexual Behavior Outside the West and the Ethnographic Imagination, 1750–1918.* New York: New York University Press.

Bolton, Ralph. 1992. Mapping Terra Incognita: Sex Research for AIDS Prevention. In Gilbert Herdt and Shirley Lindenbaum, eds., *In the Time of AIDS*, pp. 124–58. Newbury Park, Calif.: Sage.

Borri, Christopher. 1811 [1631]. *An Account of Cochin-China.* In John Pinkerton, ed., *A General Collection of the Best and Most Interesting Voyages and Travels in All Parts of the World*, 9:772–828. London: Longman et al.

Bui Thien Ngo. 1993. Organized Crime, Social Vice and Public Disorder Increasing. *Tap Chi Cong San* 1993(10): 3–6. Translated in BBC *Summary of World Broadcasts* FE/1841/B, published November 9, 1993.

Chalmers, John. 1996a. Vietnam's Communists make mark with new vice purge. Reuters World Service, January 30, 1996.

Chalmers, John. 1996b. Hanoi says fights social evils not foreign culture. Reuters World Service, February 9, 1996.

Chalmers, John. 1996c. Vietnam lugs old ideology along new road. Reuters World Service, April 22, 1996.

Chauncey, George. 1994. *Gay New York: Gender, Urban Culture, and the Making of the Gay Male World, 1890–1940.* New York: Basic Books.

Cobham, Rhonda. 1992. Misgendering the Nation: African Nationalist Fiction and Nuruddin Farah's *Maps.* In Andrew Parker et al., eds., *Nationalisms and Sexualities*, pp. 42–59. New York: Routledge.

Copley, Antony R. H. 1989. *Sexual Moralities in France, 1780–1980: New Ideas on the Family, Divorce, and Homosexuality.* New York: Routledge.

Dao Xuan Dung and Le Thi Nham Tuyet. 1996. Vietnamese Attitudes Regarding Gender, Sexuality, and Reproductive Health. Paper presented at the Asia and Pacific Regional Network on Gender, Sexuality, and Reproductive Health and

Fora on the Teaching of Health Social Science Conference. Cebu City, Philippines, January 1996.

Davidson, Michael. 1962. *The World, the Flesh, and Myself.* London: Arthur Barker.

Davidson, Michael. 1988 [1970]. *Some Boys.* London: GMP Publishers.

Demariaux, Jean-Claude. 1956. *Les secrets des Iles Poulo-Condore; le grande bagne Indochinois.* Paris: J. Peyronnet.

Eisen, Arlene. 1984. *Women and Revolution in Viet Nam.* London: Zed Press.

Farrère, Claude. 1905. *Les civilisés.* Paris: Ollendorff.

Goldberg, Jonathan. 1991. Sodomy in the New World: Anthropologies Old and New. *Social Text* 29:46–56.

Habermas, Jürgen. 1989[1962]. *The Structural Transformation of the Public Sphere.* Cambridge: MIT Press.

Hamabata, Matthews Masayuki. 1986. Ethnographic Boundaries: Culture, Class, and Sexuality in Tokyo. *Qualitative Sociology* 9:354–71.

Heiman, Elliott M. and Cao Van Le. 1975. Transsexualism in Vietnam. *Archives of Sexual Behavior* 4:89–95.

Higgins, Ross. 1995. Murder Will Out: Gay Identity and Media Discourse in Montreal. In William L. Leap, ed., *Beyond the Lavender Lexicon: Authenticity, Imagination, and Appropriation in Lesbian and Gay Languages*, pp. 106–32. Amsterdam: Gordon and Breach.

Hoang Ngoc Thanh. 1991. *Vietnam's Social and Political Development as Seen Through the Modern Novel.* New York: P. Lang.

Hyam, Ronald. 1990. *Empire and Sexuality: The British Experience.* Manchester: Manchester University Press.

Jammes, Henri-Ludovic. 1898. *Au pays annamite: notes ethnographiques.* Paris: Augustin Challamel.

Jammes, Henri-Ludovic. 1900. *Souvenirs du pays d'Annam.* Paris: Augustin Challamel.

Joleaud-Barral, J. de St. Maurice. 1899. *La colonisation française en Annam et au Tonkin.* Paris: E. Plon, Nourrit.

Junod, Henri Alexandre. 1912–13. *The Life of a South African Tribe.* Neuchatel, Switzerland: Attinger frères.

Khérian, G. 1937. Le problème démographique en Indochine. *Revue Indochinoise Juridique et Economique* 1:3–38.

Kobiet. 1953. *Nguyen-Thi-Ba; histoire d'une congai annamite.* Nancy: Berger-Levrault.

Kulick, Don and Margaret Willson, eds. 1995. *Taboo: Sex, Identity, and Erotic Subjectivity in Anthropological Fieldwork.* New York: Routledge.

La Bissachère, Pierre-Jacques Lemonnier de. 1807, see Maybon 1920.

La Bissachère, Pierre-Jacques Lemonnier de. 1812, see Montyon 1812.

Le Duan. 1976. Let Our Entire People Unite to Build Our Reunified and Socialist Fatherland. In Le Duan, *This Nation and Socialism Are One* (ed. Tran Van Dinh), pp. 175–211. Chicago: Vanguard Books.

Lewin, Ellen and William Leap, eds. 1996. *Out in the Field: Reflections of Lesbian and Gay Anthropologists.* Urbana: University of Illinois Press.

Mai Thi Tu and Le Thi Nham Tuyet. 1978. *Women in Viet Nam.* 2d ed. Hanoi: Foreign Languages Publishing House.

Matignon, Jean-Jacques. 1900. Deux mots sur le pédérastie. In his *Superstition, crime et misère en Chine*, pp. 187–209. Lyon: A. Storck.

Maybon, Charles B. 1920. *La relation sur le Tonkin et la Cochinchine de Mr. de La Bissachère*. Paris: Edouard Champion.

Meijer, M. J. 1985. Homosexual Offences in Ch'ing Law. *T'oung Pao* 71:109–33.

Montyon, Antoine de. 1812. *Etat actuel du Tunkin, de la Cochinchine et des royaumes de Cambodge, Laos et Lac-Tho par M. de La Bissachère*. Paris: Galignani.

Murray, Stephen O. 1994. The Will Not to Know: Traditional and Recent Accommodations of Homosexuality in Mediterranean and Southwestern Asian Islamic societies. Manuscript, 25 pp.

Ng, Vivien W. 1989. Homosexuality and the State in Late Imperial China. In Martin Bauml Duberman, Martha Vicinus, and George Chauncey, eds. *Hidden from History: Reclaiming the Gay and Lesbian Past*, pp. 76–89. New York: New American Library.

Nguyen Ngoc Huy and Ta Van Tan. 1987. *The Le Code: Law in Traditional Vietnam: A Comparative Sino-Vietnamese Legal Study with Historical-Juridical Analysis and Annotations*. Athens: Ohio University Press.

Nguyen Van Huyen. 1944 [1939]. *La civilisation annamite*. Hanoi: Direction de l'Instruction Publique de l'Indochine. [Written in 1939 but published only in 1944.]

Nguyen Van Phong. 1971. *La société vietnamienne de 1882 à 1902, d'après les écrits des auteurs français*. Paris: Presses Universitaires de France.

Philastre, Paul-Louis-Felix. 1909. *Le code annamite*. Paris: E. Leroux.

Poirier, Guy. 1993. French Renaissance Travel Accounts: Images of Sin, Visions of the New World. *Journal of Homosexuality* 25:215–39.

Proschan, Frank. 1990. How Is a Folklorist Like a Riddle? *Southern Folklore* 47:57–66.

Pujarniscle, Eugene. 1931. *Philoxène: ou, de la littérature coloniale*. Paris: Firmin-Didot.

Reuters. 1997. Furor Erupts Over Vietnam's First Gay Wedding. Reuters World Service, April 7, 1997.

Richard, M. l'Abbé [Jérome]. 1778. *Histoire naturelle, civile et politique du Tonquin*. Paris: Moutard.

Richburg, Keith B. 1996. Hanoi Wakes Up to Vice. *Washington Post*, January 29, 1996.

Roux, Dr. [Emile?]. 1905. Contribution a l'étude anthropologique de l'Annamite tonkinois. *Bulletins et Mémoires de la Société d'anthropologie de Paris* ser. 5, 6:321–50.

Rubin, Gayle. 1984. Thinking Sex: Notes for a Radical Theory of the Politics of Sexuality. In Carol Vance, ed., *Pleasure and Danger: Exploring Female Sexuality*, pp. 267–319. New York: Routledge.

Seizer, Susan. 1995. Paradoxes of Visibility in the Field: Rites of Queer Passage in Anthropology. *Public Culture* 8:73–100.

Sol, Bernard and Daniel Haranger. 1930. *Recueil général et méthodique de la législation et de la réglementation des colonies françaises.* Paris: Société d'éditions géographiques, maritimes et coloniales.

Stoler, Ann Laura. 1989a. Making Empire Respectable: The Politics of Race and Sexual Morality in 20th-Century Cultures. *American Ethnologist* 16:634–60.

Stoler, Ann Laura. 1989b. Rethinking Colonial Categories: European Communities and the Boundaries of Rule. *Comparative Studies in Society and History* 13:134–61.

Stoler, Ann Laura. 1991. Carnal Knowledge and Imperial Power: Gender, Race, and Morality in Colonial Asia. In Micaeli di Leonardo, ed., *Gender at the Crossroads of Knowledge: Feminist Anthropology in the Postmodern Era*, pp. 51–101. Berkeley: University of California Press.

The Struggle Against Drugs. 1982. Special issue of *Vietnamese Studies* 66:1–111.

Truong Chinh. 1977. *Selected Writings.* Hanoi: Foreign Languages Publishing House.

United States Population Census. 1990. *1990 Census of Population: General Population Characteristics: United States.* Washington D.C.: Bureau of the Census.

Vietnam Population Census. 1989. *Completed Census Results*, vol. 1. Hanoi: Central Census Steering Committee.

Voice of Vietnam. 1990. Fifth Phase of Crime Crack-Down Begins. Translated in BBC *Summary of World Broadcasts* FE/0745/B/1. Broadcast April 16, 1990; published April 23, 1990.

Voice of Vietnam. 1993. Resolution on Prostitution Control. Translated in BBC *Summary of World Broadcasts* FE/1623/B. Broadcast February 11, 1993; published February 26, 1993.

Warren, Carol A. B. 1988. *Gender Issues in Field Research.* Newbury Park, Calif.: Sage.

Whitehead, Tony Larry and Mary Ellen Conaway, eds. 1986. *Self, Sex, and Gender in Cross-Cultural Fieldwork.* Urbana: University of Illinois Press.

Williams, Walter L. 1993. Being gay and doing research on homosexuality in non-Western cultures. *Journal of Sex Research* 30.

X., Jacobus. 1893. *L'amour aux colonies: singularités physiologiques et passionnelles . . .* Paris: Isidore Liseux.

Yeager, Jack Andrew. 1987. *The Vietnamese Novel in French: A Literary Response to Colonialism.* Hanover: University Press of New England.

Private Acts, Public Space: Defining Boundaries in Nineteenth-Century Holland

11

THEO VAN DER MEER

On January 4, 1827, the High Court of the Netherlands in The Hague discharged ten men who had appealed a verdict by a court in Amsterdam. Some four months before, all of them had been found guilty of public indecencies with one another and sentenced to the maximum penalty under the law.[1] The public indecency statute (article 330) of the French penal code, which was enforced in the Netherlands in 1811 after Napoleon had annexed the country, stipulated a minimum of three months and a maximum of one year of incarceration, as well as a maximum fine of 200 French francs, usually converted to 100 Dutch guilders.[2]

Although the enforcement of this penal code officially brought along the decriminalization of same-sex behavior, it did not mean that men engaging in such behavior were set free of legal action. The appellants were by no means the only ones in the Netherlands convicted under this statute. Since 1811 prosecutors sometimes rigorously pursued sentences of this kind for "sodomites." Article 330 did not apply to same-sex behavior per se, yet men who had engaged in such behavior outnumbered by three or four to one men and women (usually prostitutes) who were accused of public sexual acts. In the case of the latter usually the minimum penalty was applied, whereas the first *always* got the maximum. Even though article 330 nowhere said anything about the gender of "perpetrators" of public indecencies, in case of male-with-male, sometimes verdicts spoke of an indecency in the "highest degree."[3] As I will show later, evidence in such cases was often rather flimsy, the indecencies themselves left much to the imagination, while the very notion of "public" in such cases was stretched to the limit. Whatever the ten appellants in 1827 had been found guilty of, they had done it inside a room.

One of the appellants, Adam Cornelissen, provided the High Court with an eloquently built legal exposé about notions of "public" and "private." He showed that neighbors who had testified against him and the others had been spying on them. He argued that there was no such thing as public indecency or public space without the presence of unwilling witnesses. Consequently the High Court discharged the appellants because it considered the charges brought against them in Amsterdam not proven.[4] Given everything that had occurred, and especially given Cornelissen's arguments, this was a half-hearted judgment at best. Nonetheless, it was Cornelissen's defense that would resound in similar cases and verdicts later in the nineteenth century. In newly fought definitions, if not just the actual, also the symbolic meanings of "private" and "public" began only in a very limited sense to refer to "inside" and "outside" or, for that matter, to physical space. "Private space" also became the representation of an interiority or subjectivity and in this case a homosexual self-awareness that had also become an inner sanctum.

In this paper I want to show that men like Cornelissen in their battles against courts compelled society into recognizing the physical, social, and cultural boundaries of phenomena that had gradually emerged since the late seventeenth century: same-sex subcultures and the existence of sodomites as a category in their own right. I also want to show that modern notions about "public" and "private" evolved in nineteenth-century Holland around trials like those of Adam Cornelissen and his friends. The outcome of the appeal of Cornelissen and his friends implies that the ramifications of his arguments go beyond a history of homosexuality that limits itself to its own singularity. Homosexuality may seem to be an obscure subject to mainstream historiography; it is sometimes pivotal to that very mainstream. Cornelissen's arguments about "public" and "private" are at the basis of any democracy: how a democratic state relates to its citizens, or for that matter, how citizens relate to one another in a democratic state. Indeed Cornelissen's arguments are echoed in modern notions about self-determination and personal integrity, that determine life in a democracy. Or to put it in other words, the state itself was redefined through legal battles such as Cornelissen's. I do not wish to suggest that Adam Cornelissen single-handedly created a democracy; I wish to make clear, however, that history—also that of the emergence of modern states—in the end is not just a history of great ideas or the battles of great men. It is also a history of common people who against the odds have compelled powers much greater then themselves to recognize them as autonomous individuals who are entitled to determine their own lives. Adam Cornelissen was just a young petty merchant from Amsterdam.

My story implies something else: since Michel Foucault published the first volume of his *History of Sexuality* in 1976, a canon in historiography has emerged that considers the medicalization of homosexuality in the second half of the nineteenth century as the most decisive source for the emergence of homosexual roles and identities. According to this canon, until then most same-sex behavior was casual, accidental, just an eruption of lust; sodomy supposedly was just an act, homosexuality on the other hand was the reflection of a personality. Apparently the medical profession provided the world with new notions about homosexuallity as a moral pathology and about the existence of a third sex: men with an innate female soul.[5]

However, sodomy was *never* considered to be "just an act"; quite the contrary! Century-old discourses on human desires—that also had roots in antiquity—claimed that sodomy was the ultimate outcome of gluttonous behavior. Each form of gluttony, or "excess of diet"—lascivious drinking and eating, or dressing, gambling, whoring—would provoke new passions.[6] Sodomy could originate in something that was "natural," a Dutch author observed in 1730. According to his and other authors' arguments, a vice once tasted singed the senses and caused a craving for more and for worse. Such an understanding of desires was rooted in Platonism and mind/body distinctions that implied only a feeble control of reason over corporal cravings.[7] As I have argued elsewhere, more than just philosophy, such ideas were part of lived experiences that even show up in court records. Once a person reached the pit of his cravings—same sex desires and behavior—he would "hold on to them," as court records of sodomy trials preceding the enforcement of the French penal code in 1811 say, over and over again, both by words of prosecutors and of those prosecuted. Such individuals would seduce others and spread the vice.

Supposedly, it was the medicalization that through its notions of a third sex first linked homosexual behavior with gender.[8] Yet again, this assertion does not stand up to scrutiny. Already in the sixteenth and seventeenth centuries, commentators spoke of an "effeminate disease" in regards to same-sex behavior.[9] The word "effeminate" linked to "disease" meant to such commentators that men who engaged in same-sex practices *morally* resembled women.

Females were supposed to be morally inferior to males because, apparently, their bodies were an inferior version of those of males.[10] At the very least, they were supposed to be endowed by nature with an insatiable lust in their wombs, that could only be controlled when they submitted themselves to the hierarchy between the sexes. By indulging in gluttony, males lost control over their bodies, and as such they resembled women. No doubt, in the late nineteenth-century discourses "the homosexual" was set apart from his heterosexual counterparts by "nature" and as such "he" became a personality. "The sodomite," on the other hand, was supposed to have developed his condition through his lack of self-control. Yet as an insatiable, effeminate being he was no less—albeit different—a personality, than his nineteenth-century successor was.

In medical discourses "the" homosexual was not "invented" as it is often claimed; his existence, which had already firm roots in common sense, was rather scientifically acknowledged and endorsed and gained a new status of indisputable scientific truth.[11] It was the fact that "sodomites" had become a category in their own right that both enabled the courts in the early nineteenth century to prosecute them the way they did, and that enabled these men to put up forms of resistance against an hostile environment. To put the nineteenth-century public indecency trials in a proper context, I will first turn to the enforcement of the French penal code in the Netherlands and I will also put these trials in an historical perspective.

Political Context of the French Penal Code in the Netherlands

For the Netherlands the last two decades of the eighteenth century and the first decade of the nineteenth century, like for most of the rest of Europe, had been turbulent years. Democratic uprisings in the 1780s—put to a preliminary end in 1787 by foreign interference (Prussian troops and English money)—had been followed by a French invasion in 1795. The French troops and local revolutionaries sealed the fate of the ancien régime of the Republic of the United Provinces.[12] This republic had been a quagmire of seven virtually independent provinces where no one or no institute (least of all the House of Orange)—except for a financial oligarchy—seemed to reign supreme, and where every city and every local court jealously guarded its age-old sovereignty. If this republic had indeed been a political quagmire—and for all its lack of a central power, a near diplomatic nightmare to John Adams, America's first envoy to the Netherlands[13]—so its criminal justice system had been. In the western province of Holland alone, there had been more than two hundred courts with jurisdiction in criminal and/or civil cases.[14] Roman law, Emperor Charles V's sixteenth-century *Constitutio Criminalis Carolina*, customary law, provincial, regional, and city statutes for centuries had decided over defendants' fates.

From the ashes of this republic in 1795 a new one arose: the Batavian Republic, named after a Germanic tribe (Batavieren) that supposedly at the dawn of the Christian era had inhabited the swamps from which the Low Countries emerged a millennium later. The tribe's freedom-loving virtues, of legendary proportions, had enabled it to rise against Roman conquerors.[15] With republican fervor, or at least with revolutionary zeal, and in the name of *liberté*, *egalité*, and *fraternité* after 1795 the reborn *citoyens* went to battle against one another over the political structure of the country. At stake was

the question how unitarian the new republic was to be. (It must be said,
however, that these *citoyens* liked their velvet: despite several coup d'états
between 1795 and 1800 the Batavian republic never suffered the explo-
sions of violence that accompanied the French Revolution.) The new republic surely was less glorious than its predecessor had been, and its lifespan
was curtailed by Napoleon. In 1806 he turned the country into one of
France's satellite kingdoms under the reign of his brother Louis, only to
annex it in 1810, because Louis failed to dance to his big brother's piping.
Yet, whatever the faults of the shortly lived Batavian republic and the even
shorter lived *Royaume des Pays Bas* may have been, they laid the foundations for the modern Dutch state. Before the eighteenth century ended the
Netherlands had a central government, an elected national convention, a
constitution, religious freedom, and a declaration of human rights. In one
thing the squabbling revolutionaries failed however: when in 1809 finally a
new unitarian criminal code was approved by the national convention, it was
too late. While this criminal code was not yet enforced because the legal system still needed to be reformed, the country suddenly found itself ruled by
an emperor in Paris and was enriched with a penal code of foreign making.

Although the end of the Napoleonic era came soon and Holland saw its
independence restored in 1813 and turned into a monarchy under the
returned House of Orange, despite many attempts to replace the French
penal code, it would last until 1886. Up to 1840 each failed new draft of a
Dutch criminal code intended to recriminalize homosexual behavior.[16]

Public Indecency Trials in Historical Perspective

Ever since the Council of Nablus in the twelfth century had declared
sodomy (anal intercourse with male or female, as well as bestiality) a crime
that could be prosecuted by ecclesiastical and secular courts, men in the
Low Countries have been prosecuted on such charges. Southern parts
(Flanders-Belgium) witnessed some severe persecutions in the fifteenth
and sixteenth centuries.[17] In northern parts (the present Netherlands)
prosecution by and large remained incidental until the late seventeenth
century. In the final quarter of that century, the number of sodomy trials
here gradually began to increase, until a rather sudden outburst of such trials occurred in 1730. Between 1730 and 1732 some 350 men were prosecuted. About 80 of them suffered the death penalty; most of the rest managed to flee their cities or the country and were prohibited to return on
penalty of more severe punishment.[18]

Aside from incidental sodomy trials, several other waves of arrests
occurred in the course of the eighteenth century: in 1764 in Amsterdam, in

1776 in several cities in the provinces of Holland and Utrecht, again in Amsterdam and other cities in the before-mentioned provinces between 1795 and 1798. Altogether, between 1730 and 1811 some 800 sodomy trials were been held here.[19] Women, aside from cross-dressers who tried to pass as soldiers or sailors and who had managed to marry other women,[20] were hardly prosecuted. It was only in Amsterdam in the 1790s that several women who were accused of same-sex acts, stood trial.[21]

The series of trials in 1730, 1764, and 1776 followed the more-or-less accidental discoveries of networks of sodomites. These trials also laid bare the existence of elaborate subcultures: numerous public and private meeting sites all over the country; forms of bodily comportment, like signs and signals used by participants in these subcultures, as well as a more-or-less specific sodomitical slang; jealously guarded love affairs; a lot of role-playing with effeminacy and travesty—went on in these subcultures.[22]

In 1730 a man in Utrecht who was to be locked away in a house of correction because of his quarrelsome behavior told the court that the year before he had seen somebody sodomizing another man. He was able to identify this "sodomite" and when the latter was taken into custody and confessed, arrests began to avalanche all over the country. Similar occurrences took place when in 1764 a soldier was arrested in Amsterdam and charged with several robberies, and again in 1776, when two men stood trial in that city for selling forged bonds.[23]

Awaiting his sentence in 1764 the soldier suddenly confessed to same-sex practices and revealed numerous names of accomplices to the court, resulting in a wave of arrests. During the 1776 trial, the warder discovered letters of a scurrilous nature in the luggage of the forgers. Investigating these letters, once again the court hit upon the existence of a network of sodomites to which the forgers themselves belonged, again resulting in a roundup of culprits.

Despite the quagmire nature of the legal system in the Netherlands and despite the wide range of criminal laws that could be applied, the courts usually painstakingly followed rules for trial procedures. Arrests could be made only if a prosecutor had clear indications of actual sexual acts committed by a suspect. Verdicts of courts all over the country closely related to the specific sexual acts defendants were accused of, the extent of the available evidence, and especially the absence or presence of a confession. Death penalties were only applied in cases involving anal intercourse; mutual masturbation was usually met with sentences to decades of solitary confinement. A confession was an absolute requirement for a death penalty and other forms of corporal punishment executed in public. Moreover, in case of the death penalty, most courts were obliged to consult jurists outside their own jurisdiction. These jurists would carefully weigh the arguments and the available evidence. Such comments, which were often published in special collections to serve as a form of jurisprudence, together with the application of Roman Law (the mother of all laws) provided a surprising unity in the bewildering number of different kinds of laws and penalties.[24]

Although suspects could be put under torture—in case of a possible scaffolding when there was abundant proof but only a confession was missing—courts were rather reluctant in applying such means. It was clearly in nobody's interest to make people confess to things they had never done. However painful the sentences were in this period, the attitudes of most prosecutors and judges may be called exemplary compared to those of some of their successors beginning in 1795.[25]

It was especially in Amsterdam when, as part of the Batavian revolution, the old guard was removed from office, that men were put on trial just for making (verbal) passes at other men. So far, as a solicitor had stated in 1730, the mere wish to commit sodomy did not constitute a crime.[26] After 1795 a new quasi-legal expression that referred to sexual intentions entered the vocabulary of the court in Amsterdam: "tentamen sodomiticam." When considered proven, such a "tentamen" was usually met with one or two years of solitary confinement.[27] Until 1798—when torture was abolished— some men charged with a "tentamen" were even put on the rack, sometimes just for things they supposedly had said. In 1797 Thomas Gouwes was sentenced to two years of solitary confinement, because he apparently had told another man that he had "wanted to fuck him." Gouwes had denied these charges also when he was subjected to a whipping.[28]

The abolishment of torture did not exactly improve the position of suspects. At the same time by decree of the National Convention, courts in parts of Holland from then on were allowed to sentence on the basis of what actually was already practice in Amsterdam since 1795. "Conviction"— basically on circumstantial evidence—could suffice to pronounce a verdict.[29] I do not want to suggest that after 1795 "innocent" people were prosecuted. Legal practice after 1795 rather shows that prosecutors and judges, if they could not accuse a suspect of actual sexual acts, could convict a suspect based on what he was presumed to be.

For those who loved others of their own sex, the enforcement of the French penal code in 1811 meant that they could count their blessings. The approved 1809 draft of a Dutch criminal code, in accordance with tradition, still had put severe penalties on homosexual acts. Yet, although the introduction of the French penal code officially implied the decriminalization of same-sex behavior, the application of the public indecency act after 1811 meant that sodomites were not set free of prosecution. In fact it meant a continuation of a legal practice that had already started in 1795. The notions of public and private, as used by the courts, were a mere excuse to prosecute men like Adam Cornelissen in 1826: men whom they knew or suspected to be "sodomites." Although verdicts in Cornelissen's and similar cases referred to article 330 in the penal code, frequently phrases like "the crime of sodomy" or "crimen nefandum" also appear in the records, despite the fact that with the enforcement of the French penal code, same-sex practices—if not in effect—had officially been decriminalized. This penal code offered one—if limited—advantage: under previous laws, it had been nigh impossible to appeal a verdict. However, most who did were, unlike Cornelissen, not very successful.

Public Indecency Trials

In 1816, following the murder in Utrecht of what turned out to be a young blackmailer, the police arrested several suspects. The prime suspect was a known sodomite. Aside from these men being questioned about their possible involvement in the murder, they were also interrogated about their sexual activities. Some of them admitted that they had had sex at squares and in public toilets in that city, and also mentioned the names of men they had encountered at such sites.[30] Like what had happened with waves of eighteenth-century sodomy trials, arrests began to avalanche, while many fled the city. Suspects were interrogated in a detailed manner, not just about their sexual behavior at public sites, but also about things they had done in the privacy of their homes. Once again the court in Utrecht laid bare the existence of a network and it even produced sociograms, describing who was acquainted with whom and who had had sex with whom.[31] Some of the names that appear in the records of these trials were already known by this or other courts since the previous century. The prosecutor specifically asked suspects about the involvement of a certain Dr. Greeve, who had died in 1815. As early as 1792 Greeve had faced sodomy charges, but had been acquitted.[32] Another suspect, Willem Bolderman, had been sentenced in his absence in 1798 by a court in The Hague.[33] Meeting sites in Utrecht mentioned in the 1816 trials were the very same that had first appeared in records of sodomy trials in 1676, 1721, and 1730. Records of indecency trials in other cities show the same procedures.[34]

The prosecutor, Pieter Willem Provó Kluit, used this information to charge 29 men (about half of them in their absence) and had them convicted for public indecency, although no witnesses had stepped forward who had ever seen them indulge in such activities. Indeed, most of these men were found guilty on the basis of confessions of those who had been arrested first.[35] As if nothing had changed, some verdicts said that "over and beyond" a public indecency, the "culprits" had perpetrated "the gruesome crime of sodomy."[36]

Elsewhere men were found guilty of public indecencies, just for making verbal passes at other men in public spaces. In many such cases there was only one witness to these indecencies, the "victim" of the "assault," while the records piously mention that decency forbade one to write the actual occurrences down on paper. Victims of such verbal assaults often were soldiers standing guard at public buildings. The frequency of such events, as well as the often scanty testimonies and also the defense of the detainees suggest that soldiers regularly engaged in prostitution and consequent blackmail.[37]

On many occasions it was rather the reputation of the defendant than his actual acts that determined a conviction or an acquittal. Sometimes defendants indeed were acquitted, when neighbors, doctors, and church ministers claimed them to be respectable citizens. This occurred to Evert Bosteen after his doctor declared in 1827 that the man was respectable and had only consulted him a few days before his arrest with complaints about his penis, and that he was not capable of any sexual act.[38] Two drunken men who one evening had been found intertwined with one another on a sidewalk were acquitted when neighbors testified that these drunks were known to be decent family men.[39] Others were found guilty when informers would testify about the bad reputations the defendants had. When in 1814 Frederik Bontjé was arrested in Amsterdam because supposedly he had made a pass at a sailor—the only witness in this case—the head of the police told the court that Bontjé was known to be guilty of this kind of "gruesome crimes."[40] Consequently Bontjé was sentenced. Recidivists especially stood no chance whatsoever, aside from the fact that in their case the maximum penalty could be doubled.[41]

And it could be worse: as late as 1846 Pieter Willem Provó Kluit, who had been in office since the late eighteenth century and who had become president of a provincial court, sentenced a man to eight years in prison and a public whipping, because when making a pass at another man in a barn, he supposedly had roughly pulled that man's arm. (Aside from the death penalty, which was abolished in 1870, it was to be one of the last corporal punishments applied in Holland.) The only witnesses were two police officers, who had been *outside* the barn and who told the court that they had heard some yelling inside.[42] While the prosecutor at first had wanted to throw the case out of court, Provó Kluit, praised by his contemporaries for his integrity and deep sense of justice,[43] had ordered him to use article 331 of the penal code, which dealt with violent acts upon the honor (chastity) of a person.

Provó Kluit's actions in this case are not devoid of a certain bitter irony.
Article 331, which put a maximum of fifteen years on violent sexual
assaults, was seldom applied to rapists. If a woman was raped outdoors,
the perpetrator, if tried at all, was more likely to be prosecuted under the
public indecency statute, with a maximum penalty of one year. Perhaps in
the best of all possible worlds, prosecutors turned to this article because
they felt a public indecency was easier to prove. However, in 1845 Provó
Kluit had rejected a prosecutor's arguments based on article 330 against a
man who was accused of the rape of a woman in a field. According to Provó
Kluit, a public indecency could never occur against a person and only with
mutual consent.[44] Aside from the fact that he considered the rape not
proven (which would have made article 331 applicable), Provó Kluit's arguments about public indecency would have made sense, only if he himself
had used them in cases against sodomites as well. Yet, on the contrary, in
cases of the many men he prosecuted in his long career for making passes
at other men, it was exactly this mutual consent that was lacking.

There may be one difference compared to the situation prior to 1811.
Even though most people prosecuted before the enforcement of the French
penal code came from the lower or lower middle classes, in many of the
trial records names were mentioned of upper-class people who participated
in the subcultures, also at the public meeting sites. Not so in 1816 or in
other "indecency trials" in the nineteenth century. That may be due to the
different type of records generated by trials before and after 1811.[45] Yet,
perhaps it also meant that upper-class people had grown less dependent
on temptations offered by the streets.[46]

The way in which the public indecency statute was used against
"sodomites" was in sharp contrast with the way in which the French penal
code in general was applied in the Netherlands. Both politicians and jurists
felt that this penal code was alien to the spirit of the Dutch nation: it was
considered to be much too harsh! Judges, especially in non-capital cases,
often put all their creativity into a mild application of the penal code. Rather
than applying the severe penalties the code required, e.g., for theft or violence, they sometimes acquitted men in their forties because, due to their
young age, they were considered to have been ignorant of the seriousness
of such crimes.[47] The French penal code was also considered to be alien to
the spirit of the nation because it did not deal with same-sex acts. Admittedly, there was some truth in this comment. Although the Parisian police in
the previous century had kept close track of "sodomites" and harassed and
lured them with decoys, most of those put under arrest did not spend much
more then a couple of weeks in jail,[48] whereas the persecutions in Holland
in the eighteenth century, however limited, were the worst in early modern

Europe. Public indecency trials in early nineteenth-century France seem to
have been much rarer than in Holland. On the other hand the legal position
of "sodomites" in the Netherlands, when arrested, may have been somewhat more solid. At least they got a trial, whereas men who suffered arrests
for public indecencies in France were often subjected to administrative
decrees, which could mean anything from being put in an asylum for a
while, a couple of months of incarceration, or being relocated.[49]

It was especially the trial of Johan Klanck, who in 1816 had murdered a
young blackmailer, that betrays the feelings of Dutch jurists and politicians
about the absence of a sodomy law in the penal code. Provó Kluit, who was
also the prosecutor in this trial, went out of his way to get the death penalty
for Klanck. Klanck one day had made a pass at 16-year-old Johan
Schroven. The boy had made him pay dearly, collecting money from him a
couple of times a week for several months. After his arrest Klanck told how
one day he had suggested that the boy should offer him sexual favors for
his money. Angrily the boy had attacked him, according to Klanck, who,
while defending himself, had accidentally killed the youth. Manslaughter
was not a capital crime unless it was preceded by another felony or misdemeanor. Provó Kluit, without a shred of evidence, managed to convince the
court that it had not been the boy who had attacked Klanck, but that Klanck
had tried a violent sexual assault (article 331) on the boy,[50] the same article
he would use thirty years later to convict a man for roughly pulling another
man's arm.

Klanck was sentenced to be hanged.[51] When his wife appealed to the
king for grace,[52] both Provó Kluit and a committee of the High Court in the
fiercest terms advised the king to reject the request. Although hardly a logical argument against the quite common royal favor, Provó Kluit advised the
king to reject the request because the discovery of "other thugs who exercise that handwork of manstupration (sic) and sodomitical filthy things"
had made it possible to force a confession from Klanck.[53] With arguments
that fitted the wish to recriminalize same-sex behavior, the High Court stated that "however difficult it may be to stop with laws the unnatural vice that
has come into vogue so much in the Netherlands, in cases like this—when
that vice results in such fatal consequences as murder or voluntary
manslaughter—it is nonetheless the indispensable duty of the judge to
apply all the vigor of the laws."[54] The minister of justice agreed with these
comments and consequently the request was rejected by the king.[55]

Just minutes before his execution Klanck confessed to have premeditat-
ed the killing of Johan Schroven, when he was at his wit's end because of
the boy's blackmail. Perhaps Klanck had wanted to cleanse his soul before
stepping into eternity, yet by admitting murder instead of manslaughter, he

also mocked the legal machinations through which Provó Kluit, backed by
even the highest legal instances, had sought his death penalty.

Provó Kluit spoke his mind about sodomites in a revealing way in 1821.
As prosecutor he then once more was to advise the king about a request for
grace. The request was put up by a Protestant church minister and the
poet laureate of the day on behalf of a man, Hendrik Herderschee, who in
1798 at the age of eighteen because of sodomy had been sentenced to
thirty years imprisonment. Although pardoned in 1815 as far as his prison
sentence was concerned, Herderschee still suffered part of his penalty. He
had also been exiled forever from the province of Holland.[56]

Herderschee's benefactors begged the king to allow him to return to his
place of birth, so that he would be able to earn himself a living. That indeed
was a difficult thing for people who found themselves in parts of the country
where they missed the support of family and friends. Herderschee's benefactors were convinced that he had mended his ways: in prison Herderschee
had taught himself French and German and had started to write pious poetry,
which, also with the help of his benefactors, was published in a booklet
called *Gezangen uit den kerker* (Songs from Prison).[57] The request outraged
Provó Kluit: "Herderschee is a villain who goes the way of all of his kind,
namely by calling every means holy to pursue their boundless vice." Provó
Kluit in insinuating terms even called into question the sexual orthodoxy of
Herderschee's benefactors. He was convinced that if Herderschee were to
return to Amsterdam, he would seek out his former friends, because, according to Provó Kluit, no one else would be willing to support him, and also
because the prosecutor was convinced "that people sick with this disease, let
themselves not be cured." A committee from the High Court dealing with the
request said that it was well known that "this vice usually remains with such
culprits into their old age."[58] Nonetheless, Herderschee was allowed to
return into the province of Holland, yet was prohibited to enter Amsterdam.

The use of the term "disease" by Provó Kluit—as indicated before, it
was already used in the sixteenth century; also in 1762 a prosecutor in
Utrecht used the very same expression[59]—probably referred to a moral or
mental condition, rather than a physical one. He thus anticipated notions
about moral pathologies that emerged in the medicalization of the second
half of the nineteenth century. Unfortunately for Herderschee, Provó Kluit
had correctly anticipated his actions. Although he was denied entrance to
Amsterdam, in 1827 Herderschee found himself once more in prison in
that city: after making passes near a public toilet at two young men, he was
convicted for public indecency.[60]

Pieter Willem Provó Kluit no doubt was a zealot (and an anti-Semite for
that matter).[61] Yet, neither did he stand alone, nor was his zealotism a mere

personal idiosyncrasy. His attitudes rather had to do with the before-mentioned social and cultural boundaries that had emerged since the late seventeenth century. These boundaries had emerged both in social and sexual practices as well as in discourses; or, as a cultural historian might say, in processes of attribution, appropriation, and transformation of meanings regarding same-sex behavior.

The contours of these discourses had by and large been set by the persecutions as they occurred in the Netherlands from 1730 onward. Prior to 1730, sodomy in every respect had been the "unmentionable vice" in Holland. Ever since the Reformation the Protestant church had been silent on this subject, except in antipapist diatribes. Dutch seventeenth-century libertine novels, unlike their French and English counterparts, never referred to sodomy. It was only jurists who published writings about sodomy for a limited professional audience. Death penalties for sodomy prior to 1730 were usually carried out within a courthouse, at least since the first quarter of the seventeenth century. In case of such death penalties usually only summary verdicts were kept.[62]

It was not a simple taboo that prevented talk about sodomy; it was a general belief that knowledge about this topic would provoke unnatural desires. Moreover, secular and ecclesiastical authorities believed (or wanted to believe) that same-sex activities were hardly practiced in the Netherlands. The Dutch had been God's new chosen people. For the sobriety and restraint its inhabitants had exercised since the Reformation, the republic had been blessed in the seventeenth century with a politically and economically powerful position in the world. In such an ontology, and with notions about what were thought to be the causes of sodomy, same-sex practices could hardly exist in Holland.[63]

The discovery of networks and subcultures in 1730 provoked a radical change. Most executions were from then on carried out in public. Trial records were kept. The prosecutions and executions were accompanied by a torrent of scholarly and popular publications. It not only meant the acknowledgment of the existence of the vice in Holland, which was considered to be of recent origin, but also that knowledge from then on was thought to serve as a necessary deterrent. Rather than wiping this vice from the face of the earth, as authorities in 1730 were said to intend, the prosecutions from that year hence marked the beginning of what Foucault called the "desire for knowledge." Persecutions throughout the century generated new knowledge and new meanings, not least of all because however severe prosecutions were in Holland, with some 800 trials over a period of 80 years, their effect remained mainly symbolical. For one thing the prosecutions gradually turned "sodomites" into gendered individuals.

In 1730 the supposedly recent emergence of same-sex practices in Holland was attributed to a rise of sinful, gluttonous behavior among the Dutch. All were to a certain extent thought to be guilty of what had happened. Therefore, the publications that appeared in 1730 all called for communal repentance. Such communal repentance would indeed take place around the scaffolds on which the "culprits" died as expatiate sacrifices.[64] By the late eighteenth century such ideas had vanished and been replaced by ideas about the personal culpability of the sinner. At that time "the" sodomite at the scaffold was to suffer only for his own sins.[65]

The discourses on same-sex behavior changed in another sense as well. Whereas at first, with notions about gluttony, desires were mainly understood to be corporal; in the second half of the eighteenth century commentators began to speak of "inner proclivities."[66] Moreover, even though sodomites for centuries had morally resembled women, very few authors in 1730 paid attention to effeminate features of the "culprits." However, in the second half of the eighteenth century, sodomites supposedly became recognizable by such features: they were said to have a whorish look in their eyes, not to grow beards on their cheeks, to have a slimy speech, to sway their hips. It were such features that were said to betray their "inner proclivities." "The" sodomite in the second half of the eighteenth century had become a gendered individual, indeed a "he whore."[67]

At the same time, men in Holland who engaged in same-sex behavior began to look for legitimations. Especially devout men would do so, because they were most at need to look at themselves as morally responsible beings. By the mid eighteenth century, they started to refer to the biblical story of David and Jonathan, while at the same time claiming to have been borne with their desires. They also appropriated discourses about effeminacy, yet bending them for their own benefit, saying their desires were innate weaknesses. Such "weaknesses" still referred to a feminine lack of self-control.[68] By the end of the eighteenth century sodomites, as much as their antagonists like Provó Kluit, thought of themselves as representing a category or a genus in their own right. Implicit notions about a third sex in parts of Europe had already firmly rooted in folk-knowledge by the end of the eighteenth and the beginning of the nineteenth centuries.

If anything, such features as sodomites had gained through the eighteenth century made them more prone to persecution as well as to public violence. It seems not unlikely that prosecutors and judges from 1795 onwards, in forming their convictions, based themselves on the physical appearance of suspects. Whereas previously sodomites had sometimes been beaten up when they were caught in the act, late eighteenth-century records show that at that time "modern" forms of "queerbashing" emerged,

which went hand-in-hand with the rise of the notion of sodomites as effeminate men.[69] "We are exposed to everything," in 1826 a man from Leiden
wrote with good reason to his lover, who happened to be one of the ten men
from Amsterdam who appealed their case at the High Court in that year.[70]
At least these men's sense of self-awareness allowed them to raise among
one another their own moral voice: "God has created no human being for its
damnation," the man from Leiden in 1826 also wrote to his lover.[71] "Everybody knows," a church minister said in 1817 in a pamphlet that he published shortly after the murder of the young blackmailer by Johan Klanck,
"that these scoundrels among their equals openly speak of their gruesome
lusts as something that is natural and proper to them."[72]

Whatever the thoughts of this minister on such "scoundrels," they themselves through a century of prosecution had built a self-awareness that had
also become an inner sanctum beyond the reach of their persecutors. To
turn one more time to the sodomy trials of the eighteenth century, one of
the things that prosecutors in those days had tried to do, especially when
they steered in the direction of a death penalty, was that they tried to gain a
hold on the culprits' souls. In many ways they were like Catholic priests
hearing confession. If not just to put their own conscience to rest (God, after
all, looked as much upon their deeds as upon anybody else's), they wanted
not just to hear a suspect tell his crimes but also to have him admit that he
well deserved his penalty. Although not always successful, especially when
the accused knew too well that members of the class to which the judges
belonged were involved in the same kind of activities but escaped prosecution, others to the delight of the courts became utterly remorseful. In 1797 a
young man, who after hearing his death sentence had nearly died of an
asthma attack, shortly before his execution told a judge that not only did he
well deserve his death sentence, but also that the members of the court
would have committed a grave sin if they had not sentenced him that way. It
was with utter tranquillity that he stepped into eternity, his prosecutor
noted.[73] When the death penalty was no longer a means to control same-
sex behavior, courts more then lost a sanction; it put the soul of a convict
beyond their control. At the same time, the—not always blessed—right to
appeal a verdict under the French penal code also enabled men like Adam
Cornelissen to stand up and defend the boundaries of their inner sanctum.

Public and Private

Especially in the first decade after the enforcement of the French penal
code, prosecutors and judges alike made a mockery of the notions of public
and private as well as of the argumentation with which they set out sen-

tence suspects in public indecency trials. As during the series of such trials in 1816 in Utrecht, following the murder of a young blackmailer, "public" just meant "outside," regardless of the question whether anybody had witnessed the activities. The conviction in Amsterdam in 1826 of Adam Cornelissen and his friends was the epitome of legal capriciousness and niceties.

Early in 1826, one of the men, Leendert Rouwenhorst, had rented a room in a house in Amsterdam's now fashionable, but then working-class district, the Jordaan. Many men used to gather in that room; visitors drank and sang until late at night.[74] Indeed one of them produced a drinking song full of sexual innuendo:

> *will only drink with deep drafts*
> *no gayety shall be shunned*
> *one may well toast with friends*
> *when champagne foams*
> *wine's always a proper comfort*
> *sometimes to divert the frats*
>
> *. . . .*
>
> *One sees the grapevine grow abundantly*
> *for him who likes to take a draft*
> *he sees the fair grape grow as well*
> *shining brighter than any fruit*
> *wine's a proper comfort indeed*
> *sometimes to divert the frats.*[75]

From the drinking-bouts that went on in that room, sometimes quarrels between visitors erupted, and one day Rouwenhorst's wife had stirred the gathering of a mob in front of the house while loudly accusing her husband of being a "sodomite." All of this happened much to the annoyance of other inhabitants of the house and consequently they took their case to the police. According to their testimonies they could not have escaped noticing what was going on in the room. When passing through the hallway through windows and a door in the room where Rouwenhorst and his likes gathered, they had been confronted with indecent acts. One day, these witnesses related, they had seen some of the defendants naked on a cupboard-bed; several others had been half naked on the floor and the rest of the visitors had been looking on while sipping *jenever* (Dutch gin). Shortly after, the police arrested several men in the room and also began to round up other known visitors. The police even confiscated personal papers—including love letters[76]—suggesting that the police were as much interested in what these men were supposed to be as in what they had done. Altogether thirteen men were arrested and, without much ado, twelve of them were

found guilty of public indecency, also those who had been merely specta-
tors drinking in the room. Especially the verdicts of the latter read like an exercise in legal creativity. The spectators were found guilty of public indecency because, according to the verdicts, while sipping their jenever, they had not stopped the activities of the other men. Again, it suggests that these men were rather convicted for what they were supposed to be than for what they had done.

Except for one, all the "culprits" appealed their case at the High Court in The Hague. The eleventh man died before he could be moved to The Hague. In those days to appeal a verdict was under any circumstance a courageous step. It meant that appellants were chained to one another and taken by foot to the other court, in this case a distance of some forty miles. Often such trains of prisoners were exposed to public mockery, scorn, and violence.[77] Probably, prisoners accused of same-sex practices were even more prone to public outrage. Already at the day of the trial in Amsterdam one of the defendants had arrived in court with his clothes torn apart. Asked by the judge why he looked that way, he told that the police officers who had walked him from his jail to the court house had taken him on purpose through crowded streets. Later on, in a letter to the High Court the man also complained about the abuse he suffered from fellow-inmates while being in custody.[78] Half way between Amsterdam and The Hague two of the other appellants got wounded when a mob hit them with stones and dirt.[79]

Adam Cornelissen presented the judges of the High Court his handwritten defense. In it, he told the court that due to nature of his supposed crime no lawyer had wanted to take his case. Nonetheless, his parents had enabled him to consult a jurist, who had obviously provided him with the required arguments. Cornelissen flatly denied all charges (which was probably a wise thing to do) yet the rest of his defense suggests that indeed he had been one of the onlookers with a glass of jenever in his hand. He challenged the court to show him the law that prohibited him to drink jenever while others committed a crime. He also challenged the court to show him the law that ordered him as a private citizen to stop others when they committed crimes. And indeed, he asked, could one call the supposed behavior of the defendants a crime? Obviously, if the other inhabitants in the house in Amsterdam had seen what they claimed to have seen, they had gone at great length to do so. The windows and the door between the room and the hallway sat ten feet high. The room could only be reached by a stairway. A room was a private space, Cornelissen stated, and what citizens did privately could not harm public decency, if there were no unwanting witnesses. In fact, he argued, there was no such thing as public space without such wit-

nesses, any less than there existed public slander without other people
than antagonists themselves being present.[80]

The outcome of this appeal gradually forced prosecutors and judges to
argue their cases. In 1833 Rudolph van Ingen was prosecuted in Amsterdam after he had assaulted a young man. The latter had lured van Ingen
into a stable in which several other young men lay in hiding, who caught
van Ingen when he put his hand in his "victim's" pants. According to the
prosecutor, van Ingen had committed a public indecency because the
doors of the stable had been open. However, the court acquitted him
because, despite the fact it considered van Ingen's behavior despicable,
there had been no other witnesses aside from those who tried to lure him.[81]

When after 1839 official registers of jurisprudence were published, verdicts by the High Court of Holland in similar cases echoed one of the arguments Adam Cornelissen had made in 1826: there is no such thing as public
indecency without people who are unwillingly exposed to "indecent" behavior. In 1839 the High Military Court in Holland acquitted a navy captain for
that very reason, when he tried to clear his name after a conviction. Although
the court was convinced the captain had "a proclivity to commit acts contrary to decency," it came to the conclusion that he had engaged in such
activities in the privacy of his cabin. It also concluded that sailors on the captain's ship had willingly exposed themselves to the captain's behavior by spying on him at night. Several decades later the High Council (the name had
changed) affirmed a conviction for public indecency of two men, because
pedestrians while passing a house one evening, because of a bright lamp
behind glass curtains, could not escape noticing what these men were doing
behind a window. And again, a couple of men who appealed their case in
1888 were acquitted because neighbors had been spying on them.[82]

Obviously, notions about "public" and "private" are related to space. Yet as
the defense by Adam Cornelissen in 1826 and the consequent verdicts by
the High Court of Holland show, the emerging boundaries between "public" and "private" did not just refer to "outside" and "inside" and they
referred to more than just space.

The boundary between "public" and "private" was set by the presence
of witnesses and even more by their intentions. In the end it meant that all
space was "private" unless people against their wish were exposed to erotic
or sexual acts of others. Or to put it the other way round, all space was
"public" when people saw themselves unwillingly confronted with other
people's sexual acts.

In the eighteenth century prosecutors and judges through an ever
threatening death penalty tried to get a hold over a suspect's soul, whereas

on the other hand "sodomites" themselves developed a self awareness
that was also an inner sanctum. Even though that inner sanctum got
beyond the reach of persecutors with the enforcement of the French penal
code, it did not set "sodomites" free of persecution, nor was the state willing to respect that sanctum. For the state, it took a battle like that of Adam
Cornelissen and his friends, to—grudgingly—acknowledge the existence
of that sanctum. Private space, as far as it referred to a physical category,
became the external representation of a subjectivity that in the course of a
century had grown into an inner sanctum. In the end, emerging legal
boundaries between "public" and "private" in nineteenth-century Holland—which were fought for by those who were most at risk—also defined
the democratic right to determine one's own life. It seems only fair to say
that this created the very basis of the emancipatory movements of the late
nineteenth century.

ABBREVIATIONS USED IN ENDNOTES

ARA: Algemeen Rijks Archief = General State Archive.
HGH: Hooggerechtshof = High Court.
GAA: Gemeente Archief Amsterdam = Municipal Archive Amsterdam.
GADH: Gemeente Archief Den Haag = Municipal Archive The Hague
GAU: Gemeente Archief Utrecht = Municipal Archive Utrecht
GAU SA: Secretariaats Archief = Secretarial Archive
HvA: Hof van Assisen = Court of Assises.
PGNH: Provinciaal Gerechtshof Noord Holland = Provincial Court North Holland
RANH: Rijks Archief Noord Holland = State Archive North Holland
RAZH: Rijksarchief Zuid-holland = State Archive South Holland
REA: Rechtbank van Eerste Aanleg = Court of First Instance.
StS: Staats Secretarie = State Secretary.

ENDNOTES

1. GAA 5074–192
2. See Theo van der Meer, *Sodoms zaad in Nederland: Het ontstaan van
homoseksualiteit in de vroegmoderne tijd* (The Hague: Nijmegen SUN, 1995), pp.
480–86, where I have listed 127 people who were prosecuted for public indecency
by courts in Amsterdam, Utrecht, and The Hague between 1811 and 1838. I limited
my research—which was an epilogue to more general research up to 1811—to that
period because in 1838 the organization of the courts changed radically. The number of public indecency trials multiplied in the second half of the nineteenth century.
Gert Hekma, *Homoseksualiteit, een medische reputatie: De uitdoktering van de
homoseksueel in Nederland* (Amsterdam: SUA, 1987), pp. 105–11.
3. RANH HvA 162, no. 394.
4. ARA HGH 395.

5. Many studies about nineteenth- and twentieth-century discourses have made this claim. In the Netherlands the most outspoken representative of this canon is Gert Hekma, *Homoseksualiteit* and "A Female Soul in a Male Body: Sexual Inversion as Gender Inversion in Nineteenth-Century Sexology," in Gilbert Herdt, *Third Sex—Third Gender: Beyond Sexual Dimorphism in Culture and History* (New York: Zone Books, 1994), pp. 213–39.

6. Cf. Theo van der Meer, "Sodomy and the Pursuit of a Third Sex in the Early Modern Period," in Herdt, *Third Sex*, pp. 179–89; Theo van der Meer, *Sodoms zaad in Nederland*, pp. 155–78.

7. Jacob Campo Weyerman, *Godgeleerde Zeedekundige en Historische Bedenkingen over den text des Apostels Pauli aen de Romeynen*, cap. 1, vers 27 (Amsterdam, 1730), pp. 3–8. Charles Taylor, *Sources of the Self: The Making of Modern Identity* (Cambridge: Harvard University Press, 1996), pp. 115–25.

8. Gert Hekma, "A Female Soul in a Male Body."

9. Henricus Carolus van Byler, *Helsche boosheit of grouwelyke zonde van sodomie* (Groningen, 1731), p. 51. Van Byler quoted a certain Josephus, probably the Italian humanist Josephus Scaliger, who in 1593 became a professor at the University of Leiden. Scaliger was one of many who, in antipapist diatribes, blamed Catholics and in particular Italians for engaging in same-sex practices. Cf. Winfried Schleiner, " 'That matter which ought not to be heard of': Homophobic Slurs in Renaissance Cultural Politics," *Journal of Homosexuality* 29, no. 4 (1994): 41–75. Eighteenth-century Dutch authors often quoted or plagiarized Scaliger on the subject of sodomy. Van der Meer, *Sodoms zaad in Nederland*, p. 373.

10. Cf. Thomas Laqueur, *Making Sex: Body and Gender from the Greeks to Freud* (Cambridge: Harvard University Press, 1990).

11. Gert Hekma, "A Female Soul in a Male Body."

12. See for this and following paragraphs about the Batavian republic: Simon Schama, *Patriots and Liberators: Revolution in the Netherlands, 1780–1811* (London: Collins, 1977).

13. Barbara W. Tuchman, *The First Salute* (New York: Ballantine Books, 1989), p. 58.

14. Florike Egmond, "De hoge jurisdicties van het 18e-eeuwse Holland. Een aanzet tot de bepaling van hun aantal, ligging en begrenzingen," *Holland: Regionaal historisch tijdschrift* 19 (1987): 129–61.

15. Leonard I. Leeb, *The Ideological Origins of the Batavian Revolution: History and Politics in the Dutch Republic, 1747–1800* (The Hague: Nijhoff, 1973); Eco Haitsma Mulier, "Between Humanism and Enlightenment: The Dutch Writing of History," in Margareth C. Jacob and Wijnand W. Mijnhardt, eds., *The Dutch Republic in the Eighteenth Century: Decline, Enlightenment, and Revolution* (Ithaca: Cornell University Press), pp. 170–87.

16. Maarten Salden, "Artikel 248bis Wetboek van Strafrecht, de geschiedenis van een strafbaarstelling," *Groniek: Gronings historisch tijdschrift* 12, no. 66 (1980): 38–48.

17. Marc Boode, "Les tres fort, vilain et detestable criesme et pechié de zodomie: homosexualité et répression à Bruges pendant la Période Bourguignonne (Fin

14e–début 16e siècle)," in Hugo Soly and René Vermeir, eds., *Beleid en bestuur in de oude Nederlanden. Liber amicorum Prof. Dr. M. de Baelde* (Ghent, 1993); and J. Decavele, "Brugse en Gentse mendicanten op de brandstapel in 1578," in Soly and Vermeir, pp. 73–93. It should be noted that many of those prosecuted in Bruges and Ghent in this period were either Italians or clerics. The latter were especially prosecuted on sodomy charges at the time of the Reformation.

18. Van der Meer, "Sodomy and the Pursuit of a Third Sex," pp. 141–42.

19. Ibid.

20. Rudolf M. Dekker and Lotte C. van de Pol, *The Tradition of Female Transvestism in Early Modern Europe* (London: Macmillan, 1989), pp. 58–63. These women seem to have been prosecuted rather for their transvestism and swindle with marriage licenses than for their sexual acts.

21. Theo van der Meer, "Tribades on Trial: Female Same-Sex Offenders in Late Eighteenth-Century Amsterdam," in John Fout, ed., *Forbidden History: The State, Society, and the Regulation of Sexuality in Modern Europe* (Chicago: University of Chicago Press, 1992), pp. 189–210; Myriam Everard, *Ziel en zinnen: Over liefde en lust tussen vrouwen in de tweede helft van de achttiende eeuw* (Groningen: Historische Uitgeverij, 1994), pp. 136–79.

22. Van der Meer, "Sodomy and the Pursuit of a Third Sex," pp. 148–69. As I have argued, these subculture emerged in northwestern Europe in the late seventeenth century, when mostly hierarchical or intergenerational forms of same-sex behavior gradually began to change into more egalitarian ones, involving adult men who could change active and passive roles. This change coincided with the transition from what Norbert Elias in his The Civilizing Process (Oxford: Blackwell, 1996) termed to be a "shame culture" into a "guilt culture" or, in more modern words, it coincided wiith the emergence of "interiority." (Cf. Taylor, *Sources of the Self*). Both imply that people from the late seventh century onward started to derive their incentives from a 'self" or a personal conscience rather than from exterior motives that were rooted in pursuits of public honor. (Cf, Theo van der Meer, "Sodom's Seed in the Netherlands; The Emergence of Homosexuallity in the Earlly Modern Period," *Journal of Homosexuality* 34, no. 1 (1997): 1–16.)

23. Van der Meer, *Sodoms zaad in Nederland, pp. 13–19, 81–89.*

24. Florike Egmond, "Fragmentatie, rechtsverscheidenheid en rechtsongelijkheid in de Noordelijke Nederlanden tijdens de zeventiende en achttiende eeuw," in Sjoerd Faber, ed., *Nieuw licht op oude justitie: Misdaad en straf ten tijde van de Republiek* (Muiderberg: Coutinho, 1989), pp. 9–23.

25. Van der Meer, *Sodoms zaad in Nederland*, pp. 134–52.

26. *Requeste en deductie mitsgaders advisen en bylagen in de zake van Joan Lucas Bouwens ingedaagde in persoon* (Amsterdam: n.d).

27. Van der Meer, *Sodoms zaad in Nederland*, pp. 93–98.

28. GAA 5061–538, pp. 373–78.

29. Sjoerd Faber, *Strafrechtspleging en criminaliteit te Amsterdam, 1680–1811: De nieuwe menslievendheid* (Arnhem: Gouda Quint), pp. 282–83.

30. RANH 162, no. 394.

31. RANH 162, no. 394; GAU REA 16.

32. GAU SA II 2244 17911.

33. GADH RA 11.

34. Van der Meer, *Sodoms zaad in Nederland*, p. 441.

35. GAU REA 16.

36. GAU REA 15b.

37. Van der Meer, *Sodoms zaad in Nederland*, pp. 442–44.

38. GAA 5074–151, 193.

39. GAA 5074–156, 199.

40. GAA 5074–274.

41. Van der Meer, *Sodoms zaad in Nederland*, p. 429.

42. RANH PGNH 114, no. 609.

43. A. J. van der AA, *Biographisch Woordenboek der Nederlanden, 1852–1878*, vol. 9, p. 251.

44. RANH PGNH 39 no. 886

45. Ibid., pp. 416–417.

46. Ibid., p. 424.

47. Sibo van Ruller, *Genade voor recht: Gratieverlening aan ter dood veroordeelden in Nederland, 1806–1870* (Amsterdam: De Bataafsche Leeuw, 1987), pp. 30–31.

48. Michel Rey, "Police et sodomie à Paris au xviiie siècle: du péché au désordre," in *Revue d'histoire moderne et contemporaine* 29(1982): 113–124.

49. Michael David Sibalis, "The Regulation of Male Homosexuality in Revolutionary and Napoleonic France, 1789–1815,"in Jeffrey Merrick and Bryant T. Ragan, eds., *Homosexuality in Modern France* (New York: Oxford University, 1996), pp. 80–101.

50. RANH HvA 162, no. 394.

51. RANH HvA 41, no. 25.

52. ARA StS 355 no. 138.

53. ARA HGH 632, no. 392.

54. ARA HGH 662.

55. ARA StS 355, no. 308.

56. See for this case and the rest of this story about Herderschee: Theo van der Meer, "Gezangen in den Kerker. De temige gedichten van een sodomiet," in *Homologie* 12, no. 1 (1990): 32–35.

57. The church minister published the poems under his own name, but with an introduction in which he told part of Herderschee's life story, leaving it however to the good reader to guess what Herderschee had been convicted for. Although Herderschee in many of his poems lamented the sins of his youth, he never referred to the actual reason for his conviction. Willem Goede, *Gezangen in den kerker: Ten voordeele van den dichter uitgegeven* (Rotterdam, 1819).

58. ARA HGH 664, no. 1.

59. GAU SA II 2244 17622.

60. GAA 5074–151, 371. Like with other recidivists his penalty was doubled. Herderschee claimed to have permission from the head of police to live in Amsterdam.

61. Cf. Van Ruller, *Genade voor recht*, p. 164. Provó Kluit often spoke in derogatory terms about Jews ("Jewish braggart"). The man who was sentenced by him to a long term imprisonment in 1846 just for pulling another man's arm, was also Jewish; that was repeatedly pointed out by the police officers who arrested him. RANH PGNH 114, no. 609.

62. Van der Meer, "Sodomy and the Pursuit of a Third Sex," pp. 139–141.

63. Ibid., pp. 178–189.

64. Van der Meer, *Sodoms zaad in Nederland*, pp. 385–95.

65. Ibid., pp. 404–8.

66. Franciscus Lievens Kersteman, *Hollandsch rechtsgeleerd woordenboek* (Amsterdam, 1768), p. 528.

67. Ibid. This author was not the only one who thought of sodomites in such terms. In 1751 a thief who was arrested in Delft and who turned out to have prostituted himself spoke in the same terms of sodomites. GAU SA II 2244 1750–51. In the final quarter of the eighteenth century, penal reformers in Holland explicitly called all sodomites effeminate and suggested that they would be scaffolded (whipping) in female attire before being incarcerated in the women's prison and be shown around for the public occasionally in their infamous clothes. Van der Meer, "Sodomy and the Pursuit of a Third Sex," pp. 193–194.

68. Ibid., pp. 195–203.

69. Van der Meer, *Sodoms zaad in Nederland*, p. 346.

70. ARA HGH 395.

71. Ibid.

72. A. Vink, *Geschied—en zedekundig verhaal, omtrent J.C. Klanck aan onnatuurlijke zonde en moord schuldig* (Amsterdam, 1817), p. 43.

73. GADH RA 12, 14–12–1797; GAU SA III 469, 15–12–1797.

74. See for this description as well as the verdicts GAA 5074–192.

75. ARA HGH 395.

76. These papers, including the text of the drinking song, rest in the files of this case at the high court, ARA HGH 395.

77. Herman Franke, *Twee eeuwen gevangen: Misdaad en straf in Nederland* (Utrecht, 1990), pp. 20–22.

78. ARA HGH 1258.

79. RAZH REA The Hague 31, no. 141.

80. ARA HGH 395.

81. GAA 5074–438.

82. Gert Hekma, "Bewaar mij voor den waanzin van het recht. De jurisprudentie met betrekking tot homoseksueel gedrag (1811–1911)," in Sjoerd Faber et al., *Criminaliteit in de Negentiende Eeuw* (Hilversum: Uitgeverij Verloren, 1989), p. 115.

"Living Well Is the Best Revenge": Outing, Privacy, and Psychoanalysis

12

CHRISTOPHER LANE

> *To make the* private *into something* public *is an action that has terrific repercussions in the preinvented world.*
> —*David Wojnarowicz*

"Terrific repercussions": It would be difficult to find a more apt or ambiguous evaluation of outing. "Terrific" suggests that abolishing the public/private distinction can generate at least two responses, the first congratulatory, the second fearful. An artist and writer who consistently spurned fear, Wojnarowicz seems to favor the first response, telling us that "each public disclosure of a fragment of private reality serves as a dismantling tool" and that words themselves "can strip the power from a memory or an event. Words can cut the ropes of an experience."[1] In *Close to the Knives: A Memoir of Disintegration* (1991), Wojnarowicz nonetheless shows that "mak[ing] the *private* into something *public*" often has devastating consequences—that refusing to distinguish between these registers turns him and his friends into objects of public scorn and hatred.[2]

This essay aims to account for the ambiguous and volatile political effects of outing—that is, revealing publicly that someone powerful, famous, possibly homophobic, and supposedly heterosexual is in fact gay or lesbian. Arguing that we cannot rid ourselves of these effects, I propose that we reframe arguments justifying outing in order to grasp the consequences of abolishing the public/private distinction. Without arguing in favor of the closet or existing definitions of privacy, I show that shattering fantasies adhering to the self-definition of groups, cultures, and even nations has profound political repercussions. Since outing aims above all to demolish homophobia, I ask whether the complexity of public and private fantasy does not in fact prevent outers from achieving this end.

Outing proponents argue that cultural hypocrisy about sexuality represents a willingness to foster elements of heterosexual desire in public forums, but an ability to tolerate homosexuality only in sublimated forms. Larry Gross, Warren Johansson, and William Percy argue of the United States and Britain (along with Michelangelo Signorile arguing of the U.S. alone) that these countries theoretically support the right to privacy for everyone, while routinely denying lesbians and gay men this right when public interest, curiosity, and perceptions of indecency are at stake.[3] These critics eloquently show that heterosexual journalists now denouncing queer activists for outing closeted homosexuals often themselves practiced outing to create scandal. Such critics argue that it is because outing challenges the general public's insistence that homosexuality be a private (and thus apparently publicly reprehensible) issue that the effects of outing are unpredictable and the results often questionable. And they conclude that hypocrisy prevents the public from grasping that homosexuality prevails throughout the world. I am sympathetic to these claims and agree that the symbolization of lesbian and gay desire is bound to be fraught, considering our culture's aversion to homosexuality—perhaps even to all sexuality.[4] At the same time, I want to complicate the idea that outing can disband or override public fantasies about homosexuality, whether benign or homophobic.

Scandal derives inevitably from the distance between public and private forms of sexual identity.[5] Such distance recurs as "common wisdom," for contemporary citizens routinely are asked to check their behavior in public. The tension between fantasized and legislated acts can therefore generate distress, tension, or furtive pleasure. Not surprisingly, this tension is the subject, even the cause, of a great many books and films.[6] Consciously overstepping the line between acceptable and forbidden sexuality—especially in public—has very significant political and legal repercussions.

The outing debates become complicated when we interpret this line, for they exist tangentially to Britain's and North America's widespread aversion to homosexual desire; their urgency also derives from the scandalous delay of both British and U.S. governments regarding the AIDS pandemic.[7] More problematic still, the vagarious enforcement of laws about consent and privacy lies in tension with these cultures' insistence on their laws' symbolic coherence. While the repercussions of breaking a law therefore vary greatly from one U.S. state to another—and certainly within Europe—the punishment specific to gay-related "crimes" overrides a general, legislative dilemma about the law's inconsistency.[8] When an act such as sodomy, which technically was grounds for public execution in Britain until 1861 and

Christopher
Lane

imprisonment until 1967, is now (under certain provisions) decriminalized, the law confronts the parameters of its legislative control.[9] Since all laws undergo forms of culturally determined revision, this last point would seem obvious, yet the repercussions of this revision for homosexuality are worth emphasizing because they aren't clear and because conservatives (and some libertarians and radicals) often assume that legal perspectives on homosexuality are unchanging and unambiguous.

The symbolic effect of this legal inconsistency may explain some of the fury surfacing after someone has deliberately broken a social code—for instance, revealing another's sexual identity. Outing someone breaks no statutory law, but it radically disregards our *culture's* insistence, however recent, illusory, or arbitrarily enforced, that homosexuality is a private affair. The drama of social fury accompanying outing may compensate for the public's inability to regulate all forms of behavior considered unacceptable: homosexual desire is much more prevalent than the public believes. And so outing inevitably reproduces in specific ways what the public suspects but does not tolerate of gay and lesbian life.

Although the line between public and private sexuality is indistinct, even nebulous (despite legal and cultural protestations to the contrary), outing tries to cancel this line's ambiguity. Those advocating outing want to revoke the argument that being gay or lesbian is something to hide. Indeed, to reveal lesbian and gay life in all its diversity, outers eschew the concept of privacy: they claim that lesbians and gay men *have* nothing to hide and therefore—at least vis-à-vis the public—no related claim to privacy. Signorile explains this strategy in his influential book *Queer in America: Sex, the Media, and the Closets of Power* (1993):

> If, as we've been saying all along, being gay is not about sex acts or about what we do in our bedrooms but is a much larger matter regarding identity and culture and community, then how can the mere fact of being gay be private? How can being gay be private when being *straight* isn't? Sex is private. But by outing we do not discuss anyone's sex life. We only say they're gay. (Signorile 79–80; original emphasis).

One might wonder, then, why Signorile uses the following quotation from Whitman as an epigraph for his book: "Out of the dark confinement! out from behind the screen! It is useless to protest, I know all and expose it."

To demystify gay and lesbian life, outing identifies closet homosexuals as part of a vast network of desires, liaisons, and relationships that prevail throughout North America, Europe, and all other countries and cultures. According to outers, the extent of this network is an "open secret" in the public's mind; according to the latter, however, the public/private distinc-

tion seems necessary (and perhaps also "successful") *until* outing renders
sexual doubt and evasion impossible.[10] In abolishing the public/private distinction, outers want to refute a widespread conviction that gays and lesbians are few, isolated, and unhappy. As the activist group Queer Nation
proudly announced when the group was founded in 1990, "We're here,
we're queer, get used to it!" (Johansson and Percy 112).

Our difficulty is not that outing tries to combat hypocrisy by promoting
clear and ethical considerations of different sexualities. It is that outing can
function *only* when the gap between public and private life is politically and
ontologically intolerable. Outers find this gap objectionable because it promotes sexual hypocrisy, given cultural aversion to public manifestations of
homosexual desire. Yet outers partly exploit this gap even as they try to
abolish it, for their strategy necessarily relies on preexisting social hatred of
lesbians and gay men. If outed into these cultures, one does not reduce the
gap between public and private sexuality; one becomes instead a *symptom*
of the cultural and political violence enforcing this gap. Outing signifies "the
return of the repressed" because it shatters our culture's demand that
homosexuality be a private affair. And while outers and queer activists consider this shattering a cause for celebration, they underestimate our culture's ongoing *attachment* to this fiction and its violent reaction to seeing
this fiction desecrated.

The general public can respond to outing with disbelief and denial; it can
also vengefully accuse the outer of *depriving its recourse to fantasy at all*. We
need only recall that the boy who insisted that the emperor had no clothes
challenged the faulty perception of adults concerned to maintain what Freud
called "the future of [their] illusion."[11] Outers—and queer activists in general—obviously hope that honesty eventually will make the public *accept* that
the emperor has no clothes—i.e., that homosexuality is a prevalent and satisfying form of desire. Yet in Hans Christian Andersen's fable "The Emperor's
New Clothes" (c. 1837), the public's need to believe that the emperor *was*
clothed demonstrates the extent to which fantasy can (and often must) override empirical evidence. This widespread suspension of disbelief might lead
us to doubt whether the public *can* accept homosexuality in any simple way
without profound, even devastating, internal or external repercussions—an
argument quite different from suggesting that its judgment is correct.

Considering this problem's magnitude, outing emerges not only as a
partial consequence of the public/private split—a split it tries erroneously to
disband—but as a symptom of the impossible reconciliation between public and private definitions of sexuality. The following sections will make clear
why I am calling this reconciliation "impossible." To avoid misunderstand-
ing, however, let me stress that arguing that the public/private split is to a

degree politically and psychically inevitable does not stop me supporting
political initiatives that *alleviate* this split. My intention is to question
whether the antagonism that outing fosters—indeed, the antagonism that
queer activism finds so compelling—can address the type of resistance
surfacing when the illusion of ubiquitous heterosexuality begins to fail. In
this respect, my argument aims *not* toward a simple reformism. It suggests
that outing enforces a type of scrutiny that often has been historically disastrous for lesbians and gay men. To support these claims, I'll revisit the outing debates in Britain before engaging related arguments that surfaced in
North America. My aim throughout will be to identify the phantasmatic and
psychopolitical repercussions of the public/private split.

Honi soit qui mal y pense

From their inception in 1990 and 1991 respectively, the British activist
groups OutRage! and FROCS (Faggots Rooting Out Closeted Sexuality)
tried repeatedly to promote clear and ethical considerations of lesbian and
gay life.[12] OutRage!'s principal spokesman, Peter Tatchell, endured ferocious hostility and homophobia when he campaigned in 1981–83 to
become a Labour Member of Parliament. Thus when Tatchell threatened to
out prominent M.P.'s and clergy in the early '90s, he was already a familiar
and despised face in British politics. *The Sun* told several million Britons in
September 1991, "Peter Tatchell squealed like a stuck pig because newspapers revealed his homosexuality when he stood as a Labour parliamentary candidate. Invasion of privacy, he protested. Now hypocrite Tatchell is
backing a spiteful campaign by gays."[13] The conditions seemed primed for
Tatchell to endure more humiliation from a nation convinced that *he* had
perpetrated sexual terrorism. Walter Schwarz of *The Guardian* summarized
this conviction by calling OutRage! a group of "outrageous tormentors."[14]
The Daily Mirror went further by declaring, "The bitches come out! I can
think of only one word to describe the 'outing' campaign by those desperately sad people who call themselves gay. Bitchy."[15]

For many in Britain, Tatchell became the symptom of a difficulty he and
OutRage! tried in vain to express. The public found their pronouncements
on others' sexuality unacceptable, not just because of hypocrisy and a wish
to enforce the closet,[16] but because the public found the evidence mar-
shaled as sexual certainty impossible to believe. The British press called
outing a "witchhunt" (*Daily Star*); "spiteful" (*The Sun*); "Bitchy and
scabrous" (*Daily Mirror*); "downright nasty" (*The Independent*); "McCarthyism" (*Daily Telegraph*); "despicable and vicious" (*Daily Mail*); and "cruel"
(*Daily Express*).[17] Like Tatchell himself, who recently acknowledged his par-

tial reliance on speculation about the people he tried to out,[18] the British public seemed torn between a desire to know and an acute resistance to further investigations into sexuality's meaning. The Bishop of London reproduced this dilemma, after he was outed, with a very British response: he called his sexuality "a gray area."[19]

Following a renewed and equally intense focus on outing during the winter of 1994 and spring of 1995, an impasse has emerged in Britain between gay activists arguing for an end to sexual hypocrisy and the closet, and the mainstream media and public (including many lesbians and gays) who sense that a more extensive and volatile issue has been broached. This concerns not only the numbers of previously closeted lesbians and gays in Britain's Parliament and Church, but the meaning attributed to sexuality in public life and the *reliability* of publicly renaming people as lesbian or gay. Outing cleaves to reliable assertion by claiming that someone has "passed" under a false identity. The Bishop of London tried to evade this principle, but outing presupposes that the outed must adopt or deny a position on either side of a supposedly well-demarcated sexual divide.

To emphasize the stable constituency and boundaries of lesbian and gay communities, lesbian and gay politics downplays that sexuality militates against clear identities. Indeed, in a strange about-face this politics often plays up—and even enforces—the distance between queers and the "heteronormative." In her recent article on our "bisexual moment," however, Lillian Faderman usefully asks, "What becomes of our political movement if we openly acknowledge that sexuality is flexible and fluid, that *gay* and *lesbian* does not signify 'a people' but rather a 'sometime behavior?'"[20] The question is ironic because political movements and subjects routinely—even necessarily—disavow what they find internally unstable. To "openly acknowledge" that "*gay* and *lesbian* does not signify 'a people'" would require lesbians and gays to accept sexual instability, especially at the level of politics and community. As we'll see, this instability undermines outing's declarative purpose of identifying the constituency of lesbian and gay communities.

Considering Britain's vehement loathing of outing and outers, a loathing more pronounced than its general hatred of queers, this debate about sexuality and coming out has important political consequences. In December 1994, at the height of the second wave of national hysteria about OutRage!, Edward Pearce published a brief article in *The Guardian* entitled "Keep the Closet Door Closed." He represented outing as "the *treacherous breaking* of privacy, the sneaking of an individual's chosen secrets, the *treason* to common decency."[21] In denouncing outing, and even gay and lesbian visibility, Pearce claimed that "hypocrisy is a great civilising force" (29).

Pearce's argument has many historical precedents in Britain; indeed,
the very idea that thought can beget evil is stamped on every British passport. The proverb "*Honi soit qui mal y pense,*" meaning "evil be to him who
thinks evil," appears on this passport beside another French aphorism:
"*Dieu et mon droit,*" or "God and my right."[22] The second aphorism con-
ceptually binds Britain's laws to the authority of its Church, but both
proverbs represent all speech and thought contravening "*Dieu et mon
droit*" as heresy and national betrayal.

Whether by intent or default, outing has become part of these aphorisms' complicated history, for it aims to revoke elements of "treachery" by
drawing clear distinctions between straight and gay. FROCS tried to revoke
hypocrisy and secrecy by dispelling every enigma about homosexuality in
Britain. Indeed, the two men in charge of this group announced to journalists in 1991 that their aim of outing 200 prominent figures was an elaborate
"hoax" designed to highlight media hypocrisy, a fact few newspapers
reported because it caused them embarrassment.[23] Nonetheless, this
demand for clarity and accountability has immense consequences in lesbian and gay politics, ironically when the term "queer" *seems* to dissolve
related problems over the gay/straight binary by emphasizing that sexuality
is fluid and mutable. Carole-Anne Tyler put this well when she remarked,
"Ours is the era of the passing of *passing* as a politically viable response to
oppression."[24]

Passing may not be viable, but sexuality's vicissitudes challenge the
gay/straight binary. And while outing advocates insist strongly on sexual
clarity, sentiments such as "Labels are for cans" are popular among
queer youth *and* queer activist groups—for instance, Homocult and Subversive Street Queers, the first an anonymous but mixed-sex collective in
Manchester, U.K., who in 1991 denounced OutRage! as an ineffective
sham; the second more closely aligned with that city's punk scene. Com-
menting on equivalent North American groups from Britain, Keith Alcorn
has written:

> Groups in Toronto, Detroit, San Francisco, and Los Angeles are now walk-
> ing away from the [gay] ghetto, arguing that gay identity is part of the
> power structure in the same way as white middle-class men and Citicorp
> bank and the Pentagon. It must be destroyed. Even Queer Nation is the
> enemy for these radicals, who believe that queers must subsume their
> identity into a movement of the powerless in American society, and that
> *sexual identity is not an axis around which any sort of political activism
> should be organised.*[25]

How does this position square with outing, which aims to pronounce the
sexual truth of "gay hypocrites"? Groups such as Queer Nation adopt a

position between queer anarchists and the "gay establishment" (a term
begging many questions, not least about intergenerational differences), but
their ensuing arguments about heterosexuality—and sexuality in general—
remain palpably unclear, because while arguing against norms they
nonetheless tend to reinstate them. From this perspective, as examples will
show, outing ironically is one way to reinstate the norm.

However difficult they are to accept or represent, these disparities in
political strategy and sexual focus profoundly affect our ability to discuss outing. While an anonymously published four-page tabloid manifesto entitled *I
Hate Straights* circulated at a recent New York Pride celebration (21–22), for
instance, other groups and publications consider "straight queers" their
allies *against* "gay conservatives" (24). *Queer Power Now,* a pamphlet distributed after the British premiere of Derek Jarman's film *Edward II,*
declared, "There are straight queers, bi-queers, tranny queers, lez queers,
fag queers, SM queers, fisting queers" (qtd. 24). According to Alcorn, "the
pamphlet included among the 'oppressors' of that identity the Stonewall
Group [a gay reformist group committed to discussion with Britain's Govern-
ment], Sir Ian McKellen, GALOP [Gay and Lesbian London Policing], and
the gay press. 'Haven't we had enough of the lies being peddled by our leaders?' the pamphlet asked. 'It's time to turn on our oppressors—gay and
straight' " (24). Many other groups reject any chance of alliance with
straights and gays, however. In 1991 the Toronto fanzine *Bimbox* declared,
in the following unfortunate words, "We will not tolerate any form of 'lesbian
and gay' philosophy . . . we will not tolerate their voluntary assimilation into
heterosexual culture . . . Furthermore, if we see lesbians and gays being
assaulted in the streets, we will not intervene, we will join in" (qtd. 22).

Eschewing all of these disputes and contradictions, Johansson and
Percy characterize U.S. queer activism as a coherent force using outing to
advance a shared political goal:

> In the new concept of a Queer Nation, . . . disloyalty through hypocritical
> perjury of one's identity seems to merit outing, *even if the closeted are in
> no other way harming fellow queer nationals.* The need for collective visi-
> bility overrules the right of privacy. . . . Vociferously condemned as it may
> be by the majority of heterosexuals and perhaps even of us, outing is here
> to stay. It will not end until the tradition of secrecy and hypocrisy in regard
> to the subject ends. . . . Those who do not learn from the past are con-
> demned to repeat its mistakes! Outing of closeted celebrities is needed for
> the good of the cause. We insist upon our right to claim them as our broth-
> ers and sisters.   (3, 4, 30; my emphasis)

Given the needs of such brothers and sisters, how should we understand
the consequences of Johansson and Percy's "even if"? The repercussions

of "hypocritical perjury of one's identity" are immense, demanding potentially that we out those who don't tell everyone they meet that they are lesbian or gay. Perjury—meaning "to be forsworn or guilty of false swearing"—
derives from the Latin *perjūrāre,* to break one's oath.[26] However, after
Faderman's question about sexuality's vicissitudes in public forums, what
does—or can—this oath mean?

Johansson and Percy admit that this question strikes at the heart of outing's political purpose: "Are we merely individual 'sinners' or 'deviates,' "
they ask, "or do we form a community or even a 'nation within a nation' with
legitimate interests that the rest of society should recognize and respect?"
(225). The first part of this question is easy to answer, though the second
part, "do we form . . . a nation within a nation?" requires more consideration. By acknowledging that sexuality often conflicts with political coherence and unity, we *can* still aim for a politics that does justice to this question's complexity without invoking "the good of the cause" to denounce the
"hypocritical perjury of one's identity" (30, 3). For the idea of "cause" often
generates egregious unbrotherly and unsisterly notions of political correction that revoke conventional definitions of community: "Now some queer
nationals believe that they have a right to out passive as well as active trai-
tors and collaborationists" (23). Given Johansson and Percy's above understanding of treachery ("disloyalty through hypocritical perjury of one's identity"), which uncannily resembles that of the British public and press,
wouldn't every bisexual—or even apolitical lesbian and gay man—represent a collaborator?

Many advocates of outing downplay these questions about sexual and
community definition as politically irrelevant; they claim that a basic
approximation to lesbian or gay desire is sufficient to render someone
accountable to his or her subculture (Signorile xi–xii; Gross 108, 121).[27] In
ways that contradict their earlier desire for "brothers and sisters," for
instance, Johansson and Percy support activists who "feel it is their moral
right or even duty to force people out of the closet, either to make them support the movement or at least to *discredit them as foes*, and also to *show
how many idols of the masses or pillars of the nation are in fact closet
queers*" (175; my emphases). This contradictory perspective leads Johansson and Percy to propose about a hypothetical Supreme Court justice who
is gay "or who even merely enjoyed gay pornography [and] worked against
gay interests": "Such a character, especially one with life tenure, which
most American judges have, should be outed as soon as possible, *even if
he (or she) is presently deciding for queer national interests*, or does so
occasionally, if only because it is time to make up for historians' failure thus
far to identify even one gay Supreme Court justice" (227; my emphasis).

Since outers and activists such as Johansson and Percy usually avoid careful analysis of hypocrisy, they downplay that outing can backfire with appalling political consequences. When queer theory and activism do theo- rize public resistance (and this is curiously rare), they tend to follow Michel Foucault's assertion that resistance, being discursive, is an implicit form of power.[28] From this perspective, outing someone—that is, naming the dis- cursive "truth" of their sexuality—implies political resistance and change. However, outing (as other queer activists realize) flies in the face of Fou- cault's insistence that we *not* consider sexuality the truth of subjectivity. "Not only did ['the society that emerged in the nineteenth century'] speak of sex and compel everyone to do so," Foucault warned, but "it also set out to formulate the uniform truth of sex. As if it suspected sex of harboring a fundamental secret."[29]

It is surely not coincidence that the famous 1890 *Harvard Law Review* article formulating "the right to privacy" as a right "to be let alone" emerged in the United States soon after Henry Labouchère's amendment to Britain's 1885 Criminal Law Amendment Act.[30] For good reason, this amendment was known as the "Blackmailers' Charter."[31] Such links between demands for privacy and sexuality's intense public scrutiny in the 1890s form an important backdrop to contemporary debates about public sexual identity. On the one hand, the growing strength of Europe's and North America's les- bian and gay communities partly transforms this history by representing outing as a collective, even seditious act.[32] Thus outing seems to defeat hypocrisy and the likelihood of blackmail by giving lesbians and gay men group dignity (Signorile 254). On the other hand, whether from public belief that outing is still blackmail or from homophobic indifference to all lesbian and gay arguments, this distinction between outing and blackmail is rarely understood or accepted in the wider culture. Usually, the media enjoy the spectacle that outing generates:[33] They relish what seem to be public sacri- fices, witnessing scenes they themselves often create under different cir- cumstances.[34]

These points contextualize broad conflicts about sexual knowledge and truth in Britain, due in part to that country's refusal to adopt a North Ameri- can model of civil rights. Traditionally, British activists have not demanded these rights, based on their assumption that such rewards would be tar- nished by co-optive legal demands to behave.[35] To understand the history of outing in Britain, then, we must return to the *Wolfenden Report*'s 1957 recommendation (enacted ten years later) that Britain's Parliament partially decriminalize male homosexuality.[36] We must also revisit the 1979 trial of Jeremy Thorpe, leader of Britain's Liberal Party until 1976. The effects of this trial not only partly informed Margaret Thatcher's homophobic policies throughout the 1980s, but dramatically reframed debates about public acts and private fantasies that in the 1990s were crucial to FROCS and Out-Rage!

The Trial of Jeremy Thorpe

Jeremy Thorpe was leader of the Liberal Party from January 1967 until May 1976. Although he never became prime minister, Thorpe played a decisive role in British politics toward the mid '70s because his party's coalition with Harold Wilson's Labour government (1974–79) increasingly was necessary for the Labour Party to retain power. Since it jeopardized the Liberal Party's awkward coalition with Harold Wilson's Labour Party, the scandal attached to Thorpe's trial contributed to the General Election in 1979 that brought Thatcher's government to office for three terms.

With three of his colleagues in the Liberal Party, Thorpe was arrested on August 4, 1978, for conspiring to murder Norman Scott, a younger man with whom he was sexually involved before the affair became a political embarrassment. Thorpe was also charged with inciting his friend and colleague David Holmes to murder Scott (he was acquitted of both charges in June 1979). In ways that confirm my previous claims about public/private identity, most of this trial aimed not to determine Thorpe's guilt but to exonerate him of blame. To this end, the judge and defense counsel focused relentlessly on the sexual behavior of Norman Scott, the plaintiff and Thorpe's accuser.[37] This focus prevailed throughout the trial, despite the court's *accepting* that Scott was the object of a conspiracy to frighten (if not murder) him. The court also accepted that Scott's dog was shot, and that Scott might have been, had his potential assassin's gun not jammed on a deserted moor in West England. Judge Joseph Cantley remarked, "That there was a conspiracy of some sort with [Andrew] Newton [the man Thorpe's colleagues allegedly hired to assassinate Scott] I don't think is disputed. I don't think Newton went on the moor with Scott just on some frolic of his own, or for some eccentric reason of his own."[38] Auberon Waugh, who witnessed the trial, remarks: "When the judge had finished chuckling to himself over this sally, he tried fitting the evidence to the idea of conspiracy."[39]

Although Thorpe faced one charge of conspiracy to murder and one charge of inciting to murder, the defense counsel and judge repeatedly characterized him as rational and honest. They did so in the hope of representing him as incapable of *participating* in homosexual acts. As we'll see, homosexuality became a hinge in the trial, determining guilt or innocence according to the manner in which Thorpe and Scott seemed "implicated" in it. Put another way, the court's deliberations turned obsessively on Thor-

pe's and Scott's ability to *enjoy* homosexual sex. Thorpe's apparent resistance to homosexuality—later interpreted by the court as an "incapacity" to
experience such desire voluntarily and with pleasure—emerged alongside
repeated emphasis on Scott's excessive enjoyment.[40] After derailing Scott's
testament about his sexual relationship with Thorpe on several occasions,[41]
for instance, Judge Cantley remarked in his summing up, with spurious
balance: "You will remember [Scott] well—a hysterical, warped personality,
accomplished sponger, and very skillful at exciting and exploiting sympathy. . . . He is a crook. . . . He is a fraud. He is a sponger. He is a whiner. He
is a parasite. But of course, he could still be telling the truth. It is a question
of belief . . . I am not expressing any opinion."[42]

Although homosexuality surfaced later in the trial as one of Thorpe's *tendencies*,[43] Thorpe's two marriages represented sufficient reparation in the
court's eyes. Waugh remarks,

> A further reason why *Private Eye* [the satirical journal]—and, for that mat-
> ter, the whole of Fleet Street—decided [initially] to leave the story alone
> was that Thorpe had married, fathered a son and been widowed in the
> meantime and was, in fact, on the point of remarrying. A bachelor might
> have been fair game, but a reformed homosexual, whose only apparent
> crime was to have had an unfortunate affair with a neurotic many years
> earlier, was safe. I stress this point because it seems important. There was
> not the slightest danger to Thorpe that any newspaper in England was
> going to print Scott's allegation [before the trial].[44]

Times have indeed changed. Yet this redemptive emphasis on marriage
endorses a conception of the homosexual as traitor; and Thorpe and Scott
had quite different relations to this fantasy.[45] The trial dehomosexualized
Thorpe by emphasizing the difference between private tendencies and
acts, and again between private acts and public testimony. In this way, it
differed radically from outing debates in the United States, which tend to
accept the subject's homosexuality but not the media's right to breach their
privacy.[46]

In Britain, projection and dissociation can derail outing so successfully
that outers (such as Norman Scott and Peter Tatchell) begin to resemble
criminals. Under fierce public scrutiny, the coherence of outing also begins to
fray: its constitutive elements—motive, knowledge, principle, and aim—are
challenged and ridiculed. On March 21, 1995, for instance, *The Scotsman*
reported: "Dozens of [M.P.'s] are widely believed to have homosexual leanings."[47] In an "Opinion" column, published the same day and entitled "The
Right to Stay in the Closet," however, *The Scotsman* scoffed at these claims:
"So, now we know. Twenty Members of Parliament, including two Cabinet
Ministers, are closet gays. Actually, we know nothing of the sort. All we know

is that the militant gay group, OutRage!, believes they are gay and has written telling them what it thinks they should do about their sexuality, which is to proclaim it. It is hard not to detect a note of menace in this tactic."[48]

Like *The Scotsman,* the 1957 *Wolfenden Report* and the 1979 trial of Jeremy Thorpe repeatedly used such terms as "homosexual leanings" and "homosexual tendencies."[49] However, neither term can be read as a simple euphemism for homosexual identity. These phrases are part of a serious belief in Britain that homosexual leanings, tendencies, acts, and identities are *not* identical, a belief seriously jeopardizing the possibility of gay and lesbian rights. Indeed, that the *Wolfenden Report* succeeded at all may be due to its careful emphasis on "the Distinction between Propensity and Behavior."[50] By corollary, outing's conflation of these terms represents something of a conceptual violence whose "culprit" (Peter Tatchell, say) aims to unify what others insist is nebulous and doubtful.[51] By questioning the relation between homosexual tendency and public identity, Britons assume that an individual's alleged "superiority" (like Thorpe's) can render these terms not only nonidentical, but—in certain circumstances—mutually exclusive. This pattern differs radically from that in the United States, where private tendencies already appear to many as public acts.[52]

For important historical and political reasons, Britain has resisted the argument advanced with some success in the United States that lesbians and gays constitute a minority, even a nation or people (repeating Johansson and Percy [225]).[53] Whatever false homogenization this ideal maintains—and the term "queer" aims to betray such imaginary unity—the U.S. media fundamentally accepted this argument in the early 1990s: there are gays and there are straights, and the closeted are just gays living erroneously or hypocritically. Distinctions between "quality" daily newspapers and supermarket tabloids do not invalidate the idea that in cases of disclosure or continued secrecy, the U.S. media understood they were simply hiding or exposing closeted gays.

In Britain, however, where legal and political distinctions between sexual identity and sexual acts frequently recur (Thorpe's 1979 trial and the Bishop of London's recent outing are only two important examples), insisting on sexual clarity raises doubts about homosexuality's consistency and fears about its persistence and likely treachery. Departing from the U.S. model, which can evacuate sexuality from gay issues without rescinding identitarian demands for equality, sexuality in Britain surfaces as a menacing specter lacking coherence and identity: its diffusion in the public realm becomes the source of its threat, and thus an apparent justification for its violent control. As the journalist Edward Pearce exclaimed, "A latent loathing of homosexuals has been raised like a small virulent poltergeist" (29).

Poltergeists combine an overabundance of "will" with an acute desire
for retribution: They punish without rationale, yet never properly materialize
(*poltern* in German means "to crash, rant, or create an uproar"). This "virulent poltergeist" shows us the raging symptom (or "outrage") prevailing as
Britain's fierce resistance to public discussion of homosexuality. Add this
specter to Britain's rigid libel laws and the historical legacy of the 1880s
and '90s purity campaigns, which tried to excise desire from public *and* private forums, and an advocate of outing rapidly becomes a symptom of
Britain's fears about its sexual unmaking. If for Pearce, "hypocrisy is a great
civilising force," then an imaginary rapport must join truth to degeneration.
The strength of this rapport makes clear why Britain's resistance to homosexuality probably will not disappear in the foreseeable future without pro-
ducing another "virulent poltergeist." The rest of my essay aims to explain
this point.

Britain's Poltergeists

When Thorpe resigned from the Liberal Party on May 10, 1976, the May 16
Sunday Mirror opined in this leader: "After he heard the news of Mr. Thorpe's resignation, Mr. Scott told reporters that he was so upset he had been
sick. It is all decent people in Britain who are sick, Mr. Scott. Sick at your
behaviour. Ugh!"[54] Given Scott's symbolic proximity to Peter Tatchell, it is
not surprising that Tatchell experienced similar sentiments, several years
later, during his unsuccessful 1981–83 campaign to become a Labour
Member of Parliament.[55]

During Tatchell's campaign, Britain's media focused relentlessly on his
homosexuality and Australian birth.[56] Unlike Thorpe, however, whose
ignominy rapidly dissolved after his exit from politics, Tatchell suffered
appalling displays of public cruelty. In *The Battle for Bermondsey,* a title
poignantly invoking "The Battle of Britain," Tatchell describes how people
delivered several hundred hate letters to him (108) and made numerous
and round-the-clock obscene phone calls (104); accused him of "involvement in terrorist activity and sexual assaults on young [children]" (104);
attempted three times to run him down in cars (106); threw bottles and
bricks at him; painted swastikas on the door of his apartment; sent him bul-
lets and white feathers (emblems of cowardice); and threatened many
times to fire-bomb his apartment (106, 108). One man boasted that "he
had a little silver bullet which he was saving to 'plant between [Tatchell's]
fucking eyes' " (qtd. 106). "We don't want sodomites you sewer rat,"
declared another (qtd. 106). And others wrote of their connection to violent
gangs and expressed limitless disgust simply at Tatchell's presence in their

neighborhood. One "ex-docker and . . . lifelong member of the Labour Party" wrote his party offices, exclaiming, "At the age of 64 with a heart complaint and therefore little to lose, I would be prepared to go to prison for the murder of this creep—don't imagine I'm a crank—far from it." The man concluded: "By the way, how did a single homosexual get a council flat to begin with?" (qtd. 72–73).

During Tatchell's campaign, ten thousand anonymous election leaflets circulated featuring two sketches: one depicted the Queen of England; the other, Tatchell wearing lipstick and makeup. Under the headline, "Which Queen Will You Vote For?," the leaflet stated:

> Peter Tatchell is an outspoken critic of the Queen and Royal Family—he believes that the monarchy should be abolished. The people of Bermondsey have always been loyal to the Crown. Many Bermondsey families lost loved ones during two world wars. They fought and died to save their country—on the other hand Tatchell ran away from his home in Australia to avoid fighting for his. Soldiers from this area also fought in the Falklands—needless to say Tatchell stabbed our boys in the back by opposing the war. Tatchell is a traitor to Queen and country. (Qtd. 139–40)

The leaflet published Tatchell's home address and phone number.

Although Tatchell's homosexuality apparently renders him effete (lipstick-wearing), his "treachery" appears to virilize him, as if the public's fantasy of Tatchell must oscillate between persecuting him and displaying a defenseless fear ("Tatchell stabbed our boys in the back"). Since Tatchell nonetheless was invoked overall as a *deficit* to his community, rather than a potential representative of it, he signified the *theft* of Britain's nostalgic relation to its past empire. He represented this nostalgia's volatile failure, confirming a point I made earlier about the trial of Jeremy Thorpe and its complex investment in fantasies about violence and homosexual enjoyment.[57]

During Britain's "feeding frenzy" on outing and Tatchell in the winter of 1994 and spring of 1995, these issues recurred with astonishing durability. In *The Guardian*, March 1995, Suzanne Moore remarked that "Tatchell has . . . been denounced as a hypocrite, a blackmailer, one of the least 'attractive characters in British public life,' a fascist, a terrorist and, in the words of *The Sun,* 'an Australian-born Vietnam draft-dodger.' "[58] Moore also argued that Tatchell's "vilification" relates implicitly to his "delving into that fragile area—the gap between what is private and what is public."[59] This "gap" signifies Britain's generic fear of sexual certainty *and* indeterminacy, making clear why a "victim" such as Tatchell can slip intangibly into a "persecutor," even an "executioner." Pearce elaborates: "[Gays] might consider that just as acceptance must evolve and deepen, it can also regress if the broad public is affronted often enough" (29).

Highlighting the resilience of this "virulent poltergeist," which sounds heterosexuality's antagonistic relation to homosexuality, outing takes us beyond the ethically expedient and politically correct. The heated exchanges prevailing throughout North America's and Europe's lesbian and gay communities during the 1980s and early '90s demonstrate that outing involves more than considerations of privacy, autonomy, and the right to self-definition, though it urgently engages all these issues. Outing also raises fundamental questions about our economy of pleasure, whose presumed superabundance, depletion, and theft have radical implications for theories of phobia and hatred.

Thus far, I have merely amplified the relative opacity of psychic pleasure and satisfaction. Such complexity requires us to consider the implicit "price" of enjoyment in an economy that has little (but not nothing) to do with wealth, rational argument, or conscious knowledge.[60] Considering this complexity, how can we discuss outing without understanding public fantasy and revenge? If outing represents an urgent need for lesbian and gay freedom, of what does freedom really consist when homosexuality—and especially homosexual enjoyment—precipitates such fear and violent reprisals? The following section tries to answer these questions, arguing that the lesbian and gay community must face these concerns without accusations of calumny: the argument on all sides of the "outing" debate leads beyond questions of treachery, though the debate's substantive focus repeats this notion with unfortunate persistence.

The Ecstasy of Bigotry

If we believe that outing is a political need with tangible rewards, what remains of the right to privacy argument? In *Queer in America,* Signorile concedes that outers oppose not only homophobes and bigots but those (including fellow gays and lesbians) who support the right to privacy (76, 80, 84–88, 128, and 254). Claiming that gay and lesbian defenders of privacy ultimately defend hypocrisy, Signorile argues that hypocrisy rescinds one's political rights. In this respect, his aim appears revolutionary (dismantling the closet to reveal homosexuality's influence on all aspects of American culture), while his *strategy* resembles that of arch-homophobes such as Judge Robert H. Bork.[61] If we accept Signorile's simplistic claim that everyone in the closet is a hypocrite, what else—besides privacy—do we lose? What fundamentally do we gain?

"Outing demands that everyone come out, and defines the closeted—especially those in power—as cowards who are stalling progress at a critical time," declares Signorile (84). While representing the straight and gay media as cowardly, Signorile maintains that he has the *implicit* approval of all those wanting to correct a political wrong. This position gains some support from Richard Rouilard, former editor of *The Advocate*, who asks us to "watch . . . double standards." But watch the following shift in Rouilard's own argument:[62]

> The closet in the 90s is too complex a historical phenomenon to be dismissed perfunctorily by the moralists and activists du jour. Clearly, it shouldn't be supported and co-opted, but neither should it be invaded or evaded without some inspection of the homophobic undercurrent that insinuates itself in all Americans' consciousness, gay or straight. So sit back, think about hurting someone, helping thousands, and feel that guilt. Another closet door will certainly be pried open soon enough. More than likely not by *The Advocate*. But that is why God made Queer Nation.[63]

Although this statement partly endorses Signorile, it implicates us all in a dilemma concerning more than political justice or cowardice. The "homophobic undercurrent that insinuates itself in all Americans' consciousness" connects implicitly with Rouilard's ironic invitation to "think about hurting someone"—that is, think about what David Mayo and Martin Gunderson have called everyone's capacity for "malice."[64] In this context, and from knowledge about the "virulence" of Conservative-Christian homophobia, the gay community's overall reticence on the subject of outing suggests not cowardice, but justifiable concern that Signorile's rejection of privacy arguments rescinds every lesbian's or gay's right to protection from the law and state, however out or closeted she or he may be.[65] Signorile argues that the state has placed privacy entirely beyond the reach of gays and lesbians, as in the Supreme Court's 1986 *Bowers v. Hardwick* ruling, and that this apparently is to our advantage:[66] we cannot maintain the closet in such a climate, he claims, for the state will not allow it (171, 396; see also Gross 142–46). The Supreme Court's ruling on May 20, 1996, against Colorado's Amendment 2 nonetheless suggests that the state's relation to lesbians and gays is complex and not predetermined.[67] However, is *Signorile's* position to our advantage?

If we heed the words of rights advocates, the demand for privacy represents more than a naive quest for equality; it stems from a realization that some distance from the law is a prerequisite for sexual emancipation. More sophisticated privacy arguments, such as Jed Rubenfeld's recent article in the *Harvard Law Review*, question the political efficacy of fighting a "reverse discourse" for the autonomy of homosexuals while recognizing that malice and prejudice prevent us from disbanding this discourse entirely, and that legal protection from homophobia is a vital aspect of freedom from the state.[68] Rubenfeld put this conceptual dilemma well: "Once personhood's

logic is extended to the 'communal aspects' of our identity, the right to privacy of the intolerant—or simply of those committed to prevailing values—
will always conflict with the right to privacy of the iconoclast. . . . [T]he identities that personhood strives most vigorously to protect are themselves likely to impinge upon others' self-definition. . . . [T]he neighbor's private life is
precisely not one's own" (766–67, 770).

This argument has profound implications for community justifications of
outing. While outers ignore group and community intolerance (theirs and
others') by eclipsing complex aspects of sexual identity and public fantasy,
Rubenfeld asks pointedly of homophobe and gay activist alike: "Is homosexual sex said to be self-definitive simply because it is sex, or especially
because it is *homosexual* sex?" (777–78). Such distrust of personhood
leads Rubenfeld to a Foucauldian position that is strangely underrepresent-
ed in outing debates: "In the very concept of a homosexual identity there is
something potentially disserving—if not disrespectful—to the cause advo-
cated. There is something not altogether liberating" (779).

Rubenfeld inadvertently turns the queer outing argument on its head:
he demonstrates that outing someone into rigid distinctions between heterosexuality and homosexuality has conservative implications: "The mere
act of being homosexual is seen as definitive in itself precisely because of
its supposed abnormality, and it remains categorically definitive regardless
of what sort of partners or sexual encounters the homosexual pursues. . . .
Thus personhood, at the instant it proclaims a freedom of self-definition,
reproduces the very constraints on identity that it purports to resist"
(780–81; my emphasis).

Despite this argument's political and conceptual value, Rubenfeld stalls
on questions of interiority versus exteriority, following his incorrect characterization that for Freud "sexuality . . . delineates an inner boundary of the
strictly personal that the state ought not to be able to cross" (770–71),[69]
and on the social and psychodynamics of "theft," given his Foucauldian
understanding of power (783). With its attention to fantasy and identification, psychoanalysis would dispute Rubenfeld's confident assertion that
"the neighbor's private life is precisely not one's own"; indeed, as the previous section demonstrated, both outers and homophobes ceaselessly confront the enigma (and occasional horror) of the neighbor's demand. I return
to this point.

"There *is* something fundamental at stake in the privacy decisions,"
Rubenfeld claims, "but it is not the proscribed conduct, nor even the freedom of decision—it is not what is being taken away. The distinctive and sin-
gular characteristic of the laws against which the right to privacy has been
applied lies in their *productive* or *affirmative* consequences" (783–84; orig-

inal emphases). We cannot dispute that such laws "*take over* the lives of
the persons involved: they occupy and preoccupy" (784; original emphasis), but such claims ignore how laws *also* operate by detraction, impediment, and prohibition. To consider *Bowers v. Hardwick* solely a mechanism
that "forceably [*sic*] channel[s] certain individuals—supposing the law is
obeyed—into a network of social institutions and relations that will occupy
their lives to a substantial degree" (799–800) provides only a vague
account of the incident precipitating the Supreme Court's 1986 ruling: a
state such as Georgia apparently can make homosexual sodomy a criminal
offense *without violating either man's right to privacy.*

This returns us to Signorile's argument, while casting his claims in a
more complicated light. After the Georgia police arrested Michael Hardwick
for having anal sex with another man in his bedroom, they invoked a statute
that renders sodomy illegal; more important for our reading, they did
"deprive [him] of something deeply important to [him]," perhaps also "crucial to [his] happiness" (799). Psychoanalytic theory adds this dimension to
Rubenfeld's argument to consider the extent to which laws negotiate
between desire and impediment. This negotiation may "affirm" and "produce," in a strictly Foucauldian sense, but it also raises urgent questions
about the *law's* vagarious enforcement and implicit "pleasures," and the
ease with which such pleasures override our own (as in the *Bowers v. Hardwick* ruling) precisely *because* they deprive us of sexual freedom. For quite
different reasons, then, Rubenfeld and Signorile ignore this dimension of
the law: Rubenfeld, to shift privacy debates away from prohibition and personhood; Signorile, to downplay the consequences of outing people to prej-
udicial media and homophobes.

Signorile tries to destroy the homophobic myth that lesbian and gay sexuality renders us inhuman—a myth that would quickly turn privacy into a
need—but outing does not fulfill this aim (indeed, it often confirms the
myth by highlighting rifts within the lesbian and gay community). The price
we pay for disbanding all claims to privacy—as all who agree to outing,
however fervently or halfheartedly, eventually concede—is an astonishing
absence of any recourse to legal and state protection. Reproducing the
worst excesses of public surveillance between the 1890s and 1990s, outing can represent lesbian and gay desire only as a public affair. This renders the outed—and, by default, every lesbian and gay—a symptom of
social hatred: the outed is subject entirely to the Other's jouissance, the
agent that tries to steal our pleasure by insisting that we renounce and sacrifice this pleasure.[70] This may explain why we commonly hear that we do
not deserve rights, homes, or life (recall what Tatchell endured for standing
for office). William F. Buckley Jr.'s fantasy of tattooing people with HIV and

AIDS, echoed by Pat Robertson's infamous pronouncement, "AIDS is God's
way of weeding his garden," are brutal examples of the Other's jouissance.
Since outing cannot detach itself from this jouissance, despite Signorile's
and Gross's claims to the contrary, why do we consider it progressive?

All sides of the outing debate downplay the extent to which jouissance—
which I am calling "the ecstasy of bigotry"—lies at the heart of this issue.
Jouissance is not a force or pleasure pertaining only to the outlaw; it
includes the homophobe who considers himself an *agent* of the law. Consider Fran Lebowitz's important concerns about outing, which echo fear
about Bork and his allies: "[Outing is] damaging, it's immoral, it's
McCarthyism, it's terrorism, it's cannibalism, it's beneath contempt. . . . To
me this is a bunch of Jews lining up other Jews to go to a concentration
camp."[71] Like Lebowitz, psychoanalysis asks us to consider the jouissance
operating in these scenarios and the dilemma that rights and outing advocates face over sexuality's "treacherous" relation to identity.

Without theorizing homophobia and sexual aversion, Signorile asks us to
rescind all "benefits" related to the closet—including compromised forms
of privacy—because they are hypocritical and contingent on whatever
power is at stake. By displaying our collective visibility, he argues, we will
compel the state to recognize our numbers and accord us human rights.
Ignoring the present legal paradox in which states such as Massachusetts
and Minnesota have antidiscrimination legislation for lesbians and gay men
as well as sodomy statutes (Minnesota also has legislation defining gay
bashing as a hate crime),[72] Signorile claims that outing and mass coming
out will make the closet redundant: "Outing is a natural process that will
eventually make itself obsolete" (83). However schematic this sounds, it
highlights a conceptual understanding of the closet that has tremendous
importance for queer activism: that the state often (though not exclusively)
relegates every lesbian and gay to a legal outcast, living below or beyond
society's minimal terms of inclusion. Briefly eschewing his idealistic vision
of homosexuality's eventual mass acceptance (83)—that is, post-outing,
Signorile gives us a perspective on lawlessness that not only justifies anger,
but also deems homosexual desire axiomatically rebellious, even seditious.

Signorile's conviction that most lesbians and gay men naively defend the
right to privacy ironically repeats Judge Bork's and others' claims that
homosexuality rescinds lesbians' and gays' human rights, and—by a
bizarre twist of projection—that it fosters a need for protection among *heterosexuals.* Signorile seems to grasp this political and psychic issue only in
his Afterword to *Queer in America*, when he cautions against assuming that
greater opposition is a sign of our imminent victory. Similarly, Johansson
and Percy acknowledge only in the preface to their book's second printing,

"time has also shown that progress in gay rights seems always to be dogged by backlash" (xxxi). This leads them to admit, somewhat remarkably, given their prior hypotheses and statements about "hypocritical perjury of one's identity" (3): "We feel that at this time the non-English speaking areas— even France and most of the other areas of Western Europe, with their long-time cultural traditions of respect for privacy, longtime decriminalization of sodomy, and their strict libel laws, are perhaps not ripe for outing" (xxxiii).

"Progress in gay rights seems always to be dogged by backlash": unfortunately, Signorile reproduces this situation in his book when defining lesbian and gay politics by strict binaries between honesty and deceit, ally and enemy, hero and collaborator. The stakes of hypocrisy logically escalate here—reproducing the problem I identified earlier in Johansson and Percy's work—to the point where no one can feasibly participate in politics *without foreclosing on the indeterminacies of their sexual identity, fantasies, and past.*[73] This is not a pro-closet argument; what concerns me are the broader implications of outing, public malice, and our assumption that desire must correspond publicly to identity for our politics to be cogent. As Alan Sinfield remarks of comparable issues in Britain: "We don't know how many straights are confirmed in their malice by Queer and how many are impressed by its boldness. We don't even know how far we should be bothering about what straights think anyway."[74] Arguing that "we don't need to produce our own villains; the straight media will do that for us," and that "community doesn't mean establishing a party line," Sinfield usefully adds, "if you are struggling to be Gay [in rural England], the last thing you want is someone living in more fortunate circumstances telling you that you don't measure up because you can't think of yourself as Queer."[75]

Those emphasizing outing's political and symbolic necessity often defend it on the grounds that it not only defeats political hypocrisy and provides role models, but corrects a distorted self-image by demanding communitarian involvement. This argument represents coming out not only as a *right* but as a *duty*; it assumes, primarily, that being closeted is a manifest betrayal of others, while coming out is itself politically reparative.

Perhaps not surprisingly, such outing advocates in Britain and North America maintain a strong—but still contentious—belief that political hypocrisy disbands all related concerns about outing's efficacy. Invoking hypocrisy inaugurates a zero-sum strategy, however, in which the debate's many sides rapidly diminish to two: for or against. When philosophers such as Richard Mohr argue vigorously for the right to out the closeted, for instance, they simplify the issues and gloss over the fact that outing can (and has) cost lesbians and gays dearly in happiness. Mohr unusually concedes that "vindictive outing *is* like McCarthyism: such outing feeds gays to the wolves, who thereby are made stronger. And to the extent that outing is viewed as punishment of any sort . . . [it] seems to pander to the values and punitive instrumentalities of the dominant culture, giving them at least the appearance of credence."[76] But he insists: "The point of outing, as I have defended it, is not to wreak vengeance, not to punish, and not to deflect attention from one's own debased state. Its point is to avoid degrading oneself" (36).

Mohr doesn't seem to realize that the motivation behind his argument hinges not only on agency and intention, but on unconscious predicates. Since he theorizes only conscious intention, Mohr urges "the outer . . . not [to] pledge allegiance to the phobia-driven cyclone of hate that admittedly is sometimes a foreseeable consequence of outing" (36–37). Nonetheless, his section on "Outing as Vindictiveness and Punishment" ends by vacillating: "What *is* troublesome is the *doubt,* the possibility, that some outing is indeed motivated by lingering self-hatred on the part of the outer" (37; second emphasis mine). The point is surely that outing cannot *avoid* this "phobia-driven cyclone of hatred" by goodwill, strategy, or radical intention; its risk lies precisely in the immense volatility of public reaction to homosexuality.[77] To this extent, what happens to the right to self-determination *even in* examples of manifest hypocrisy, *even when* anticipating that such hypocrites will eventually join the gay and lesbian community? Since the principle of self-determination often vanishes at this point (it must for outing to seem justifiable), how can we accept the communitarian argument and distinguish justification from punishment and humiliation? We read such confident assertions as Mark Chekola's: "[A]ny loss of 'privacy' entailed by coming out of the closet can be more than compensated by the rewards of casting off implications of worthlessness."[78] Why does privacy require quotation marks in this citation? Chekola's point may be true, but it doesn't take us far enough; troubling questions still remain. How, for example, can privacy vanish so quickly from discussion? And what is at stake in insisting on unequivocal and public forms of sexuality?

Those advocating outing often respond that the closet is either an annoying symptom of sexual reticence or, as Leo Bersani has put it quite differently, a widespread *aversion* to sex.[79] But to do justice to Bersani's argument, we must ask whether outing (or even coming out) can resolve sexuality's difficult—perhaps impossible—relation to identity and public symbols. Is there not something at stake in the tenuous quality of outing and coming out that militates against final closure, stable understanding, and even lasting satisfaction?

In Bersani's essay, aversion is not limited to the phobic; it is a drama afflicting us all.[80] Mayo and Gunderson argue relatedly that we need protection—however imaginary or limited in practice—not only from prejudice, but from our capacity for "malice" *against* "our own"; that is, from our jouissance and aversion.[81] These arguments complement, not contradict, the contention of many queer activists and writers that coming out should *not* be reconciliatory, but a trenchant statement about the differences (and surely the agonistic similarities) between straights and gays.[82] Since this argument also engages differences among gays, we must consider the role of jouissance here; class and racial politics tell us only half the story.

Ironically, Signorile—in language that now would probably make him cringe—once offered a related assessment of these differences: "Be part of the solution instead of the problem. If not, then get the fuck out of our way. Because we're coming through and nothing is going to stop us. And if that means we have to pull you down, well, then, have a nice fall" (73). Whatever we think about this statement, it troubles Signorile's and Gabriel Rotello's related but nonidentical efforts to replace the term "outing" with one they consider fairer: "equalizing" (78).[83] Here, the obstacle to "equalizing" relations between straights and gays is not simply the closet, hypocrisy, class, or "power"; it is also "the ecstasy of bigotry." Thus Signorile writes of Rouilard, former editor of *The Advocate*:

> Rouilard's change of mind is fairly typical for gay men and lesbians: First, they're adamantly opposed to outing; then it's okay, if the person to be outed is involved in blatant and vicious homophobic actions. Finally, most come to the conclusion that a person's sexuality should be discussed whenever it is pertinent to a news story. Often opinion swings 180 degrees, so that *in a vindictive stage we stretch circumstances to say that the person being outed has engaged in the most horrendous, ruthless activities imaginable. I did this sometimes myself*—often in capital letters—in my *OutWeek* columns. Even lawyer Sandra Lowe did it, at first adamantly opposed to outing, then comparing [then Assistant Secretary of Defense Peter] Williams to "a Jew in the SS." . . . . It's hard to say if *The Advocate's* demonizing him actually helped or hurt the story. I confess that it made me uneasy.   (128; my emphasis)

Signorile does at least realize here that outing's *political* certainty conflicts with the psychic ambiguities that inform it; this is quite a concession. To grasp this point's repercussions, however, we should note that when Edward Pearce tried to point up outing's psychic underpinnings, he offered this homophobic perspective on "malice" in *The Guardian*: "I suspect that if we had a wave of vicious anti-homosexuality here [in England], with politicians on the right picking it up as they have picked up the cheap nationalism of anti-Europeanism, some gays would be deeply, contentedly, blissfully happy. It seems that self-pity and masochism are kissing cousins" (29).

Pearce's argument rests on the fantasy that such "a wave of vicious anti-homosexuality" is elsewhere—that it has not already occurred on British soil (Tatchell's parliamentary campaign proves otherwise). Such imaginary distance blinds Pearce to the recurrence of violence in his own article, where lesbian and gay anger converts magically into sexual self-debasement. The point is that Pearce's rhetoric *anticipates* this pleasure, though he leaves others to act it out. And so, like Signorile, he indicates why jouissance—"the ecstasy of bigotry"—recurs in contemporary politics.

Pearce returns us to the French proverb *"Honi soit qui mal y pense"* ("Evil be to him who thinks evil"), which every British passport reproduces and which Pearce would rewrite as "Evil be to him who outs others." Mayo and Gunderson actually touch on this proverb's implicit violence when arguing, "Respect for privacy is a mechanism we adopt to . . . ease this tension [i.e., the] . . . prejudice and malice we might experience—and practice—if we knew how different we are from each other."[84] Seen in this light, privacy is less a means of perpetuating the closet than a form of protection we may all require, given our astonishing and agonistic proximity to others. If the closet formerly ensured this protection (or something close to it), the outed—like all lesbians and gay men—require an analogous defense against the ecstatic bigotry that Bork, Buckley, and Robertson are only too keen to realize: the imagined annihilation of all lesbians and gays. Consider a "benign" example of this fantasy, a letter written by two parents to their son after they had all vacationed together: "We're devastated that you're a homosexual. When we found out, we felt that if our plane had crashed on the way back from Hawaii, our whole family would have been better off than this" (qtd. in Signorile 250).

This example reinforces my earlier points about public desire and private retribution: The parents believe that when they "lost" their son to homosexuality, their lives (and those of other passengers and the airplane crew) became worthless. This belief takes us beyond conscious statements about loss and grief; it gestures toward imagined theft, as if the gay community has robbed these parents of satisfaction (and their son). This fantasy strengthens perceptions that gay men have robbed others to have too much pleasure, sex, and disposable income. In this fantasy's most volatile form, we see a grotesque rationale for the humiliation or death of gay men and lesbians; such fantasies become the stuff of genocide. Again, that this fantasy appears *credible* to this family and so many others clearly warrants our concern.

This link between malice and enjoyment recurs whenever we reflect seriously on the political and psychic stakes of outing lesbians and gay men. Thorpe's trial and Tatchell's persecution demonstrate that we cannot practically distinguish outing from the public's fantasies of vengeance (this also applies, albeit differently, to the United States). Hence the complex aphorism in my title, "Living well is the best revenge," attributed to George Herbert's *Jacula Prudentum* (1651), which radically implies that "living well" can deprive others of pleasure.[85] This aphorism relates enjoyment to how we tolerate and live with others. Herbert of course was not alone in formulating this notion; the Germans invoke the term *Schadenfreude* to express the pleasure of another's hubristic failure.

The idea that another's pleasure *depletes* us asks us to rethink a long and turbulent sexual history, of which outing is merely the latest symptom. But materialist accounts of homophobia can take us only so far in interpreting these links between pleasure and annihilation. By corollary, psychoanalysis can add much to this complex debate about sexual identity, political resistance, and public fantasy, for its emphasis on the differences between social and psychic resistance highlights the insufficiency of Foucauldian conceptions of power. Rather than claiming that naming sexual categories and revealing hypocrisy are inherently radical, psychoanalysis implies that these acts can have conservative, even disastrous, consequences. Psychoanalysis also argues that despite political differences between outing and blackmailing, these acts may be inseparable in public fantasy.[86] As Shane Broomhall, spokesman for FROCS, acknowledged, apparently without seeing his group's strategy as exacerbating this difficulty, "It's the homophobia that needs changing. Journalists can help do that, but the majority of them prefer to attack us, victimise us, tie us with paedophilia and say we are disgusting people, and make money out of that."[87]

The question therefore remains: Does outing diminish homophobia? I think it does just the reverse. Since unconscious factors prevail in outing cases with astonishing force, it is vital to rethink the claim that outing disbands psychic enigmas and political deceit. Highlighting a crucial difference between "Foucauldian" notions of power and psychoanalytic accounts of defense, aporia, and difficulty, I have tried to conceptualize outing within specific theories of resistance and identification. Without focusing solely on assertions of individual hypocrisy and group accountability, I have stressed that widespread fantasies of retribution make outing unpredictable and an unlikely way of diminishing homophobia; both outcomes are a political concern.

Discussions of outing quickly expand into debates about identity politics, ethics, sexual fantasy, accountability to groups and subcultures, class conflict, and political freedom. I will conclude, however, by reminding us that the gap between the "out" and the "closeted" influences sexual politics beyond our conscious comprehension and control. This gap, which only approximates to public/private distinctions, highlights our political and psychic resistances, sometimes undermining our cherished beliefs about sexual desire, identity, and community. Standing in for related enigmas about fantasy, this gap points up a difficult lesson: what we want as a community is frequently not what we desire.

By assuming that the death of privacy is our goal, however, and by directing outing toward this ideal, lesbian and gay politics is tending to ignore public reactions to outing, with their varied and unpredictable effects. As my essay has repeatedly shown, there are clear signs that we cannot overcome resistance in this way. Moreover, desire's complex relation to identity, activism, and public symbols concerns every subject, regardless of political or sexual orientation. This argument does not imply defeat or quietism; on the contrary, it challenges us to find new ways of combining sexual freedom with social equality.

ENDNOTES

I thank Larry Gross for sharing his press cuttings, and Carlos A. Ball, Leo Bersani, Tim Dean, Jason Friedman, Kevin Kopelson, Bill Leap, Robert McRuer, Chris Reed, and Vince Samar for invaluable comments on an earlier draft. The reference staffs at the New York Public Library and the University of Pennsylvania's Van Pelt Library and Biddle Law School were immensely helpful on a number of occasions. I also thank the English Department at Penn for inviting me to present an earlier version in November 1995, and the Unit for Criticism at the University of Illinois, Urbana-Champaign, for hosting my visit in March 1997.

1. David Wojnarowicz, *Close to the Knives: A Memoir of Disintegration* (New York: Vintage, 1991), pp. 121, 153.

2. In telling us that "Words can cut the ropes of an experience," Wojnarowicz is detailing what is most liberating about "mak[ing] the *private* into something *public*" (pp. 153, 121). Elsewhere, however, he is more attentive to the violent repercussions of this revelation, endorsing the thoughts of his friend Johnny, who "talked about the thin line people contain, which they can instantaneously cross to become windmills of slaughter" (p. 178). Wojnarowicz ends his memoir thus: "Meat. Blood. Memory. War. We rise to greet the State, to confront the State. Smell the flowers while you can" (p. 276).

3. Larry Gross, *Contested Closets: The Politics and Ethics of Outing* (Minneapolis: U of Minnesota P, 1993), pp. ix-x; Warren Johansson and William A. Percy, *Outing: Shattering the Conspiracy of Silence* (Binghamton, N.Y.: Harrington Park, 1994), p. 1; Michelangelo Signorile, *Queer in America: Sex, the Media, and the Closets of Power* (1993; New York: Doubleday, 1994), pp. 79–80. Subsequent references to these books give pagination in main text.

4. See Leo Bersani, "Is the Rectum a Grave?" *AIDS: Cultural Analysis/Cultural Activism*, ed. Douglas Crimp (Cambridge: MIT, 1988), p. 197. I return to this point at the end of my essay.

5. See William A. Cohen, *Sex Scandal: The Private Parts of Victorian Fiction* (Durham: Duke UP, 1996), pp. 5, 7, 12.

6. The film *Personal Services* (dir. Terry Jones, 1987) is a useful example because it depicts British sexual hypocrisy. The film adapts the real-life story of Christine Painter, a British waitress, who later managed a successful brothel catering to prominent English lawyers and businessmen.

7. The title of my essay derives in part from Andrew Holleran's thoughts about living with AIDS, in *Ground Zero* (New York: Morrow, 1988), p. 74.

8. My point about homosexuality's varied legal status is not equivalent, however, to a claim for legal relativism and voluntarism.

9. England and Wales's first legal statute against sodomy dates from 1533. Under Henry VIII, this statute endorsed and superseded ecclesiastical law by condemning all acts of buggery as "crimes against nature" punishable by hanging. Although one of the last enactments of this statute was in England in February 1816, when four crew members of H.M.S. *Africaine* were hanged for buggery after a major naval scandal, the statute remained part of English and Welsh law until 1861 and Scottish law until 1889: The 1861 Offences Against the Person Act removed the death penalty for buggery, "replacing it by sentences of between ten years and life"; see Jeffrey Weeks, "Discourse, Desire, and Sexual Deviance: Some Problems in a History of Homosexuality," *The Making of the Modern Homosexual*, ed. Kenneth Plummer (London: Hutchinson, 1981), p. 85. See also note 36 below.

10. D. A. Miller, "Secret Subjects, Open Secrets," *The Novel and the Police* (Berkeley: U of California P, 1988), pp. 192–220.

11. Sigmund Freud, *The Future of an Illusion* (1927), *Standard Edition of the Complete Psychological Works of Sigmund Freud*, ed. and trans. James Strachey (London: Hogarth, 1953–74), 21:3–56.

12. OutRage! was founded in 1990 by Tatchell and others in response to the murder of gay activist Michael Boothe, who was kicked to death by a gang in West London ("Teachings by the Church Underpinned Persecution," *The Guardian* [March 14, 1995], p. 3).

13. *The Sun,* Editorial, reprinted in Terry Sanderson, "Media Watch," *Gay Times* (London; September 1991), p. 19.

14. Walter Schwarz, "Prepare for Sins of the Father to Shock the Parish," *The Guardian* (March 15, 1995), p. 22. See also Lawrence Donegan, "OutRage! Threatens to 'Out' MPs Who Fail to Admit Homosexuality," *The Guardian* (March 21, 1995), p. 2; "The Right to Stay in the Closet," *The Scotsman* "Opinion" (March 21, 1995), p. 12.

15. *The Daily Mirror*, reprinted in Sanderson, "Media Watch," *Gay Times* (September 1991), p. 19.

16. See Signorile, *Queer in America*, pp. 68, 75–76, and Eve Kosofsky Sedgwick, *Epistemology of the Closet* (Berkeley: U of California P, 1990), pp. 56–57.

17. All quotations in Sanderson, "Media Watch," *Gay Times* (September 1991), p. 18.

18. "The Right to Stay in the Closet," *The Scotsman,* p. 12; Alex Duval Smith, "Everybody's Talking about . . . Outing!" *The Guardian* (December 2, 1994), p. 3;

and Schwarz, "Gay Demonstration Names 10 Bishops," *The Guardian* (December 1, 1994), p. 8, which quotes Tatchell as saying "We cannot always be certain that all 10 bishops are gay. We do know there have been persistent reports in Church circles which claim a present or past homosexual orientation."

19. Qtd. in "Bishop Attacks Gay Campaign to 'Out' Him," *The Herald* (March 14, 1995), p. 4.

20. Lillian Faderman, "A Bisexual Moment," *The Advocate* 689 (September 5, 1995), p. 43.

21. Edward Pearce, "Keep the Closet Door Closed," *The Guardian* (December 10, 1994), p. 29, my emphasis. Subsequent references give pagination in main text. See also two responses by *Guardian* readers: "Outing as an Expression of Impatience, Frustration, and Pain," *The Guardian* (December 12, 1994), p. 19.

22. Both aphorisms also appear on the European passports that British citizens now receive. Following the convention of non-Francophone usage, I have altered the spelling of the French participle "*honni.*"

23. David Smith, "Stopping Them in Their Tracks: David Smith Talks to Shane Broomhall, One of the Men behind the Great Outing Scam," *Gay Times* (September 1991), p. 9.

24. Carole-Anne Tyler, "Passing: Narcissism, Identity, and Difference," *differences* 6, nos.2–3 (1994): 212.

25. Keith Alcorn, "Queer and Now," *Gay Times* (May 1992), p. 22, my emphasis. Subsequent references give pagination in main text.

26. T. F. Hoad, *The Concise Oxford Dictionary of English Etymology* (Oxford: Clarendon, 1986), p. 347.

27. See also Taylor Branch, "Closets of Power," *Harper's Magazine* (October 1982), pp. 35–50.

28. Michel Foucault, "Power and Strategies," *Power/Knowledge: Selected Interviews and Other Writings 1972–1977*, ed. Colin Gordon, trans. Gordon, Leo Marshall, John Mepham, and Kate Soper (New York: Pantheon, 1972, 1980), p. 142.

29. Foucault, *The History of Sexuality*, vol. 1, trans. Robert Hurley (New York: Pantheon, 1978), p. 69.

30. Samuel Warren and Louis Brandeis, "The Right to Privacy," *Harvard Law Review* 4.5 (1890): "Political, social, and economic changes entail the recognition of new rights, and the common law, in its eternal youth, grows to meet the demands of society. . . . [W]ith the recognition of the legal value of sensations, the protection against actual bodily injury was extended to prohibit mere attempts to do suol [*sic*] injury; that is, the putting another in fear of such injury. . . . So regard for human emotions soon extended the scope of personal immunity beyond the body of the individual. . . . Recent inventions and business methods call attention to the next step which must be taken for the protection of the person, and for securing to the individual what Judge Cooley calls the right 'to be let alone' " (pp. 193–95). In 1885, however, Section 11 ("The Labouchère Amendment") of Britain's Criminal Law Amendment Act designated *all* male homosexual acts, *whether public or private*, illegal and punishable for a "term not exceeding two years, with or without hard labour"

(previously, only buggery was illegal). See Weeks, *Coming Out: Homosexual Politics in Britain, from the Nineteenth Century to the Present* (London: Quartet, 1977), p. 14, and F. B. Smith, "Labouchère's Amendment to the Criminal Law Amendment Bill," *Historical Studies* 17 (1976), pp. 165–73.

31. Weeks, *Coming Out*, pp. 14, 22.

32. Concerning the presumption that homosexuality is intrinsically radical and seditious, however, see Bersani, "Is the Rectum a Grave?" p. 205: "To want sex with another man is not exactly a credential for political radicalism."

33. Media hypocrisy is not a sufficient basis to justify equal opportunity scandal, however. For the reverse claim, see Signorile, *Queer in America*, pp. 60–61: "We weren't 'pushing the envelope.' We were having our own Carnival every night. . . . Our only recourse was to create a spectacle, something the media could sell."

34. Ibid., pp. 183–87. See also pp. 42–43, which refers to the psychology of scandal for lesbians and gay men: "Perhaps because information is power, gay people, traditionally powerless, love to revel in gossip and dish."

35. For a summary of these arguments, see Richard Smith, "Papering over the Cracks," *Gay Times* (May 1991), pp. 28–29.

36. The 1967 Sexual Offences Act did not fully legalize male homosexuality in England and Wales. It stated, "Subject to the [following] provisions . . ., a homosexual act *in private* shall not be an offence provided that the parties consent thereto and have attained the age of twenty-one years" (The Sexual Offences Act 1967, Chapter 60, 1.1, *The Public General Acts and Church Assembly Measures 1967, Part II* [London: HMSO, 1967], p. 1269; my emphasis). The age of consent for heterosexual sex was (and remains) sixteen in England and Wales while that of lesbian sex is normally the same (the legal status of lesbianism in Britain is notoriously vague), but the 1967 act stipulated a higher age for homosexual consent because, the 1957 *Wolfenden Report* argued, "We should not wish to see legalized any forms of behaviour which would swing towards a permanent habit of homosexual behaviour a young man who without such encouragement would still be capable of developing a normal habit of heterosexual adult life" (*The Wolfenden Report: Report of the Committee on Homosexual Offenses and Prostitution,* intro. Karl Menninger [New York: Stein and Day, 1963], p. 50). Departing from the law's wider provisions for heterosexual sex in public and private, the 1967 act insisted not only that sex between men occur "in private," but that it be *unseen.* If a neighbor or window-cleaner happened to see two (or more) men having sex, for instance, the act would be illegal and revised elements of the 1885 Criminal Law Amendment Act would apply. In February 1994, Britain's Parliament voted into law that men aged eighteen and above could legally consent to gay sex.

37. See Auberon Waugh, *The Last Word: An Eye-Witness Account of the Trial of Jeremy Thorpe* (Boston: Little, Brown, 1980): "By generously supporting the more favourable interpretation of Scott's motives, Mr. Taylor [leading counsel for the Crown] may have encouraged the misapprehension of which Scott himself frequently complained—that he was on trial as much as Thorpe, and the jury were being invited to choose between the two" (p. 97).

38. Judge Cantley, qtd. in ibid., p. 229.

39. Waugh, ibid.

40. See Judge Cantley's insistence that while Thorpe's letters to Scott indicated an affectionate relationship, "you [the jury] must not assume that mere affection necessarily implies buggery" (qtd. in ibid., 11); and Thorpe, "The Lies of Norman Scott, by Jeremy Thorpe," *Sunday Times* (March 14, 1976), qtd. in ibid., pp. 162–63.

41. See, for instance, Waugh, *The Last Word*, p. 101: "In 1963 . . . [Scott's] relations with Thorpe continued as before. At this point the judge interrupted to ask a question about [Scott's national insurance] cards, saying he did not want to hear about the relations."

42. Ibid., pp. 223–25. On the fifteenth day of the trial, Waugh remarks with characteristic understatement: "I began to watch Mr. Justice Cantley rather more closely. What had seemed a healthy scepticism, at the beginning of the trial, now began to seem alarmingly one-sided" (p. 142). Waugh's title for his eyewitness account derives from Judge Cantley's astonishing boast at the end of the trial: "Remember, I have the last word."

43. Ibid., p. 184: "Mr. Thorpe in 1961 was a bachelor with homosexual tendencies." See also George Alfred Carmen, QC, and leading counsel for Thorpe, in alluding to the same fact: "He [Thorpe] is human like us all. We learn, do we not, that idols sometimes have feet of clay? . . . There are people who have propensities which we personally may not understand. To them we have to extend tolerance, sympathy and compassion," Mr. Carmen, QC (qtd. in ibid., pp. 206, 208).

44. Ibid., p. 19. Waugh later speculates "about a possible agreement between prosecution and defence, with or without the judge's knowledge, that no evidence of Thorpe's homosexual background would be called provided Thorpe was prepared to acknowledge homosexual tendencies at the relevant time" (p. 49).

45. Here we can consider the relevance in national myth of such figures as Guy Burgess, the Cambridge graduate who famously defected with Donald Maclean to the Soviet Union in 1951. To the British public, Burgess's homosexuality confirmed his treachery. We might also consider the relevance of Roger Casement's homosexuality to his trial and execution for treason in 1916 for assisting the Irish during its "Easter rebellion."

46. The media's relation to privacy is changing all the time, however. For accounts largely contemporaneous with the first wave of outing in the United States (Malcolm Forbes was outed in March 1990), see Suzanne Garment, *Scandal: The Culture of Mistrust in American Politics* (New York: Times, 1991), pp. 191–97, and Larry Sabato, *Feeding Frenzy: How Attack Journalism Has Transformed American Politics* (New York: Free Press, 1991).

47. James Hardy, "Gay Lobby Urges MPs to Admit Homosexuality," *The Scotsman* (March 21, 1995), p. 9.

48. Editorial, *The Scotsman* (March 21, 1995), p. 12.

49. *The Wolfenden Report*, p. 128; Waugh, *The Last Word*, p. 117. For related accounts of Thorpe's trial and checkered career, see Lewis Chester, Magnus Linklater, and David May, *Jeremy Thorpe: A Secret Life* (London: Deutsch, 1979); Barrie

Penrose and Roger Courtiour, *The Pencourt File* (New York: Harper and Row, 1978);
and Peter Chippindale and David Leigh, *The Thorpe Committal* (London: Arrow,
1979).

50. *The Wolfenden Report,* pp. 27–30.

51. In the Glasgow *Herald,* the Right Rev. Michael Turnbull, Bishop of Durham,
who was "given a conditional discharge 26 years ago after admitting committing an
act of gross indecency in a public lavatory" is quoted, after denying he is gay, as saying that a gay lifestyle is "incompatible with full-time stipendiary ministry," qtd. in
"Bishop Attacks Gay Campaign to 'Out' Him," *The Herald* (Glasgow; March 14,
1995), p. 4. See also Schwarz, " 'Inconsistent' Bishop Dismays Campaigning
Group," *The Guardian* (September 28, 1994), p. 3, and Schwarz, "Bishop Urges
Dismissed Gay Clergy to Appeal," *The Guardian* (November 7, 1994), p. 6.

52. Implicit in the current U.S. administration's "solution" to lesbians and gay
men in the armed forces, "Don't Ask, Don't Tell, Don't Pursue," is a correlation
between desire and act, in which *desire* already renders one unfit for military service.
For explication of this assumption, see Marc Wolinsky and Kenneth Sherrill, eds.,
Gays and the Military: Joseph Steffan versus the United States (Princeton: Princeton
UP, 1993).

53. Faderman's doubts, cited earlier, may recur in recent queer *theory,* but they
are relatively uncommon in U.S. lesbian and gay politics.

54. The *Sunday Mirror* (May 16, 1976), qtd. in Waugh, *The Last Word,* p. 161.
See also Frank Pearce, "The British Press and the 'Placing' of Male Homosexuality,"
The Manufacture of News: Social Problems, Deviance and the Mass Media, ed.
Stanley Cohen and Jock Young (1973; London: Constable, 1981), pp. 303–16.

55. See Peter Tatchell, *The Battle for Bermondsey* (London: Heretic, 1983). Subsequent references give pagination in main text.

56. It is interesting, and perhaps symptomatic, that the same press struggled to
ignore all scandal attached to *Thorpe's* homosexuality only two to four years earlier,
until his trial inevitably publicized it. Waugh emphasizes this in *The Last Word*: "It is a
fact that for the five years up to the dog-shooting, there had been no mention of
Scott's allegations in any national newspaper, despite strenuous attempts by Scott
and the [South African] journalist Gordon Winter to get them printed" (p. 161).

57. I advance this argument in *The Ruling Passion: British Colonial Allegory and
the Paradox of Homosexual Desire* (Durham: Duke UP, 1995), pp. 229–31. For a
related but nonidentical argument about contemporary Britain, see Salman Rushdie,
"The New Empire within Britain" (1982), *Imaginary Homelands: Essays and Criticism 1981–1991* (London: Granta, 1991), pp. 129–38.

58. Suzanne Moore, "Straight Talking," *The Guardian* (March 10, 1995), p. 5.

59. Ibid. See also Quentin Crisp's witty article "Let Sleeping Men Lie," *Guardian*
(April 7, 1995), p. T4.

60. Concerning this last issue, Weeks has usefully characterized superficial
accounts of homophobia as follows: "Hostility towards homosexuality has usually
been seen as an arbitrary figment of men's unreason, which would soon be thrown
out on the junkyard of prehistory. . . . A more radical view of homosexuality will have

to take account of the varieties and diversity of sexual expression, of the arbitrariness of social labels, of the cultural moulding of gender and sexual identities; in short, of the historical creation of sexual beliefs and attitudes" (*Coming Out*, p. 7). Since Weeks's work, much theoretical work in lesbian and gay studies and queer theory has usefully enumerated this "radical view" but not always examined its psychic underpinnings or effects.

61. See Robert H. Bork, *The Tempting of America: The Political Seduction of the Law* (New York: Free Press, 1990), pp. 117–26, and *Slouching Towards Gomorrah: Modern Liberalism and American Decline* (New York: Regan Books, 1996), pp. 112–14.

62. Richard Rouilard, editorial, *The Advocate* 587 (October 8, 1991), qtd. in Gross, *Contested Closets*, p. 317.

63. Ibid.

64. David J. Mayo and Martin Gunderson, "Privacy and the Ethics of Outing," *Gay Ethics: Controversies in Outing, Civil Rights, and Sexual Science,* ed. Timothy F. Murphy (New York: Haworth, 1994), pp. 50, 53.

65. See Anya Palmer, "Cornered in the Confessional: Outing Is the Issue Which Splits the Gay Community," *The Guardian* (March 15, 1995), p. 22.

66. *Bowers v. Hardwick*, 478 U.S. 186 (1986).

67. See John Gallagher, "High Drama: The Supreme Court Takes a Powerful Stance on Gay Rights," *The Advocate* 710 (June 25, 1996), which quotes Justice Anthony M. Kennedy as arguing, "We must conclude that Amendment 2 [which would have prohibited Colorado from ever passing a nondiscrimination law, also voiding existing ones] classifies homosexuals not to further a proper legislative end but to make them unequal to everyone else. This Colorado cannot do. A State cannot so deem a class of persons a stranger to its laws" (p. 24).

68. Concerning the first issue, Jed Rubenfeld argues bluntly in "The Right of Privacy," *Harvard Law Review* 102, no. 4 (1989): 755: "There has been a peculiar willingness simply to state or to assume—as if it required no explanation—that matters of sexuality go straight to the heart of personal identity." Subsequent references to Rubenfeld's article give pagination in main text. For slightly different accounts of privacy and outing, see Susan J. Becker, "The Immorality of Publicly Outing Private People," *Oregon Law Review* 73, no. 1 (1994): 159–234; Andrea Austen and Adrian Alex Wellington, "Outing: The Supposed Justifications," *Canadian Journal of Law and Jurisprudence* 8, no. 1 (1995): 83–105; Vincent J. Samar, *The Right to Privacy: Lesbians, Gays, and the Constitution* (Philadelphia: Temple UP, 1991), esp. pp. ix–xii; and Janet E. Halley, "The Politics of the Closet: Towards Equal Protection for Gay, Lesbian, and Bisexual Identity," rept. in Jonathan Goldberg, ed., *Reclaiming Sodom* (New York: Routledge, 1994), pp. 145–204.

69. Rubenfeld elaborates on this "Freudian" argument, which he attributes to advocates of personhood: "In sexuality lies the hidden truth of our identity, and for the sake of our identity, society must not be allowed to repress that truth or to prevent us from discovering it" (pp. 770–71). Such characterizations betray the voice and convictions of Anglo-American Foucauldians unaware of Foucault's ambiguous rela-

tion to psychoanalysis. Freud's *Civilization and Its Discontents* (1930 [1929]), *Standard Edition* 21:57–145, argues strongly that sexuality can never delineate an inner boundary and that our "discontent" derives precisely from "civilization's" insistence that its satisfactions must override our own. To this extent, and in a way that Foucault downplayed in his later writing, much of Freud's work would support Rubenfeld's concerns about the state's encroaching on our lives. What psychoanalysis gives us, moreover, is a way of reading public fantasies that cannot simply be classed as political aims or strategies.

70. "Jouissance" is beyond the pleasure principle—it refers to psychic drives that are ontologically satisfying but subjectively destructive (Tim Dean, "The Psychoanalysis of AIDS," *October* 63 [1993]: 110–16). See also Jacques Lacan, *Four Fundamental Concepts of Psycho-Analysis*, ed. Jacques-Alain Miller and trans. Alan Sheridan (New York: Norton, 1978), pp. 174–200.

71. Rebecca Lewin, "A Few Minutes with Fractious Fran," *The Advocate* 554 (July 3, 1990), p. 63.

72. "Various Sexual Prohibitions and Pro-Gay Rights Legislation, by State," *Harvard Gay and Lesbian Review* 2, no. 3 (1995): 27.

73. Signorile acknowledges, for instance, that while working with ACT UP, "my closet wasn't totally open. I was, of course, out in Manhattan, but I wasn't out on Staten Island. I had convinced myself that I had once told my parents I was gay" (*Queer in America*, p. 63).

74. Alan Sinfield, "What's in a Name?" *Gay Times* (May 1992), p. 27.

75. Ibid., p. 26. Richard Smith also notes about queer activism in Britain, "Under this pretence of bringing us all together there were also some who appropriated the word [*queer*] to signal an elite—that they comprised a select band of sussed queers who had gone beyond being Good As You [i.e., gay, pleading equality], beyond being different to them, to thinking themselves better than the rest of us. "Queer" for them became a show of contempt for ordinary lesbians and gay men. Oddly enough their main allies were the main critics of queer" ("Papering over the Cracks," p. 28).

76. Richard D. Mohr, *Gay Ideas: Outing and Other Controversies* (Boston: Beacon, 1992), p. 36. Subsequent references give pagination in main text.

77. While urging outers and activists to take this claim seriously, I do acknowledge that outing can have different repercussions in Britain and the United States—indeed, my essay began precisely from a concern to theorize these differences. For instance, as Carlos A. Ball and Robert McRuer of the University of Illinois usefully observed when responding to an earlier version of this paper, the recent (1996) outing of Republican Representative Jim Kolbe of Arizona—following his support for the 1996 Defense of Marriage Act—was singularly unspectacular, allowing Kolbe to insist that being known publicly as gay has not, and will not, affect the way he votes or legislates. Kolbe's response prompts me to repeat my claim above that "the U.S. model . . . can evacuate sexuality from gay issues without rescinding identitarian demands for equality." The argument here is conceptual, but the fact that outing has not encouraged *Kolbe* to advance "identitarian demands for equality" must be noted. If outers acknowledge in advance the strong

possibility that the outed's politics will *not* in fact change in the lesbian and gay
community's favor, outing represents only the satisfaction of highlighting hypocrisy
without substantive gain.

In contrast to Kolbe's outing, a recent (March 1997) copy of Britain's *Gay Times*
contains two lead stories on outing, both endorsing my argument that outing in
Britain can generate very different issues. In "Out the Homophobes," Peter Tatchell
"explains why two-faced gay M.P.s should be outed" (p. 4). And, more significant, in
"Stoned Love," "a 24-year-old former Tory activist, Paul Stone, [explains why he] det-
onated a bombshell in the pre-election campaign with his claims of an underage
affair with a Tory M.P." "But why did he do it?," asks *Gay Times*. "Is he merely a
tabloid patsy, in it for the money? Or is he a crusader against establishment
hypocrisy?" (p. 20). The article notes significantly that although *The News of the
World* was not particularly homophobic in its coverage (perhaps because Stone sold
them his story!), subsequent reports in other British papers—including the nationwide lesbian and gay *Pink Paper*—denounced Stone for being opportunistic and
treacherous rather than communitarian—that is, for preferring self-interest to a conscious attempt to rescind hypocrisy and advance gay and lesbian rights. This is
merely a condensed version of the wider problem all lesbian and gay communities
face when attempting to justify outing. Sadly, the same issue of *Gay Times* includes a
sarcastic letter from Peter Tatchell responding to its national readership, which in
1996 voted him "Gay Shame of the Year" (p. 104).

78. Mark Chekola, "Outing, Truth-Telling, and the Shame of the Closet," *Gay
Ethics*, p. 67. Consider as an example Signorile's account of OutPost's "Absolutely
Queer" campaign: "The anti-outing charges came mostly from older gay and lesbian
writers, and from closeted ones. However, on the streets during Gay Pride Week,
crowds of young gays, many in their teens, gathered around the posters. None were
upset or spoke about privacy [!]; most of them were thrilled and excited to find that
some of their heroes and heroines were gay" (*Queer in America*, p. 88). This quotation obviously contradicts Signorile's claim on p. 81 that he rejects the idea that outing can generate role models.

79. Bersani, "Is the Rectum a Grave?" p. 198.

80. Ibid.: "I'm interested in . . . *something both camps have in common*, which
may be a certain *aversion*, an aversion that is not the same thing as a repression and
that coexists quite comfortably with, say, the most enthusiastic endorsement of poly-
sexuality with multiple sex partners" (first emphasis mine). For elaboration of this
point, see Bersani, *Homos* (Cambridge: Harvard UP, 1995), p. 1.

81. Mayo and Gunderson, "Privacy and the Ethics of Outing," *Gay Ethics*, pp. 50,
53.

82. Gregg Bordowitz, "Picture a Coalition," *AIDS: Cultural Analysis/Cultural
Activism*, pp. 183–96; Wojnarowicz, *Close to the Knives*. See also Joshua Gamson's
interesting essay, "Must Identity Movements Self-Destruct? A Queer Dilemma,"
Social Problems 42, no. 3 (1995): 390–407.

83. See also Gabriel Rotello, "Theory and Practice: Commentary: Why I Oppose
Outing," *OutWeek* (May 29, 1991), reprinted in Gross, *Contested Closets*, p. 278.

84. Mayo and Gunderson, "Privacy and the Ethics of Outing," *Gay Ethics*, p. 50;
see also p. 53: "The violation of privacy involved in outing someone is—or at least is
very much like—theft. It is theft from that person of control of private information.
When someone loses control of that information, he or she may very well suffer serious harms, especially if that information triggers responses of prejudice, intolerance,
and malice in others. Moreover, unlike most thefts, it may be irreversible." For related
discussion that aided many of my arguments about privacy and jouissance, see
Dean, "Hart Crane's Poetics of Privacy," *American Literary History* 8, no. 1 (1996):
83–109; and Joan Copjec, *Read My Desire: Lacan Against the Historicists* (Cambridge: MIT Press, 1994), pp. 191 and 215–16.

85. George Herbert, *Jacula Prudentum, or, Outlandish Proverbs, Sentences &c.*,
sel. Mr. George Herbert (London: T. Maxey for T. Garthwait, 1651).

86. Gross acknowledges: "Still others in the gay and lesbian community have
claimed that outing anti-gay politicians is blackmail. This is not, perhaps, an untrue
statement but one which falls flat since most people realize that *all* politics are fought
with threats and blackmail of some sort" (*Contested Closets*, pp. 269–70). In this
move from the particular to the general, Gross downplays the strength of feeling
accompanying outing from the gay and lesbian community and straight media—the
precise degree to which outing does not—and must not—"fall flat" because its purpose is to engender reaction, whether confrontation, surprise, denial, shock, acceptance, or contrition. Thus Signorile avows, in *Queer in America*: "Going over the top
was the only way to get a lot of attention" (p. 72).

87. Shane Broomhall, qtd. in "Stopping Them in Their Tracks," p. 9.

REFERENCES

Alcorn, Keith. "Queer and Now." *Gay Times* (London; May 1992): 20–24.
Bersani, Leo. "Is the Rectum a Grave?" In Douglas Crimp, ed., *AIDS: Cultural Analy-
sis/Cultural Activism*. Cambridge: MIT Press, 1988. 197–223.
——— . *Homos*. Cambridge: Harvard University Press, 1995.
Chekola, Mark. "Outing, Truth-Telling, and the Shame of the Closet." In Timothy F.
Murphy, ed., *Gay Ethics: Controversies in Outing, Civil Rights, and Sexual Sci-
ence*. New York: Haworth Press, 1994. 67–90.
Cohen, William A. *Sex Scandal: The Private Parts of Victorian Fiction*. Durham: Duke
University Press, 1996.
Copjec, Joan. *Read My Desire: Lacan Against the Historicists*. Cambridge: MIT
Press, 1994.
Edge, Simon. "Stoned Love." *Gay Times* (March 1997): 20.
Faderman, Lillian. "A Bisexual Moment." *The Advocate* 689 (September 5, 1995):
43.
Foucault, Michel. "Power and Strategies." In Colin Gordon, ed., *Power/Knowledge:
Selected Interviews and Other Writings 1972–1977*. Trans. Colin Gordon, Leo
Marshall, John Mepham, and Kate Soper. New York: Pantheon, 1972, 1980.
——— . *The History of Sexuality*, vol. 1 (1976). Trans. Robert Hurley. New York: Pan-
theon, 1978.

Freud, Sigmund. *The Future of an Illusion*. 1927. In James Strachey, ed. and trans., *The Standard Edition of the Complete Psychological Works of Sigmund Freud*. London: Hogarth Press, 1953–74. 21: 3–56.

——. *Civilization and Its Discontents* (1930 [1929]). *Standard Edition*. 21: 57–145.

Gross, Larry. *Contested Closets: The Politics and Ethics of Outing*. Minneapolis: University of Minnesota Press, 1993.

Herbert, George. *Jacula Prudentum, or, Outlandish Proverbs, Sentences &c*. Selected by Mr. George Herbert. London: T. Maxey for T. Garthwait, 1651.

Hoad, T. F., ed. *The Concise Oxford Dictionary of English Etymology*. Oxford: Clarendon Press, 1986.

Johansson Warren and William A. Percy. *Outing: Shattering the Conspiracy of Silence*. Binghamton, N.Y.: Harrington Park, 1994.

Lacan, Jacques. *Four Fundamental Concepts of Psycho-Analysis*. Ed. Jacques-Alain Miller, trans. Alan Sheridan. New York: Norton, 1978.

Lewin, Rebecca. "A Few Minutes with Fractious Fran." *The Advocate* 554 (July 3, 1990): 63.

Mayo, David J. and Martin Gunderson. "Privacy and the Ethics of Outing." In Timothy F. Murphy, ed., *Gay Ethics: Controversies in Outing, Civil Rights, and Sexual Science*. New York: Haworth Press, 1994. 47–65.

Miller, D. A. *The Novel and the Police*. Berkeley: University of California Press, 1988.

Mohr, Richard D. *Gay Ideas: Outing and Other Controversies*. Boston: Beacon Press, 1992.

Moore, Suzanne. "Straight Talking." *The Guardian* (March 10, 1995): 5.

Pearce, Edward. "Keep the Closet Door Closed." *The Guardian* (December 10, 1994): 29.

The Public General Acts and Church Assembly Measures 1967, Part 2. London: HMSO, 1967.

Rubenfeld, Jed. "The Right of Privacy." *Harvard Law Review* 102, no. 4 (1989): 737–807.

The Scotsman. Editorial. "The Right to Stay in the Closet." (March 21, 1995): 12.

Sedgwick, Eve Kosofsky. *Epistemology of the Closet*. Berkeley: University of California Press, 1990.

Signorile, Michelangelo. *Queer in America: Sex, the Media, and the Closets of Power*. 1993. New York: Doubleday, 1994.

Sinfield, Alan. "What's in a Name?" *Gay Times* (May 1992): 25–27.

Smith, David. "Stopping Them in Their Tracks: David Smith Talks to Shane Broomhall, One of the Men Behind the Great Outing Scam." *Gay Times* (September 1991): 9.

Smith, Richard. "Papering Over the Cracks." *Gay Times* (May 1992): 28–29.

Tatchell, Peter. *The Battle for Bermondsey*. London: Heretic Press, 1983.

——. "Out the Homophobes." *Gay Times* (March 1997): 16.

——. "Am I Really Such a 'Gay Shame'?" *Gay Times* (March 1997): 104.

Tyler, Carole-Anne. "Passing: Narcissism, Identity, and Difference." *Differences* 6, nos. 2–3 (1994): 212–48.

"Various Sexual Prohibitions and Pro-Gay Rights Legislation, by State." *Harvard Gay and Lesbian Review* 2, no. 3 (1995): 27.

Warren, Samuel and Louis Brandeis. "The Right to Privacy." *Harvard Law Review* 4, no. 5 (1890): 193–220.

Waugh, Auberon. *The Last Word: An Eye-Witness Account of the Trial of Jeremy Thorpe.* Boston: Little, Brown, 1980.

Weeks, Jeffrey. *Coming Out: Homosexual Politics in Britain, from the Nineteenth Century to the Present.* London: Quartet, 1977.

———. "Discourse, Desire, and Sexual Deviance: Some Problems in a History of Homosexuality." In Kenneth Plummer, ed., *The Making of the Modern Homosexual.* London: Hutchinson, 1981. 76–111.

Wojnarowicz, David. *Close to the Knives: A Memoir of Disintegration.* New York: Vintage, 1991.

Wolfenden Report, The: Report of the Committee on Homosexual Offenses and Prostitution. 1957. Intro. Karl Menninger. New York: Stein and Day, 1963.

Index

AIDS/HIV, x, 2, 14, 16, 61, 72, 76,
111–13, 115–16, 133, 136, 138,
141, 142, 151, 166, 183*n*9, 215,
217*n*5, 265–66
Alcorn, Keith, 253, 274*n*25, 281
Aronson, Jacob, ix, 18*n*7, 203–21

Bangkok, 176–78
Barnett, Alan, 112–13
Bell, David, 3, 9, 19
Bergman, David, ix, 5, 8, 95–114
Bersani, Leo, 77, 93
Bok, Sisela, 9, 11, 19
Bolton, Ralph, vii, 14, 19, 70*n*1, 70,
72, 93, 138, 142, 150, 152, 154,
158, 182, 185, 215, 218
Bowers v. Hardwick, see *Hardwick*

Chauncey, George, 62, 217*n*9, 218
China, legal attitudes toward homosex
in, 204–5
Cherry Grove, 95, 97, 98, 99, 100, 102
Christopher Street, 95, 190
Clatts, Michael, ix, 5, 8, 15, 138,
141–55
Colonialism, homosex and, 205, 206,
217*n*10
Community, formation of through pub-
lic sex, 65–66, 187–202
Community, gay, 8, 12, 184, 188, 189
Cosgrove, D. E., 7, 19, 115, 139

Cruising, 8, 31–33, 56–57, 58–60,
191, 209

de Certeau, Michel, 6–7, 17*n*6, 19,
70*n*3
Delaney, Samuel X., 89, 93, 190, 201
Delph, Edward, 18*n*10, 19, 70*n*2, 70,
127, 139, 187, 188, 196, 198,
200*n*4, 201
Decter, Midge, 96–97, 113

Edelman, Lee, 10, 16, 19, 20
Eigo, Jim, 17*n*3, 20, 72, 93

Faderman, Lillian, 252, 277*n*53, 281
Fag bashing, *see* Gay bashing
Fire Island, 5, 8, 95–114
Foucault, Michel, 70*n*1, 224, 256,
271, 274*n*28, 278*n*69, 281
Freud, Sigmund, 264, 273*n*11,
278*n*69, 282

Gay bashing, 60–61, 135, 166,
236–37, 266
Gay liberation, 73, 195
Goodwin, Joseph P., 198, 201
Great Britain, 251–62
Greenwich Village (New York City), 5, 8,
12, 142–49
Gross, Larry, 248, 255, 272, 272*n*3,
280*n*83, 281*n*86, 282

Habermas, Jurgen, 217*n*8, 219
Hardwick, 9, 18*n*7, 72, 263, 265,
278*n*66
Hekma, Gert, 242*n*5, 245*n*82
Herdt, Gilbert, vii
Higgins, Ross, ix, 5, 8, 187–202, 213,
219
Hirsch, David, 7, 20
Holland, 5, 12, 223–45
Holleran, Alexander, 86, 95, 97, 98,
102, 104–5, 106–7, 112, 113, 197,
201, 273*n*7
Hollister, John, ix, 5, 15, 55–71
Homosex as treason, homosexual as
traitor, 235, 258, 261, 276*n*45
Humphreys, Laud, x, 5, 13, 18*n*11, 20,
23–27, 29–54, 55, 58, 63, 70*n*1,
71, 151, 155, 162, 185, 187, 201

Johansson, Warren and William Percy,
248, 249, 254, 255, 259, 272*n*3

Kinsey, Alfred, 187, 190, 200*n*3
Kramer, Larry, 97, 98, 99, 107–9, 114

Lane, Christopher, x, 18*n*7, 247–83
Landscape, 11, 125, 138*n*1; sexual,
6–8, 12, 59, 72, 116, 136
Language and homosex: nonverbal,
24, 33–34, 60, 65, 72, 82–83, 84,
168, 170, 210, 228; verbal, 33–34,
89, 95, 119, 133, 145, 169, 208,
209, 211, 214, 217*n*10, 228, 229,
231, 235
Leap, William L., x, 1–21, 69, 115–40,
182, 185, 223, 225, 229, 272
Leavitt, David, 106
Lewin, Ellen, x, 20, 139, 215, 219
Leznoff, Maurice 197, 200*n*2, 201*n*12,
201

Mohr, Richard, 9, 11, 20, 73, 94,
182*n*2, 185, 267–68, 279*n*76, 282
Montreal, 5, 8, 187–202
Mordden, Ethan, 112, 114

Murray, Stephen, x, 5, 10, 15, 17*n*3,
20, 66, 71, 189, 194, 199, 201,
207, 213, 217*n*9, 220

Nardi, Peter, x, 5, 18*n*11, 20, 23–27
Newton, Esther, 18*n*9, 98, 99, 114

Outing, 247–83

Pearce, Edward, 252, 259, 261,
269–70, 274*n*21
Picano, Felice, 99, 101, 107, 110, 114
Pines, The (Fire Island), 95–114
Police, gay harassment/arrest by, 25,
41, 43, 60–61, 163, 194–95, 203,
207, 208, 214
Policing Public Sex, 3–4, 19
Privacy (sexual): as concealment, 9,
87, 119, 125, 135, 215, 216; as fictional construction, 4, 11, 12,
17*n*8, 73, 157–59; as
protection/safety, 9, 72, 92, 135,
165, 211, as restricted access, 77,
129–30; "right" to, 161, 224,
238–40, 248, 256, 262–72
Public, definition(s) of, 9
Public sex:
—"aging crisis" and, 37–39, 43, 62
—anonymity and, 14, 25, 33, 62, 74,
127, 135, 150, 161–62
—class and, 11, 34, 36–37, 44, 77,
87, 117, 125, 195, 232
—drug use and, 101, 144, 148, 151–52
—gay taxonomies of sites for: 61, 90,
123, 126–27, 136–37, 146,
180–182, 200*n*9
—identities (sexual) and, 3, 11, 25, 26,
32–33, 35, 39, 44–46, 63, 69, 71,
78, 92, 121, 124–26, 179, 187,
213, 217*n*9, 224, 253
—"invention" of "homosexuality" and,
224–26, 243*n*22
—legal inconsistencies toward, 228,
237, 248
—observed sex, 157–82

—race and, 31, 34, 77, 87, 117, 118, 129, 132
—research, *see* Studying public sex
—safety and, 141–55
—sexual risk and, 2, 111, 150–54
—sites for: backrooms, 12, 15, 116–20, 127–35; bathhouses, 5, 8, 10, 12, 71–94, 157, 169, 171, 181, 195; beaches, 12, 162–63, 167, 174–85; cinemas, 10, 191, 196; health clubs ("straight"), 12, 15, 116–20, 121–27; "Meat Rack" (Fire Island), 98–99, 102, 104, 109; parks, 8, 135, 163, 165, 191, 196, 203, 207; rest areas, highway, 5, 12, 15, 55–71; restrooms, 10, 29–54, 144, 192, 193–94, 196, 198; (steam)baths, 71–94, 195; "trucks," 190
—site-specific activity, as, 2, 34, 65–69
—social reproduction of sites for, 65–69
—"straights' " taxonomies of sites for, 125–26, 137
—watching/ witness(es), importance of, 164–67, 168, 171, 175–76, 240
—women and, 11, 17*n*6, 18*n*9, 65
Public vs. private: boundary between debated and contested, 1, 2, 4, 8–12, 63, 72, 73, 98–100, 136, 163, 247–51, 264, 270: court debates over, 9, 18*n*7, 72, 230, 232, 237–41, 257–60, 263, 265, 278*n*66; importance of witnesses and, 240; media debates over, 258, 275*n*33, 279*n*77

Queer activism, 253–56, 266
Queer bashing, *see* Gay bashing
Queer theory/theorists, 26, 69, 212

Rechy, John, 90, 94, 141, 154, 155
Rotello, Gabriel, 2, 6, 17*n*1, 17*n*2, 21, 269, 280*n*83
Rubenfeld, Jed, 263–65, 278*n*68, 278*n*69

Rubin, Gayle, 183*n*13, 186, 213, 217*n*9, 220

Sanzio, Alain, 198
Sex workers (male), 143–44, 146–49, 152
Signorile, Michelangelo, 2, 6, 17*n*1, 17*n*2, 21, 248, 249, 255, 262–72, 272*n*3, 275*n*33, 279*n*73, 282
Silence: as public response to homosex, 204–5, 208, 235; during "public" sex, 24, 33–34, 61–62, 72, 84
Sodomy trials, 18th-19th–century Holland and, 223–45
St. Marks Baths (New), 12, 75–93
Studying public sex: ethics in, 13–16, 19*n*13, 52–54; methods used in, 2, 4, 12–16, 18*n*10, 52–54, 57–58, 66–69, 120–21, 128, 188, 197; problems of representation in, 2, 15–16
Styles, J. 18*n*10, 21

Tatchell, Peter, 251–57, 260–262, 282
Tattelman, Ira, x, 5, 8, 71–94
Tearoom Trade, ix, 5, 13, 16, 18*n*11, 20, 25–27, 58
Thorpe, Jeremy, 257–60
Tourism, gay, 214, 218*n*12

van der Meer, Theo, x, 5, 223–45
Vietnam, 5, 8, 18*n*7, 203–21
Violet Quill (writer's project), 97–114

Warren, Samuel and Louis Brandeis, 256, 274*n*30
Weinberg, Martin S. and Colin J. Williams, 18*n*10, 71, 74, 94
White, Edmund, 96, 97, 98, 103, 104–5, 114
Whitmore, George, 100, 105–6, 114
Williams, Raymond, 7, 115, 139, 189, 202
Wolfenden Report (Great Britain), 256, 275*n*36, 276*n*49, 277*n*50, 283

Between Men ~ Between Women
Lesbian and Gay Studies
Lillian Faderman and Larry Gross, Editors

Rebecca Alpert: *Like Bread on the Seder Plate: Jewish Lesbians and the Transformation of Tradition*
Edward Alwood, *Straight News: Gays, Lesbians, and the News Media*
Corinne E. Blackmer and Patricia Juliana Smith, editors, *En Travesti: Women, Gender Subversion, Opera*
Alan Bray, *Homosexuality in Renaissance England*
Joseph Bristow, *Effeminate England: Homoerotic Writing After 1885*
Beverly Burch, *Other Women: Lesbian Experience and Psychoanalytic Theory of Women*
Claudia Card, *Lesbian Choices*
Joseph Carrier, *De Los Otros: Intimacy and Homosexuality Among Mexican Men*
John Clum, *Acting Gay: Male Homosexuality in Modern Drama*
Gary David Comstock, *Violence Against Lesbians and Gay Men*
Laura Doan, editor, *The Lesbian Postmodern*
Emma Donoghue, *Poems Between Women: Four Centuries of Love, Romantic Friendship, and Desire*
Allen Ellenzweig, *The Homoerotic Photograph: Male Images from Durieu/Delacroix to Mapplethorpe*
Lillian Faderman, *Odd Girls and Twilight Lovers: A History of Lesbian Life in Twentieth-Century America*
Byrne R. S. Fone, editor, *The Columbia Anthology of Gay Literature: Readings from Western Antiquity to the Present Day*
Linda D. Garnets and Douglas C. Kimmel, editors, *Psychological Perspectives on Lesbian and Gay Male Experiences*
Lynda Hart, *Between the Body and the Flesh: Performing Sadomasochism*
renée c. hoogland, *Lesbian Configurations*
Ellen Lewin, *Recognizing Ourselves: Ceremonies of Lesbian and Gay Commitment*
Richard D. Mohr, *Gays/Justice: A Study of Ethics, Society, and Law*
Sally Munt, editor, *New Lesbian Criticism: Literary and Cultural Readings*
Timothy F. Murphy and Suzanne Poirier, editors, *Writing AIDS: Gay Literature, Language, and Analysis*
Noreen O'Connor and Joanna Ryan, *Wild Desires and Mistaken Identities: Lesbianism and Psychoanalysis*
Don Paulson with Roger Simpson, *An Evening in the Garden of Allah: A Gay Cabaret in Seattle*
Judith Roof, *Come As You Are: Sexuality and Narrative*
Judith Roof, *A Lure of Knowledge: Lesbian Sexuality and Theory*
Claudia Schoppmann, *Days of Masquerade: Life Stories of Lesbians During the Third Reich*

Alan Sinfield, *The Wilde Century: Effeminacy, Oscar Wilde, and the Queer Moment*

Jane McIntosh Snyder, *Lesbian Desire in the Lyrics of Sappho*

Chris Straayer, *Deviant Eyes, Deviant Bodies: Sexual Re-Orientations in Film and Video*

Dwayne C. Turner, *Risky Sex: Gay Men and HIV Prevention*

Ruth Vanita, *Sappho and the Virgin Mary: Same-Sex Love and the English Literary Imagination*

Thomas Waugh, *Hard to Imagine: Gay Male Eroticism in Photography and Film from Their Beginnings to Stonewall*

Kath Weston, *Families We Choose: Lesbians, Gays, Kinship*

Kath Weston, *Render Me, Gender Me: Lesbians Talk Sex, Class, Color, Nation, Studmuffins . . .*

Carter Wilson, *Hidden in the Blood: A Personal Investigation of AIDS in the Yucatán*

Jacquelyn Zita, *Body Talk: Philosophical Reflections on Sex and Gender*